W0254192

SOUTH ASIA
Traditional
and
Non-Traditional Threats

SOUTH ASIA
Traditional and Non-Traditional Threats

Edited by
Shekhar Adhikari

PENTAGON PRESS

South Asia: Traditional and Non-Traditional Threats
Shekhar Adhikari (Ed)

ISBN 978-81-8274-808-8

First Published in 2015

Published by
PENTAGON PRESS
206, Peacock Lane, Shahpur Jat
New Delhi-110049
Phones: 011-64706243, 26491568
Telefax: 011-26490600
email: rajan@pentagonpress.in
website: www.pentagonpress.in

Branch:
Flat No.213, Athena-2,
Clover Acropolis,
Viman Nagar,
Pune-411014
Email: pentagonpresspune@gmail.com

Printed at Avantika Printers Private Limited.

Contents

Section II

NON-TRADITIONAL SECURITY THREATS

Preface

After the end of Cold War and thereafter, with the nuclearization of the sub-continent, South Asia has attracted the attention not only of strategic experts but also of academicians. Society and culturally, the peoples of South Asia have shared centuries old common heritage and have contributed towards renewal of these bonds despite their emergence as new nation-states. But, internally independent India, Pakistan, and Bangladesh face religious, ethnic, and sectarian strife. In their perception, this development along with the existing patterns of power relationship, large conventional military strength and different kinds of political systems have intensifies the potential for conflict in South Asia. Overall, South Asia presents a picture of marked contrast in all fields-politically, economically, and military.

Politically, the entire South-Asia region, with the exception of India, has witnessed convulsive politics in the last fifty years. While India has managed to keep its democracy alive, the other nations of South Asia have experimented off and on with democratic processes. Democratic political institutions if they had been allowed to mature could have contributed to building up of regional trust and confidence. Unfortunately, democracy has been an exception amongst South-Asian states rather than the rule.

South Asia, in terms of economic development and regional economic co-operation, offers very attractive prospects due to the richness of natural and energy resources within the region and the potential for cheap hydroelectric power. But one finds that increasing population worldwide has resulted in competitive survival of human beings on the earth. Except in a few developed nations, availability of food material has become a big challenge. Without food, societies become breeding grounds for instability, civil unrest, terrorism, and demagogues. The region will need to produce twice as much food by 2050, given demands and rising populations.

Military, South Asia is a conflict prone region where the two largest countries fought four wars. This conflictual environment has largely affected the financial resources which could have gone for economic and social development. New military dangers grew in 1998 with the nuclear weaponizations of South Asia. Thus, the possibility of future conflict has become a cause of great concern which affairs not only to regional actors but also international actors. The existing military environment has affected the process of the evolution of regional co-operation and development in South Asia.

South Asia, therefore, present a picture of a troublesome environment so far military, political, economic, and social issues are concerned. In such a situation, what is essential, is to explore meaningful conflict resolution initiative and measures so that peace and stability can prevail in the region. In the absence of any such positive initiatives, the region has become a global concern which would in turn has involved other regions such as the Middle East, South-East Asia great powers like USA, Russia, China, and European Union.

Thus, conflict resolution in South Asia is a pre-requisite for establishing any meaningful regional co-operation and the ultimate emergence of South Asian Economic Community akin to the European Economic Community. South Asia, however, continue to be a prisoner of the past in political and military terms, i.e., political divisiveness and military conformation arising from the formative stages of nation building. In political and military fields, therefore, it may be difficult to achieve mutual confidence and trust. Simultaneously, building fresh economic and social structures in South Asia and reinforcing mutual co-operation could proved a holistic model for peace and development in South Asia.

The step already taken by the countries of the region are not sufficient for the consolidation of peace and co-operation in the region. Therefore, there is a need to closely observe and study the entire region in a much holistic manner.

With this aim the book on South Asia: Traditional and Non-Traditional Security Threats has been written. It has been divided into two sections: (1) traditional security threats; and (2) non-traditional security threats. The book contains various articles contributed by distinguished scholars in their own respective areas.

Shekhar Adhikari

Acknowledgements

At the outset, I would like to extend my sincere gratitude to all contributors who have come together to discuss very crucial issues of South-Asian Security. I must acknowledge my heartfelt gratitude to Prof. A.K.Singh, Vice- Chancellor, University of Allahabad, Allahabad for his constant encouragement and support. My thanks is also to Dr. Shalini Chawala, Dr. Sanjay Kumar, and Dr. Dhirendra Dwivedi for their active support. My special thanks goes to Mr. Rajan Arya, Pentagon Press, who was kind enough to publish the book in a short span of time. Last, but not the least, I am grateful to Pratibha Adhikari who have kept her patience cool in order to complete the book in time.

Contributors

1. Dr. Diwakar Kaushik is an Associate Professor, Department of Political Science, University of Allahabad, Allahabad, U.P.
2. Lt. Gen. V.K. Narula is a Director General of Artillery, New Delhi.
3. Dr. Shekhar Adhikari is a Professor and Head, Department of Defence & Strategic Studies, University of Allahabad, Allahabad, U.P.
4. Dr. Shalini Chawala is a Senior Fellow, Centre For Air Power Studies, New Delhi.
5. Group Captain Biswajeet Bose is a Research Associate , Centre For Air Power Studies, New Delhi.
6. Dr. Rajpal Budania is an, Associate Professor, Department of Political Science, University of Allahabad, Allahabad, U.P.
7. Mr. Rohit Kumar is a Researcher, Centre for Studies in International Politics and Governance, School of International Studies, Central University of Gujarat.
8. Dr. Saurabh Sharma is an Assistant Professor, Centre for Studies in International Politics and Governance, School of International Studies, Central University of Gujarat.
9. Ms. Tseyang Lhama is a Research Associate, Centre For Air Power Studies, New Delhi.
10. Dr. Uttam Kumar *Jamadhagni*, is an Associate Professor, Defence & Strategic Studies, University of Madras, Chennai, Tamil Nadu.
11. Mr. Ramakrishnan Ramani is a Research Scholar, Defence & Strategic Studies, University of Madras, Chennai, Tamil Nadu.
12. Dr. Sanjay Kumar is an Associate Professor, Department of Defence & Strategic Studies, Meerut College, Meerut, U.P.

13. Brig. Narendra Kumar is a serving Army Officer.
14. Dr. Atul Mishra is a Researcher, Department of Defence and Strategic Studies, University of Allahabad, Allahabad, U.P.
15. Dr. Shreesh K.Pathak is a Research Scholar, Centre for South-Asian Studies, School of International Studies, Centre for South Asian, New Delhi.
16. Col. Jaibans Singh is an Editor- Defence info.com, New Delhi.
17. Dr. P.S. Harish is an Assistant Professor, Department of Medieval and Modern History, University of Allahabad, Allahabad, U.P.
18. Lt. Gen. R.N.Singh, PVSM, AVSM, SM, VSM, is a Director General of Military Intelligence, New Delhi.
19. Dr. Raj Kumar Upadhyaya is a Professor, Department of Defence and Strategic Studies, University of Allahabad, Allahabad, U.P.
20. Dr. Dhirendra Dwivedi is an Assistant Professor, Department of Defence and Strategic Studies, ISDC, University of Allahabad, Allahabad, U.P.
21. Col. Jaspal Singh is a Research Scholar, Department of Defence and Strategic Studies, University of Allahabad, Allahabad, U.P.
22. Mr. Amar Singh is a Researcher, Centre for South-Asian Studies, School of International Studies, JNU, New Delhi.
23. Dr. Shivendra Shahi, is a Project Fellow, Department of Defence and Strategic Studies, University of Allahabad, Allahabad, U.P.

Section I

TRADITIONAL SECURITY THREATS

1

South Asia: A Unique Region and Modi's Diplomatic Priority

Diwakar Kaushik

A region has several connotations. Geographically a region is more than a country and less than a continent. Politically a region is a half-way house for a time when the utility of a single nation is doubted but the world is not yet ready for unity. On the whole, therefore, within the region there is close proximity among nations, they have common historical perceptions on which common historical experiences, on which similar perceptions of the world and developmental strategies might be based. Regionalism in South Asia cannot be studied with the help of European models because South Asia is a unique region and the situation here is different from that of Europe in many ways.

Geographically, South Asia is bounded on the north by the Pamir knot and the great chain of mountains which flow out from it the Himalayas, Karakorum, Hindukush, and in the south by the Indian Ocean. Historically, from the earliest times, the peoples of this region have been intimately linked by race, culture, religion, and sometimes by political allegiance. Indic civilization in its many forms Dravidian, Harappan, Vedic, Buddhist, Brahmanic, Indo-Islamic, Anglo-Islamic is distinct from Sinic civilization in its various manifestations to the east, and from the civilizations of Persia, Sumer, and Egypt in their evolutions to the west. Cultures overlap in border areas where peoples mix and migrate.[1]

Main Features of South Asia

The region of South Asia is different from that of Europe and other regions of the world because the countries of this region had to face colonial legacies, regional divides, ethnic problems and are least developed economies LDC. The countries of South Asia have not solved their problem of nation-building, sovereignty, legal order, legitimacy, etc. This had been solved much before by West Europe before they embarked on regional co-operation and Furthermore, South Asia had been ravaged by the role of external forces, such as, Super Power competition in the Cold War, North South conflict and its implications, etc. hence, any analysis of South-Asian region should be different from the European perspective.[2]

Dr S.D. Muni, regards South Asia as an Indo-Centric region because India is central to it geographically and in terms of the socio-cultural and economic infrastructure of the region. However, in order to understand the problems of the region, it is necessary to underline its principal characteristics. Indo-Centric means that almost all the countries of the region like Bangladesh, Bhutan, Burma, Nepal, Sri Lanka all have a common border with India. They are also related to India separately and individually in terms of their cultural identities, economic patterns, philosophical trends, and historical experience, i.e., there is a bit of India in every other country of South Asia but on the other hand there is anything of significance between one of India's neighbours and another. If anything it is India that is common between them, e.g., Tamils in Sri Lanka, Bengalis in Bangladesh, Paharis in Nepal and Bhutan, Mohajirs and Sindhis in Pakistan, etc. Moreover, most South-Asian countries have common borders with India. Furthermore, all nations of South Asia are related to India by history, ethnicity, culture, religion, philosophical trends, economic patterns, etc.

Another characteristic of the South-Asian region is that it has an unbalanced and asymmetric power structure in favour of India. The nature of this imbalance and asymmetry is such that India stands as the dominant power in the region and any future plan of regional co-operation necessitates India's positive and meaningful role. In terms of size, population, resource base, potential for economic growth, military strength, and viability of the constitutional and political system, nuclear capability, India is far too superior to any of its neighbours.[3]

Thus, it becomes abundantly clear that South Asia is not only Indo-centric but also an India-dominated region. This makes India the proverbial Big Brother with all the negative connotations of that expression for the healthy growth of regionalism on the sub-continent. Its negative consequence is demonstrated in the fear of India's lesser neighbours. The small neighbours look to China to balance the power of India thus, inviting an extra-regional power in this region and clearly demonstrates "big power' vs "small power "syndrome. Moreover, it is recognized by all governments specially those of Bhutan and Nepal that they lie within India's defence parameters and India's defence establishment also reflects its responsibility to defend most of its South Asian neighbours in fact an *ad-hoc* military co-operation also underlies India's relation with Myanmar against a possible Chinese attack on it.

The disparity in power between India and its neighbours has certainly generated legitimate and understandable apprehensions in the latter. Things become more aggravated with India declaring herself as a nuclear power and America signing a civil-nuclear co-operation with her. It cannot be disputed that such apprehensions create difficulties in the way of regional co-operation. However, we should be careful in analyzing the implications of power imbalances for the growth of regionalism in any given region because it would be misleading to emphasize the negative implications alone ; for the primacy of any particular power in a region may even make for stability, peace, and co-operation in that region.

Regionalism in South Asia

Regionalism in South Asia should be looked from a historical perspective. Its post-colonial history is characterized by conflict and tensions in relations between the various countries of the region. The major sources of conflict in the region can be traced back to colonial rule. Colonial rule have left three significant legacies.

Firstly, an unnatural and absurd state system was brought into being by means of a partition of the sub-continent and the creation of a disjointed Pakistan. The British rulers played a significant role in this partition, which, led to a series of conflicts and hampered co-operative ventures in the region.

Secondly, state boundaries between India and its neighbours were left undemarcated by the Britishers in the region. However, after independence there arose several major territorial disputes, and these strained bilateral relations in the region. Many of these disputes have been solved after protracted and difficult negotiations requiring much diplomatic efforts. But now, cross-border and state-sponsored terrorism has thrown up a new challenge.

Thirdly, in almost every country of South Asia, there are ethnic minorities who have their origin in another country of the region—as, for example, the Tamils in Sri Lanka, the Hindus in Pakistan, Bangladesh, and Afghanistan, the Biharis in Bangladesh, and Nepal, the Nepalese in Sikkim (until Sikkim's integration into India) and India, the Indians in Burma, Bangladeshi and Chakma tribals in India, Mohajirs in the Sindh province of Pakistan, Pakistani's in Punjab and Kashmir, and so on.[4] In this era of globalization, a country's borders have become meaningless. In addition, the presence of religious and linguistic minority groups across national boundaries continues to be a sensitive issue in intra-regional relations.

Strategy of South-Asian States

Conflict and tension arose in South Asia because of the different paths and strategies adopted by the various South Asian states for their social, economic, and political development. These economies also manifested strong tendencies of mutual competition and incompatibility owing to their differing growth potentials and directions of development.

Moreover, as regards nation-building in South Asia, there emerged in the South-Asian countries a clear emphasis on particularistic religious, ethnic, and linguistic components of the social fabric rather than on universalistic goals and tendencies in the nation-building processes. The emphasis in Pakistan was on Islam and Urdu, in Bangladesh on Islam and Bengali, in Sri Lanka on Buddhism and Sinhalese, in Nepal on Hinduism, and in Burma and Bhutan on Buddhism of different sects and varieties. In India also, under the umbrella of secularism as a goal of polity, politics largely turned on communal, regional, and linguistic considerations. All this resulted in the emergence of dominant ethnic groups in the countries of South Asia. Consequently, the politics of nation-building in each of these countries gave rise to many complex problems with repercussions extending across national boundaries.

Furthermore, the differences in the strategies of economic development adopted by the various South-Asian countries arise from their initial differences in terms of stage of development, resource base, and growth potential. Being comparatively well-placed, the Indian economy has grown faster; so has the Indian state structure and the bourgeoisie as compared with their counterparts in South Asia.

Thus, we see that different paths and strategies have been adopted by South-Asian states for economic, political, and social development. They have adopted different strategies with regard to nation-building. The elitist South-Asian states, such as, Pakistan, Bangladesh, and Nepal feel that they have drawn heavily from Indian civilization, therefore, they underline their differences with India in order to build a separate identity with India so that they can play a meaningful role in the international system. Instead of universalistic goals they emphasize on particularistic components like religion, ethnicity, language, etc., this has led to domestic conflicts which have reverberated the region, e.g., Hindu-Muslim relations affect Indo-Pak and Indo-Bangla relations; Sinhala-Tamil relations affect Indo-Sri Lanka relations.

With regards economic development, there is a difference in strategy, resource base, and style of development with the result that Indian economy is at a higher stage of development than the neighbours. They are afraid that in the guise of economic co-operation the Indian counterpart will swamp them due to firstly, the inherent strength of Indian economy and secondly, because of the Marwari psyche of Indian businessman (Marwari is a businessman who is selfish and intent on making quick and disproportionate profits). The result is that South-Asian nations co-operate with the West and not with India—this is detrimental both to India and South-Asian states.

Moreover, as regards the internal political process in South Asia we find that the peripheral states, the elites are afraid of India. The failure of development process in the peripheral states has led to the emergence of military elites in Bangladesh and Pakistan; the elites in Bhutan and Nepal were monarchistic while Sri Lanka has an authoritarian UNP or SLFP rule. However, India has democracy with mixed economy both serve as examples of anathema to South-Asian nations and ruling elites therein. This feeling of insecurity in our neighbours and the ruling elites therein leads them to feed anti-Indian feeling in order to mobilize support for their own regimes. This is detrimental to regional co-operation. Furthermore, the Cold War conflict between the Soviet Union and the United States, the Sino-Soviet rift, the North-South conflict, the Arms Race, etc., have all impinged upon the sub-continent.

The sibling rivalry between India, Pakistan, Bangladesh has had a unique effect on South Asia. The Muslim League and the Indian National Congress both before independence contested for the rewards and affection of the British, but now, they contest for the rewards from Super Powers to the detriment of each other.

Co-operation in South Asia

We always talk of co-operation in South Asia but the question which arises is what do we mean by co-operation? The concept of co-operation connotes acting together in agreement to achieve certain common ends. It is an antonym of conflict (though nations may pursue co-operation and conflictive ends simultaneously). Co-operation may be eager or reluctant, extensive or limited, but co-operation certainly means something more than indifference or non-action. It needs to be stressed, however, that co-operation is something less than integration. No merging of identity or function is necessary for co-operation to take place in the economic, cultural, or political realms of human endeavour.

What is needed is the political will to overcome obstacles that lie in the path of co-operation. There are five sets of circumstances which compel the urgent consideration of Regional Co-operation in South Asia:

Firstly, the global circumstances of political and military rivalry between the US and the Soviet Union, and the Soviet Union and China, impinge directly on the countries of South Asia. Every fratricidal dispute on the sub-continent since 1974 has provided ingress to outside powers; every breakdown in friendly relations has also provided access to outside influence.

Secondly, the circumstances of world trade, investment and economic assistance place all developing countries (South) at a disadvantage in their dealings with advanced industrial countries (North). The thrust of the movement to build a New International Economic Order (NIEO) has been to improve the individual and collective self-reliance of the South so as to enhance its bargaining power with the North. All the countries of South Asia have contributed to the NIEO movement. The inequality of current economic arrangements with the North is a strong argument in favour of regional co-operation.

Thirdly, the familial and religious ties that cut across political boundaries in South Asia. If the peoples of the region were asked their opinions, not many would be likely to opt for the endless bureaucratic formal bureaucratic formalities they have to undergo before being able to fulfil some deeply felt obligation, such as: marriage of an offspring to a member of the same community, but different nationality; attendance at the death bed of a parent; pilgrimage to holy places including the birth place of the Buddha, or Guru Nanak, or Sheikh Salim Chisti; study and enjoyment of related fields of music, art, literature, architecture; competing in sports events. Going one step further, one may well ask if government should, or can, prevent their peoples from walking across borders to seek a wage, or make an investment?

A fourth set of circumstances is created by the ecology of South Asia. The squeeze of population growth combined with rapacious attitudes towards the environment threatens soil, water, forests, and wildlife. No one country in the region can tackle the problems without co-operating with others. The problems of soil salinity in Bangladesh caused by tidal waters flowing inland will ease only when the waters of the Ganges river system are augmented; the problems of flooding and soil erosion in Uttar Pradesh and Bihar will become more acute until Nepal controls deforestation and harnesses its fast-flowing rivers. The beaches and fisheries of the region will be subjected to pollution and marauding until all the countries co-operate in looking after them. Because of India's unique position in the region, co-operative arrangements made bilaterally between India and any neighbour could benefit the region as a whole. India, as the largest and most powerful country in the region, bears the major responsibility for shaping it. Without India's interest and active participation, regional co-operation will remain an inadequate response to the imperatives.

Fifthly, co-operation in South Asia is necessary to prevent the positioning of external forces within the region. To position the armed forces on the borders of the sub-continent against extra-regional enemies, rather than to maintain the present positioning of armed forces vis-à-vis each other like India versus Pakistan, India versus Bangladesh, etc., and to be able to pressurize for the abandonment of military and naval activity in the Indian Ocean.

India is the largest and most powerful country in the region of South Asia and without India's interest and active participation, regional co-operation will remain an inadequate response to these imperatives.

Firstly, the uniqueness of the region is itself an obstacle. No other region in the world exhibits such vast disparities among its members; few regions share such cultural bonds as South Asia. There is a vast disparity in power and mineral resources between India and its neighbours. The crux of the problem is that while the neighbours suspect Indian domination in the guise of regional co-operation therefore they posit internationalism against regionalism on the other hand, India suspects the neighbours of ganging up against her and therefore she posits bilateralism as against regionalism. Both sets of fears and tendencies are harmful for regional co-operation and have to be countered.

Secondly, there are the links of history, religion, race, language, and culture between India and its neighbours. These create identity problems for states who are culturally close but politically distant from India. Consequently, the actions of smaller neighbours antagonizes India and this acts as an obstacle to regional co-operation in South Asia.

Thirdly, obstacle to regional co-operation is due to the dissimilarity in the strategic perceptions held by different governments in the region. The imperative of jointly protecting the region from outside interference is ignored while the governments separately assess the intentions and capabilities of outside powers to harm or benefit them. Divergences are the result of (i) past history, e.g., partition between India and Pakistan. Pakistan believes that India is out to undo partition. (ii) Different political systems, particularly the authoritarian political system in the neighbours exacerbate differences with India in order to bolster their regimes.

Fourthly, there are tremendous disparities in economic resources through the region creates several obstacles to co-operation, such as—

- Fear of domination by India
- Lack of common developmental strategies
- Low level of intra-regional trade

But there is economic limit to co-operation, e.g., India cannot meet the developmental needs of all its neighbours hence, the neighbours co-operate more with World institutions, West, China, Soviet Union from where they get aid. The result is disadvantageous to the region as a whole as well as to the recipient country. There is also political limit to co-operation, e.g., Pakistan will not take wheat, coal from India which is across the border, though it is much cheaper here because for political reasons. It appears that fruitful regional economic co-operation will follow improved relations and economic prosperity rather than precede them.

Finally, the lack of an appropriate model of regional co-operation in South Asia is also an obstacle. Neither history nor the contemporary world provides India and its smaller neighbours with readymade answers to their problem. If their leaders succumb to mutual suspicions, their countries will surely languish separately. If they come together, the countries might progress collectively. The only certainty is that the fate of India and its neighbours is inseparable.

In the past, South Asia was described by Peter Lyon as a 'region without regionalism'. It is a home of four major world religions; Hinduism, Buddhism, Sikhism, and Islam. World Bank statistics show that all countries in the region belong to the lowest income category, i.e., the total number of people who live below the poverty line, is roughly equivalent to the number of inhabitants of the African continent. South Asia is called the 'Earth's poor house' besides, in child mortality, malnutrition, and illiteracy it stands at the bottom end of International statistics.

Among the countries of this region, there are geographical, economic, and military dissimilarities decisively influenced by India. India has got the biggest army and the largest potential of scientific, technical manpower after U.S. and U.S.S.R. Indian population is more than three times larger than the population of neighbours and more than eight times than that of Bangladesh. India covers 72% area of the entire region and is four times larger than Pakistan. India possesses 100% of the region's uranium, copper, gold, lead, and silver resources and has 78% of the aggregate of South Asian GNP.

Despite cultural proximity and the common colonial period and Indian pre-dominance triggered reservations among its neighbours, while India perceives neighbours as being integral to its own security, the neighbours perceive India as a threat against which security is necessary.

SAARC

All Indian activities were interpreted by those affected as an expression of India's striving for hegemony while the actions of the other states was always viewed by the Indian side as an attempt to establish foreign powers in the region. SAARC as established in 1985 at Dacca and had seven original members namely, Bangladesh, Bhutan, India, Maldives, Pakistan, and Sri Lanka. Afghanistan was later included as a permanent member at the 14th summit held at New Delhi in 2007. The last summit (17th) was held at Addu City (Maldives) and the next summit is proposed to be held in November 2014 at Nepal.

SAARC is an important regional discussion forum where contentious bilateral issues are not to be raised, and if raised, should be resolved. On a closer examination, it is understandable why controversial issues are to be bypassed within the framework of regional co-operation. Almost all states have conflicting interests with India, hence, such a discussion would have led to a confrontation and isolation of India and thus a breakdown of all efforts. On the other hand, a successful regional co-operation cannot be meaningfully realized without India, bearing in mind its political and economic significance.

South Asia Preferential Trade Area (SAPTA) was made operational in December 1995 but as of today the intra-regional trade is roughly 3% and there are two reasons for it firstly, many of SAARC members have very limited items in their export basket and secondly significant portion of trade is based on practical convenience. SAARC secretariat was established at Kathmandu in 1987, while the SAARC Chamber of Commerce and Industries was established at Dhaka in 1991. South Asia Free Trade Area SAFTA came into existence from January 1, 2006 without much significance. It was also decided that the decade from 2001-2010 would be designated as the Decade of the Right of the Girl Child. There is a need of a SAARC bank and Parliament.

Today, SAARC stands at crossroads faced with diverse sets of incentives, compulsions, and pressures as well as difficulties in the further growth and advancement of its objectives. End of Cold War has turned the International atmosphere conducive to and compelling for co-operation and understanding at the regional level in South Asia. Cold war rivalries and tensions are no longer relevant, the countries need not get divided on partisan issues, over regional rivalries and suspicions have surfaced with greater vehemence, e.g., India-Pakistan. India's relations with its South Asian neighbours have unfortunately been far from satisfactory. This has weakened its position to such an extent that it may well be viewed as India's Achille's heel.[6]

This year's historic elections in Pakistan and its P.M. Nawaz Sharif coming to Delhi at the swearing ceremony of Narendra Modi has given rise to expectations of an improvement in bilateral relations. Pakistan High Commissioner to India Salman Bashir said: 'The logical course of the history to proceed is for these countries to become good neighbours, friends and that is not only for people of Pakistan and India but also forms a critical ingredient in realizing the vision of a prosperous and peaceful South Asia'.[7]

There are contradictions in India's global policy and its regional approach. At the international level, India rejects balance of power and exclusive sphere of influence but clings to them at the regional level. It is strongly opposed to intervention by major powers in the internal affairs of the weaker ones, but it provided security to smaller nations and their regimes, India was all for multilateralism at the global level yet in the region it insisted on bilateralism. Moreover, India castigated the West for its protectionist policies, yet in the region it had liberal arrangements with Nepal and Bhutan but was closed to others like Sri Lanka and Bangladesh—we protested at the global level but managers of security order in the region.

Contradictions can be seen since 1990s,—India's tough stand of imposing trade embargo against Nepal and its interventions in Sri Lanka and Maldives—contributed to India's image of a 'regional hegemon' after this neighbours became uneasy and anti-India feeling acquired greater strength. India was miffed at the cussedness of its neighbours and their attempts to mobilize support from China and Pakistan and to encourage or ignore activities hostile to India.

One of the unintended consequences of globalization was ending the economic partition of 1947 and the ossified system of regional economic separation got its first challenge. Pressures from IMF, World Bank, and the dynamics of WTO and GATT demanded the region to adopt policies at export promotion. While the economic reforms moved forward in the 1990's it was apparent that India would be the natural engine of growth in the region.

In the beginning, India was cool to the idea of SAARC and regarded it as a forum designed to isolate India politically in the region but by the turn of 1990's India began to emphasize the importance of economic co-operation. Pakistan had been the slowest camel to set the pace of economic caravan because she insists that there can be no economic progress unless political issues are resolved. An important option for India is to advance economic co-operation in the region—with Pakistan if possible, and without Pakistan if necessary.

There is a growing interest in the Indian private sector and the Asian Development Bank (ADB) to promote economic co-operation in the region and the concept of a South-Asian Growth Quadrangle SADQ involving Nepal, Bhutan, Bangladesh, and India's north-eastern states. It is high time we tightened up our cultural diplomacy as an important tool to supplement our diplomatic and economic efforts.[8]

The post cold war changes have compelled states across the globe to reorient their foreign policies to face the new challenges. The same is true of South-Asian states. The cold war period was marked by a higher degree of anti-India feelings largely due to unresolved disputes compelling the smaller states to seek the involvement of external powers in their dealings with India. In the post cold war period through the traditional security concerns persist there is a dilution of anti-India rhetoric and greater willingness to engage in dialogue to address all areas of dispute.[9]

Neither history nor the contemporary world provides India and its smaller neighbours with readymade answers to their problems. If they succumb to mutual suspicions, then their countries will surely languish separately. But if they come together, the countries will progress collectively. The only thing certain is that the fate of India and its neighbours is inseparable. Our destinies are inextricably linked and we have to work together to lift our lives out of underdevelopment and conflict to peace and prosperity, because India will not be able to realize its own destiny without the partnership of its South-Asian neighbbours.[10]

Indian Express writes, by inviting the leaders of neighbouring countries to attend his swearing in as Prime Minister of India, Modi has challenged the entrenched negative perceptions, at home and abroad, about his world view.

Modi's terrific move should help generate a more realistic appreciation of India's foreign policy trajectory in the coming years. Modi has sought to project a balanced approach to the neighbours ever since he was anointed the BJP's prime ministerial candidate last year. While expressing concerns about cross-border terrorism from Pakistan or illegal migration from Bangladesh, he also underlined the importance of joining hands with the neighbours in fighting poverty and underdevelopment in the sub-continent.

It is a more self-assured government in Delhi that is ready to engage the neighbours without standing on protocol and precedent. Unlike, his predecessor, Manmohan Singh, Modi, as PM, must travel frequently to the neighbouring countries, including Pakistan. Routinization of such diplomatic engagement will not solve all of India's problems with its neighbours. But it will certainly create a more conducive environment for purposeful negotiations on outstanding issues.

Prime Minister designate Modi pulled off a coup off sorts by inviting all leaders of the SAARC countries, including Pakistan's Prime Minister Nawaz Sharif for swearing-in ceremony. If India improves its relations with its neighbours, it will not just benefit the region economically but also make it a safer place. At the moment, SAARC has been held hostage to the hostilities between India and Pakistan and the new PM will have to work his way around this. The invitations will also assuage fears that India wants to play the role of a big brother. Rather, the message that is being conveyed is that India will be the locomotive that will pull the region ahead. This a sound and positive foundation on which to build a new, proactive foreign policy.[11]

Narendra Modi is stepping in the right direction by looking to strengthen ties with China. India announced a Look East policy in 1992, years after the Southeast Asian 'tiger economies' had surged into the global limelight. Over time, the governments of East and Southeast Asia joked India's policy was better described as 'look east, then look away.' New Delhi has struggled to put meat on the bones of this policy. Its relatively closed economy, overstretched military and inability to match China in any sphere meant that India remains a two-tier foreign partner for these countries. 2013 has seen East Asia beating a path to India. Japanese Prime Minister Shinzo Abe was the country's Republic Day chief guest. He had been preceded by the first joint summit between India and the ASEAN. The election of Prime Minister Narendra Modi and the sense that the past five years of inertia may have come to an end have only accelerated this sub-continental drift. China's new leader, Xi Jinping, has already signaled his desire to visit India in 2014.

The neighbours are eager to grasp what it means for them and their own interests. It was not easy for Prime Minister Nawaz Sharif to make the journey from Islamabad, but if he was courageous enough to do so—though not before clearance came from the Pakistan Army and hawkish sections of his own party—it was because he hoped that the new dispensation in Delhi would match that gesture in some way. In the event, the visit has ended up not making Mr. Sharif's position in Pakistan any easier. He refrained from bringing up the Kashmir issue in public while in Delhi, and for the first time, a Pakistani delegation did not hold a meeting with the Hurriyat. In keeping with the spirit of the occasion, Mr. Sharif called for attitudes to change from "confrontation to co-operation." The Indian side highlighted that Mr. Modi gave no quarter on the issue of terrorism emanating from Pakistan, and on speedy action in the 2008 Mumbai attacks case. Mr. Sharif had to go into damage-control mode when he returned to Pakistan. It cannot be emphasized more that India's interests on the terrorism issue, as well as its expressed keenness to move towards "full trade normalization" with Pakistan, are better served by strengthening Mr. Sharif's hands.[12]

Delhi has been unwilling to confront and address the reasons for the steady loss of Indian influence in the region over the last many decades. An India that fails to reclaim its primacy in the sub-continent, Modi can now see, can really make a lasting impression on the world beyond. If Modi is luckier than Manmohan Singh and Atal Bihari Vajpayee, he might make some sustainable progress with Pakistan. As a realist, however, Modi should be aware that major breakthroughs are unlikely amid the current political flux within Pakistan and Sharif's deteriorating relations with the all-powerful army. Modi's determination to pursue a vigorous regional diplomacy appears to rest on five foundations.

Firstly, Modi has appreciated the much neglected fact that foreign policy begins at the nation's borders. India's traditional diplomatic discourse is obsessed with grand concepts such as non-alignment and the elusive quest for the leadership of the global South. It has been rather easy for the Indian strategic community to forget the critical importance of tending one's own neighbourhood in the sub-continent and the Indian Ocean. Worse still, Delhi has been unwilling to confront and address the reasons for the steady loss of Indian influence in the region over the last many decades. India that fails to reclaim its primacy in the sub-continent, Modi can now see he can really make a lasting impression on the world beyond.

Secondly, Modi has understood the importance of discarding the diplomatic formalism that has bedeviled India's engagement with the region. In inviting the regional leaders for his inauguration, Modi is suggesting that contacts with neighbours should be made a matter of routine rather than be treated as exceptional occasions. In his interactions with the South-Asian leaders after the swearing in, Modi must tell them he is ready to visit all neighbouring countries, including Pakistan, at the earliest and will order his cabinet colleagues to do the same.

Thirdly, Manmohan Singh had a clear vision that India's destiny is inextricably linked with that of her neighbours. But Manmohan Singh was unable to overcome the political resistance within the Congress Party. If the Congress had put narrow electoral considerations above India's national interests in the region, Modi seems ready to uphold the Central government's responsibility to conduct foreign policy. Modi's rejection of the protests from the BJP's allies and others in Chennai against the visit of Sri Lankan President Mahinda Rajapaksa not only underlines India's new resolve but also improves Delhi's negotiating leverage with Colombo on the question of Tamil minority rights in Sri Lanka.

Fourthly, in inviting the prime minister of Mauritius to the swearing in ceremony, Modi is acknowledging Delhi's special relationship with the island nation and its Indian Diaspora. The new PM is acutely aware of the urgent need to reverse the UPA government's wanton destruction of this relationship at the very moment when Mauritius was re-emerging as the strategic pivot of the Western Indian Ocean.

Fifthly, Modi appears to have recognized that India's ability to deal with great powers like the United States and China will significantly improve only if and when Delhi can reconstitute the geopolitical unity of the sub-continent. For decades, India has complained about US and Chinese strategic partnerships with Pakistan. More recently, India has watched warily as China's political influence rose rapidly in the sub-continent. Delhi must accept a large portion of the blame for making it easier for outsiders to limit its influence in the region.

Instead of whining about external intervention in the sub-continent, Delhi needs a strategy that builds on India's natural geographic advantage, economic complementarity, historic role as the regional security provider and a shared cultural inheritance. If Manmohan Singh talked the talk on restoring India's regional primacy, Modi might have the political will to walk by resolving long-standing political disputes and promoting economic prosperity across the sub-continent.[13]

By inviting the South-Asian Association for Regional Corporation (SAARC) leaders to his swearing –in ceremony, Prime Minister designate Narendra Modi has sent out a powerful message on foreign policy. To give the South-Asian neighbourhood such importance right at the start of his term is indeed a significant step. The other important move he has made is calling all economic ministries, to which the external affairs ministry could soon be included, to send in reports on policies that the United Progressive Alliance (UPA) failed to implement, as well as the impractical policies it adopted. In fact, there are many parts in his predecessor's foreign policy book that Mr. Modi might well want to take a leaf out of.

The first is Dr. Singh's creative thinking on the neighbourhood. It was Dr. Singh's focussed drive for better relations with Pakistan, or Indian concessions on trade with Bangladesh, or the massive reconstruction and infrastructure building efforts undertaken in Afghanistan and Sri Lanka, India's SAARC engagement has helped its standing in the region.

Perhaps the part of Singh's foreign policy that Mr. Modi will most want to take forward will be the focus of the economist prime minister on economic diplomacy. Modi has been most positive about it. Even at a lecture he delivered at the University of Madras last year entitled "India and the World" "Modi emphasized that a strong economy is the driver of an effective foreign policy." He is quoted as saying, "We have to put our own house in order that the world gets attracted to us".

Mr. Modi's swearing in could well serve as a kick-off point for a new foreign policy regime for South Asia; that is, if he desires to make a break with past precedents. "For time and the world do not stand still", said U.S. President John F. Kennedy in his famous "Change is the law of life" speech delivered in Frankfurt in 1963. "And those who look only to the past or the present are certain to miss the future".

Narendra Modi's decision to invite Pakistan Prime Minister Nawaz Sharif for his swearing in ceremony and Sharif's acceptance has raised hopes among weary mainstream and separatist parties of Kashmir. "It's a positive beginning and would generate hope among the people belonging to the large peace constituency in South Asia. He (Modi) has actually sent out an encouraging signal that he is serious to follow former prime minister, Atal Behari Vajpayee initiatives of friendship towards Pakistan.

India needs to provide its neighbours with a sense of reassurance that it has vital stake in regional peace and security and the new government's first priority has to be the revitalization of the ceremony through structural rectification in the manufacturing sector to create the millions of jobs that India's young population expect as their rightful due. Nearly 45% of our GDP is accounted for by international trade. The priority therefore, must be to rejuvenate the economy and then to leverage the growing economy to conquer poverty equally rapidly and create the biggest middle class, labour, and consumer market in the world. We will need to become a manufacturing, agricultural, and services hub that generates the jobs, income and purchasing power that people and the economy need. This will require harnessing the talent of India's enormous pool of human resources in empowering and enabling people, especially youth and women. This, in turn, will strategically lay the basis for addressing the global challenges of the environment and climate change.

The last ten years were characterized by hesitation, indecision bordering on neglect and lack of vision, which together looked like strategic confusion. This was most conspicuous in our immediate neighbourhood where our bilateral relationships, each more important than the other, are without exception crying out for urgent attention and repair. As the larger country in South Asia, we need to provide our immediate neighbours with a sense of reassurance that we have a vital stake in sub-regional and regional peace and in their security and well-being. Enlightened co-operation can facilitate a co-prosperity sphere, which we should underwrite through instruments of trade policy. Other important relationships, particularly those with the P5 and other members of the G4 also require a healthy dose of encouragement.

Within a day of winning the elections, Modi had proffered the invitation to the all SAARC neighbours. The invitation went down in Indian history, and became a part of global parlance, for the boldness of the move and the all-round praise it received. Many were surprised but everyone lauded the initiative calling it a masterstroke, a strategy with vision. When it was announced that the Foreign Secretaries would meet in Islamabad on August 25, it seemed in line with Mr. Modi's grander strategy of squiring a new future for the entire neighbourhood, one that would be launched at the SAARC summit in November in Kathmandu.

It was another day of acrimonious exchanges between India and Pakistan on August 20, 2014 with the External Affairs Ministry rejecting Pakistan High Commissioner Abdul Basit's statement that the Hurriyat was a "stakeholder" in the peace process. The statement came after Mr. Basit held a press conference, defending his meetings with the Hurriyat leaders on August 18 and 19 that made India cancel the talks between the two nations. "The objective of interacting with Kashmiri leaders is precisely to talk to all the stakeholders to find a viable, peaceful solution", he said. Ministry spokesperson Syed Akbaruddin said: "There are only two stakeholders on the issue of Jammu & Kashmir—The Union of India and the Islamic Republic of Pakistan.

Indian officials say Pakistan will have to recognize the "new reality." While they can continue to meet whoever they like, they can no longer attempt to triangulate the talks by openly and brazenly speaking to Kashmiri leaders just before their talks with India", a government source said. With India Pakistan hardening their positions on the meetings Pakistan High Commissioner Basit Ahmed had with Hurriyat leaders, the immediate casualty seems to be the possible talks between Prime Minister Narendra Modi and his Pakistani counterpart, Nawaz Sharif, on the sidelines of the United Nations General Assembly meeting in New York in September.

Mani Shankar Aiyar writing in *Indian Express* on August 20, 2014 that there was nothing to be gained from making an issue of such a trivial matter. Nothing earth-shattering, either for us or the Pakistanis, has resulted from earlier meetings of the Hurriyat with the Pakistanis, including visits of Hurriyat leaders to Pakistan that we ourselves had permitted. From a Pakistani point of view, meeting the Hurriyat is an excellent way of selling to the Pakistani public the explanation that 'Kashmiri' wishes are not being ignored in the dialogue process. From the Indian point of view, the 'separatists', who are Indian citizens, whatever their view, are of such significance as to have warranted our 'interlocutors' talking to them.[14]

The *Hinduatan Times* in its editorial believes that it is time Pakistan did something that would be in its own interest if it is indeed interested in peace. And that would be to tell the Hurriyat leaders that unless they have something substantive to contribute to the dialogue, they should not drop in for a cup of tea and a chat before any significant bilateral talks.

New Delhi called off the August 25 bilateral talks after Basit went ahead with his meetings with the Hurriyat leaders. Stressing that the two sides should keep the "diplomacy doors ajar" and "diplomacy is the art of the possible", Basit said, "We need to engage with all stakeholders. It is not a question of either or as far as we are concerned. We are engaging with India to find peaceful ways". He was responding to New Delhi's stand that Pakistan should choose between dialogue with separatists or with the Indian government. Stating that he "did not breach any diplomatic protocol" by meeting the Hurriyat leaders, he said such meetings have been a "longstanding practice" since the Kashmir issue is a "dispute" between the two countries.

Reacting to his statements, the Ministry of External Affairs official spokesperson Syed Akbaruddin said that after 1972 and the signing of the Simla Agreement by the Prime Ministers of India and Pakistan, there are only two "stakeholders" on the issue of Jammu & Kashmir—the Union of India and the Islamic Republic of Pakistan. "This is a principle which is the bedrock of our bilateral relations. This was reaffirmed in the Lahore Declaration of 1999 between Prime Ministers Nawaz Sharif and Atal Behari Vajpayee", he said.[15]

Prime Minister Narendra Modi's decision this week to cancel the foreign secretary level talks with Pakistan has drawn much political flak at home and generated some international concern that the NDA government might be departing from its proclaimed commitment to improve relations with the neighbours. Both Pakistan and the separatists pressed for a trilateral dialogue. Delhi rejected a table for three. The Modi government is now saying that there is no place for the Hurriyat in the peace process with Pakistan.

Any number of busy bodies will want to mediate between Delhi and Islamabad on Kashmir. While internationalizing the Kashmir question has always been part of Pakistan's strategy, preventing external intervention has been a major Indian political objective. It is India's careful engagement with Pakistan and a dialogue on Kashmir that have kept the major powers at arm's length. Any serious breakdown of the peace process will bring the great powers back into play and undermine Modi's new emphasis on bilateralism.

Under criticism from the United States, Jammu and Kashmir political leaders and the Opposition over its decision to cancel talks with Pakistan, the government sought to explain its stance, saying the problem was not the talks themselves, but the sequencing of talks. "We have always said that you can change your friends but not your neighbours", said senior Minister Ravi Shankar Prasad. "They chose to talk to the separatists first in spite of clearly being told that if this persistence is there, it will be difficult to pursue the dialogue". "Here the PM walked the extra mile to meet the leader of Pakistan. And in spite of being told it would not be fair, they went ahead".

A new Modi administration will adequately appreciate the close links between good governance, national economic development, internal security and importance of trade, investment, foreign and security policy. The 21st Century belongs to India. Our foreign policy will be robust, strategic and proactive, not inert and defensive.

REFERENCES

1. S. Mansingh, *India's Search for Power*, Sage Publications, New Delhi, 1984, p. 265.
2. B. Prasad, *India's Foreign Policy*, Vikas Publishing House Pvt. Ltd., Ansari Road, New Delhi, 1979, pp. 107.
3. Ibid, p. 108.
4. Ibid, p. 110.
5. See n. 1.
6. M. Dubey, *India's Foreign Policy: Coping with the Changing World*, Pearson, Dorling Kindersley (India) Pvt. Ltd, Delhi, Chennai, Chandigarh, 2013, pp. 52-60.
7. *The Times of India*, July 17, 2014.
8. In Strategic Analysis by Dr. Rabindra Sen, Prof. of International Relations at Jadavpur University, Kolkata, Vol 38, No. 1, Jan-Feb 2014.
9. L.A. Pandit, *India and Her Neighbours: Changing Perceptions*, World Focus, Vol 378, June 2011.
10. S. Tharoor, *"Pax Indica" India and the World of the 21st Century*, Thomson Press, India Ltd., New Delhi, 2012.
11. *Hindustan Times*, May 25, 2014.
12. *The Hindu*, May 29, 2014.
13. "Five Point Someone" by C. Raja Mohan, *Indian Express*, May 26, 2014.
14. "Being a Bully" by Mani Shankar Aiyar, *Indian Express*, August 20, 2014.
15. *Indian Express*, August 21, 2014.

2

Sino-Indian Political, Economic and Strategic Interest in Asia

V.K. Narula

Introduction

It is believed that history repeats itself. 16th century saw China and India together generate more than 50 per cent of the world's GDP. These were the magnificent empires of the agricultural wave of the world history. Of course, the onset of the industrial wave revolution in Europe overtook and tilted this status towards itself. Subsequently, India was colonized and China spent a century of humiliation at the hands of foreign powers. However, the resultant aftermath of this colonization and humiliation helped in strong but different in character and ideology and nations emerged as major powers.

By the middle of the 20th century, both China and India had again re-emerged as major states, this time joined with Japan, resulting in the Euro-centric orientation once again undergoing a significant shift of paradigm, forcing the world to call the 21st century as the Asian century; holding within itself, the world's second, third and the fourth largest economies and whole range of second tier players on the rise. The industrialisation and urbanisation of Asia has not only led to foreseeable growth but also amplification of nationalism, exceptional and persistent military and naval build up. The same situation in Europe saw two highly destructive world wars. It is highly possible that the hunger for resources of energy and other critical inputs to maintain the Asian hegemony and power status may lead to hostilities in the near future, with the epicenter in Asia.

While military concerns remain important, they are no longer the only impetus. Much of the present emphasis has economic roots, recognizing that modern states are not self-sufficient and face a myriad of economic problems. International cooperation offers the only hope for solutions to shortages and mal-distribution of food and raw material, friction caused by competing political systems, and potential dangers posed by environmental decay.[1] China and India as the epicenter of the Asian comprehensive growth has to be seen in that light and priority.

DIMENSIONS OF SINO-INDIAN BILATERAL RELATIONS

Political Interaction

India and China restored ambassadorial relations in August 1976. Higher political level contacts were revived by the visit of the then External Affairs Minister, A.B. Vajpayee in February 1979 which was reciprocated by the Chinese Foreign Minister Huang Hua in June, 1981. Indian PM, Rajiv Gandhi's visit in 1988, Premier Li Peng visited India in December 1991 and PM Narashima Rao's visit to China in 1993 were more oriented towards boundary issue.

The visit of President R. Venkataraman to China in May 1992 and President Jiang Zemin's reciprocal state visit to India in November 1996 gave impetus to the political interaction between the two countries. India conducted its second series of nuclear tests in May 1998, which took the relations back to the square one. However the External Affairs Minister Jaswant Singh visited China in June 1999. It was reiterated that neither country is a threat to the other. Further visit of President K.R. Narayanan to China in May-June 2000 put the relations back on the track which was confirmed by a return visit of Premier Zhu Rongji in January 2002.

A landmark visit by Prime Minister A.B. Vajpayee to China in June 2003 is considered as an important event in the relations of both the countries.[2] During this visit, a Declaration on Principles for Relations and Comprehensive Cooperation was signed. This was the first comprehensive document on development of bilateral relations at the highest level between India and China. Both countries concluded a border trade protocol to add a border crossing between Sikkim and TAR. The two Prime Ministers appointed Special Representatives to explore the border issue from a political perspective.

Prime Minister Dr. Manmohan Singh visited China on 13-15 January 2008 during which a joint document, "A Shared Vision for the 21st Century of the Republic of India and the People's Republic of China", outlining common positions on a number of international and some bilateral issues, was signed. This was followed by another visit by the Indian Prime Minister in October same year to participate in the 7th Asia-Europe Summit held in Beijing. In May 2010, Mrs. Prathiba Patil, the President of India paid a state-visit to China and met Chinese top leadership. Besides this, she attended the reception to mark the 60th anniversary of diplomatic relations between both the countries which was jointly organized by CPAFFC and the Embassy of India. She also visited Luoyang to inaugurate the Indian style Buddhist Temple which was dedicated as a gift from India to the people of China.

The above visit was reciprocated by Chinese Premier Wen Jiabao who paid a three day official visit to India from 15-17 December 2010.[3] He met the top leaders of Indian government as well as the leader of opposition. He also interacted with the children in the Tagore International School and addressed India-China business cooperation summit. He also attended the closing ceremony of the Festival of China in India along with the Prime Minister of India.

Six agreements on cultural exchange, green technologies, media exchanges, hydrological data, and banking were signed and a Joint Communiqué was released. During this visit, a bilateral trade target of 100 billion USD was set to be reached by 2015.[4] A Strategic Economic Dialogue and a CEO Forum were established; and 2011 was declared as 'Year of India-China exchange'. The establishment of hotline between the Indian PM and the Chinese Premier, was established. Such, almost regular interactions did showed, that different perceptions on boundary should not hamper the bilateral relationship which is necessary to built a multilateral relation for both the countries.

Economic Interactions

The Asian giants China and India were economically the most strong and flourishing countries in the world, contributing almost 50% of the world's GDP. If there had been no boundary problem between both, the economic marriage would have continued. After the 1962 war, the trade relations between both the countries resumed only in 1978. Chinese GDP was lower than that of India in absolute terms in 1978 but caught up with India in the very next year. IMF predicts that in 2014, India and China together would account for 22.8% of world GDP, although China's share will be much bigger than India's. This is shown in Table 1.

The size of Chinese economy (in 1991) was 1.47 times that of India and in 2008, the size of Chinese economy became 3.58 times that of India. The growth rate of China in the pre-reform period was 5.5 and post-reform period was 10.1, whereas India's was 5.7 and 5.9 respectively. India had avoided the pitfalls of the Great Leap Forward and the Cultural Revolution.[5] Though after the Reforms of

Deng Xiao Ping since 1978, China was way ahead of India in all the economic and social parameters.

Table 1: World GDP Shares by G-7 and BRIC Countries, 1980–2014

Country	*1980* (%)	*1985* (%)	*1990* (%)	*1995* (%)	*2000* (%)	*2007* (%)	*2014** (%)
Advanced economies	64	64	64	64	63	56	49
Developing economies	36	36	36	36	37	44	51
G-7 countries	51	51	51	50	49	43	37
Canada	2	2	2	2	2	2	2
France	4	4	4	4	4	3	3
Germany	6	6	6	6	5	4	3
Italy	4	4	4	4	3	3	2
Japan	8	8	9	9	8	7	5
United Kingdom	4	4	4	4	4	3	3
United States	22	23	23	23	23	21	18
BRIC	15	16	17	16	17	23	29
Brazil	4	3	3	3	3	3	3
Russia/CIS	8	8	8	4	4	5	5
India	2	2	3	3	4	5	6
China	2	3	4	6	7	11	15
World	100	100	100	100	100	100	100

Note: Project estimates in 2014. Total may not appear to add due to rounding. GDP based on PPP.

Source: IMF, World Economics Outlook, Oct. 2009.

China and India both started their liberalization, privatization and globalization during the early 1990's. China dashed forward without any hindrance; even though being a communist state, it switched over to cent percent capitalist policy and kept the Deng Xiaoping's dictum alive; "I don't care whether it is a white cat or a black cat. It is a good cat as long as it catches mice."

India on the other hand could not follow the same system being a democracy. The ideologically same communists in China, who practiced hard core capitalistic policy in China, opposed the liberalization in India. In 1984 the two sides signed the Most Favored Nation Agreement.[6]

FDI which gives impetus to the economic growth of a country was adapted in China but faced problems in India initially. The Annual average inward FDI into China was US$ 48.79 billion (from 1991 to 2008) which accounted for 6.25% of the total annual average. Inward FDI into world is US$ 780.312 billion, whereas the annual average inward FDI into India was US$ 7.46 (from 1991 to 2008) which accounted for 0.96% of the total annual average inward FDI into world and 15.29% of the total annual average inward FDI into China. India got two-thirteenth of Chinese annual average inward FDI into China. At the beginning of 1991, India's inward FDI flow amounted to 75 million US Dollar. In other words, when India's inward FDI flow was one US$, Chinese was 58.21 US$ in the same year 1991; whereas at the end of the year 2008, India's inward FDI flow amounted to 41554 million US$. In other words when India's inward FDI flow was one US$, Chinese was 2.66 US$ in the same year.[7]

In 1991, China's industrial strength, infrastructure and vast pool of skilled labour made it a natural choice for the manufacturing sector. India, on the other hand, with booming information technology sector and its huge reserves of English-speaking graduates, was a better option for outsourced service and technology development facilities.

India has established itself unequivocally as the back office to the world and played a major role in business transformation by offering an unbeatable combination of low-cost and high value. India has now emerged as a major manufacturing hub, because of cost-effective production and skilled work-force. "The great untapped resource of technical and scientific knowledge available to India is the economic equivalent of the untapped continent available to the U.S 150 years ago."

In 1994, a Double Taxation Avoidance Agreement was signed between India and China which further brought both countries closer not only in bilateral trade but also had a cascading affect on the relations with the ASEAN forum.

India-China bilateral trade was as low as US$ 2.92 billion in 2000. The socio-economic indices of India are dismal compared to China. Infant mortality is 65 per thousand in India, while 30 per thousand in China. Life Expectancy is 65 years in India and 75 years in China. Literacy is 65% in India and 91% in China. Even the Human Development Index (HDI) which is a composite index prepared by UNDP using longevity, education and income as key components, China ranked 92, while India's was 134 in 2009. India, thus, has a poor HDI record as compared to China.

In June 2003, a JSG was set up after Prime Minister Vajpayee's visit to China. Both China and India have also consciously strengthened their economic relations within Asia as indicated from their dialogue partnership with ASEAN and signing of framework agreements for closer economic cooperation with it in 2002 and 2003 respectively. Bilateral trade and investment between the two countries have grown rapidly over the past few years pointing towards the presence of a vast potential for further growth.

Sino-Indian ties face a "Deficit of Trust". Although there is a positive outcome from the above economic engagements, there is a requirement to diversify the trade basket since 50% of exports of India to China is iron-ore and bilateral trade accounts for 7% of our global trade, but it is only 1.2% of China's trade volume. Therefore, India should diversify her export portfolio to more value-added products, apart from iron-ore—moving up the value-chain to reduce the gap in trade deficit. In 2010, bilateral trade between the two countries was in excess to the time of 60 billion dollars with the balance of trade tilting heavily in favour of China. The trade deficit for India in the same year stood at more than $ 20 billion. In 2009, it was $ 15.87 billion while in 2008 the trade deficit was $11.18 billion. Urgent steps are needed to boost the production and diversify the number of items which are to be exported. China dominates export of labour and intensive products world-wide; India does not, except in gems and jewellery. Chinese manufactured goods exports as percent of GDP was 18% as against 4% for India in 1999-2000. India's demographic profile is a key factor to India's future.

India is the most competitive producer of steel, automotive components, pharmaceuticals and chemicals, besides traditional strengths in textiles, gems and jewellery in the world.

In 2005, a MoU signed between both countries on liberalisation of air links to increase trade and other economic activities was a boost to the economy.[8] This agreement provides for major liberalisation of air links between India and China to cater for carriage of trade goods in plenty. The Memorandum is designed to have unlimited third, fourth and fifth freedom traffic rights with unlimited capacity entitlement for dedicated cargo services. In terms of frequency, the liberalized civil aviation agreement allows for 42 flights a week. Cities linked are Beijing-New Delhi; Guangzhou-New Delhi, Shanghai-New Delhi, Mumbai-Shanghai, Kunming-Kolkata and Chengdu-Bengaluru. Shanghai Airlines has also expressed keen interest in operating flights to India. In September 2010, the Ministry of Foreign Affairs, People's Republic of China authorized Hainan Airways to operate direct flights between India and China as per the 1988 ASA concluded between the two countries in Beijing.

There are a number of Chinese companies in India and vice-versa, doing good business. Although the balance of trade tilt is towards China and it is the major beneficiary at present. There are steps to be taken to reduce this as far as possible. India and China also have an understanding on Financial Dialogue. At this point of time, the economy of China and India affects the world economy. Therefore, during the Financial Dialogue, both sides exchanged views on the global macro-economic situation and policy responses, with specific reference to current risks to the global economy and the role of India and China in the post crisis recovery phase. Many bank branches of both countries have been opened to help business transactions of both countries.

There are many similarities and commonalties in administrative and economic activities. China and India are amongst the five biggest countries in the world in terms of area, geographical diversity, population, market-size and economy measured in terms of purchasing power parity. Both countries were colonized by western powers, and attained independence within a few years of each other in the mid twentieth century. They both pursued socialist models of development before opening up gradually, China from 1978, and India from 1991. China and India are presently the fastest growing major economies of the world, although the majority of the population continues to be dependent on agriculture as both have a large base in agriculture sector. The state sector continues to dominate economic activity in both countries and at the same time the role of private enterprise is expanding fast. In a research paper number 2008/13, on 'Comparing Regional Development in China and India' by Yanrui Wu of United Nations University explains how inspite of rapid economic growth, regional economic disparities have widened in both China and India.

Both China and India face serious fiscal problems and ballooning domestic debt and contingent liabilities. They need major public-sector adjustments in the foreseeable future. However, much of India's public sector deficit has been absorbed directly by the government, whereas China has relied more heavily on the banking system to fund the deficit. Therefore, while India has higher fiscal deficits, China's banking system has more non-performing assets.[9]

India-China Bilateral Trade: In 2008, bilateral trade between India and China stood at US $51.8 billion, which made China India's largest goods trading partner, replacing the United States of America. By the end of 2009, as a result of the world economic slowdown, bilateral trade dropped to US$ 43.27 billion. Also the trade deficit which was increasing since 2005 were affected even more. However, at the same time, while within a short period, China became India's single most important trading partner, India itself has reached at an unsustainable bilateral trade deficit of US$ 26.3 billion in 2010 (IMF, 2012a).

A JTF of India and China which was constituted to study the feasibility and the benefits of a possible China-India RTA, on the recommendations of the JEG, finalised its report in its sixth meeting held on 21st and 22nd October, 2007. The Prime Minister visited China during 13-15 January, 2008 and discussed the findings of this report with the Chinese Prime Minister. Both the Prime Ministers decided to refer the report for consideration to the JEG headed by the Trade and Commerce Ministers of the two countries. The report of India-China JTF was considered by the two Commerce Ministers at the 8th Session of India-China JEG held on 19th January, 2010 in Beijing. No decision was taken on the recommendations of the JTF.

In 2010 bilateral trade between China and India reached US$ 61.74 billion, a growth of 43% compared to the same period last year. India exported goods worth US$ 20.86 billion (+52%) to China and imported goods worth US$ 40.88

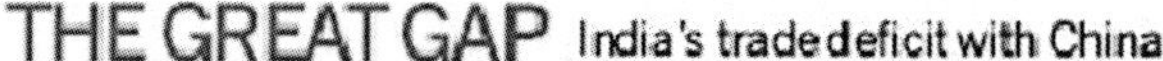

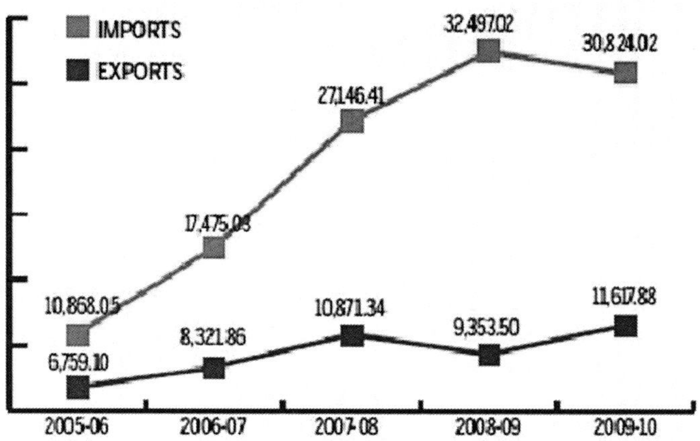

Source: DGCIS; figures in $ million

EXPORTS

Top 10 principal commodities

Commodity	%Share*
Iron Ore	44.48
Cotton Raw Including Waste	9.57
Other Ores and Minerals	5.54
Non-Ferrous Metals	5.03
Plastic and Linoleum Products	3.82
Gems and Jewellery	3.74
Machinery and Instruments	2.91
Ferro Alloys	2.39
Electronic Goods	2.15
Marine Products	1.84

IMPORTS

Top 10 principal commodities

Commodity	%Share*
Electronic Goods	30.78
Machinery Except Electronic	14.71
Organic Chemicals	7.63
Project Goods	6.69
Iron and Steel	4.15
Other Commodities	4.10
Electrical Machinery	3.69
Transport Equipment	3.12
Medicinal & Pharma Products	2.35
Textile, Yarn, Fabrics	1.93

*Share in total exports to, and imports from, China: source: DGCIS

billion (+38%) from China, resulting in an adverse balance of trade of US$ 20 billion.

In 2010 during Chinese Premier Wen Jiabao's visit to India both countries agreed to set up the India-China SED meant to discuss strategic macro-economic issues. It would also facilitated and shared their individual best practices and in handling challenges where emphasis was on domestic economic issues and to identify specific fields for enhanced cooperation, learning and experience sharing. At the SED, the Indian side is by Mr. Montek Singh Ahluwalia, Deputy Chairman, Planning Commission, while the Chinese side was led Mr. Zhang Ping, Chairman, NDRC.

Trade between the two ancient civilizations was not limited to the purely simple forms of transaction of primitive societies. The three main patterns of trade include reciprocity, redistribution and exchange. Applying these categories to the ancient Sino-Indian trade one finds that all the three main forms of transaction co-existed.[10]

A recent study by Goldman Sachs shows that India will take a long time to catch up with China; may not catch up even by 2050. This is because China has a much larger base than India; therefore, even smaller relative increases in income for China would mean higher absolute increase than India.

However, China is on the eve of a demographic shift that will have profound consequences on its economic and social landscape. Within a few years the working age population will reach a historical peak, and then begin a precipitous decline. This fact, along with narratives of rapidly rising migrant wages and periodic labor shortages, has raised questions about whether China is poised to cross the Lewis Turning Point, a point at which it would move from a vast supply of low-cost workers to a labor shortage economy. Crossing this threshold will have far-reaching implications for both China and the rest of the world.

SINO-INDIAN BILATERAL MILITARY RELATIONS

The PLA: Political-Military Paradigm

The date of the Nanchang Uprising—August 1, 1927—is taken as the birth date of the PLA. PLA and the CCP have survived many trials as these two entities have been intimately linked for little less than a century, and it sometimes has been hard to identify where one ended and the other one began. Both the PLA and CCP have together gleaned from each.[11]

Both China and India realized that their growth story can further be exploited to look for regional and subsequently global power status. One of their most potent weapons, the Armed Forces, should be allowed to interact with each other and work whenever situation requires. However it is important to note that the system of functioning of both, the PLA and the IA are quite different, historically as well as in the contemporary times. Historically, the relationship between the Communist Party of China and the People's Liberation Army has always remained that of mutual benefit and dependence. Lack of functional and clear institutional framework further compounded the problems. Actually, it was more in Mao's interest to keep it in that state, to serve his own interests of mass mobilization. He nurtured the army and invented a tailored-made compartment to mould the army into an essential ingredient of the Chinese politics. Since the inception of the PLA, in 1927, "political loyalty" has been the bedrock of its existence. The same can be proved by looking into the various events like; Cultural Revolution

(1966-1976) and the Tiananmen Square incident in 1989. Even a study by David Shambaugh suggests that Tiananmen signified a qualitative shift in the approach and stature of the PLA in domestic politics, transforming its task from military to political.[12]

Due to the emergence of a stronger economy, the subsequent years also saw a definite shift in the modernisation of the PLA and requirement of a stronger Air Force and Navy. While keeping history as the bedrock of inception of PLA, the modernisation plan was implemented so as to meet the requirements of the new world order. In the 40's while Mao did not feel the requirement of a bomb,[13] changed in late 50's and early 60's.

The PLA has moved towards smaller and more mobile forces. It has disbanded dozens of heavy divisions and created smaller brigades-producing a core of mobile mechanised forces and motorised functions. PLA has also established 'special mission battalions' for quick-reaction missions and rapid deployment units known as the **'fist'** units.[14] The formation of 'combined battalions,' from a company-sized unit to a dozen different branches of the armed forces, has significantly improved the operational flexibility of the PLA. The integration of the civilian transport network into PLA's logistical infrastructure has provided efficient troop transport and dramatically increased the mobility of PLA's ground formations, especially in Southern Tibet and along the disputed Sino-Indian border. The civil-military cooperation has allowed PLA to deploy its key formation faster, thus enhancing its military might along the borders and consolidating more effective control in remote regions. This modification is nothing but reinventing Chinese history of Tang Dynasty during which a system called 'fubing system' was invented for faster mobilisation of troops and the units were known as **"Zhechougfu"**.

Over the last decade China has committed itself to a deliberate and focused expansion of PLA's capabilities, aimed primarily at acquiring the necessary platforms to serve area-denial strategy. The Chinese Central Military Commission and the PLA headquarters visited 14 neighbouring countries in 2011, and had profound cooperation in military exercises. This is indicative of military diplomacy projecting PLA's military might in the region. China continues to focus on developing its military operations within Asia and invest in long-range power projection by investing in aircraft carriers, heavy bombers, strategic transport, amphibious assault vehicles by 2025 PLA will definitely be a formidable force to reckon within Asian and global contexts. People's Republic of China will gain formidable regional power-projection capabilities and PLA's ground forces would be at the forefront of this hard-power projection wherewithal, courtesy its defense spending.[15] The PLA is preparing itself to checkmate US, which would automatically take India into its fold.

Indian Armed Forces: A political Colonial Past and Present

During the British occupation of India, the British Indian Army was central in the occupation and policing of India. As a result, the army establishment had become synonymous with the image of British rule over India. This led to a general distrust within the political circles against the armed forces, who did not believe that the armed forces should occupy a central position in the running of the nation. India created, under the Home Ministry, a large numbers of para military forces ostensibly to man the borders, wage war on malcontent Indian citizens and so on.

The main motive though was the "Nehruvian" inferiority complex driven suspicion of the military which was, in his day, led by British educated and trained King's Commissioned Officers who were far superior to his pitiful Civil Servants and politicians like himself. The para military, the politician-bureaucrat nexus hoped provided them a bulwark against the Indian Armed Forces.

An immediate consequence of this was that the armed forces were relegated to a position below the political leadership. In addition to this, the Indian Armed Forces all come under the umbrella of the Indian Defense Ministry, headed by a Defense Minister who is more of a bureaucrat than a strategist.

It is mandatory for the armed forces to seek the approval of the ministry in all matters of acquisition. In essence, there is a two-layer system of checks and balances; the first layer is the strict loyalty of the armed forces to the elected leaders of the country and the second is the Defense Ministry. This ensures that the army is always kept under very strict civilian control. In 1957 for example when General K.S. Thimayya was appointed COAS and Krishna Menon was appointed Defense Minister, much was expected out of this relationship, but differences soon emerged and as a testament to post-independence India's suspicions of the armed forces, it was Menon the bureaucrat who emerged as Nehru's favourite.

It was Nehru's belief in peaceful rapprochement with his neighbours, coupled with a strong civilian control over the military that led to the neglect of the Indian Armed Forces. From 1947, the armed forces of India faced depleting capabilities and a withering arsenal for 15 years. However, this method of international relations was seen by many as too naïve to last. This organisation of the Indian Armed Forces was in stark contrast to what we see in India's neighbours such as China and Pakistan. In both these countries, the armed forces play a key role in governing the nation.

The offensive role by the Indian armed forces during the 1971 war was however, sometimes overlooked, despite having a clear military and strategic advantage against Pakistan (West). At that time, India did not choose to push forward into Pakistani territory or seek a forceful resolution to Kashmir, which goes to show that even in the wake of a victory, India's leaders and by extension of it's armed forces demonstrated the Nehruvian ideal of **'strategic restraint'.**

It was during Rajiv Gandhi's time that some strategic and visionary attitude was encouraged in building of the Armed Forces. Even this was short lived when he retrieved to coerce Pakistan with the military might India had at that point of time, during Brasstacks, once again showing the policy of restraint.[16] The Indian Army has been a political since inception. Thus, the difference in the cultural and historical up bringing of the Armed Forces emerging out of situations created by history of both the countries show a drastic difference in conceptual thinking.

The early years after independence were to enhance the capability of India towards self-sufficiency. The Nehruvian peace theory neglected the building of armed forces. However, soon this policy changed with the eventful wars waged against India by both its neigbhours, China and Pakistan. Contemporary India had no other option but to carry out modernisation programme of the Indian Armed forces although at a slow pace.

The Indian Army has been for long making a case for having its own fleet of attack helicopters which would be integral to the Cold Start Doctrine-designed to cut down the time taken to mobilise troops.

It has become necessary to achieve interoperability with U.S. and other friendly armed forces for joint operations in India's area of strategic interest due to unconventional threat. The Indian military is taking steps to modernise and create force structures that are capable of undertaking network-centric warfare on land, at sea, and in the air. Gradually, but perceptibly, the Indian armed forces are upgrading their capabilities, enhancing their kinetic effectiveness and command and control, and improving interoperability.[17] The fifteen year and five-year long modernisation programme has been given the green signal by the Indian government.

Force Comparision: China and India

The collapse of the Soviet Union in 1991 proved to be a boon to China. Apart from a formidable enemy being neutralised, many displaced scientists, engineers and technicians from the erstwhile Soviet Union found employment in the Chinese military industrial complex. The Russian aircraft industry struggling to survive was more than willing to sell modern aeroplanes and technology to China. And the booming Chinese economy could afford to import the best that was on offer.

Two of China's seven Military Area Commands (MACs)—Shenyang, Beijing, Lanzhou, Jinan, Nanjing, Guangzhou and Chengdu—are responsible for the Indian border. The Lanzhou MAC, which includes the 21st and 47th Combined

India vs China: Military Expenditure

	Defence Expenditure US$ m		Defence Expenditure per capita US$		Defence Expenditure % of GDP	
	India	China	India	China	India	China
2008	31,540	60,187	28	46	2.52	1.33
2009	38,278	70,381	33	53	3.11	1.41
2010	30,865	76,361	26	57	1.89	1.3

China has been stepping up its military expenditure steadily over the years. Though India has been following suit, the expenses are nowhere near those of China.

Corps (earlier known as Group Armies), is responsible for operations on the Ladakh border. The Chengdu MAC, which includes the 13th and 14th Combined Corps, is responsible for the Sikkim and Arunachal Pradesh borders.[18] These four Chinese combined corps musters nine divisions and five mechanised brigades. The Indian Army matches that with nine divisions on the Sino-Indian border—one in Ladakh, three in Sikkim, four in Arunachal and two in Nagaland and Manipur. In addition, India plans to raise a mountain strike corps during the 12th Defence Plan (2012-2017), which would add two more divisions. These would be stationed in the Brahmaputra Valley for launching offensive operations into Tibet.

China's road and rail infrastructure allows it. The major advantage of Chinese troops that they can move troops rapidly, even from other MACs. This would permit the PLAA to quickly concentrate a large number of troops in a small area, attack and overwhelm the Indian defenders at that point. Since the Sikkim and Arunachal roads are poor and railways non-existent, the Indian Army would find it difficult to move defenders as quickly to the threatened sector. The White Paper reveals that the PLAA has extensively practiced concentrating troops in a conflict zone. The document says, "since 2010, a series of campaign-level exercises and drills code-named "Mission Action" for trans-MAC maneuvers have been carried opposite the Indian border along Tibet. India has always estimated that the PLA Army (PLAA) numbers 1.6 million soldiers but the White Paper says the PLAA was just 850,000 strong. According to the White Paper, the the PLA Air Force (PLAAF) has 400,000 airmen, while the PLA Navy (PLAN) has 235,000 sailors. These figures of the white paper, however, does not seem to be matching with any other report available in the environment. **(See report of IISS)**

Many analysts make the mistake of comparing China's armed forces with those of India on item to item basis which is very simplistic. A country's military potential must be viewed against the backdrop of its will to fight, determination

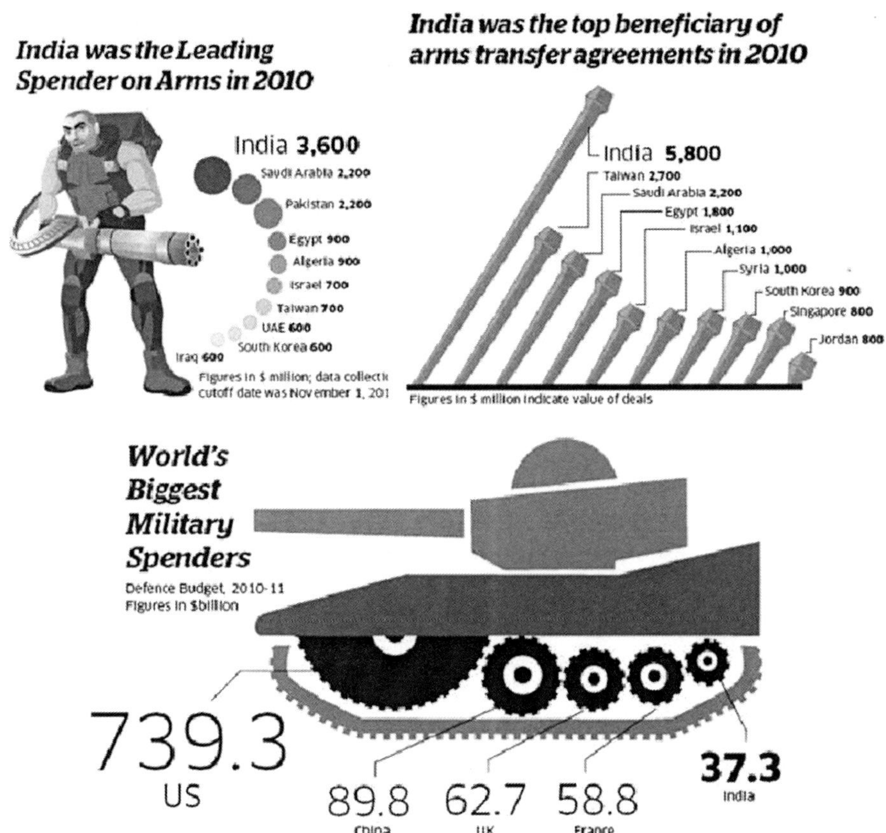

to win, ability to absorb punishment, innovative ideas and ingenuity of its leadership. However for comparative analysis it is mandatory to figure out the force levels. (**See IISS data of China and India's force levels.**)

Modus Operandi: Future War

Colonels Qiao Liang and Wang Xiangsui in one of their books have described 'assymetrical warfare' as the best option of war. This includes methods of non-military warfare including inter-alia hacking into websites, targeting financial institutions, engaging in terrorism and using the media, (psychological warfare). In an interview, with Zhongguo Qingnian Bao, Qiao stated that "the first rule of unrestricted warfare is that there are no rules, with nothing forbidden".

The evolution of Chinese strategy can be traced back to its written history itself. The military strategy of China is identified with its pre-eminent military strategists like Sun Tzu, Sun Bin and others. However, starting from Confucius and other contemporary thoughts of Mao gives a broader spectrum of options in which assymetrical warfare certainly gives examples of successes, where wisdom rather than valour was used to subdue the opposing forces e.g., D-3 viz. diversionary tactics, deception and disinformation is used as a potential tool.[19]

The other option as the US strategists think is the A2/AD i.e., 'area assess and area denial' concept. It is a concept of 'drawing the enemy into place and time of own choosing' at a tactical level. One could also safely conclude by this; make the enemy fight the way you want him to fight. Li Bingyan gives an good example of this. First, he asks how an inferior force could fight a technologically superior opponent. Using the example of a weak mouse (i.e., China) trying to keep track of a huge cat (i.e., the U.S.), he asks, "How could a mouse hang a bell around a cat's neck?" His answer: "the mouse cannot do this alone or with others. Therefore, the mouse must entice the cat to put the bell on himself". Second, he asks, "How can you make a cat eat a hot pepper?" His answer: "you can stuff a pepper down a cat's throat [the most difficult], you can put the pepper in cheese and make the cat swallow it, or you can grind the pepper up and spread it on its back. The latter method makes the cat lick itself and receive the satisfaction of cleaning up the hot pepper."[20] The cat is oblivious to the end goal either in case of the bell or the hot pepper. This deception reflects idiosyncratic Chinese strategy and, at least so far as how an inferior force might defeat a superior force, it evinces their mind-set.[21]

Sino-Indian Military Interactions

Amongst difference of opinion on the border, during various meetings between Dec 1988 and Jun 1993, progress was made in reducing tensions on the border via CBMs, including mutual troop reductions, regular meetings of local military commanders and advance notifications of military exercises. During Shri Sharad Pawar's visit to Beijing in July 1992, the first ever by an Indian Defense Minister, it was agreed to develop academic, military, scientific and technological exchanges. A senior level Chinese military delegation aimed at fostering CBMs between the defense forces of the two countries made a six day goodwill visit to India in Dec 1993. The visit was reciprocated by Indian Army Chief Gen BC Joshi's visit to China in July 1994. Since then regular exchanges have been taking place at various levels. The CNS, Indian Navy visited China in March 1996.

The Chief of Air Staff of the Indian Air Force visited China in May 2001. Another visit by Defense Minister, Mr. George Fernandes, to China in Apr 2003 only goes to show the politico-military relationship between the two countries.

This was followed by a return visit by Chinese Defense Minister Gen Cao Gangchuan in Mar 2004. In Dec 2004, Gen NC Vij, the then COAS visited China, the first by an Indian COAS in a decade, during which, both the countries agreed to deepen defense cooperation. In May 2005, the Chinese CGS visited India, a further sign of warming relations between the two countries. The Indian

Defense Minister Mr. Pranab Mukherjee visited China in May 2006 and signed the first ever MoU on Defense Exchanges between theArmed Forces of India and China.

The MoU envisaged the establishment of a mechanism to ensure frequent and regular exchanges between leaders and ministers of Defense Ministries and the armed forces of the two countries. The two developed an annual calendar for holding joint military exercises and training programmes. The defense ministers visit to the Lanzhou Military Area Command, which is the largest of the Chinese seven military regions and also controls the nuclear research and missile testing facilities, was a significant step in the process of building bilateral trust.[22] The Commander of PLA Air Force visited India in October 2006. In May 2007 Gen JJ Singh, Chairman COSC and COAS visited China. This was the first time that Chairman COSC visited China and was hosted by the CGS of the PLA. The first Defense Dialogue was held in November 2007.

The First Joint Training Exercise between the Indian Army and the PLA, 'HAND IN HAND 2007' was conducted at Kunming, China. One Company each from the Indian Army & PLA participated in the exercise which was based on the theme of Counter Terrorism. Simultaneously, the Commander PLA Navy paid a visit to India in Nov 2008. The Second India China Joint Training Exercise was held in India (Belgaum) in Dec 08 based on the same theme and participation level. The Ex Hand-in-Hand 2008 aimed at expanding and strengthening military-to-military ties between the two armed forces.

During the course of joint training, the Chinese troops from the 1st Company of Infantry Battalion of Chengdu Military Area Command and the Indian Army troops from 8 Maratha Light Infantry Battalion, participated. Suryakiran Aerobatic Team (SKAT) participated in the 7th International Aviation and Aerospace Exhibition at Zhuhai, China in 2008. This was followed by the second round of Defense Dialogue. The chairman COSC and CNS, Admiral Suresh Mehta visited China in 2009. The third Defense Dialogue was held in January 2010.

Nuclear Paradigm

Mao's China which pledged a nuclear free nation in early 50's describing nuclear nations as "paper tigers" took a U-turn under the same Mao. He started believing in a minimum nuclear deterrent to sort out its Taiwan policy in relation to the US. The reliability factor on USSR, for active nuclear help was probably not in the pipeline, and self-reliance was thought to be a viable option. It was Deng Xiaoping who performed the difficult job of linking the Maoist ideology for reasons of legitimacy while departing from it for practical purposes. China developed and possessed weapons of mass destructions, including chemical and nuclear weapons and conducted its first nuclear test on 16 October 1964.

Immediately after explosion, it committed itself to "no first use", which was also done by India, however China opposed any deal with India on 'minimum deterrence' in return of joining CTBT.[23] It exploded its first Hydrogen bomb in 1967. The tests continued till it signed the CTBT in 1996. On October 27 1966, it conducted the first successful missile trial test, and ratified the CWC in 1997. It acceded to the BWC in 1984.

China had built its Special Artillery Corps as far back in 1958, and then on July 1, 1966, it established its Second Artillery Corps with the approval of the Central Military Committee (CMC). The Second Artillery Corps today is a well-trained strategic missile corps with a certain level of nuclear counter attack capability.[24]

In its 2004 White Paper, China pledged not to be the first to use nuclear weapons at any time or under any circumstances. This "no-first-use pledge" was explicitly and unconditionally included in each of China's defense White Papers, from the first, in 1998, to the sixth and every year thereafter. It was among the strongest assurances in the world of no-first-use, a stance that the United States has never taken.

However, Xi Jinping, in a speech to the Second Artillery Force, which is responsible for China's land-based nuclear weapons, in a significant rhetorical shift, is reported to have said that nuclear weapons create strategic support for the country's status as a major power and did not repeat China's no-first-use promise this time probably a shift in national doctrine in context to the US doctrine in this matter.[25] In 2002 China ratified the IAEA additional protocol and was the first nuclear weapon state to do so. In 2004, China joined the NSG and ratified the Chemical Weapons Convention in April 1997. It has been experienced in case of nuclear issues that, a nuclear test is either preceded by or near simultaneously followed by a nuclear doctrine of the nation. However, in case of China, there didn't seem to be a coherent nuclear doctrine at least in public perception.[26]

The Chinese have certainly concluded that their current nuclear capabilities are not enough for credible minimum deterrence. Survivability and secrecy are absolutely critical to retaining the deterrent capability of Chinese nuclear forces. This is the primary reason that the Chinese nuclear forces are being modernized on such a large, wide-ranging scale. China believe of mixed ideology and practicality and headed towards a"nuclear deterrence with strong mass support".[27]

China does not plan to only increase the number of forces but also enhance their survivability simultaneously. Chinese had always called the disarmament of US and Russia as "Sham Disarmament". Thus Banning Garrett and Bonnie Glaser has described China's arms control approach as of "limited security interdependence. "They say that China has not only learnt the importance of nuclear weapons from the USA and the USSR but also that "continued arms competition and further qualitative enhancement of nuclear forces go hand-in-hand with arms control agreements".[28] Since China is a signatory to the CTBT, it would restrict in its quantitative production. China doesn't disclose the size of its nuclear arsenal, but U.S. officials and experts estimate it at around 240 warheads. Beijing has never sought to match U.S. nuclear capabilities, but has tried to establish "minimum deterrence"—sufficient nuclear forces to survive a nuclear attack on Chinese soil and to conduct a retaliatory "second strike." Alexei Arbatov, an expert on nuclear issues at the Carnegie Moscow Centre believes China was the only country that, by adding multiple warheads to its missiles, could expand its nuclear arsenal to the same level as the U.S. and Russia within 10-15 years.[29]

India's first PM, Pandit Jawaharlal Nehru had said, "as long as the world is constituted as it is, every country will have to devise and use the latest devices for its protection. I have no doubt India will develop her scientific researches and I hope Indian scientists will use the atomic force for constructive purposes. But if India is threatened, she will inevitably try to defend herself by all means at her disposal".

In response to the testing by China in 1964, immediately preceding the 1962 war, India was left with no option but to be self-reliant. India tested its first nuclear device in 1974, which was code-named "Smiling Buddha". The test was followed by number of sanctions imposed by United States. India became a member of the IAEA but did not sign the NPT or the CTBT, due to its objection to the lack of provisions for universal nuclear disarmament "within a time-bound framework."

India also demanded that the treaty also ban laboratory simulations. In addition, India opposed the provision in Article XIV of the CTBT that requires India's ratification for the treaty to enter into force which India argued was a violation of its sovereign right to choose whether it would sign the treaty. In early February 1997, Foreign Minister I.K. Gujral reiterated India's opposition to the treaty, saying that "India favors any step aimed at destroying nuclear weapons, but considers that the treaty in its current form is not comprehensive and bans only certain types of tests."

India is an original signatory to the CWC. In June 1997, it acknowledged that it had a dedicated chemical warfare production programme. The second series of tests were conducted by India on 13 May 1998 code named "**operation Shakti**". The tests were India's first since 1974, and reversed the previously ambiguous nuclear posture where Indian officials denied possession of nuclear weapons. Indian officials cited a perceived deterioration of India's security environment, including increasing Pakistani nuclear and missile capabilities and perceived threats from China, to justify the tests.

In August 1999, the Indian government released a proposed nuclear doctrine prepared by a private advisory group appointed by the government. It stated that India will pursue a doctrine of 'credible minimum deterrence'. The document states that the role of nuclear weapons is to deter the use or the threat of use of nuclear weapons against India, and asserts that India will pursue a policy of "retaliation only."

The draft doctrine maintains that India "will not be the first to initiate a nuclear strike, but will respond with punitive retaliation should deterrence fail." The doctrine also reaffirms India's pledge not to use or threaten to use nuclear weapons against states that do not possess nuclear weapons. It further states that India's nuclear posture will be based on a triad of aircraft, mobile land-based systems, and sea-based platforms to provide a redundant, widely dispersed, and flexible nuclear force. Itty Abraham argues that it was not until roughly 1986 that India could be considered a "nuclear weapons-capable state."[30] At that time, advances in Pakistan's efforts to acquire nuclear weapons and the oblique nuclear threats issued by Islamabad in the wake of the 1986 to 1987 Brass tracks crisis appear to have persuaded Prime Minister Rajiv Gandhi to authorise weaponisation of India's nuclear capability. In 2007, India's national security interests recommended"a comprehensive and integrated nuclear defense capability," taking into account the persistent political instability in the region and China's continued nuclear cooperation with Pakistan.[31]

China's Interest in East Asia

The growing prowess of China is the result of China's and other nation's interdependency on each other from historic times. When Mao Zedong died in September 1976, China was, in many respects, already an East Asian great power. It had already fought a politico-military war with United States to draw in the Koreans; it had developed a soft nuclear deterrent capability. It had subjected its neighbors with its typical and traditional concept of the 'Middle Kingdom', which included Burma, Thailand, North Vietnam, North Korea and even Pakistan to accommodate its interests in territorial security in exchange of perks from China.

Politically it superimposed itself in the resolution of regional conflicts like, 1954 war in Indochina, 1962 settlement of the Laotian civil war and the U.S.-North Vietnamese war and subsequently, agreement and its unification. However, in the post-Cold War era, the focus still remains on the prospects for regional tension and heightened power conflict. It is felt that tension may increase due to the absence of liberal democracies, economic interdependence and multilateral institutions. East Asia has the world's largest and the most dynamic economies as well as great power competition.[32] The dangerous combination of economy and strategy leads to preoccupation in East Asian balance of power. The most important factors in the Chinese rise in the East Asian strategic dynamics would be; firstly, how will China counter the US hegemonic capacity in East Asia vis-a-vis it is not very conducive to relations with its maritime neighbours, secondly, its maritime security, thirdly, modification of its PLA in a superfast mode, fourthly, its role in regional integration, fifthly, the Cross-straits relationship with Taiwan and continental Tibetan separatism.

The difficulties coming in the way of China's rise was a negative legacy from Mao Zedong in China's support for the Khmer Rouge and the invasion of Vietnam. Second, China has been too tough on territorial issues, such as with Taiwan in the 1990s. Third, China's relations with some of its Asian neighbours are not as good as they could be. Ties with Japan have improved only in trade but are still not warm. The relationship with India and Russia are worse than they were in the past. Ties with South Korea were much closer in 2004 than they are currently. The same could be said about Australia and Indonesia. The exception was where China has made progress with Taiwan.

The overall objective of China's regional strategy for East Asia was to push for more regional integration. The continuing emphasis is that China affords ASEAN+1 (China-ASEAN) as a venue for cooperation; China's plans for numerous projects to connect the infrastructure of neighbouring countries, the building of cooperation mechanisms, such as the Chiang Mai initiative and the regional economic surveillance system. China's economic aid to Southeast Asian countries most affected by the financial crisis and China's willingness to engage Japan during its change in leadership. East Asia is bipolar because of location of China in East Asia and hegemonic presence of U.S. From early 1970's till the end of cold war, there were three actors in the strategic triangle in East Asia i.e., U.S., China and Russia. However after the cold war the Chinese have filled up the vacuum for Russia in Korean peninsula and Vietnam. The bipolar regional component is the Chinese dominance of mainland of East Asia and U.S. dominance of maritime East Asia.[33]

In further assessing China's influence, trade and investment were major strengths for China, as were its bilateral and multilateral relations, which asked little of neighbouring countries. China also derived power from its cultural influence in the region, including overseas Chinese. In terms of weaknesses, China's nationalism conflicted with other nationalistic countries in Asia. China's territorialism, military expansion, authoritarianism and lack of transparency have also weakened its ability to have stronger influence. Further, China was unwilling to undertake the risks necessary to address these weaknesses.

US on the other hand exploited these shortcomings of China to gain the dependency of these nations for a secure environment. However, it was the global financial crises which brought China into limelight. In order to achieve its national ambition of development set during the 16th CCPC in 2002, China decided to abolish its previous model of keeping at a controlled level tensions in relation with its neighbours in favour of building benign relationship with them; the most important of them being the building of positive relationship with ASEAN on the basis of partnership and cooperation. Variety of agreements were signed which helped to foster closer relations with other Southeast nations as well.[34]

China is aware that in wake of its ascendency, other countries are likely to follow a path of hedging. Some of the strategies could be as follow:

(a) A traditional balance of power and a containment policy through the forging of military alliances against Beijing;
(b) Diplomatic and political "soft-balancing", engagement and hedging; maximizing relations with US, India and in some cases European Union (EU);
(c) Bilateral and multilateral cooperation in form of an incipient EAC; strengthening ASEAN; promote ASEAN+3, ARF and EAC;
(d) Be accommodative to the Chinese sentiments and core interests;
(e) Follow a policy of appeasement and show neutrality and even bandwagoning;
(f) Make alliance with China and become its satellite state and accept tributary status in an emerging Sino-centric order to enjoy the influence, suzerainty and hegemony in East Asia.

Unlike US, China has not sought or maintained any military bases beyond its borders in East Asia, so far, which may be a little soothing. But making military use of these commercial coastal areas in near future cannot be ruled out, lest we forget that East India Company and the colonisation of other countries by Britain and other European countries. In the given situation, there are not very many countries prepared to accept **Pax Sinica**, even the most likely cases of North Korea and Myanmar. They also keep the rise of India in mind. Japan, South Korea, Philippines, Thailand and Singapore remain quasi-allies of the US.

China has accommodated its East Asian neighbours, to reassure them of accepting a multilateral approach to the territorial disputes in the Spratley in the South China Sea, and actively participate in regional processes such as APT, ARF, APEC and EAS. The Chinese soft power may grow in East Asia but at the same time US and Japan can also exercise soft power. Even smaller regional players display soft power. The mutual benefits of economic interdependence between China and small actors are probably more attractive than Chinese soft power. The authoritarian nature of Chinese regime may turn out to be an Achilles heel and will have little appeal beyond North Korea, Laos, Vietnam and Myanmar. Thus, the East Asian countries seek to be friend and a partner based on mutual respect but not its vassal state.

China's enjoys hegemony over North Korea's economy and security due to its geographical contiguity and its strategic and economic isolation because of the nuclearisation. China also enjoys not only conventional military superiority on the Sino-Russian border but also advantages over Russia over its border states of Kazakhstan, Kyrgyzstan, and Tajikistan. China has a dominant influence in Southeast Asia. Burma has been a de facto Chinese protectorate. Thailand has also more or less aligned with China after U.S. presence in Southeast Asia mainland diminished. Vietnam and Cambodia also saw a leaning towards China. All these changes saw China achieve dominance over the mainland of East Asia with the exception of South Korea, which also practices comparative hegemony between the U.S. and China, in its national interest. On the other hand the U.S. still retains domination in maritime East Asia, inspite of loosing its bases in Thailand in 1975 and withdrawing from bases in Philippine in 1991 because of its advanced and technologically superior air and naval projections facilities in Singapore, Malaysia, Indonesia and Brunei.

China and India's Common Interest: South China Sea (SCS)

South-China Sea is an area of important concern. There is a dispute over territory and sovereignty over ocean areas and the Paracel and the Spratly—two island chains claimed in whole or in part by a number of countries. The area consists of dozens of uninhabited rocky outcrops, atolls, sandbanks and reefs, such as the Scarborough Shoal. China claimed the entire SCS and made its first effort to include the region as a "core national interest", similar to Taiwan, Tibet and Xinjiang province, relating it to 2000 years of history when the Paracel and Spratly island chains were regarded as integral parts of the Chinese nation by submitting claim to the UNCLCS in May 2009.

China's aggressive attitude on the SCS affected India after Beijing denounced an Indian company ONGC Videsh's venture for off-shore oil exploration in water's belonging to Vietnam (not recognized by China). It showed China's double standards. While China opposes India's entry into the SCS on commercial issues initiated by Vietnam, it unilaterally insists on building strategic projects in POK and on deploying troops there.

In view of India not withdrawing from its commitment, China announced plans to expand maritime exploration of 10,000 sq km of seabed in Southwest Indian Ocean. The afore-stated developments need to be seen in the context of India's stated naval doctrine. The Indian Navy document (2007) "Freedom to use the Seas: India's Maritime Military Strategy", lays down clearly that India's area of interest which "extends from the north of the Arabian Sea to the South China Sea".

In the ARF meeting in 2010, India along with many more countries backed the United States' multilateral approach, instead of China's "bilateral approach" for resolution of the SCS disputes and that the SCS should remain open for international navigation. The SCS is not only a strategic maritime link between the Pacific and the Indian Ocean, but is also a vital gateway for shipping in East Asia. Almost, 55% of India's trade with the Asia Pacific transits through the SCS. Apart from helping secure energy supplies for countries like Japan and Korea, India has the unique distinction of shipping oil from Sakhalin to Mangalore through sea routes of the region. China, naturally, does not welcome the ASEAN move to interact militarily with India.

In 2010, the Indian Navy carried out Milan series of maritime exercises in the Andaman and Nicobar Islands with almost all ASEAN countries. India helped Malaysia in building up its Coast Guard. India has a strong Navy with technological credibility that can be leveraged by ASEAN. Collaboration on missile technology, radar systems, defense component systems and supporting hardware are again areas where ASEAN countries can work in partnership with India. India has also shown keenness to sell Brahmos missiles to friendly countries including the neighbouring Southeast Asian countries. Most of the ASEAN countries have engaged in a defence modernisation programme, assistance in weapons up-gradation and systems integration, with India due to its long experience in using Russian products and giving this service cheaper.[35]

China and India's Interest in Indian Ocean

Consideration of China's strategic objectives in the Indian Ocean is an imperative discussion and a matter of analysis as to the intents of the Chinese. It boils down to two possibilities. Firstly, that China is genuinely seeking to sustain its economic development and achieve its goal of being seen as an emerging and responsible world power; and therefore has to secure its energy routes. Secondly, it is seeking to expand its influence aggressively by consolidating its presence through the acquisition and construction of military and naval facilities and by improving relations with Indian Ocean island and littoral states, thus isolating India and reducing the role of the United States in the region; in which case it fulfills both the criteria of securing its energy routes and containing India. China's naval presence in the Indian Ocean began in earnest in 2006, when Chinese vessels joined the international task force aimed at curbing Somali piracy in the Gulf of Aden and securing pivotal global shipping routes.

By the foregoing it is evident that China is embarked on a multi-phased strategy of expanding along the Chinese coast from Japan to Taiwan, the Philippines and Borneo to include portions of the northern Yellow Sea, the East China Sea, the South China Sea and, eventually, the northern Pacific, keeping in mind the protection of sea lanes from the Middle East. In this regard the development of a naval base at Sanya, on the southern coast of Hainan Island is an example.[36]

After almost two decades, in 2010 China raised its defense budget by only 7.5 percent. Shen Dingli, a professor at Fudan University in Shanghai, believes that, it is the ability of other states to block China's trade routes that poses the greatest threat to China, and not terrorism or the piracy. To prevent this from happening, he advocates not only a blue-water navy but also overseas military bases to cut the supply costs. In this context, the Chinese no longer accept the Indian Ocean as only an ocean of the Indians and advocate a new naval strategy of "far sea defense", that include the Indian Ocean.

Deployment of its Jin class submarines in 2008 at a submarine base near Sanya in the southern tip of Hainan raised alarm in India, as the base is merely 1200 nautical miles from the Malacca Strait which is the closest access point to the Indian Ocean. The base also has an underground facility that can hide the movement of submarines which makes them difficult to detect. The concentration of strategic naval forces at Sanya could propel China towards a consolidation of its control over the surrounding Indian Ocean region (IOR).

The presence of access tunnels on the mouth of the deep water base is particularly troubling for India as it will have strategic implications in the IOR, allowing China to interdict shipping at three crucial chokepoints in the Indian Ocean—Bab el Mandeb, the Strait of Hormuz, and the Strait of Malacca. More important point of concern is what has been termed China's "string of pearls" strategy that has significantly expanded China's strategic depth in India's backyard.

In January 2009 an Indian Kilo class Indian submarine and Chinese warships, on their way to the Gulf of Aden to patrol the pirate-infested waters, reportedly engaged in rounds of maneuvering as each tried to test for weaknesses in the others' sonar system. The Chinese media reported that its warships forced the Indian submarine to the surface, which was strongly denied by the Indian Navy.[37] China has activated its maritime geo-political interests by earning contracts with various littoral states/coastal countries in Pacific and Indian Ocean.

It struck a deal with Pakistan in March 2002 to construct its port at Gwadar, which is strategically located on the western end of Baluchistan coast on the opposite end of the Gulf of Oman, an important route for oil tankers bound for Japan and western countries out of Gulf. It is a centerpiece as a gateway to Strait of Hormuz. Lately, the port has been handed over to China to be operated by state-run Chinese firm—China Overseas Port Holding Company (COPHC). Many Indian and other world strategists feel that in the long run there is a possibility of Pakistan allowing China to make military use of this port.

Another Chinese investment in the Indian Ocean is the construction of Sri-Lankan Port of Hambantota, also known as 'Magampura' which is situated about 19 nautical miles north of the key shipping route between the Malacca Strait and the Suez Canal. It links Asia and Europe. The construction of phase-1 commenced in 2008. An estimated 36,000 ships including 4500 oil tankers use this route annually. It is a deep water port unlike most of the Indian ports and is in close proximity to the most intense sea lanes in the world. 85% of the cost of construction was funded by the Export-Import Bank of Republic of China and constructed by China Harbor Engineering Company and Sino Hydro Corporation. Hambantota is projected to have a liquefied natural gas refinery, aviation fuel storage facilities, three separate docks giving the port a Tran's shipment capacity and dry docks for ship repair and construction. The project also envisages that when completed the port will serve as a base for bunkering and refueling. The port at Gwadar also has similar characteristics is a point of concern.

Dr. Hasan Mahmud, Bangladesh State Minister for Environment and Forests stated that China had agreed to fund and help to modernize the Chittagong port, which handles around 92 per cent of the country's import-export trade, and in building a new deep-water port facility at Sonadia, located near Cox's Bazaar. Chittagong's strategic location serves as an important access point for Chinese commerce, as recently confirmed by Shanghai Institute for International Studies' South Asia director, Zhao Gancheng, who stated: 'Developing the port is a very important part of China's co-operation with Bangladesh, and China is aware of its strategic significance.' He added: 'While there is currently no oil pipeline running to Bangladesh, access to Chittagong will be of greater importance in the future when this infrastructure is put in place'. With the development of China's transportation of goods and energy in the Indian Ocean, China will certainly continue to attach more importance to this Port' and construct Chittagong-Kunming Highway via Myanmar. Dr. Hasan Mahmud, the State Minister for Environment and Forests had stated. Although in its present form, no military use of the port is envisaged, but future use will depend on the geostrategic environment prevailing at that point of time.

The coastline of Burma provides naval access in the proximity of one of the world's most strategic water passages, the Strait of Malacca. It is the narrow ship passage between Malaysia and Indonesia. It links the Indian and Pacific Oceans, and is the shortest sea route between the Persian Gulf and China. It is the key chokepoint in Asia. More than 80% of China's oil passes through the Malacca Strait. The narrowest point is the Phillips Channel in the Singapore Strait, only 1.5 miles wide at its narrowest. Themistocles, a Greek writer, once said that, "he who commands the sea has command of everything." "Whoever controls the Indian Ocean dominates Asia.... in the 21st century the destiny of the world will be decided on its waves." It is being attributed to Mahan. Both China and India's growing military ambitions and maritime power build-up in seeking the control of Indian Ocean have the potential to destabilise the region.

For those who are positioned between these rising powers, amid Grotian notions of the oceans and Mahanian visions of sea power, there remains an historic challenge as well; the member states of the ASEAN must find fresh ways of averting confrontation and facilitating co-operation that would contribute, in sum, to the rediscovery of equilibrium.[38]

Of all the Southeast Asian states, Burma occupies the most sensitive position between India and China, giving rise to routine descriptions of a 'Sino-India rivalry'. If the strait were closed, nearly half of the world's tanker fleet would be required to sail further, leading to arise in freight rates worldwide. The region from Burma to Banda Ache in Indonesia is fast becoming one of the world's most strategic chokepoints. In 1992, China and Burma agreed that China would modernise Burmese naval facilities, in return for permitting the Chinese navy to use the Small and Great Coco Island.

Since then, Chinese experts have built an electronic intelligence station on Great Coco Island, vastly improved and militarised the Burmese port facilities in the Bay of Bengal at Akyab (Sittwe), Kyaukpyu and Mergui, and constructed a major naval base on Hainggyi Island near the Irrawaddy river delta. China assists in constructing a naval base in Sittwe (Akyab), a strategically important seaport close to eastern India's largest city and port, Kolkata. The day may not be too far off when a Chinese aircraft carrier makes routine pit stops at cities along the Indian Ocean littoral.

It also funds road construction linking Rangoon and Akyab, providing the shortest route to the Indian Ocean from southern China. It has also built an 85-metre jetty, naval facilities and major reconnaissance and electronic intelligence systems on the Great Coco Island which is located 18 kilometers from India's Andaman and Nicobar Islands. It gives Chinese capabilities to monitor India's military activities, including missile tests. Access to Burma's ports and naval installations provide China with strategic influence in the Bay of Bengal, in the wider IOR and in Southeast Asia. To keep its presence felt, India, in 2004, signed an agreement in Yangon by the foreign ministers of India, Burma and Thailand to develop transport linkages between the three countries. This included a 1,400 km highway connecting North-Eastern India with Mandalay and Yangon, and on to Bangkok, which would contribute to opening up trade between the countries and give India access to Burmese ports. India is also spending $100 million to fund a deal linking Burma's Sittwe port with an Indian one, perhaps Calcutta. A planned deep-sea port in Dawei, together with a new highway connecting it to Kanchanaburi in Thailand would no doubt contribute further to commercial links.[39] Seychelles off late has been in limelight due to more Chinese commercial and military activities. Although Chinese relations with Seychelles date back to 1976 and were of little interest till 2007 when President Hu Jintao visited this island nation as a part of his eight-nation tour of Africa. These were only inconsequential diplomatic and economic ties between the two nations till this visit. Hu's visit signaled China's strategic interests in the region for the first time. Chinese Defense Minister General Liang Guanglie led a 40-

member military delegation to Seychelles; a nation with just a 500-strong SPDF does raise uneasy questions. As a part of developing military ties, China gifted the SPDF with two Y-12 aircraft for surveillance and anti-piracy duties and its hospital ship 'Peace Ark' visited Seychelles in November 2010. China is also training 50 soldiers of the SPDF in China as part of a military cooperation agreement signed in 2004.[40]

India has a major interest in Seychelles. Besides a fair sized diaspora, mainly from Tamil Nadu to Gujarat, India has actively supported Seychelles in training the SPDF. It provided a Dornier aircraft, two Chetek helicopters (1981 vintage) and a fast attack craft. Indian ships regularly visit Victoria and have been active in combating piracy in the waters around Seychelles. The Indian Foreign and Defense Ministers visited Seychelles in 2010 underlining the importance of having friendly relations with Seychelles.[41] The Indian Navy has actively been guarding the EEZ (Exclusive Economic Zone) of this island nation since 2009 following a request from the Seychelles government. Warships and maritime aircraft of the Indian Navy stationed in this island country have also been spearheading anti-piracy operations in the IOR.

Chinese intent of spreading their tentacles in the IOR and trying to outstrip the historical Indian presence in these coastal areas indicates Chinese intent of overshadowing the Indian monopoly in the region. In 2004, a team of think-tanks in the United States ; Booz-Allen reported, of a concept of China's purported plan to establish naval bases and intelligence stations throughout littoral South Asia; adherents to this perspective argue that Beijing has spent the past decade trying to forge closer diplomatic relations with many Indian Ocean nations. It is yet to be analysed whether "Asia Pivot" provided impetus to term called "Strings of Pearls"[42] or visa versa. But it is quite evident from the above that both the terms involve Sino-Indian relations, good or bad, time will dictate.

The "Strings of Pearls" theory is probably based on the fact that China possesses one of the world's largest commercial shipping fleet and relies very heavily on international maritime commerce. Since its energy requirements traverse long treacherous sea's coupled with the dangers of piracy, it is pertinent that China seeks for security of its important energy by means of establishing economic and military relations. While, immediate economic relationship for a long duration is visible and seen; the long term interest of these bases for military use remains a dilemma. There are two schools of thought; one, that in the game of power politics, China does not want itself to be contained by any nation, in the present scenario, it is the US; two, it wants to be the most powerful. However, in either case, India gets entangled. Keeping the experience of 1962 and related incidents still lingering, a small part of the brain gets activated to think of the intent of China past of "Middle Kingdom" and "Mandate of Heaven", its present of "Peaceful Rise" and its future of "Global Power".

Conclusion

Concepts of international politics based solely on poweful nations pursuing their own interests, with opposing power blocks as the only deterrent and competing power blocs maintaining peace through mutual fear are now obsolete. Power remains an important element (perhaps the most important) in relations among nations, but no state now has sufficient power to impose its will on the international community. Therefore, the self-interest of the mighty as well as the weak is best served through cooperative efforts to solve security problems be they military, economic or political.[43]

The Chinese have very often practiced hard sui generis realpolitik, and strategic doctrines. In the period of strength, the diplomacy of the Middle Kingdom was an ideological rationalization for imperial power and during the period of decline, it served to mask weakness and helped China manipulate contending forces. China has the ability, skill and the political will to coax people surrounding it. Foreign policy has always been fundamentally affected by domestic politics and ideological fixations. China's international behavior has been subject to the pressures of anarchy and the associated search for security. Chinese policy makers have always kept the domestic politics at the back of their mind for ensuring global political survival. In the present geo-political scenario, the Chinese policy in Central Asia is intended to hold political stability through economic growth, and rule rather than deter its opponents. The Chinese display their character in a popular game they play; Wei qi, meaning, "a game of surrounding pieces"; implies a concept of strategic encirclement.[44] China mainly relied on its traditional resources: the analytical abilities of its diplomats, and the endurance and cultural confidence of its people, rather than on technology or military power to wither away pressures from Europeans. Europeans today feel twenty first century to be an Asian century. A decade can make a great difference. A little more than a decade earlier, the Asian financial crisis seemed to spell the end of the "Asian miracle", while now, a little more than 10 years later, the region is one of the few bright spots in the global economy. The Asian crisis was also claimed to be the catalyst for increasing integration in the region.

However, the issue of whether economic growth, as a presumed consequence of further regional integration, can be separated from the discussion of security has been raised, especially in the aftermath of the crisis coupled with Chinese hegemonistic and assertive attitude. India perceives the relationship between China and India has very often than not, revolved around bilateral issues like boundary and off late, water. There are reasons to believe that since the late 1950's hostility and confrontation had featured in its relations.

After 1988, perceptions varied greatly on improvement, since bilateral ties showed positive graph only in trade, that too imbalanced. Strong economic relations are no insurance against political, military and strategic confrontations of China and India. India believes that friendship cannot be either little or more, it has to be complete and in doing so, no barriers or constraints should be acting as a catalyst. The barriers of unresolved boundary dispute, only with India, when same with other countries have been solved, the nuclearisation and arming of Pakistan with an aim to destabilise India and strategic aim of creating water scarcity or using water as a blackmail tool in future are all but causing trust deficit and, therefore, a perceived threat rather than friendship from China. With the trust deficit in the background the overlapping spheres of influence seem to forestall the chances for genuine Sino-Indian rapprochement.

REFERENCES

1. R.D. Bernard, Nuclear Weapons and Limited War, Washington, 1986, pp. 123.
2. M. Rasgotra and V.D. Chopra India's Relations with Russia and China: A New Phase, Gyan Publications New Delhi, p. 180.
3. F. Burton and B. West, A Closer Look at India's Naxalite Threat, 8 July 2010. Available at (http://www.stratfor.com / weekly / 20100707 closer look indias naxalite threat assessed on 9 July 2013.
4. A.J. Anoop, China-Naxalite linkages: Guaging Its Dimentions, 25 March 2011. http://www.vifindia.org/article/2011/march/25/China-Naxalite-linkages-Gauging-its-dimensions assessed on 2 Aug 2013
5. S.R.Gen Chowdhury (Retd), "To Combat Red Terror, Tackle its Root Causes", *The Asian Age*, April 21, 2009
6. *Economic Watch*, 30 June 2010
7. Journal of Contemporary Research in Management, January-March, 2010, pp. 132-133.
8. Ministry of External Affairs, Government of India official site.
9. China's Economy Yearbook, Vol.-2, Ed, Chen Jiagui, p. 83.
10. L.Xinru, 1988 second impression, 1997, Ancient India and Ancient China; Trade and Religious Exchanges AD 1-600, Oxford University Press, New Delhi, p. 77.
11. Mao Tse-tung, 'Problems of War and Strategy', from the Selected Works of Mao Tse-tung, Peking: Foreign Language Press, 1967, p. 219.
12. P. J. Panda, China's Path to Power; Party, Military and the Politics of State Transition, Pentagon Press, New Delhi, 2010.
13. R.P. Pillai, The Dragon's Fire: Chinese Military Strategy and Its Implications for Asia, Rupa and Co, New Delhi, 2009 p. 17.
14. Ibid, p. 113.
15. For more details see National Defense Research Institute, Rand, article at http://www.rand.org/content/dam/rand/pubs/monographs/2011/RAND_MG1009.pdf. assessed on 2 July 2013.
16. S. Saher, 10 Aug. 2011, Indian Defense: Role and Function of the Indian Armed Forces. www.indiandefense.com/role-function-indian-armed-forces-1068/ assessed on 24 May 2013.
17. An article by G. Kanwal in National Bureau of Asian Research: India's Military Modernization: Plans and Strategic Underpinnings, Sep 2012. http://www.nbr.org/research/activity.aspx?id=275#.UdJffthHjfI assessed on 2 July 2013.
18. An article in Business Standard written by A. Shukla.
19. A. Seghal, China and the Doctrine of Asymmetrical Warfare, Indian Defence Review, Oct-Dec, 2002.
20. Bingyan li, "Applying Military Strategy in the Age of the New Revolution on Military

Affairs," in The Chinese Revolution in Military Affairs, ed., Shen Weiguang China: New China Press, 2004 pp. 2-31

21. Excerpts taken from the article "The Chinese Military's Strategic Mindset" by Lt Col T.L. Thomas, U.S. Army (Retd).
22. R.N. Das IDSA Monogram No.19, May 2013, India-China Relations: A New Paradigm.
23. "China opposes minimum Nuclear-Deterrence to India", *The Hindu*, Delhi, 28 Jan 1999.
24. Major General Y. Huan, "China's Strategic Nuclear Weapons", Defense Industry of China 1949-89, Beijing: National Defense Industry Press, 1989 excerpted in Michael Pillsbury (ed.) Chinese View of the Future Warfare, Institute for National Strategic Studies, 1990.
25. J.M. Acton, April 2013, Is China Changing its Position on Nuclear Weapons, *International Herald Tribune*, assessed on 20 May 2013.
26. Alaistar Iain Johnston, Prospects for Chinese Nuclear Force Modernization: Limited Deterrence versus Multilateral Arms Control in David Shambaugh and Richard H. Yang (ed.) China's Military in Transition Clarendon Press, Oxford, 1999, p. 288.
27. A.I. Johnston,"China's New Old Thinking", *International Security*, vol.20, no.3, p. 19.
28. Banning N. Garret and Bonnie S. Glaser," Chinese Perspectives on the Nuclear Arms Control", *International Security*, vol.20, no.3, Winter 1995/96, p.74.
29. Page Jeremy, April 2013, *The Wall Street Journal*; US-China Nuclear Silence Leaves a Void. available at http://online.wsj.com/article/SB10001424127887324695104578416960963213342.html assessed on 13 May 2013.
30. I. Abraham, "Interpreting the Meanings of India's Nuclear Tests," in S.D. Sagan, ed., Inside Nuclear South Asia Stanford: Stanford University Press, 2009.
31. G. Perkovich, India's Nuclear Bomb: The Impact on Global Proliferation Berkeley: University of California Press, 1999.
32. Z.S. Hussain, October 2009, No China dam over Brahmaputra-PM assures Arunachal, *Thaiindia News*, assessed on 20 May 2013.
33. *The Tribune*, 04 Aug 2000.
34. *India Today*, June 25 2001.
35. B. Challaney (2011), Water: Asia's New Battleground, Washington D.C., p.160, Georgetown University Press. *The Times of India*, New Delhi 23 April 2013, China's New War Front.
36. The Guardian Sunday, 20 Dec 2009, Copenhagen Summit: China's quite satisfaction at tough tactics and goalless draw.
37. N. Gokhale, March 06 2012, The Diplomat India, China and the Pirates. http://thediplomat.com/2012/03/06/india-china-and-the-pirates/assessed on 22 May 2013.
38. N. Gokhale April 19, 2011, The Diplomat.
39. R.S. Ross, Chinese Security Policy: Structure, Power and Politics, Routledge, Oxon 2009, p. 45.
40. R.S. Ross, Chinese Security Policy: Structure, Power and Politics, Routledge, Oxon 2009, pp. 46-47.
41. V.P. Malik and J.Schultz, The Rise of China: Perspectives from Asia and Europe, Pentagon Press, New Delhi, 2008, p.141.
42. US National Security Doctrine Paper released in 2002.
43. Tucker Nancy Bernkopf, China's Relation with the West: The Role of Taiwan and Hong Kong. Vol 13, No 7, May 2008.
44. R.S. Ross, Chinese Security Policy: Structure, Power and Politics, Routledge, Oxon, 2009 p.160.

3

India-Russia: Problems and Opportunities

Shekhar Adhikari

Since the disintegration of the Soviet Union in 1991, there has been paradigm shift in the nature of relations among countries. So far India and Russia are concerned, they have found a new basis for establishing their close and friendly relations. At the outset, it should be made clear that Indo-Russian relations are governed by certain distinct features. First, geographically, both the countries do not share common borders. Second, past records show that these countries never had a historical legacy of hostilities. And, third, what is more important, is the domestic set up and the role of political decision makers in bringing each other much closer as both the countries believe in the principle of federalism and democracy.

The historical context within which Indo-Soviet and Indo-Russian relations have moved had deep impact on global strategic environment. Reassessing the strategic environment after 1945, in brief, one thing becomes clear that the term 'polarity' had to be addressed in proper perspective. Polarity in international relations refer to the arrangement of power politics within the international system. The concept arose from bipolarity, as spelt by Morton Kaplan. During the cold war period, the international system was dominated by superpowers. However, the term bipolar was more frequently used by Joseph Stalin who saw the international system as bipolar world or two camp world with two opposing ideologies and power bases.

The Soviet foreign and security policies toward India during Stalin was seen in a negative sense as the Soviet Union rejected Nehru's non-alignment policy.

The change in the Soviet's attitude towards India soon occurred after Stalin's death and under Khrushchev regime. It was, then, seen India's anti-imperialist and anti-western stand as an asset in the Soviet propaganda offensive against the United States of America. Furthermore, the Sino-Soviet rift, US-Soviet détente in 1950s' and 1960's, the Chinese nuclear weapon test and cultural revolution and the Sino-American ping-pong diplomacy in early 1970's brought India and the Soviet Union more closer and they cemented their relations with a defensive treaty of 1971. This was essential for both the countries because of the strategic development that was taking place among the USA, China and Pakistan in South Asia.

The Indo-Soviet ties remained stable and strong until the collapse of the Soviet Union, although the Soviet intervention in Afghanistan in 1979 created a wrinkle of strained relations between them. The Afghanistan's crisis forced the Soviet political decision makers to re-assess their foreign and security policies as it affected their economy. A new era was dawn in the 1980s in the form of rise of Gorbachev and his famous reforms such as restructuring, democratic set-up and new thinking in foreign policy. Inspite of Gorbachev's reforms, the Soviet Union disintegrated into several independent states.

SOVIET UNION AFTER 1991

Political Relations

Since the disintegration of the Soviet Union, Russia is still a formidable power inspite of early political and economic setbacks. The initial two years (1991-93) was rather difficult years in Indo-Russia relations. The reason was constant debate in Russian foreign policy regarding the future course of action. At that time, there were two options left for Russia: (1) to pursue a pro-western policy and (2) to maintain a balance among the old and new partners. It delayed the evolution of a concrete foreign policy, as Russia, economically was passing through a transitional phase from socialist economy to market system. The transition swept the whole society and Russia was not fully prepared for such a drastic change.

As I have said that Russia's transition to western market openness was met with criticism from certain quarters. On the political front, various Russian scholars and political leaders criticized pro-western orientation of Kozyrev, George Kundaze and others. Kozyrev stressed the distinction between "the normalization of relations with other countries and normal relations with them." He explained that while Gorbachev had begun the first task it was up to Russia to complete the second.[1] They also argued against retaining the special relationship with India that the Soviet Union had cultivated during the cold war period. On the other hand, there were certain Russian strategic experts who argued that it was a major mistake of Russian diplomacy to renounce the special relationship with India by giving more emphasis on western economy. The Russian scholars even accepted the status of India as a rising power. Moreover, the 1971 treaty was replaced by a new treaty of Friendship and Cooperation in 1993 which dropped security clauses meant for the USA and China.

In the past, India had wide and extensive cooperation with different Republics under the overall umbrella of Indo-Soviet cooperation. The government thus undertook the task of disaggregating in Republic wise Indo-Soviet ties. In September 1992, India recognized the independence of three Baltic States and accorded diplomatic recognisation to all the Republic of the former Soviet Union.

Another positive features in 1990s was that India offered humanitarian assistance to the Russian Federation amounting to Rs 15 crores. The purpose was that the money to be utilized for the urgently needed items like baby food, rice, standard medicines, including sulphur drugs and antibiotics. India also contributed some US$ 250,000 for those victims who were affected by the Chernobyl disaster.

A decade later Putin's remark was that "Russia view of itself as a great power means that it consider itself to be in a very different category from all other European post-communist states, and hence refuse to accept the tutelary role of western institutions that in one way or another have imposed conditionality processes on its neighbours.[2]

Putin's rise to power in 2000 placed Russia in a more comfortable position despite various problems. His efforts to rebuild the relations on a new and strong foundation was a tough work for him. When we compare the trend before and after 1991 then one thing becomes clear that we have moved from block politics to more specific bilateral relations in the form of strategic partnership. In case of India, the signing of the "Declaration of Strategic Partnership" and ten more agreements in various areas provided a very solid base to cooperate in the political, economic, defence, science and technology and cultural spheres. Annual summits and regular ministerial level meetings have led to political intensification between the two countries. This is quite reflected in our cooperation in fighting international terrorism, the uprising in Kashmir and Chechnya, the evolving situation in Afghanistan, Central Asia and Middle East. Efforts were also made to work for a multipolar world and a democratic world order. Russia was the first major country to support India's candidature for a permanent seat in the UN Security Council.

Putin's task of pushing India further got a boost from the next President Medevdev's. The President Medevdev's visit to India in December was symbolic because he was the first world leader to visit India after the terror attacks in Mumbai. Medevdev promised to "work with India on a whole spectrum of problems and provide supports in all directions. He also called upon all the perpetrators, master mind's sponsors and even those who were connected with the barbaric act."

Economic Cooperation:

Economic cooperation which had declined during the 1990-92 period somehow revived. An agreement signed in 1993 terminated the rupee trade arrangement and mandated all bilateral trade transactions to be conducted on hard currency basis. On the issue of repayment of civilian and military loans to India, the rouble credit was denominated in rupees and repayment schedule was drawn up. It was agreed that India will pay some Rs 3000 crores annually to Russia for 12 years from 1994 and that Russia would use the rupees to buy Indian goods. Later on, it was resolved between the two countries that this amount could be put to auction to Russian and third party enterprises at discount to make Indian goods more economically viable. Today, Indo-Russian trade is based on payments in freely convertible currencies. All Russian exports to India follow the new system. So far India is concerned about 20% of Indian exports follow the new pattern and the remaining are financed through the renegotiated rupee-debt repayment mechanism. Though Indo-Russian trade declined sharply in the last decades, it was only $ 1.5 billion which accounted for only 2.5% of India exports and about 1.3% of imports. But, the trade balance was in favour of India. The real volume of bilateral trade made rapid stride from 2005 onwards. In 2008, Indo-Russian trade crossed $ 8bn and achieved the $ 10bn figure by 2010.

Economic relations between India and Russia also went structural changes. The new Russia eliminated state monopoly over foreign trade. So far India was concerned, the decline of India's most important international benefactor coupled with a dramatic rise in world energy prices during the Gulf War I presented a grave challenge to India's quasi-socialist economy. It is interesting to note that during 1990s three vital issues surfaced on India's politics. These were 'Mandir', 'Mandal' and 'Market Reforms.' Confining to market reforms, the then Indian Foreign Minister, Man Mohan Singh, started a series of liberalizing trade, investment and market reforms so that it could revamps the country's competitiveness. The result was impressive. India's GDP growth increased from 3 to 4% in 1980s to 5 to 7% in 1990s and reached 9% growth in mid 2000's.

Inspite of these developments, Indo-Russia trade was more focused on traditional items. The main items of traditional export from India were tea, readymade garments, drugs and pharmaceuticals coffees, tobacco, rice and leather goods. Traditional imports from Russia include fertilizer, iron and steel, non-ferrous metals, newsprint, synthetic rubber and chemicals. The Indo-Russia trade during this period could be seen from the following table.

Table 1: Indo-Russian Trade (1993-1994 to 1999-2000)

Year	*Total exports to Russia*	*% Share in total exports*	*Total Imports from Russia*	*% share in total imports in dollar's millions*
1993-94	648.80	2.92	256.89	1.10
1994-95	807.80	3.07	504.54	1.76
1995-96	1046.55	3.29	857.53	2.33
1996-97	811.84	2.42	628.96	1.61
1997-98	954.12	2.72	679.02	1.63
1998-99	702.26	2.14	654.42	1.29
1999-2000	952.60	2.53	618.23	1.31

Source: CMIE.

But, these statistics do not give the clear picture. Many imports from Russia, particularly metal, metal scrap, fertilizer, paper products were sourced through international suppliers. Hence, they do not reflect in the figure. Similarly, many Indian goods entered Russia via "Shuttle trade" or through third countries. What was important in 1990s that the future of Indo-Russia economic cooperation would be determined by two factors: first, by sustained growth of the Russian economy and second, competitiveness of India industry, commerce and services.

Thus, one thing became quite clear that, throughout 1990's, one saw the negative trend in Russia as she was struggling as an economic power. On the other hand, India was better placed and enabled her rise as a responsible and effective international actor.

Defence Cooperation

So far defence cooperation is concerned, Indo-Russian relations in early 1990s were not so smooth because Russia had set-up her own priorities and as such had to choose between old and new partners. On the other hand, India was careful in improving the relations with Russia. The conditions became more favourable for India with the rise of Bhartiya Janta Party (BJP). The BJP was more committed to economic liberalization and assertive nationalism which in a way was quite a reversal of Nehru's policy of secularism and socialism. Furthermore, the BJP emphasis on military power to promote security objectives was also one way of defending her nuclear option. Earlier, in November 1991, Russia voted for Pakistan's sponsored UN resolution calling for the establishment of a South Asian nuclear free zone. Russia also urged India to comply NPT agreement and in March 1992 decided to apply full scope safeguards to future nuclear supply agreements.

India's position on this issue was clear and India did not acceded to the NPT in 1996 when the treaty was indefinitely extended. India, in May 1998, also conducted a series of nuclear tests and declared itself a nuclear weapon state outside the NPT preview. There was worldwide condemnation, except by France and Russia. The Russian government viewed that, as a party to the NPT, Russia did not officially recognize India's status as a nuclear weapon state but refrained from imposing any kind of sanction. Moreover, Russia cooperated more and more with India in nuclear energy and space research.

Inspite of nuclear test explosion by India and Pakistan there was worldwise criticism. But it did not deterred India and Russia from entering into defence agreement. In September 1992, India and Russia finalised a deal worth $ 466million for the purchase of 20 MIG-29M and 6MIG-29UM Fulcrum multirole fighters. On June 30, 1994, a bilateral agreement was signed to form the Indo-Russian Aviation Private Limited as a joint venture between the HAL and ICICI and MAPO.

But, there was one such issue, i.e., cryogenic engine for developing India Geo-Synchronous Satellite Launch Vehicle (GSLV), met with criticism from western world. The USA protest was that the transfer of Russian missile and technology to India would violate the MTCR provisions. From Indo-Russian perspective, the cryogenic engine deal was legal under the MTCR as it did not violate the support of peaceful space venture.

The US attempt to block the sale was financially motivated since General Dynamic and French Arianespace were out bidden by Glavkosmos. Inspite of Yeltsin's assurance to India but the US diplomatic pressure to apply sanctions and in 1993, Russia agreed to suspend the transaction and to alter the nature of the transfer of sale of only cryogenic engine and not the technology.

From mid 1990s, the relations did improved as a comprehensive arms sales agreements from January 1993 to February, 1996 were signed. According to Russian sources, during the past four decades the total value of Russia Indian military technical cooperation had exceeded $ 3.5 billion.[3]

For a brief period, it appeared that Indo-Russian relations would buckled down under western pressure. But this did not last long when in January 1996. Primakov took over as the Russian Foreign Minister. His political approach was different from Kozyrev's pro-western stand. A year later, an agreement was signed to build two Russian light water nuclear reactors in India despite Nuclear Supplier's Group Ban. The two countries also signed an accord which payed the way for the construction of two—1000 Mw light water nuclear reactors at Kundankalam in Tamil Nadu. On 17 August, 1999, India's National Security Advisory Board was set up with a draft copy of nuclear doctrine. The draft document refueled the debate within the USA over the future course of US policy towards India. The US State Department warned that it would be unwise for India to move in the direction of developing a nuclear deterrent due to action-reaction cycle for a South Asian arms race. The Russian government response, on the other hand, was opposite and said "we shall carefully study the draft and in due time clearly state our opinion." There was a behaviourable difference between the USA and Russian approaches towards India. The Clinton administration took aggressive stand against India and pushed for continuation of sanctions. Meanwhile, Russia was negotiating with India for the sale of TU-22BM striker bombers. This contrast in the US and Russian approach towards India security needs and compulsions signify Indo-US and Indo-Russian relations over the past five decades.

The Russian arms sales still remain India's most important element of their overall relations. Even in 1990s, almost half of the major surface combatants and combat submarines for Indian navy were developed in Russia. The Indian army had also acquired almost T-72 tanks and hundreds of BMP-1 and BMP-2 armoured vehicles.

It was under Primakov that Indo-Russian relations showed signed of positivism in the conduct of security policy. Primakov spoke highly of India as a global partner and priority partner for Russia. Moreover, Russian leaders did not considered India's nuclear weapons status as a threat to Russia or even to its allies. In 2003, the Indian Prime Minister Atal Behari Vajpayee made it clear that there was all party consensuses in India on the need to develop stable and strong relations with Russia.

Furthermore, under Putin, Indio-Russian's strategic partnership's expectation was to move it beyond a buyer-seller relationship. Putin commented that the military and technological cooperation between them was confined not only to the supply of modern Russian equipments but was expanded to joint research and development of military projects. In 2001, both the countries signed a joint protocol to augment and define the long term programmes of defence cooperation till 2010. Russia had delivered $ 10 bn worth of arms and other military hardware and technology. During Putin's period, Russia had also empasised the importance of Indian Ocean by conducing the first ever large joint naval exercise, code named Indra-2003 in May-June. The Russian side was represented by the guided missile cruise Moskva, 2 larger anti submarine ships of the Pacific fleet, Marshal Shaposhnikov and Admiral Panteleyev, the tankers Ivan Bubnov and Vladimir Kolechistsky, strategic bombers, 4 Ka-27 anti submarine warfare helicopters and a maritime surveillance helicopter.[4] Such exercises have become a regular features.

Thus during the 2000s, the Russia arms sales to India and China were 60-70%. However, India position was better than China as India focused on technological know-how and China on quantity. On January 24, 2007, the Sixth Meeting of the India-Russia Inter Government Commission on Military Technical Cooperation was held where India emphasized on the need of license production and technical documents for RD series Aero Engines and protocol of intent for the joint development and production of multipole role of transport aircraft.[5] In 2007, the Indian government ordered an additional 347 Russian manufactured T90s Main Battle Tanks which were intended to match US Abrams M2.[6]

Like Putin, his successor Demitry Medvedev also focussed on arms sale to India. Both India and Russia had extended their long military and technical agreement for the period 2011-2020. India and Russia inked an agreement for navy and Nerpa class nuclear submarines leased for 10 years by the Indian Navy which was inducted in Indian water in Feb 2011. India and Russia also signed two documents relating to nuclear power production. This road map added 4 more reactors to the existing 2 rectors at Kundankulam and develop another site in Haripur in West Bengal. In 2009, Russia had also offered India the option of participating in the International Uranium Enrichment Centre in Angrsk, Siberia which would guaranteed fuel supplies. The only setback Russia got in term of arms purchase was that when Russian MIG failed to make short list for India's single large defence procurement deal, a tender to purchase 126 fighter jets under the Medium Multi Role Combat Aircraft.

With the return of Putin to power again, both the countries elevated their relationship to a "Special and Privileged Strategic Partnership" status. On 24 December 2012, Putin visited India and signed a series of facts on defence cooperation and also reached consensus to develop economic and trade relations. During his visit, Putin signed with Indian government an arms deal worth $ 2.9 bn. The deal included India purchase of 42 Sukhoi, 30 MK fighters and 71 MI-17V5 military choppers. Putin also spared no effort to retain the dominant position of Russia holding the 2/3 of India's defence market much against the growing competition from other countries. Defence exports are the major source of hard currency earning for his country. Putin was successful in his policy which was clear from the fact that India had virtually overtaken the position of China as the largest customer of Russian's defence machinery and equipment.[7]

Thus, the Russian political, economic, and defence cooperation in the Russian foreign policy were characterized by conformity to the realities of power politics in the international system coupled with a redefinition of what constitutes Russia' s national interest. Russia under Putin sought to emphasis the necessity of international system and that too on its terms. Hence, as such in analyzing the Indo-Russian engagement it becomes necessary to identify those international actors which could act as a stumbling block or could enhance Indo-Russian bilateral cooperation.

Changing Strategic Relations

After 1991, four such international actors became important, i.e., the USA,

Russia, China and India, in shaping international system The pertinent question is how they view the strategic environment of post Cold War era. The USA wants a unipolar world and multipolar Asia. China wants a multipolar or even bipolar world and unipolar Asia. Russia and India believe in both multipolarity in world and Asian affairs.

The changed global strategic calculation could be viewed from two different perspectives; First, the strange relations that was emerging between the USA-China and India and second, the growing concern amongst India-China-Pakistan.

At the outset, it should be made clear that the US involvement in the Asian politics made the Indian political decision makers more skeptical. Initially, India was much worried about the USA foreign policy orientation towards Pakistan and China. During the President Barak Obama's first tenure, many democrats believed in the promotion of the settlement of Kashmir issue. Other democrats saw Bush's policy of pushing India as a counter weight to China as something dangerous.

It was rather Bush who pledged to work with India as a rising power that had the potential to reshape the Asian balance of power and contribute to the management of major global crisis. This declaration was followed by two important agreements. First was ten year defence cooperation that opened up to sale of more advanced US weapons to India and defined 'Joint Military Exercise'. And second was the civil nuclear cooperation that sought to end India's isolation from the global non-proliferation regime. Not surprising, China opposed the Bush nuclear initiative and tried to promote similar deal with Pakistan.

Given this background, President Obama's during the initial phase tried to ease some of India's concern but not completely. For example, Obama dropped the issues of Kashmir and India-Pakistan mediation and were more careful to frame US policy towards India and China.

So far China was concerned, the story was different. Obama's visit to China in November 2009 was seen by strategic experts as an attempt to create Sino-US condominium over Asia. The reason cited by the US administration was that, as compared to India, China was far more stronger in the global economy. Hence, the USA underlined the importance of a creation of a new structure of Sino-US cooperation. This even led historian Fergusson to call such kind of Sino-US relations as "Chimerica" or "G-2". But, China made it clear that their interest lies elsewhere and not in the formation of "Chimerica" as China was confident about its own military and economic strength. China, in recent years, has gone through the biggest, fastest industrial revolution in human history. Through its sheer size, developmental "advantages of backwardness", entrepreneurial people, history of imperial statehood and manifest individual and collective hunger for "wealth and power" China will become relatively stronger and so, since all power is relative, the USA will become relatively weaker.[8] As such, China would play her card according to its own term for strategic cooperation with the USA.

In such a situation, what was India's position. India had to be more careful in developing relations with the USA and Russia. Initially, India was reluctant to sign such agreements like communication and information agreement and logistic support agreement. This stemmed from India's traditional approach to international politics by opposing the US hegemony that could have eroded India's strategic autonomy. But, later on, realities of international politics has enabled India to reassess its priorities and policies and found that stable understanding with the USA may suit its objective as it may balance a more assertive China.

Indo-Russian Engagement at Regional Context

The crux of Indo-Russian engagement also lies in the compatibility of their vital interests in Central and South Asia.

A noteworthy features that was witnessed was the emergence of Central Asian States as independent entities. The Central Asian States are surrounded by major influential countries. Russia, China and Iran have strong cultural and ethnic bond. Afghanistan is a defunct state. There are second order neighbourhood. Pakistan has deep historical contacts with the region. India is the civilization destination of Central Asia. Turkey was the land of forefather and was also a source of ancient trade linking China, India, the Middle East and the fringe of Europe.

The region is rich in energy and other sources. From the viewpoint of competing geo-politics, there are two horizontal powers: Russia in the north and the USA in the south of Central Asian region and Caspian Sea. The presence of Russia is because of her geo-political position since ancient times and the US is the external power that made her presence in this unstable region through sheer military force without the fear of a possible confrontation.

The Russian involvement in the region is greater because of the penetration of Islamic extremism. Hence protection of the southern periphery of the Commonwealth of Independent States have assumed great strategic significance for Russia. The thrust of the Russian policy is economic, political and military relations with them. There is a Collective Security Treaty Organization (CSTO) comprising of Russia, Belarus, Armenia, Kazakhistan, Kygrystan, Tajikistan and Uzbekistan. The CSTO has also bases in Kygrystan and Tajikistan.

From Indian perspective, in the changed strategic environment, India began to look upon the five states of Central Asia as part of its extended neighbourhood. Since the majority of the people of Central Asia are muslims, Indian interest lays primarily in seeing that the secular fabric of these states remain intact.

Like Russia, India is facing the problem of terrorism and separatism. The cause of the Indian governments worriness was the ouster of Mohd. Najibullah by the forces of religious extremism led by Burhaunddin Rabbani. From here, we saw the beginning of Afghanistan emerging as the hub of extremism and terrorism. Moreover, civil war in Tajikstan in 1992 which lasted for five years signaled a new phase of growth of religious extremism.

One cannot also ignore our immediate neighbours Pakistan activities in Afghanistan. Pakistan's interest lies in creating a bridge between the Central Asian region and the rest of the world. In other words, Pakistan wants to create a "strategic integrated region" with religious orientation. India's concern was that these Central Asian states are depended on Russia for their security. Today, India and Russia are facing similar problems in Kashmir and Chechnya.

But the main problem arose in the wake of the event of 9/11. One saw the presence of international forces led by the USA which, in a way, has altered the geo-political situation in Central Asia. The Taliban has been defeated but has not completely wiped out. Besides in the wake of 9/11, there was a change in their attitude in all Central Asian states. All states had not only supported the campaign against terrorism but had also offered military facilities. For example, the presence of US in Khanabad or the K-2 air in Uzbekistan. Kygrystan had earlier opened its Manas air base for the US troops. In Tajikstan, coalition forces of France and US were stationed.

The pertinent question was why US wanted to intervene in the affairs of the Central Asian States? One reason was, perhaps, that the Central Asian States felt that the existing security arrangements provided by Collective Security Treaty Organisation was inadequate. As one Uzbek observer earlier stated that the majority of the people regarded the US presence as a gift from Allah. He also felt that Russia had no money to protect us and the economic assistance from West would be helpful to them. Besides this, all the five states of Central Asia are members of organisation for Security and Cooperation in Europe. They are also members of Partnership for Peace, a programme of NATO.

By the end of the 20th century, deterioration in relations were also soon seen in US with some of the Central Asian states. As such Uzebekstan asked the US to vacate the base and in November 2005, the US forces left Uzebekstan. In July 2005 at Shangi Cooperation Organisation meeting, the US were also asked for time bound withdrawal of its forces from Kygrystan.

In such a situation, Indian and Russia interest lay in ensuring stability and security of the Central Asian region. Given its friendly ties with Russia, India favours Russia as the sole guarantor of security in the region. Besides the security issue, India and Russia have economic interest in the region. Hence, new areas of cooperation have nevertheless emerged. Both the countries will benefit by increasing their economic involvement in the region. The proable areas are textiles, light industry and agriculture in the form of new farming techniques. India has vast experience in operating a Soviet type of industrial infrastructures. Similarly, Indian management skill can be matched with Russian expertise in upgrading, modernizing and developing new enterprises in the medium and small scale sectors. India has already invested some $ 2.7 billion in Sakhalin project on natural gas. Given the strategic nature of bilateral cooperation, India should move ahead for bigger investments in the Russian energy sector in order to meet our requirements in future. In 2012-13 India-Central Asian Trade reached $746 million and Russia-Central Asian trade was $ 28 billion.[9]

Indio-Russian engagement in the development activities of Central Asia can be further 'increased if they can provide the landlocked countries access to the outside world. In this regard, North-South corridor connecting St. Petersburg with Mumbai will be the best option. The corridor, a combination of sea, rail and road routes was planned in 2002 with Russia, Iran and India and they agreed to this ambitious project. Russia has already constructed a container terminal at Olia and Makhachkala on the Caspian Sea. On July 1, 2003, Kazakhstan also joined the North-South Corridor because one branch of the corridor goes to Aktau on the Kazakh side of the Caspian Sea. From the Russian side, it is much cheaper and easier to provide this Eurasian region with goods from India than from Europe. This route is expected to reduce the cost of movement of goods between India and Russia. To make it more effective 3rd Coordination Council Meeting of the INSTC was held in October, 2005 in New Delhi and the 4th meeting at Aktau, Kazakhstan in October 2007 to streamline the operation of the corridor.[10]

Although the North-South Corridor is operational, it is not functioning up to a desired level. It is also important to point out that the Siberian part of Russia should also be made a part of the project because it will give this isolated region access to the outside world. This could be possible if one branch of the Trans Siberian Railway from Omsk Oblast could be connected to Aktau in Kazakstan. If this is possible, then a whole new vista for Indian goods could open up not only in Central Asia but in Siberia as well. The landlocked Siberia would also be able to interact with Southeast Asia and Africa. More important than this, the opening of the Siberian region via the North-South Corridor would facilitate Indian labourers in the region. In Siberia, because of topography there is much demand of labour. India labourers are well known for their efficiency and hence could play an important role in the development of Siberia.

China in Indo-Russian Strategic Calculation

Let us analyse China as a factor in Indo-Russian relations. In terms of Asian geopolitics, the Chinese role cannot be ignored or minimised. For example, China shares border with Kazakhstan, Kygrystan and Tajikstan which form part of Central Asian region. In South Asia, the region is earmarked by boundary dispute between India and China. The role of Russia-China-India in international politics become important as all these states have shown their eagerness to come together and play a more dominant role. One way of playing positive role is in the form of cooperation rather than competition.

Shanghai Cooperation Organisation: In order to play more positive role in regional security arrangements China came up with the proposal of Shanghai Cooperation Organisation (SCO). The objective of the organisation was to fight against three evils-terrorism, religious extremism and separatism and at the economic level it meant improving economic relations with India.

So far India is concerned, India was admitted as an observer to the SCO at the Astana Summit. Indications from the Chinese side is that they would support full membership for India in SCO.[11] India's support was to develop economic cooperation, ensure stability and combat terrorism, religious extremism and separatism. Some specific areas which have been extensively debated in various SCO meeting have influenced the nature and behaviour of Indian foreign policy. These are:

- evolving security situation in Afghanistan
- capacity building in Central Asian region
- connectivity with the European region
- counter terrorism and anti narcotism
- energy cooperation

Although SCO has emerged as a dynamic and active group but the success of it would also depend on the nature of Indo-Russian relations. As the Russian and Central Asian States move towards democracy and openness, the pertinent question is how these countries view SCO and its functioning. Moreover, equally important is how SCO looks at CSTO? The common theme of India-Russia-China is to maintain peace, stability and good neighbourliness on its common borders. The CSTO has also emerged as an active group but its emphasis is on defence and security cooperation.

How India can play an effective role in SCO? On June 16, 2009, the then India Prime Minister Manmohan Singh remarked at SCO at Yekaterinburg, Russia. He said that "the SCO represents a vast land mass rich in cultural diversity, creativity and resources. India has the privilege of having excellent bilateral relations with each of the members of the Organisation. Our relations with them rest on solid civilization, cultural and economic linkages that have flourished over centuries. As an Observer State, we have following the evolution of the SCO with keen interest. We wish to see peace, prosperity and stability in the region that the organisation represents. It is in this spirit that we approach our engagement with the organisation and its different organs and bodies. The growth of Indian economy has enabled us to generate high investible resources to cater the needs....Against this background, the Russian President's initiative to focus on the themes of regional security and sustainable development are more appropriate. The threats we face to our security are global in nature and require a global response. The prevalence of poverty and underdevelopment in large parts of the world continue to threaten global security. We believe that with the resources available with us, the SCO and India can mutually reinforce each other's efforts towards the economic emancipations of our region."

Furthermore, since independence India's contribution towards peace and security cannot be ignored. Similarly, the Chinese President recently said that China and India are long lasting strategic and cooperative partners rather than rivals. The President further stated that he is willing to work with the new Indian government to enhance China-India strategic and cooperative partnership to a high level and jointly safeguard strategic period of opportunities as well as peace and stability of the region and the world.[12]

Moreover, India has a vast experience in multilateral diplomacy. India is the founder member of NAM and also member of G-77, South-South Cooperation. India has also vast experience in combating terrorism, religious extremism and separatism. India would like to emphasis on people to people contacts, exchange of business persons and scholars, and trade and investment, technology flows. Cooperation in the fields of energy and food security and infrastructure would bring them closer for some fruitful dialogues and concrete result.

BRICS: Against the backdrop of this trend, Russia and China attempted to evolve a fresh financial architecture, including a proposal for a new global currency to replace the dollar as a way to check another financial crisis. It was Russia's initiative that Brazil, India and China should joint hands as part of the Brazil, Russia, India, China forum (BRIC) to push the idea and overcome the economic crisis.

BRIC was coined in 2001 by the then head of asset management at Goldmn Sachs, Jim O'Neill, with a paper entitled "Building the Better Global Economic BRIC's". In his analysis, O' Neill singled out Brazil, Russia and China as the largest emerging markets, whose rate of growth he saw as challenging the leading role of the G-7 economies.[13] Later on, South Africa was inducted as another important member of BRIC. Now it is known as BRICS.

The BRICS countries collectively represent almost 3 billion people (43% of world population) with a combined GDP of $ 14.8 billion (about a quarter of global income), 17% of world trade and an estimated $ 4 million in combined foreign reserves.

The fundamental characteristic of BRICS is that they have different political structures. The BRICS comprise four democracies and one totalitarian country (China). China and India have been forced to an uneasy cohabitation, due to long standing geopolitical rivalries, including territorial disputes over Tibet.[14] On a positive side, Brazil, India and South Africa have traditionally supported a progressive human rights agenda. But, on many occasions China and Russia have systematically opposed it.

In economic terms, the basic feature of BRICS is that they are export driven economies. But the nature of export is different. On the one hand, Brazil, Russia and South Africa are exporters of minerals and energy and on the other hand, China and India because of low labour costs tend to increase market shares in service and manufacturing sectors. Inspite of this sharp differences, these countries maintain equitable relationship. The need for more raw materials in India and China can also boost the GDP of Russia, South Africa and Brazil.

Since 2009, when the BRICS heads of states and governments met for the first time, there have been six consecutive summits. In 2013, the BRICS heads agreed for the new "development bank". It is bank set up by the world's leading emerging economies aimed at funding infrastructure projects in developing countries. In July 2014, the heads of the states agreed that the New Development Bank will be based in Shanghai, China. India will preside over its operations for the first five years, followed by Brazil and then Russia. It is scheduled to start lending in 2016. The bank will begin with $ 50bn divided equally between its five founder members. Another $ 50bn will come from new members. The aim was to mobilise resources to the tune of $ 4.5 trillion over an initial 5 year period for recycling surpluses into investment in developing countries for infrastructure and sustainable development projects. Besides this, in Durban the BRICS created a 'Contingent Reserve Agreement' to pool reserves. The five countries will set up $ 100bn pool of currency reserves to help countries forestall short term liquidity pressures. In this, China's contribution was $ 41bn, Brazil, India and Russia $ 18 each and South Africa $ 5bn.[15]

The recent Fortaleza (Brazil) summit should be regarded as the most successful BRICS summits so far. Three Cs—common vision, coordination and cooperation—mark the Fortaleza declaration. The vision is to promote peace, security, development and cooperation. The BRICS agenda is to work for world economic governance which is contrary to neo-liberalism and western dominance approach. Hence, the BRICS have to play a bigger role in international relations so that they can forge a credible political understanding and a credible union which can be useful for global governance. This is more important when the USA is moving ahead with Trans Pacific Partnership (TPP) and has given priority to diverse economies of Asia and Asia-Pacific region. Moreover, Russia and China reiterate the importance of other BRICS countries—Brazil, India and South Africa—in international affairs and also support their aspiration to play a greater role in the UNO. If this kind of understanding is developed among the BRICS countries the US unilateral action can be checked to a great extent. It is also important to mention that India will host the 2017 summit. India can try to bring the South Asian countries together so that they can interact with BRICS. This could be seen from Prime Minister Narendra Modi's bilateral meeting with the President of China and Russia which drew immense attention.

But, BRICS is met with certain limitation. Till now, the explanation from Russia and China to play a greater role in world geopolitical and strategic issues has not come out clearly. Hence, the BRICS countries need to take more positive step in resolving political issues, particularly when both Russia and China are permanent members in the Security Council.

CONCLUSION

As stated above about the limitation of an author to discuss Indo-Russian engagement covering the entire global issue in totality, therefore, I had touched some of the issues which had far reaching consequences on our relations with Russia. What is necessary for us to maintain a harmonious relations and once this happens it will be easy to progress further in a more positive manner. As a collective body, the emphasis should be to promote peace and stability in the disturbed regions. More stable and positive relations between India and Russian cooperation would depend upon following measures:

- As a major supplier of military equipment and technology to both India and China, Russia must ensure that the clash of interest and rivalry between the two Asian giants are minimised or contained. Furthermore, India should convince Russia that her arms and technology transfer are not aimed against India and also see that the Russian defence equipments given to China are not transferred to Pakistan.
- Dialogue among Russia, India and China should not be broken at any cost. It is true that the apprehensions do persist amongst them. Moreover, each state has economic and trade transaction with the western countries on a much larger scale. However, two things become important; first is Russia's deep engagement with China and second is the improved Sino-India relations to such a point where the two do not see each other as threats.
- In the era of strategic partnership, hostile alliances are to be avoided in future. Continued multidimensional friendship between India and Russia serve both the countries long and short term interests.
- Russia has repeatedly committed itself to support the case of India for the permanent membership of UN Security Council. India membership can be possible in a cooperative rather than competitive world order.
- In terms of trade and economic investments, both have not move at promising note. Inspite of several dozen agreements, their trade and

economic relations constitute the weakest link in their growing strategic partnership. Despite efforts to double the trade turnover target over the last decade, bilateral trade volume does not indicate significant growth. Hence, efforts must be made to bring the private economic players of both the countries to play a more positive role inorder to increase trade and economic relations. The time has come to draft a bilateral Comprehensive Economic Cooperation Agreement or think of free trade agreement in order to infuse new blood into the stagnating bilateral trade and economic cooperation. It is good on the part of India and Russia that they have agreed for free trade agreement. Moreover, rapid activation of the North-South transport corridor will enhance cooperation in bilateral trade.

- The USA, on the one hand, has opposed the vision of a multipolar world and it is also true that in the emerging world order the USA and China will dominate international proceedings. In this case, India and Russia must come more closer because at this stage India cannot and must not ignore such a dependable partner like Russia. To sum up, Kautilya, the famous India strategic thinker, once said that "there is some self interest behind every friendship and there is no friendship without self interest." This Kautilya's vision of diplomacy fits well in case of Indo-Russian relations.

REFERENCES

1. Nezavi Simaya, 1 April, 1992, p.3.
2. See S. Prozorov, Understanding Conflict Between Russia and the EU: The Limits of Integration, Basingstoke, Palgrave, Macmillan, 2006.
3. W. Minnick, Russia Fights Increased Cooperation in India, Defence News, 13 February, 2009.
4. Glvashentsov, India: Strategic Partnership in Action, International Affairs, 2004, p. 162.
5. http://www.india.defence.com/reports/2834.
6. *The Hindu*, 18 August, 2011.
7. http://www.mainstreamweekly.net/article3950html.
8. *Hindustan Times*, 9 November, 2012.
9. URL: http://idsa.in/policybrief/IndiaandCentralAsiaagupta141013.
10. F. Gordon, Trade Route of the Future. India, Iran and Russia are pushing North-South Transportation Corridor to reach Northern Europe, *The Journal of Commerce*, 4. 21, 2003.
11. *Hindustan Times*, 16 July, 2014.
12. *The Times of India*, 17 July, 2014.
13. J.O. Neil, Building Better Global Economic BRICS, Global Economic Paper No. 66, Goldman Sachs, London, 2001.
14. http://www.dailymaverick.co.za/article/2012-03-30-brics-summit-exposes-the-high-wall-between-india-and-china//UGZ00445VP8
15. http:www.theguardion.com/comment.isfree/2013/apr/02/brics-challenge-western-supremacy.

4

China-Pakistan Strategic Nexus: Challenges for India

Shalini Chawla

Undoubtedly, China and Pakistan have been complementing each other's strategic requirements in spite of different cultures, political systems and social values, not to talk of different history. There is a growing consensus within Pakistan not only amongst the ruling elite but also masses that that their relationship with China is indispensable because of sustained Chinese military, strategic and economic assistance and also their belief, that Pakistan and China share common strategic interests. Pakistan's military needs, attributed to its perceived threat from India have been by and large fulfilled by China. Over the years, China has provided Pakistan wide range of conventional weapon systems and Pakistan's nuclear and missile built up is primarily with the Chinese assistance. While, Pakistan turned towards Beijing as a trusted a 'all weather friend' in dealing with its 'implacable' enemy India, China, on the other hand, found a feasible option in Pakistan to contain India and also expansion of the US dominance in the region. China's added incentive has been to cater to its growing energy requirements from the Persian Gulf and Central Asia through Pakistan.

The Early Years

China-Pakistan strategic partnership which started as early as 1951 has continued to grow and both the nations have enjoyed the mutually beneficial relationship. Pakistan, in fact, is one of the first groups of countries that recognised People's

Republic of China (PRC) on May 21, 1951, when the two nations officially established their contacts.

In the early years after the establishment of the Sino-Pakistani diplomatic relations, Pakistan, being a military ally of the West maintained a general link with China. It was during the Bandung Conference in 1955, Premier Zhau Enlai held two friendly talks with the Pakistani Prime Minister Mohammad Ali, and exchanged the idea that the cooperation between the two nations should be strengthened in various fields.[1] China's aim was to wean Pakistan away from the military alliance led by the United States against the Soviet-PRC military alliance. The Conference assisted in building the relationship between China and Pakistan and initiated high level exchange of visits between the two nations.[2] Zhau Enlai assured Field Marshal Ayub Khan that there was no need for Pakistan to be apprehensive about China as it has no plans of aggression against Pakistan.[3] Pakistan, on the other hand was looking for a support in order to build its capacity to cope up with the Indian military and diplomatic posture.

It was as early as in 1959 when Ayub signalled to Beijing his interest in demarcating Sino-Pakistani border in northern Kashmir.[4] Further boost to Sino-Pak relationship was post Sino-India border war in 1962. China displayed ample interest in extending support to Pakistan despite its membership of the US alliance system against China and the Soviet Union. Pakistan received economic, military and strategic support from China and, in return, China was guaranteed a foothold in the subcontinent and also assurance of support from the Islamic world west of Pakistan.[5]

The informal Sino-Pak alliance grew and a border agreement was negotiated between the two nations in 1962. In March 1963, the two countries signed the boundary agreement on "China's Sinkiang and the contiguous areas the defence of which was under the actual control of Pakistan"[6]

In Article 6 of the agreement, interestingly, China made the agreement conditional in that:

> "the two parties have agreed that after the settlement of the Kashmir dispute between Pakistan and India, the sovereign authority concerned will reopen negotiations with the Government of the People's Republic of China on the boundary..."[7]

The agreement was under consideration for some time but it certainly received impetus after the Sino-India War in 1962. Khalid Bin Sayeed has talked about the reasons as to why, both China and Pakistan went for the agreement. Explaining the Chinese side he states, "...obvious answer was that since they (PRC) had been branded in the West as an aggressor in their border dispute with India, they were interested in changing this image and presenting themselves as a reasonable and friendly power"[8]

India kept on strongly objecting since 1962 that Pakistan was in illegal occupation of the territory, hence it would not be incorrect to say that the treaty was illegitimate that Pakistan sought to give legal status to its illegal occupation. The agreement becomes very important in the history of Sino-Pakistan relationship as it provided the base for the future defence and military collaborations between the two nations.

The 1965 India-Pakistan war marked an important landmark in the Sino-Pakistan relations providing it a new dimension. China demonstrated support for Pakistan which was a member of SEATO, basically constructed to counter communist expansion. China overtly threatened India and started firing on the border to apply pressure on India when Pakistan was losing the war. Post 1965, the Chinese military assistance and in the 1980 the nuclear assistance has been at an uninterrupted pace.

Chinese Nuclear and Missile Assistance to Pakistan

One of the most important outcome of China-Pakistan strategic nexus is China's extensive support to Pakistan in building up its nuclear capabilities. Nuclear proliferation analyst, Gary Milhollin, was not wrong when he argued, "If you subtract Chinese help, there wouldn't be a Pakistani program."[9]

China offered to supply nuclear weapons to Pakistan in 1965, but General Ayub turned down the proposal. Pakistani leadership started systematic and aggressive efforts for acquiring nuclear weapon capability after the India-Pakistan war in 1971 and creation of Bangladesh. Bhutto propagated the religious ideology to seek assistance for Pakistan's nuclear programme on the global platform. Nuclear weapons were expected to "neutralize" India's conventional military superiority and hence increase Pakistan's military and psychological capacity to continue it's fight for Kashmir. The nuclear weapon programme started from 1972, continued to develop under the leadership of Gen Zia-ul-Haq in the 1980s. Pakistan sought external assistance for its nuclear weapon programme and China has been the most important source for nuclear exports to Pakistan. China, allegedly provided direct assistance to Pakistan's nuclear weapon programme in the past, which includes the supply the warhead designs and also highly enriched uranium (HEU).

China proved to be Pakistan's crucial partner in its nuclear programme and in the 1970s and 1980s there were definitely state-to-state deal and Pakistan's former top Pakistani nuclear scientist and proliferator nuclear scientist Abdul Qadeer Khan, was the key intermediary.[10] Pakistan received help with reactor, weapon design and nuclear material. A Q Khan visited China on a regular basis and the Chinese scientists were present at Kahuta possibly helping the Pakistani scientist.[11]

In 1986, China also, concluded a comprehensive nuclear cooperation agreement with Pakistan and in the same year, reportedly, Chinese scientists began assisting Pakistan with the enrichment of weapon grade uranium. Pakistan also received tritium gas from China, that could be used to achieve fusion in hydrogen bombs and boost the yield of atomic bombs. The amount of gas transferred to Pakistan was apparently sufficient for making 10 nuclear weapons.[12]

China adopted an extremely supportive posture in the development of Pakistan's nuclear weapons and supplied with it a variety of nuclear products and services, ranging from uranium enrichment technology to research and power reactors. China involved the Pakistani scientists in a nuclear test at its Lop Nur test site in 1983. Pakistan's Foreign Minister Yakub Khan was also reportedly present at the site. The Chashma nuclear power plant project which was previously initiated and cancelled by France in the 1970s, was resumed in the early 1990s. The nuclear plant was under the IAEA safeguards with China Nuclear Energy Industry Corporation (CNEIC) as the foreign supplier and the reactor is based on China's first indigenous reactor, Qinshan-1.[13]

There was significant pressure building up in the region and from Washington on China to restrain its nuclear assistance. In 1993, in fact, China and the International Atomic Energy Agency (IAEA) signed an agreement to apply IAEA safeguards to the Chinese nuclear power station sold to Pakistan (INFCIRC/418).[14] Despite these measures and pressure from the US, Chinese assistance in this direction continued including the assistance in the construction of a 40 MW reactor at Khushab.[15]

A 1997 report by the director of Central Intelligence stated that China "was the primary source of nuclear-related equipment and technology to Pakistan" during second half of 1996.[16] Although, China has always denied its direct assistance in this direction, there are official and unofficial fact and reports, which clearly bring out China as the prime contributor in Pakistan's nuclear bombs. Further clarity and conclusive evidence came from the revelations from the Libyan files and very recently, confessions by AQ Khan. He indicated in a letter that China provided Pakistan with nuclear-weapon materials and schematics.

"We put up a centrifuge plant at Hanzhong, (China)," Khan wrote in the 2004 letter to his wife. "the Chinese gave us drawings of the nuclear weapons, gave us 50 kg of enriched uranium, gave us 10 tons of UF6 (natural) and 5 tons of UF6 (3 percent)."[17]

China became the full member of the IAEA in 1984, signed the Non-proliferation Treaty (NPT) in 1992 and Comprehensive Test Ban Treaty (CTBT) in 1996, but continued the assistance to Pakistan. It was in 1995 when Chinese supplied ring magnets to Pakistan for the production of HEU. Pakistan's economy in the 1990s was on a total downslide with a decreasing GDP growth rate which stood at an average of around 2.5%. But ironically, Pakistan nuclear programme was kept up and acquisitions from China for the bomb continued. Pakistan went for overt nuclear tests in 1998 and has been expanding the nuclear arsenal. China has continued its support for the nuclear programme. Nuclear reactor Chashma-1 (also known as CHASNUPP-1) in Punjab was started in 2000 with the Chinese support. Chashma-2 commenced in 2005 with the Chinese technical and financial assistance. The enriched fuel for the pressurised power reactor (PWR) is imported from China. In 2008, Pakistan announced the plans for the construction of two new reactors—Chashma-3 and 4 with the Chinese assistance. China has agreed to provide 82% of the total cost at an extremely low interest rate.[18] Reportedly, in 2010, PAEC has signed a construction agreement with China National Nuclear Corporation (CNNC) for the fifth unit at Chashma.[19]

China's Missile Exports to Pakistan

Pakistan's missile development programme has been primarily carried out with the Chinese assistance and to some extent from North Korea after the United States imposed sanctions on China. Chinese missile assistance to Pakistan ranges from providing equipment, training to transferring the complete missiles. In 1989, Lt Gen Talat Masood, Chairman of Pakistan's Ordnance Factories (POF) board (1981-1988) admitted Chinese active role in Pakistan's missile programme, in an interview.[20] US Assistant Secretary of State Winston Lord was not wrong when he wrote a letter to Senator Robert F. Bennett stating "The entire strategic weapons program should be stamped "Made in China".[21]

The Chinese M series of SRBMs commenced development in the early 1980s and the three versions are known as, the M-9, M-11 and M-18. These designations were apparently used for the export versions.[22] Information from various sources indicates that Pakistan had negotiated the deal for the M-11 during Zia's regime. According to the US officials, Pakistan agreed to pay China $15 million as a partial payment on its 1988 contract with the state-owned China Precision Machinery Import-Export Corporation (CPMIEC) for an undetermined number of M-11 missiles, launchers, and support equipment.[23] China reportedly, started discussing the transfer of M-11 missiles to Pakistan in the early 1990s. In the same period Pakistan, reportedly acquired complete though unassembled M-11s and possibly an undisclosed number of M-9 Short Range Ballistic Missiles from Beijing.[24]

M-11 is a single stage, solid fuelled missile with a reported range of 300 km and payload of 800 kg. In 1989, Pakistan test-fired a 150 kg multi stage rocket at an altitude of 640 km. This was followed by the testing of short range, solid propellant, Hatf-I and Hatf-II missiles, for which China provided vital assistance. Pakistan went in for the longer range missiles as these missiles were unable to target Pakistan's prime objective, New Delhi.[25]

The technology for the M-11 was used to develop future missiles by Pakistan. Technical evaluation of the missile Hatf-3 (Ghaznavi), tested for the first time in 2002, suggest that Hatf-3 is a version of M-11 or may be even a repainted M-11. Reportedly, the production facilities of these missiles have been set up with Chinese assistance.[26]

Hatf-4 or Shaheen-1 is believed to be a scaled up version of M-11 missiles supplied to Pakistan in 1993. Shaheen is a single stage, solid propellant missile with an inertial guided system and has a maximum range of 750 km.[27] Ghauri missile, was developed with the North Korea assistance. Ghauri missile, which resembles the shape of the Russian 'Scud B' is an outcome of a coordinated inputs from both North Korea and China. There were reports regarding an arrangement made between Pakistan, China and North Korea whereby China would provide with soft technology and engineering for Ghauri, North Korea would act as an agent for the transfer of Chinese technology and would provide hardware and components from its Nodong missile programme.[28] The first flight test for Ghauri, single stage, liquid propellant missile was in April 1998 with a range of 800-1200 km. Hatf 6, test fired in 2004 and has maximum range of up to 2500 km is believed to be based upon the earlier Chinese two-stage solid propellant missile M-18 which was demonstrated in 1998. Also, Pakistani cruise missile Babur, (tested in 2005) which is an air, ground, ship and submarine launched short range, turbojet powered, single warhead cruise missile, does have a Chinese technical input.

Chinese Conventional Weapons to Pakistan

China began arms aid to Pakistan in 1965 after the US embargo on Pakistan, when the leadership in Islamabad felt the need of diversifying its sources of weapon supply.

China is today Pakistan's largest defence supplier. Pakistan has not only imported the maximum types and number of defence equipment from China but managed to build up its indigenous defence capability with the Chinese assistance. Chinese equipment turned out to be much cheaper as compared to equipment from the West and the Chinese sales were further facilitated by availability of credit from China on easy repayment terms. In the 1960s, and later in the 1970s also, Pakistan received interest free economic aid and also a significant amount of free weapons from China and became the only non-Communist third World country to receive generous assistance from it.

Pakistan did manage to acquire high technology equipment from the US in the 1950s and early 1960s which prompted it for its aggression in 1965 against India. It was mainly the US equipment which was used by Pakistan in the 1965 war.[29] The Chinese F-6 entered the PAF's inventory in 1966 followed by other systems. In the late 1960s, Pakistan received MiG-19 fighters from China, apart from the substantive infantry equipment. China supplied 115 F-6 fighters between 1971 and 1981. Chinese military assistance came in not only in the form of arms but also development of infrastructure for repair and overhaul.

On the naval front, after the 1971 war, the Pakistan Navy opted for a modest acquisition programme in the form of new Chinese built missile/torpedo attack crafty. Between 1972 and 1980, 12 Slaughter class attack FPBs, 4 Hunaim class attack craft and 4 Huchwan class hydrofoil craft were delivered to Pakistan.[30] Pakistan's naval acquisitions in the late 1970s focussed on building surveillance and targeting capability and, thus, the deal for French Atlantiques was finalised.

In the 1980s, Army inventory included significant numbers of Chinese equipment including the T-59 MBTs, T-60 Light Tanks and T-63 Light Tank and Type 531 APC. About 90 A-5s were obtained in 1983-84 for the price of $1 million per aircraft. Q-5 Fantan A. Acquisitions of 95 F-7 series aircraft was started, adding to the quantitative element in the PAF.[31] By the early 1980s, China had provided Pakistan with roughly about 65 per cent of its aircraft and roughly 75 per cent of its tanks.

The decade of 1990s was a setback for Pakistan's military modernisation due to the American sanctions and also Pakistan's crippled economy. Economic growth recorded a steep decline and Pakistan was under severe pressure from the international financial institutions to reduce fiscal deficit and hence cut down the spending on defence. Despite the US sanctions, low GDP and a collapsed democratic structure, Pakistan tried hard to acquire the defence equipment.[32]

Sino-Pakistan defence collaboration flourished under the umbrella of the US sanctions and, in the process, the two nations entered into deals for the co-development of a fourth generation fighter aircraft, the JF-17 (earlier called the FC-1), the K-8 jet trainer had earlier been jointly produced. The JF-17 is designated to be a low cost, high multirole combat aircraft to meet the tactical and strategic requirements of the Pakistan Air force with the reduced reliance of Pakistan on imports. The JF-17 is co-developed by Pakistan and China and is being built by China's Chengdu Aircraft Industry Corporation (CAC) and Pakistan Aeronautical Complex (PAC) Kamra. Pakistan has also increased its initial target of buying 150 JF-17s to acquiring up to 250 aircraft.[33] This represents a quantum jump in Pakistan aircraft industry. With the production of JF-17 Pakistan has joined the exclusive club of the few nations manufacturing fighter aircraft. Pakistan has also concluded the deal for the purchase of two squadrons of Chinese J-10 which, along with the JF 17, would form the backbone of the PAF according to the Pakistan Air Force Chief.[34] Various media reports suggest the ongoing negotiations for J-11 between the two nations.

Pakistan signed in 2008 a deal for the purchase of Chinese AWACS (ZDK-

03) for $ 278 million. Pakistan is the first country to buy the Chinese AWACS system which China only started to produce only in 2004. Pakistan has been focused on the acquisitions of force multipliers and this deal with China is in addition to the Saab Turbopop platform equipped with Erieye, from Sweden.

China's support to the Pakistan Navy has been significant and in 1984, four Huangfen Class missile attack crafts were transferred from Beijing for about $20 million per piece. It is interesting to note that the Chinese naval equipment being inferior in quality was less desired but Pakistan obtained the missile crafts mainly, with a longer term objective of striking a deal of technology transfer in the future for indigenous production of the missile crafts.[35]

Pakistan's naval acquisitions from China, in the current decade, include 24 C-802/CSS-N-8 anti-ship missiles and 4 Jiangwei-II class frigates. In 2006 Pakistan Navy ordered four F-22P type frigates from China with the value of the deal at $600 million.[36] The first destroyer, PNS Zulfiqar, was delivered in 2009 and the second one in 2010. The F-22P which is a modification of a Chinese frigate that uses a Russian-designed main gun rather than a Chinese model is armed with eight C-802 anti-ship warfare missiles, eight FM-90 surface-to-air missiles (SAM), one AK-176M main gun and two Chinese 30 mm close in weapon systems (CIWS). The frigates can be loaded with one Z-9EC helicopter.[37] Fourth F-22P PNS ASLAT was inducted in the PN in September 2013. PNS ASLAT is the first Frigate of the Navy which has been indegenously built at the Karachi Shipyard and Engineering Works (KS&EW). The production was done in collaboration with the China Shipbuilding and Trading Company.[38]

Other defence production plans on the naval front include 4 modern corvettes which are planned to be built alongside with F-22P in Karachi Shipyard & Engineering Works (KS&EW). The Navy also plans to manufacture and procure additional mine hunters, tankers, missile and patrol boats.[39] China has also confirmed the sale of six ship-based medium sized Z 9C helicopters to the Pakistan Navy.[40]

China and Pakistan's Arms Industry

General Zia-ul-Haq accorded high priority to building up of defence capability. Domestic capability build-up was boosted but this was not at the cost of equipment technology acquisition arrangements with the USA and China, but complimentary to them. The 1980's and the 1990's saw a wide expansion of defence production activities and a large number of varied projects were undertaken in this period. China has been the main support in establishment of defence production units in Pakistan often provided free of cost. Some of the major defence production units established with the Chinese assistance are as follows:

Heavy Industries Taxila (HIT)

This facility is located near Taxila, set up with the help of China in 1971. Until mid-1960s Pakistan was receiving imported tanks, initially from the US (the M-47 and M-48 Patton class in the 1950s and the 1960s) and then from the Chinese (the T-59, which was produced in China from the Soviet T-54 design built under licence).[41] In 1971, a Heavy Rebuild Factory Project (P-711) was conceived with Chinese assistance and technology to rebuild T-59 tanks. When the production started in 1981 the HRF had the capacity to rebuild 100 tanks and 250 engines every year and by October 1990, that capacity had been able to service 1,000 tanks and 2,000 engines.[42] It is claimed that out of 11,000 components used in the overhaul of the T-59 approximately 8,000 are now manufactured locally. The overhauling of the Patton tanks and the upgrading of the T-59s was being done in critical areas with technical assistance from China, America and the British.

HIT, witnessed a rapid growth in 1980s when it started to produce the T-69 MBTs with Chinese help. The T-69 11MP tank is fitted with a special engine and also special armour to enhance armour protection.[43] The current and future planned production of the HIT includes various products, some of which are with the Chinese assistance: Some of the major productions at HIT include: Tank 'Al-Khalid', Tank 'Al-Zarrar', Infantry Fighting Vehicle 'Al-Hamza', and WZ 653 series ARV.

The F-6 Rebuilt Factory (F-6RF)

Pakistan Aeronautical Complex, established in 1973 is dedicated to the overhaul and rebuild of Chinese and French aircraft in the Pakistan Air Force inventory. The F-6 Rebuilt Factory i.e.; the F-6RF, in the Pakistan Aeronautical Complex (PAC), is an important facility at Kamra, established with Chinese assistance in 1980. The primary purpose of F-6RF has been the overhaul of PAF's Shenyang F-6 aircraft and their accessories. (Soviet Mig-17 built under licence in China and sold to Pakistan).

Heavy Mechanical Complex LTD. (HMC)

Heavy Mechanical Complex Ltd. (HMC), located in Taxila is not officially part of defence production establishment, since it is a major heavy engineering subsidiary of the State Engineering Corporation (SEC), controlled by the Ministry of Industries and Production, Government of Pakistan. This was established in 1979 with Chinese assistance and is the largest undertaking of this type in Pakistan.[44] HMC is capable of undertaking the designing, engineering and manufacturing of industrial plants and machinery.

Development of the Gwadar Port

Gwadar has been developed with the Chinese assistance and the primary project has been the construction of deep sea port expanding its maritime role and to allow the trade to and from the land locked Central Asia. More importantly, the port would have the conversion facilities to allow the movement of the natural gas for the Turkmenistan-Afghanistan-Pakistan natural gas pipe-line when completed. Gwadar offers the geo-economic and geo-strategic pivot to China and Pakistan. It is strategically located on the south-western coast of Pakistan between three increasingly important regions of the world; South Asia, Central Asia and oil-rich Middle East. Gwadar, which is overlooking the Gulf of Oman and the entrance to the Persian Gulf region is just 180 nautical miles from the Straits of Hormuz. Thus Gwadar would eventually emerge as the key shipping hub providing mass trade to Central Asian Republics through Pakistan and China, and important naval base. China's involvement in Gwadar is undoubtedly a response to China's emerging energy requirements, China being world's second largest oil importer. Approximately 70% of Chinese oil supply comes from the Middle East and Africa through sea. China is expanding its energy procurement efforts and the strategy of series of ports along the oil shipment routes which would allow China to safeguard and monitor energy flows. Gwadar being built in Baluchistan coast, would enable Pakistan take control over the world energy jugular and interdiction of Indian tankers.

China's Support to Pakistan in its Dispute with India

China provided legitimacy to Pakistan's illegitimate occupation of the valley in 1963 itself by signing the Shakesgham valley agreement. China's overt position on Kashmir sat the international front has undergone many twists and turns. In October 2009 China took the decision of issuing separate visas to Indian passport holders from Jammu and Kashmir and also, very importantly projecting the disputed territory as an independent country in other ways. Visitors to Tibet and journalists in particular have received handouts where Kashmir is indicated as a country separate from India.[45]

China has been shifting its stand on Kashmir in favour of Pakistan. The 1963 Sino-Pak Frontier agreement allowed transfer of Shakasgam valley of J&K to China, which was certainly legitimisation of Pakistan's occupation of parts of J&K (south of Xingjiang). However, accepting (in 1962-63) that J&K was disputed area and Pakistan did not have sovereign rights over the valley, China made the treaty conditional to the final decision on sovereignty of the area south of Shakasgam. Chinese stand on Kashmir, which turned in favour of Pakistan in the early 1964 was certainly one of motivating factors for Pakistani thinking which believed in exploring military solution for Kashmir. In 1964, China accepted POK as part of Pakistan and constructed the Karakoram Highway.

China did extend support to Pakistan during and after the 1965 and 1971 war. During the 1965 war, China not only supported Pakistan diplomatically and also pressurised India during the war when it started firing on the border. Ayub Khan secretly flew to Beijing from Peshawar in the middle of the 1965 war requesting China for military help. Ayub Khan was accompanied by Bhutto and had two meetings with Zhou En Lai and Mshl Chen Yi.[46] China was of the opinion that India's numerical superiority could be neutralised in a prolonged war even if it was at the cost of one or two major Pakistani cities. China gave complete assurances to Ayub Khan when Zhou En-Lai said, "And don't forget that we will be maintaining our presence all the time".[47] Chinese weapon supply to Pakistan obviously grew at a faster pace after the 1965 war, facilitating Pakistan with relaxed payment modes for the acquisitions.

During the 1971 war, Pakistan did not receive any military equipment from China, but did provide Pakistan economic, political and moral support after the 1971 war. Two factors could be held responsible for China's approach during the 1971 war:

- India had signed the Indo-Soviet treaty in August which had security clause.
- War took place in winter in December and the passes were closed.

In 1972, China used its first ever veto to hold the recognition of Bangladesh as a gesture to support Pakistan. In the 1980s China's position turned less aggressive in its support to Pakistan on Kashmir and it held the view that Kashmir was a bilateral issue between India and Pakistan that should be solved peacefully. But during the 1980s China's nuclear assistance to Pakistan strengthened Pakistan's aggressive posture and Pakistan Army Chief Aslam Beg declared the doctrine of "offensive defence" in 1989. With the acquisition of the nuclear bomb, Pakistan's covert activities increased tremendously not only in the valley but also in other parts of India. Even though, China adapted neutral posture on Kashmir in the 1980s, its nuclear assistance did add to Pakistan's illegal activities in Kashmir.

During the Kargil war, China maintained absolute neutrality and Pakistan did not receive any direct military assistance during the war. But what is more important is that—Post-Kargil War, Pakistan has been extremely focused on building its air force, which it realised was one of the reasons for its defeat, and maritime strike capabilities of the Navy, primarily, with the Chinese supplies and the US equipment post 9/11.

Chinese stand on Kashmir is now witnessing significant change which has obviously added to New Delhi's concerns and discomforts.[48] In August 2009, China signed a Memorandum of Understanding with Pakistan on building a 7,000-megawatt hydropower project in Bunji in the POK. Also, China also agreed to build Diamir-Bhasha dam on the Indus river in the POK.[49] China has undertaken to support number of projects in the POK including the upgradation of the Karakorum Highway. Reportedly, 10,000 Chinese workers are presently engaged in the various activities in the area. Apart from mounting pressure on India over Arunachal Pradesh, China's disturbing acts in the past of issuing separate visas to Kashmiris clearly projects China's posture of treating/questioning/protesting Kashmir's status as an integral part of India. Also, the new Chinese map projects Arunachal Pradesh as part of China which raised serious concerns amongst the Indian leadership. Indian foreign ministry dismissed the new map stating that "the cartographic depiction did not change the reality that Arunachal Pradesh was part of India."[50]

Probability of a Two Front War?

China-Pakistan strategic nexus has no doubt strengthened Pakistan's military and nuclear muscle. Past experience of China's role in extending support to Pakistan during conventional confrontation with India and also consistent tensions with China on the border dispute raise numerous questions about the probability of a two front war in the future. Pakistan has made three attempts in the past and has initiated aggression. The aggressive covert war tactic of Pakistan is unlikely to change and in fact, it is likely to intensify post 2014 after the US and NATO troops withdrawal unless the ruling elites especially the military alters its strategic calculus and exempts terrorism as a foreign policy tool. With China, India has had a bitter experience in 1962 and the tensions with China have never really settled down.

Looking into the probability of the two front war for India the obvious question arises as to why and when can India potentially face a two front war? This has to be analysed keeping in mind the aims, objectives and policies of both the Pakistan and China vis-a-vis India. Following hypothetical scenarios can be drawn:

Scenario A: If China starts a war with India on a small scale or large scale, then, will Pakistan take advantage of the situation and initiate an aggression? There has been a divided opinion on this issue in Pakistan and the military and political leadership has perpetually debated the fact they missed an opportunity during the 1962 China-India war. Pakistan's aggression in 1965 was a fallout of the fact that the Pakistani leadership felt that India was weak and vulnerable post 1962 and the time was right for attacking India. Thus, in a scenario where China initiates an aggression, the probability of Pakistan trying to take advantage of the situation is extremely high.

Pakistan would also be encouraged to accelerate the terrorism in case India is involved in a conventional confrontation with India. The whole strategy of Pakistan has been to "bleed India through thousand cuts" and thus, a vulnerable

India would be better platform for the state sponsored terrorist outfits to intensify their activities in India.

Scenario B: The next scenario could be the reverse of the first scenario where India and Pakistan face a military confrontation, and China tries to take advantage and initiates an aggression. However, the Indo-Pak confrontation can occur under two circumstances and in both the cases China is expected to react differently.

One of the scenarios for India-Pakistan confrontation could occur if India decides to take military action against Pakistan in response to a terrorist act like 26/11, which has been conducted with support from Pakistan. In this kind of a scenario the likelihood of China actually supporting Pakistan militarily is extremely low.

This assumption is strengthened by the fact that Pakistan now has been fully acknowledged as a ground for breeding terrorism and also it patronage to the terrorist outfits is well known. Osama bin Laden's killing in the in the military compound where apparently he was staying for the last six years, well demonstrated the support system Pakistan has to cater the terror outfits and its leadership.

Secondly, China's own position on terrorism has changed in the last ten years. Till 9/11 terrorist attack, the Chinese government was not open about the existence and the extent of the jihadist activities within China. It viewed these activities as a law and order and police issues and believed that reporting of these incidents which have been occurring in the Xingjiang province would start another spark of violence in the country.

Anti-Chinese fighters have operated Afghan-Pakistan border and also on the Afghan territory (from the mid 990s) getting their funding and training from al-Qaeda. The East Turkistan Islamic Movement (ETIM) received financial and training assistance from al-Qaeda. Later, in 2007 Turkistan Islamic Party (TIP) emerged with similar objectives as the ETIM to liberate Xingjiang. TIP has been involved in a series of terrorist attacks on the Chinese soil and the organisation has support groups in Pakistan. The Chinese government has been increasing concerned regarding this issue and has been putting pressure on Pakistan to cooperate.

The terrorist activities on the Chinese soil did prompt it to for the formation of Shanghai Cooperation Organisation (SCO) in June 2001. The SCO has a terrorist monitoring centre and Chinese position on terrorism does project a shift. In which case, probability of China's support to Pakistan, in case of India retaliation for a Pakistan sponsored terrorist attack, is very low.

Second Scenario—If Pakistan launches an aggression like in Kargil. In this situation chances of China extending the diplomatic support to Pakistan is much higher. During the Kargil war, China did extend diplomatic support to Pakistan. China may not necessarily resort to a military action unless Pakistan starts losing a war.

Conclusions

Pakistan's military modernisation and its evolving military muscle owes significantly to the Chinese assistance. Pakistani association with China started in the mid 1950s and was intensified in the 1960s. Pakistan's reliance on China has remained unaffected with the frequent changes of regimes in Pakistan, and both military and civilian leadership have been equally enthusiastic about Chinese assistance in various fields.

Sino-Pak nexus and Chinese assistance to Pakistan in varied fields has multiple implications for India. For the last six decades Pakistan has been following the strategy of covert war against India. The reason why Pakistan adopted the route for covert war has been India's conventional military superiority which has deterred Pakistan in its illegitimate claim for Jammu and Kashmir. Even, with the realisation of India's military strength Pakistan in its offensive postures launched three wars against India and lost all of them. The prime reason why Pakistan went for the Chinese assistance was the fact that Pakistan needed to build up its conventional force and with the suspended western supplies and China was probably the only option. Study of the Pakistan's covert activities in the Indian territory clearly brings out the fact that the covert activities increased with the build up of the Pakistan's conventional military capability. China, has contributed significantly in building up Pakistan's conventional military capability in the previous three decades, which undoubtedly, implies that it has enhanced and will further enhance not only Pakistan's capability, but also the will to carry on covert war through terrorism in India, without the fear of being defeated in the retaliatory Indian aggression.

Although, Pakistan has been rewarded heavily (for the third time since 1954) by the US in the last nine years and has received substantive US equipment, it no more feels threatened with any future US arms suspension. Chinese equipment, has improved in quality owing to the input from Russian and Israeli technology, is no more inferior to the weapons from the West, and thus is adding not only the quantity but also quality to the Pakistan's inventory.

Chinese nuclear assistance to Pakistan has been a matter of deep concern and has altered the security situation globally. Pakistan's nuclear posture today, has generated deep concern with the risks and dangers of a nuclear holocaust. Chinese assistance in building up Pakistan's long-range nuclear missile capability poses political and psychological threat to India. Even though one finds the possibility of a nuclear war a remote phenomenon, Pakistan's acquisition of nuclear weapons have strengthened its confidence to continue its strategy of "bleed India".

China's assistance in the development of the Gwadar port is an issue of international attention and mostly interpreted in terms of China's strategy of "string of pearls" in areas far from its territory. But what is perhaps of greater significance for India is the implication of a much expanded and technologically advanced Pakistan Navy (and its aerial capability) deployment at the port abeam the major trade and oil transportation routes, besides its proximity to the Strait of Hormuz through which passes more than 50 per cent of the world's crude oil. The bulk of India's oil supplies coming from the Persian Gulf through this choke point would then pose a new challenge of vulnerability that would have to be addressed on priority. Similarly, more than four million Indian expatriates work in the Arab states of the gulf region. The political implications of potential influence/control by Pakistan on the sea routes between India and the Gulf ports would have to be carefully examined.

Pakistan with the full knowledge of the reality that India had superior military capability, launched a number of covert and overt wars against India since 1947. China played a crucial role in holding out threats to India during the 1965 war(including deploying military forces on the border and opening fire at Indian troops) launched by Pakistan on 1st September 1965, after three weeks of covert war in Kashmir.

With the current realities the probability of two front war are under one scenario:

> If China launches a small scale or large scale aggression India, then chances (strong) of Pakistan taking advantage of the situation do exist. In the other scenarios, Pakistan might not receive direct Chinese military assistance but China's diplomatic and political support will certainly exist for Pakistan. This assumption is strengthened with the Chinese announcement to provide 50 JF-17s to Pakistan, free of cost immediately after Osama's killing in May 2011. China's unstinted support to Pakistan has no doubt evolved its military and nuclear (missile) power. This has given Pakistan confidence to continue its strategy of covert war against India. This has also reduced Pakistan's reliance on the West for future military assistance and thus, it is less bound to adhere to the western pressure to alter its strategic calculus.

REFERENCES

1. "The Bandung Conference of 1955", *China Daily*, at, http://www.chinadaily.com.cn/english/doc/2005-04/20/content_435929.htm
2. In October 1956, at the invitation of the Chinese government, the then Pakistani Prime Minister H. E Sulawadi visited China and in December 1956, Zhaou Enlai visited Pakistan.
3. Although China had been showing certain parts of Pakistan as part of China in 300 miles

long undefined border between Xinjiang and Pakistan occupied Kashmir.

4. D. Kux, *The United States and Pakistan 1947-2000: Disenchanted Allies,* New York, Oxford University Press, 2001 p.113.
5. S. Yasmeen, "China and Pakistan in a Changing World", ed. K Santhanam and S.Kondapalli, *Asian Security Review 2003, Asian Security and China 2000-2010,* New Delhi, Shipra Publications, 2004 p. 310.
6. *The Boundary Agreement Between China and Pakistan,* 1963.
7. Ibid.
8. K.B. Sayeed, 'Pakistan's Foreign Policy: An Analysis of Pakistani Fears and Interest' in Hameed A.K. Rai, ed., Readings in Pakistan's Foreign Policy, Vol. 1, Lahore Aziz Publishers, 1980, p. 53, as cited in S. Sinha, "China in Pakistan's Security Perceptions", in S. Singh, ed, *China-Pakistan Strategic Cooperation : Indian Perspective* (New Delhi, Manohar Publishers, 2007), p 82.
9. Gordon Corera interview with Gary Malhollin, Eashington, D.C., December 14, 2005, as cited in Gordon Corera, *Shopping for Bombs,* (New Delhi, Foundation Books, 2006), p. 45.
10. Ibid, p.45.
11. Ibid.
12. "Incidental Intelligence: China Emerging As Third World Weapons Supplier," *Asia-Pacific Defence Reporter,* September 1991, p. 19; G. Milhollin and G. White, "Bombs From Beijing: A Report On China's Nuclear And Missile Exports," May 1991, p. 17; *The Risk Report,* May 1995, p. 8; G. Milhollin and G. White, "A New China Syndrome: Beijing's Atomic Bazaar," *Washington Post,* 12 May 1991, pp. C1, C4. As cited in, "China's Nuclear Exports and Assistance to Pakistan", *NTI,* at http://www.nti.org/db/china/npakpos.htm
13. "Pakistan's Nuclear Weapons Programme Development", at http://nuclearweaponarchive.org/Pakistan/PakDevelop.html
14. "China's Nuclear Exports and Assistance to Pakistan", *NTI,* at http://www.nti.org/db/china/npakpos.htm
15. Ibid.
16. Ibid.
17. "Pakistan received Chinese Nuclear Weapon Assistance, Khan Letter Asserts", *NTI,* at http://www.globalsecuritynewswire.org/siteservices/print_friendly.php?
18. See, "Nuclear Power in Pakistan" at http://www.world-nuclear.org/info/inf108.html
19 Ibid.
20. R. Frost, "Pakistan's Procurement Chief on New Programs", *International Defence Review,* June 1989 p. 765.
21. B. Gertz, "China Plays A Major Role in Expanding the Nuclear Club", *Washington Times,* 29 May 1998.
22. "Nuclear Weapons Database: Pakistan's Possible Nuclear Delivery Systems", at http://www.cdi.org/nuclear/database/panukes.html
23. B.Gertz, *Washington Times,* 4 October 1994, p. A8; Barbara Starr, *Jane's Defence Weekly,* 15 October 1994, p. 6as cited in "China's Missile Exports and Assistance to Pakistan – Statements and Developments" at http://cns.miis.edu/archive/country_india/china/mpakchr.htm
24. "Missile Overview" *NTI* at http://www.nti.org/e_research/profiles/Pakistan/Missile/index_3066.html
25. B. *Pakistan's Nuclear Weapons,* London, Routledge, 2009, p. 69.
26. S. Chandrashekar, Arvind Kumar and R. Nagappa. "An Assessment of Pakistan's Ballistic Missile Programme : Technical and Strategic Capability", *NIAS* study, 2006, p. 10.
27. *Jane's Strategic Weapon Systems* Issue 48-2008, p. 112.

28. J. Bermudez, "A Salient Partner", *Janes Defence Weekly* (Coulsdon Surrey), 20 May 1998.
29. A. Siddiqa-Agha, *Pakistan's Arms Procurement and Military Buildup, 1979-99: In Search of a Policy* London: Palgrave, 2001, p. 105.
30. "Pakistan Navy" at http://www.globalsecurity.org/military/world/pakistan/navy-intro.htm
31. A. Siddiqa-Agha, n 29, p. 161.
32. In 1990, fifty Mirage 3 (as indicated in the Table 2) were acquired from Australia for a paltry sum of $28 million along with engines and spares.
33. Interview, Air Chief Marshal, Tanvir Mahmood Ahmed, Pakistan's Chief of Air Staff, 4 April, 2007, *Janes Defence Weekly*, p.34
34. Ibid.
35. Ayesha, n 29, p. 159.
36. B.H. Khan, "Pakistan Navy Modernization Program", *Pakistan Military Consortium*, at http://www.pakdef.info/pakmilitary/navy/pn_,odernization.html
37. Ibid.
38. "Navy gets fouth F-22 Frigate", *The Nation*, September 4, 2013, at http://www.nation.com.pk/karachi/04-Sep-2013/navy-gets-fouth-f-22-frgate
39. "Pakistan Navy" *Pakistan Defence*, at, http://www.defence.pk/pakistan-navy/
40. *The Military Balance 2005-2006, IISS* London, Taylor and Francis, 2005 p.230
41. J. Kaniyalil, "Defence Industries in Pakistan", *Strategic Analysis*, May 1993, pp 229-247.
42. M. Hussain, "Pakistan's Heavy Armour; Upgradation/modernisation programme," *Defence Journal*, October 1990, p.7, as cited by Aabha Dixitt, "Defence Production in Pakistan", *Asian Strategic Review 1991-92* (IDSA, New Delhi, 1992), p. 293.
43. A.Dixit, Ibid, pp 293-94.
44. FAS, Taxila, http://www.fas.org/nuke/guide/pakistan,facility/taxila.htm
45. "China opens a new front in Kashmir", *Asia Times South Asia,* October 21, 2009.
46. A.Gauhar, *Ayub Khan: Pakistan's First Military Ruler* Karachi, Oxford University Press, 1996, p. 236.
47. Ibid, p. 237.
48. "India warns China over Kashmir", *Asiaone,* October 14, 2009, atwww.asiaone.com.sg
49. Ibid.
50. "India reacts to reported Chinese claim on Arunachal Pradesh", *Hindustan Times*, June 28, 2014.

5

Strategic Dimension of Pakistan, China, and Myanmar's Relations

Biswajit Bose

Introduction

The geopolitical subsystem commonly called South Asia comprises of the group of nations like India, Pakistan, China, Myanmar and Bangladesh. The study of this region has become essential due to the daunting challenges which confront this region especially after 9/11 and the recent era of globalization. Prior to the tragic event of 9/11, the world was becoming US centric. Things began changing when non –state actors directly challenged the military, economic and technological superiority of the US. The message was loud and clear that it is the geopolitical or geo-economics' which will be responsible for shaping the decisive factors for nature and pattern of international relations. The geopolitical and security environment in South Asia has undergone an amorphous and ambiguous transformation with China's dramatic ascent to global power status, which has attracted a great deal of attention throughout the world. During the past couple of years, China's presence in Myanmar's Coco island, Gwadar deep sea port in Pakistan, arms sales to Sri Lanka to fight the LTTE and signing of two key development projects worth $350 million in Aug 2009 to gain access to the port of Hambontota in its southern coast are all part of a long term strategy to encircle India. These are not at all comforting to India's security, strategic, economic and investment interest.

A comprehensive study of the might of two of the friendliest nations

(Myanmar and Pakistan) will be worthwhile to understand the political equation being played to dominate the Indian Ocean by China. It needs to be clarified that except China as a sole opponent no other country in this subsystem can match the might of the Indian Armed forces. A general awareness of the possible weapons available and future acquisitions of these countries can prove to be valuable for gauging the influence China has on these neighbors of India.

PAKISTAN

Defence and Security

Pakistan which was once a part of Indian subcontinent, has throughout its existence maintained an aggressive posture towards India. This has resulted in three wars—1948, 1965 and 1971. The 1971 war led to the creation of Bangladesh which was earlier known as East Pakistan. Further on, there have been many low intensity conflicts like the Kargil war in 1999. Pakistan has always maintained a sizable military force since its creation in 1947. It ranks seventh in the world in terms of active armed personal. The armed forces of Pakistan constitute the Army, Navy and the Air force. The country has built up a large conventional armed force, though its size and strength pales in comparison to India's military power. A ratio of one is to three is maintained between these two neighbouring countries. By possessing the nuclear weapon, Pakistan has tried to gain technological superiority over India due to its "No first use" policy. Drawing lessons from the past wars with India, Pakistan while maintaining that it follows a defensive military doctrine, however has realized the need for an "offensive defence strategy" to counter the superior conventional might of the Indian military. India is considered as Pakistan foremost rival in South Asia. Pakistan has also increasingly inclined itself towards China to procure advanced arms and weapon. The two countries have a strategic partnership to contain India from becoming a global power.

Other than India, Afghanistan also recently has been involved with Pakistan in small skirmishes, mostly on border issues. Pakistan's attempt to establish a 'proxy regime" in Afghanistan to gain strategic benefits have also caused tension between the two countries. Though their military conflicts have not taken any serious proportions so far but an unstable Afghanistan could pose a serious threat to Pakistan.

Strategic Relations

China: China has remained Pakistan's most important strategic and military ally for the last sixty years. China has supplied several key defence equipments, jointly developed sophisticated weapons systems and conducted joint military drills with Pakistan. Chinas assistance to Pakistan is mostly aimed at building up the indigenous military power with a thrust on air combat and naval capabilities. Most of Pakistan's nuclear arsenal and missile technology have been provided by China. The recent contract between the two nations include MBTs, naval frigates, combat jets, fighter bombers etc. This contract also includes the transfer of technology of these military equipments. This was widely demonstrated in December 2008 when Pakistan and China signed a landmark agreement that sought to further escalate existing bilateral military cooperation. The agreement signed in Beijing between Pakistan's Chairman Joint Chief of Staff Committee, General Tariq Majid and People's Liberation Army's Chief of General Staff, General Chen Bingde, was in furtherance to the forum of Defence and Security Talks instituted way back in 2002. It was well established by the early 2009 that nearly 65 percent of Pakistan's aircraft and 75 per cent of its tanks were supplied by China. Pakistan's Chief of Naval Staff, Noman Bashir, held discussions for the purchase of JF-17 fighter planes (which Pakistan is co-producing with the Chinese) and four Jiangwei-class frigates. The JF-17, better known as the Thunder fighter jet (FC-1) is a lightweight multi-role combat aircraft similar in design to the US F-20 Tigershark and is being distinctively projected to be sold in the developing markets thus replacing the outmoded and obsolete fleet of the MiG-21, F-7, and F-5 fighters. Notably, there are estimates that Islamabad could ultimately end up purchasing as many as 250 of these aircrafts. In addition, Pakistan reportedly has placed an order for as many as eight F22P frigates from China in the past few years and now is graduating on to a considerably larger model. The first of the four F22P frigates ordered by Pakistan was delivered in July 2009. In fact, the delivery of the shipment coincided with Pakistan Defence Minister, Chaudhry Ahmed Mukhtar's visit to Beijing in July 2009. Vowing to augment military ties between their two countries, Chinese Defence Minister, Liang Guanglie stated, "China values the relationship with Pakistan and is engaged in boosting bilateral ties from a strategic and long-term perspective." Significantly, the Pakistani warships now possess all-round capability to target surface ships, aircrafts as well as submarines. Islamabad is exploring possibilities for an advance range of ammunition and weapons for which it is likely to seek crucial Chinese assistance, including missiles. Pakistan is the recipient of the C-801/C-802 anti-ship cruise missile also known as the Yingji (Eagle Strike) YJ-8 and YJ-82—capable of being launched from ship, land or aircraft. As Pakistan is fast on track so as to hone its asymmetric military capabilities, Chinese surface-to-surface missile sales to Islamabad raise grave apprehension for India. Incidentally, it is a well-known reality that China sold the DF-11 (the M-11s) to Pakistan. Beijing has indeed traveled a long distance in the realm of conventional arms sales since the decade of the 1990s when the protracted Iran-Iraq war provided it with the perfect opportunity of becoming a key supplier of 'economical' weapon systems to developing nations. Since that time, the value of China's arms export transfer agreements with developing nations hit a pinnacle in 2007 at $3.8 billion. The production of the J-17 fighter aircrafts could well be credited for constituting a considerable chunk of this figure. According to reports, China's overseas arms sales have averaged more than $2 billion a year in the recent past, which is considerably higher in comparison to the decade of the 90s, when Beijing averaged less than $1 billion annually in arms exports. In the time period ranging 2000-2007, China exported $7.8 billion worth of arms globally.[1]

A single-engined light fighter aircraft designed by Chengdu with assistance from MiG, the JF-17 was Pakistan's first experience of manufacturing fighter aircraft. So far, the PAF has produced about 40 JF-17s at the Pakistan Aeronautical Complex (PAC) north of Islamabad, but there are plans to eventually manufacture upto 150 aircraft. While it was originally an assembly and test-flight facility, PAC is now manufacturing 60% of the airframe and 80% of the avionics. Although the JF-17 was initially visualized as a second line of defence to fly alongside the US-manufactured F-16, senior PAF officers said they do not discount the possibility of the PAF one day relying almost exclusively on China for its frontline fighters.

The PAF has previously revealed discussions with China of the purchase of up to 36 Chengdu J-10 fighter aircraft, although IHS Jane's understands that a final agreement has been on hold since early 2012 due to Pakistan's fraught finances. One way to finance the J-10 purchase could be to export the JF-17s in partnership with China to third countries. In early 2012 IHS Jane's reported that China and Pakistan expect to sell 300 JF-17s to markets across Africa, Asia and the Middle East by 2017, marketing the aircraft as a cost-effective alternative to surpass US Air Force or other second-hand F-16s that they might otherwise consider. In mid-2012 Pakistan's ambassador to Indonesia was quoted by Indonesian media confirming that Islamabad had made an offer to sell a batch of JF-17s to the Indonesian Air Force, which faces this situation.[2]

USA: The US military assistance to Pakistan dates back to 1950 when the two countries signed the Mutual Defence Assistance Agreement in 1954 and the US later supplied a large number of F-86 Sabre fighters to the PAK Air force. The military cooperation between the two countries was further enhanced after the 9/11 terror attacks. A key ally of the US in the war against terror-Pakistan has received a number of sophisticated equipment including fighter like F-16s, surveillance aircraft, attack helicopters, naval crafts and anti missile defence systems. In 2006 US arms sales to Islamabad topped $3.5 billion, nearly matching total purchases by Pakistan from the US during the fifty years prior to 2001. According to a US Congressional report, the total Foreign Military sales agreement with Pakistan was worth about $5.4 billion for FY2002-FY 2010. Islamabad since 2001, has received $7.9 billion worth of military equipment.[3]

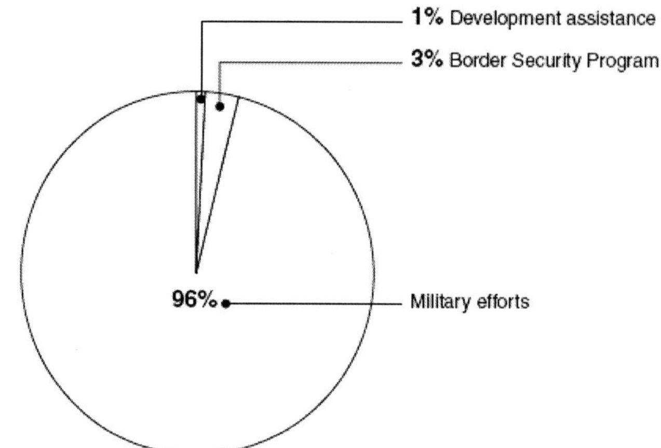

Source: GAO analysis of Defense, State, and USAID data.

Percentage of US funding directed towards Military, Border security and development activity in Pakistan in the period of 2002-07

Year	*Military (USD in billions)*	*Economic (USD in billions)*
2002	1.36	1.233 for 2002 to 2004
2003	1.500	1.233 for 2002 to 2004
2004	1.200	1.233 for 2002 to 2004
2005	1.313	.338
2006	1.260	.539
2007	1.115	.567
2008	1.435	.507
2009	1.689	1.366
2010	1.232	1.409
2011	1.685	unknown
Total	11.740 billion	6.08 billion

Iran: Some of the Islamic nations had maintained cordial relations with the South Asian countries for the last five decades. Defence cooperation between them has generated joint development of armored vehicles, tanks, helicopters and unmanned systems. Iran and Pakistan relation has had a clandestine angle in which the latter has supplied nuclear technology to the former, which had raised concerns in the international community.

Saudi Arabia: Saudi Arabia has provided extensive financial and other aid to Pakistan who in turn has provided military expertise and aid to them. The most recent development has been the secret attempts by Pakistan to provide nuclear technology to Saudi Arabia. The two sides have pledged to maintain strategic relationship amongst each other.

Turkey: The two countries were once the members of Central Treaty Organization during the cold war era. Today they have maintained this relationship in order to facilitate the transfer of technology for combat vehicles, naval vessels and unmanned aerial vehicles.

Defence Capabilities

Army

The Pakistan army which constitutes the ground forces was established in 1947 following its creation. It is the largest branch of the PAK armed forces and is a voluntary force. It is at present being commanded by Genaral Raheel Sharif. The present force level of the Army can be broadly described as follows.

Active Duty: 619,000
Reserve: 550,000
Paramilitary Forces:

National Guard	185,000
Pakistan Rangers	35,000
Frontier Crops	35,000
Anti Terrorist Elite Force	Exact Number Classified

Organization

Corps Headquarters	9
Infantry Divisions	19
Artillery Divisions	1
Aviation Squadrons	17
Special forces Group of 3 Battalions	1
Armored Recce Regiment	3
Independent Mechanical Infantry Brigades	6
Independent Armored Brigades	7
Artillery Brigades	9
Air Defence Command	3
Air Defence Groups,	
AD Brigades	1
Engineer Brigades	7
Armored Divisions	2

Corps:

I Corp at	Mangla
II Corp at	Multan
IV Corp at	Lahore
V Corp at	Karachi
X Corp at	Rawalpindi
XI Corp at	Peshawar
XII Corp at	Quetta
XXX Corp at	Gujranwala
XXXI Corp at	Bahawalpur

The army is broadly divided in six commands spread in a geographical/functional distribution in the entire country. The various equipment of the army is given as below.

New Acquisition/Procurement

The army is in the process of modernizing its inventory by inducting the following equipments:

(a) The Chinese made T-59 tanks are being upgraded and named "Al Zarar."
(b) 300 Al Khalid are on order.
(c) Pakistan and China have signed a deal in 2012 for manufacturing Al Khalid the latest version of the existing Al Khalid MBT. The new combat vehicle will have improved capability and system.
(d) Development work is going on for the advanced Al Khalid-II which is expected to be ready by 2019.
(e) The US has delivered four refurbished Russian origin Mi-17 helicopter to the PAK Army in 2010. The US funded maintenance overhauls for 24 Mi-17 in the Pakistan Army has been completed for 12 and returned to Pakistan in 2009.

Navy

The naval wing of the Pakistani armed forces also constitutes the maritime forces and the coast guard. It operates a few submarines, frigates, corvettes and missile boats with some aircrafts and helicopters. The exact description and number are given in to this article. The primary task of the navy is to protect and defend the countries territorial waters and guard Pakistan's sea frontiers, sea trade and maritime interest. A big modernization drive is taking place in Pakistan Navy which will include the induction of submarines, frigates and spy planes. The major naval bases of the PAK navy are Ormara, Pasni, Gwadar, Karachi Jiwani, Ahsan, Jinnah, Makran, Mehran and Qasim. The present Chief of Naval staff is Admiral Asif Sandila.

The force level can be broadly specified as follows:

Maritime Security Agency 2,500
Coast Guard Exact Number Classified
Total of 20000+

New Acquisition/Procurement

The navy is in the process of modernizing its inventory by inducting the following equipments:

(a) The Chinese made fast attack craft (FAC), PNS Azmat armed with missiles was inducted into service in Jun 2012. The second ship in this class was built in the Karachi shipyard and engineering works(KSEW) known as PNS Dehshat and was launched in August 2012.

(b) China has delivered three F-22 frigates armed with latest missiles and weapons while the construction of the fourth is underway at the Karachi Dockyard.

(c) The Pak Navy has commissioned a refurbished US naval frigate the USSMC Inerney (FFG-8) and renamed it as PNS Alamgir.

(d) Two indigenously built small tanker-cum-utility ships, PN Madadgar and PN Rasadgar have been commissioned in 2011.

(e) Pakistan has plans to replace its ageing French origin Agosta 90 B submarines with the modern and better equipped Chinese submarines. Discussions for six of these are underway with the Chinese agencies.

(f) Delivery is underway for nine P-3C Orion maritime patrol aircraft.

(g) 12 Harbin Z-9C helicopters are on order to equip the new Chinese built F-22 Frigates

(h) The first squadron of indigenously built Uqab-II unmanned aerial vehicles (UAVs) has been commissioned in July 2012.

Strategic Force Command

On 2 Feb 2000 Pakistan has formed this National Command Authority (NCA) to manage its nuclear and strategic assets. The NCA comprises of the Strategic Plan Divisions (SPD) and the strategic force command of the three services. These agencies are controlling the haft series of missiles with various ranges for deployment of the nuclear arsenal.

While China has been an all weather friend and Chinese imports have taken precedence in Pakistan's import list in the last two decades, the United States became Pakistan's major arms supplier since 9/11. Pakistan did manage to get more than US$ 20 billion of the US aid between 2002-2010. The future of the US aid and equipment, obviously remains uncertain due to the increasing mistrust between the two nations. The Obama administration has already declined the forthcoming aid of US$ 800 million. On the other hand, anti-American sentiments in Pakistan have risen and surprisingly, for the first time have surpassed anti-India sentiments.

MYANMAR

This is the poorest country in the South-east Asia region, inspite of emerging as a natural gas producer as well exporter. The socio-economic conditions have deterioted due to mismanagement. The Parliament which has about 100 seats reserved for defence forces member lacks governmental control, has inefficient policies, corruption and excessive rural poverty. The United States, European

Union and Canada had imposed financial and economic sanction against this country which after the election in 2011 has been lifted. The government under President Thein Sein has taken steps towards reforming and opening up the economy by lowering taxes, easing restrictions and reaching out to international organisation for assistance.

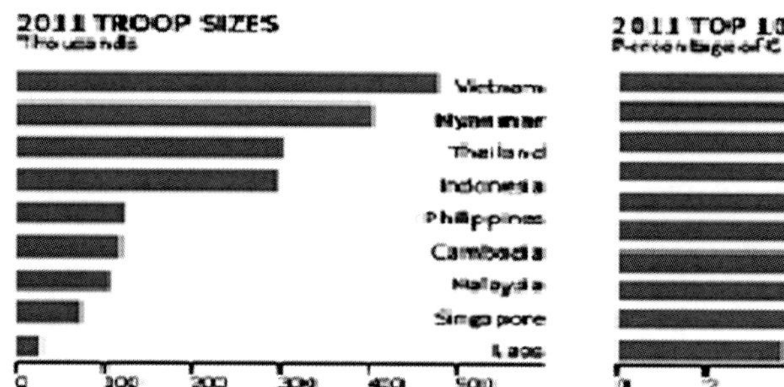

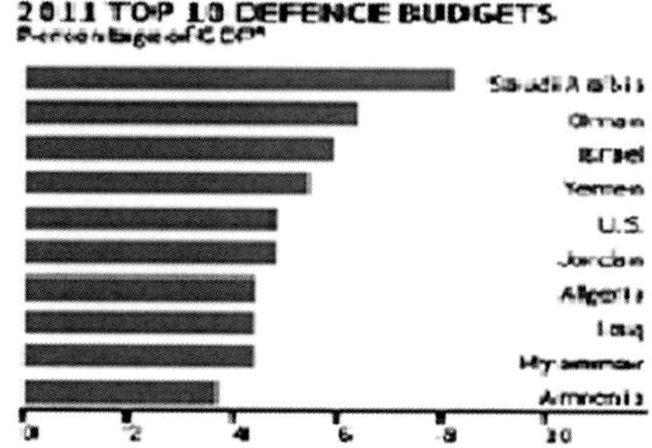

International Disputes

As the country is surrounded by Bangladesh, India, China, Laos and Thailand and is not well governed the disputes lead to a constant state of unrest in the bordering area. Some of the serious disputes are as follows.

(a) The Naf river on the border with Bangladesh serves as a smuggling and illegal trade route.

(b) Myanmar is constructing a 200 km wire fence to deter illegal cross border tensions with Bangladesh since 2010.

(c) Bangladesh has referred to India and the International tribunal the claim of Myanmar on the maritime jurisdiction as it violates their SEZ.

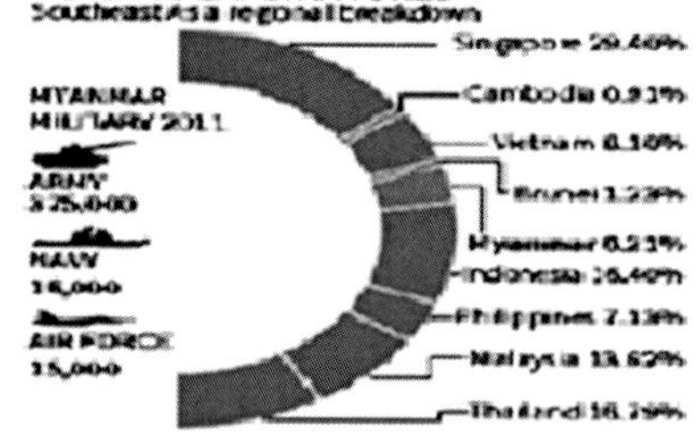

Source: The Military Balance 2012

(d) To prevent influx of illegal immigration by Myanmar a fence with its border with India near the state of Manipur is also being constructed.

The Defence Forces

The Myanmar Armed Forces, officially known "Tatmadaw" is the military organization of Burma, also known as Myanmar. The armed forces are administered by the Ministry of Defense and comprises of the Army, the Navy and the Air Force. Auxiliary services include Myanmar Police Force, People Militia Units and Frontier Forces, locally known as Na Sa Kha. Currently, there is no military draft. Thus, all service personnel are volunteers in theory, although there is a law on the books (the People's Militia Law) that allows for conscription if the President considers it necessary for Myanmar's defense that the provisions of the law be activated. In practice, it has been claimed that the Tatmadaw conscripts adults and children and uses civilians as forced labour and even human mine-sweepers.[6] The Tatmadaw has been engaged in a bitter battle with ethnic insurgent sand the narco-armies[7] since the country gained its independence from Great Britain in 1948. All this is likely to change after the newly elected government (2011) starts taking charge of the parliamentary proceedings. An official publication has revealed that almost one-quarter of Myanmar's new national budget will be allocated to defense. The Government Gazette reports that 1.8 trillion kyat (about $2 billion at free market rates of exchange), or 23.6% of the 2011budget will go to defense.[8]

Defence Industry

The Myanmar Defence Industries (DI) consists of 13 major factories throughout the country that produce approximately 70 major products for Army, Navy and Air Force. The main products include automatic rifles, machine guns, sub-machine guns, anti-aircraft guns, complete range of mortar and artillery ammunition, aircraft and anti aircraft ammunition, tank and anti-tank ammunition, bombs, grenades, anti-tank mines, anti-personnel mines such as the M149 pyrotechnics, commercial explosives and commercial products, and rockets and so forth. DI has produced new assault rifles and light machine-guns for the infantry. The MA series of weapons were designed to replace the old German-designed but locally manufactured Heckler & Koch G3s and G4s that equipped Burma's army since the 1960s. The List of equipment manufactured by the Myanmar DI is given in details in

Heavy Industries (HI)

Heavy Industries were established with Ukrainian assistance mainly to assemble the BTR-3U fleet of the Myanmar Army. Total of 1,000 BTR-3U wheeled APCs are to be assembled in Burma over the next 10 years from parts sent by Ukraine.[9] The BTR-3U is fitted with a number of modern weapon systems including 30 mm gun, 7.62 mm coaxial machine gun, 30 mm automatic grenade launcher and anti-tank guided weapons. HI has also built APC/IFV such as MAV 1, MAV 2 and BAAC APCs. Little is known about MAV infantry fighting vehicles but it appeared that only 60% of the components are produced locally and some vital components such as fire control systems, turrets, engines and transmissions are imported from China NORINCO industries. Apart from BTR 3Us, MAVs and BAACs, HI is also producing a number of military trucks and jeeps for the Army, Navy and Air Force.[10]

Strategic Partnership

China: China's strategic perception of Myanmar has undergone different stages since the establishment of diplomatic relations between the two countries. At various times, Myanmar's importance to China has fluctuated. In 1949, just after the founding of the People's Republic of China, Burma, was the first non-socialist country to establish diplomatic relationship with Beijing. Myanmar also helped China to break its international isolation from 2000, political friendship (or paukphaw friendship) was the one—and almost only—highlight of bilateral relations. Political ties were strong, but other factors, such as economic cooperation, lagged behind. During this period, Burma was seen as China's political friend. Around 2000, as China began to seek new resources and markets, the economic cooperation between the two countries picked up speed. Myanmar, conveniently located along the Chinese border and rich in natural resources (such as hydropower, minerals, timber, and jade), turned out to be a natural destination for Chinese investment and business. First led by border trade, the economic campaign soon became dominated by large Chinese state-owned enterprises seeking energy and mineral supplies from Myanmar. By 2010, China became Myanmar's biggest investor and second largest trading partner. During this period, Myanmar, as a supplier of natural resources and raw materials, achieved a highly important status as an economic partner to China. Thus, political friendship and economic cooperation were the two cornerstones of China's relationship with Myanmar, with little or no specific mentioning of the country's strategic importance. Analysts and officials talked about Myanmar as a corridor into the Indian Ocean, but the purpose was mostly for trade and transportation routes. China did not hesitate to provide military aid to the ruling Military Junta in these years. Eager to win allies in the region following the crackdown in Tiananmen Square, China began to supply vast amounts of military material to Myanmar in 1990. This was at a time when the government in Yangon (formerly Rangoon) was also being condemned by the rest of the world for its abysmal human rights record, and most Western powers had imposed a de facto arms embargo on Yangon. Now, however, Myanmar is trying to diversify its sources of military hardware, in spite of a seemingly never-ending stream of Chinese arms have been pouring into Myanmar. These generally comprise of equipments like 200 light and medium tanks, including T-63, T-69IIs, the Chinese version of the Soviet PT-76 light amphibious tanks (T83), armoured personnel carriers and infantry fighting vehicles, at least 30 Norinco Type 63 107mm multiple rocket launchers, a sizeable quantity of 37 mm single barrel anti aircraft guns, HN 5A shouldered-fired surface to air missiles. The aid amounts to about US$290 million worth including smaller items the likes of light arms and ammunition, artillery pieces, radio sets for military use, night vision devices, nearly 1000 5t jiefang trucks, and radar equipment.[11]

The air force has also been boosted by the delivery of Chinese-made F-7 jet fighters, with the first squadron arriving in early May 1991. Today, Myanmar has acquired or is ordering from China a total of three squadrons of F-7 fighters and two squadrons of NAMC A-5M close support aircraft. A Burmese squadron consists of 12 aircraft, and the F-7 Batch includes 30 single-seat versions and six twin seat trainers. In addition, in September 1992 China delivered two SAC Y-8D medium range transport planes, with a further two on order. The navy has so far received 10 Hainan-class naval patrol boats, plus radar equipment. The naval craft have been accompanied by 70 Chinese naval personnel—over half of whom are middle rank officers—to assist the Burmese in operating the boats, training local crew and maintaining newly installed radar equipment. At the same time, Myanmar's naval strength doubled to 15,000 men including a battalion of naval infantry. The navy has also ordered three 1,865 ton Jianghu 053 frigates but the delivery has been delayed because of technical problems.

In late 1992, US satellites detected a new, 150 ft antenna for signals intelligence at the naval base on Coco island, a Burmese possession in the Indian ocean. The suspicion that this new equipment was likely to be operated at least in part by Chinese technicians led to fears that Beijing's intelligence agencies would monitor this sensitive maritime region. Recent intelligence reports indicate that the Chinese are pressing the Burmese to allow them access to three major strategically located listening islands along Myanmar's coast on Ramree south of Sittwe, the western Arakan State, on Coco Island in the Indian Ocean, and at Zadetkyi Kyun (or St. Matthew's Island) off the southeastern Tenasserim coast. The last is especially sensitive as this long, rugged island is located off the coast of Myanmar's southernmost point, Kawthaung or Victoria Point, close to the northern entrance of the Strait of Malacca. India especially was viewing the developments with increased concern. Coco Island is located barely 30nm from India's naval base on the Andaman Islands. Any sophisticated signals intelligence equipment on Coco island would also be able to observe India's missile tests at Chandipur-on-sea on the northern coast of the Bay of Bengal. India is known to have made several diplomatic representations to Yangon on the issue.

Even Burmese themselves, perhaps feel the heat from their neighbours. The country has become much worried about the extent of the Chinese-influence economically, politically and militarily. Credible intelligence reports indicate that many middle-ranking officers, especially at the prestigious Defence Service Academy in Maymyo at internal meetings and seminars expressed their dissatisfaction with the unprecedented dependence on China.

Singapore: The next country after China to enter the Burmese arms bazaar was Singapore. Western intelligence sources in Southeast Asia also assert that private companies in Singapore have arranged for several more shady arms deals since the first shipment, often acting as a middle-men with countries which would not normally sell weapons to Myanmar. These practices caused embarrassment in Lisbon in late 2001 when it was discovered that Singaporean middle men had arranged for the shipment to Myanmar of US$1.5 million worth of 120mm and 81mm mortars manufactured in Portugal. The shipment violated the European Community arms embargo on Myanmar's military regime, but there was not much Lisbon could not do much as it had little influence over the private company—Companhia de Polvoras Mounicoes Barcarena SA—which had arranged for the almost untraceable trans shipment via Singaporean middle-men.[12]

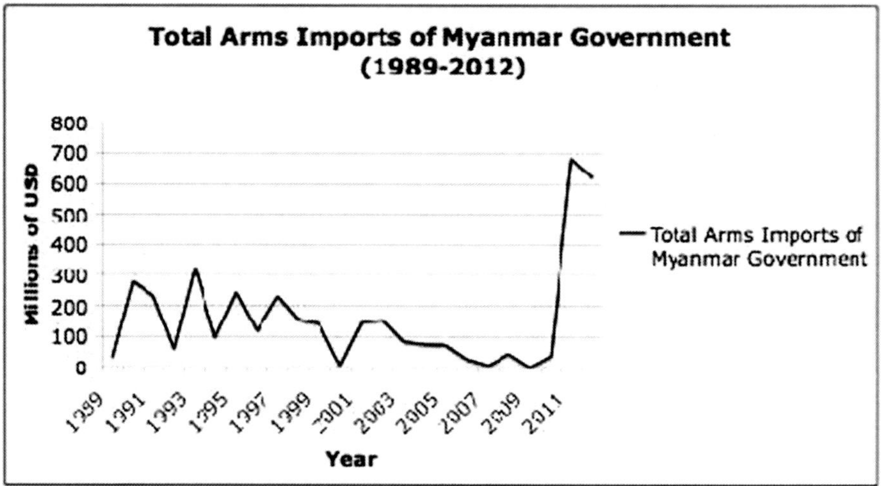

Source: Stockholm International Peace Research Institute (SIPRI).

New Acquisitions/Procurements

The Majority of modernization has taken place for the Navy. In 2012, Myanmar Navy has taken delivery of 2 Type 053H1 class frigates from China. These 2 ships were upgraded extensively by Myanmar Navy. Upgrades to frigates include the replacing of HY 2 anti ship missiles by more lethal C 802 missiles and installing of new sensors. First indigenous frigate, F11 Aung Zeya has entered service in 2011 and took part in joint exercise with Indian Navy ships off Visakhapatnam in early 2013. Second ship of Aung Zeya class, F 12 Kyan Sit Thar, enters service in 2012 and which is the Myanmar Navy's first stealth frigate. Third ship is under construction at Myanmar Navy Dockyard (Thilawar) and expected to enter service in 2014. Myanmar Navy plans to build 6 frigates. Myanmar Navy frigates combine Russia, India, China and western weapon system. These ships are equipped with Kh-35E anti-ship missiles, Oto Melara 76 mm Super Rapid Cannons, AK-630 6-barrel 30 mm CIWS guns and Chinese ASW rockets and torpedoes. Radars and electronic systems are mainly from Bharat

Electronics of India. Myanmar is more interested in building their own ships with the help of Chinese engineers. 2 Type 053H1 they bought recently are just as a stop-gap before their own frigates are ready. Myanmar acquired SAMs and ASHM from PRC for its newly built frigates and OPVs. Myanmar Navy Shipyard which is acquired from PRC in late 1990s is one of the most modern shipyards in the region. Many Myanmar naval engineers underwent shipbuilding training in PRC and Russia. They also acquired some technology from their biggest allied PRC. However, Myanmar is very much interested in buying at least one Type 54A for reserve engineering.

Defence Production and R&D

Myanmar has upgraded its arms industries to produce light armoured vehicle and mobile rocket launchers and is looking to become more self sufficient in small production. The country is still heavily dependent on foreign suppliers for much of its heavier arms and ammunition. It has invested substantially in making a large weapon factory at Htonebo, Paduang and Nyaung Chiduak. Military supplies are being produced in factories at Yango, Intaing and Madalay.

Following the commencement of Myanmar's "democratic transition" in 2012, which led to the lifting of international economic sanctions, India's government and some of its private companies saw a strategic opportunity to influence the subcontinent's periphery. Indian firms such as ONGC Videsh, Jubilant Oil and Gas and the Century Ply-Star Cement group commenced operations in Myanmar. Total Indian investment in the country now approaches $300 million. Yet this is a small fraction of the total $43 billion in foreign direct investment (FDI) that has reached Myanmar and the majority of its FDI continues to originate from China. While a decrease in Chinese FDI in Myanmar has ensued since 2012 the government in Naypyidaw remains dependent on China (and Russia) for its military armaments. Here, India is simply not in a position to compete, and probably will not be for many years to come—if at all.[13]

Conclusion

Southern Asia is, as of now, influenced by a major policy convergence. The foreign policies of China, the United States, India, Myanmar, and the nearby countries of ASEAN, are all pro-economic growth, pro-international trade, against the retention of excessive governmentally-imposed barriers to trade and growth, and generally against tensions and conflicts that may inhibit trade and growth. These policies are backed by commitments by governments to facilitate economic liberalization at home, and to achieve high economic growth through market-oriented methods. The fact that China and the ASEAN countries have been strongly rewarded for adopting these foreign and domestic economic strategies, while India and Myanmar have reaped at least some more modest rewards, augurs well for the long-term continuation of these particular policies, and works against things that might substantially alter or negate them. So do the economic travails of Pakistan. Among the things which could disrupt the convergence would be new or renewed efforts by an India, China, or U.S. to practice military and political hegemonies', and thereby generate diplomatic and military resistance by smaller countries. Another dangerous item would be takeovers by extreme nationalist leaders of key governments that are either inside Southern Asia or are closely involved in Southern Asian affairs. These would be Chinese, Indian, Pakistani, or American leaders that are interested in military and diplomatic status more than trade. Whether such things will happen is more dependent on the internal political dynamics of these countries than anything else. Those dynamics are not predictable, and no calculation of seeming national economic self-interest and rationality by either current decision-makers or foreign observers can make them so. But perhaps one may venture the optimistic opinion that nationalist extremism is highly unlikely to be in power in all of these countries at any one time, and that the nefarious influences of one government's extremism might well be checked by the practice of moderation elsewhere. The suspension of the controversial Myitsone Dam project by Myanmar and refusing to accept China to act as a referee for conflict resolution between the two ethnic groups Kachin Independence Army (KIA) and United Wa State Army (UWSA) are indication that Myanmar wants to start a process of self governance by its own recently elected mixed leadership.

There are ample analyses in China calling for a more active Indian Ocean strategy and for turning Pakistan and Myanmar (two of China's most loyal friends) into outposts of China's strategic outreach into the Indian Ocean. To facilitate this goal, many assert that China must go beyond the existing security and military cooperation ties with Myanmar and pursue political and economic cooperation more. Some hardliners even go as far as calling for the expansion of China's naval forces and the establishment of a military base in the Indian Ocean to protect the security of communication sea lines, as well as to maximize China's geopolitical interests. By comparison, the bridgehead strategy[14] seems to be the least threatening, among all the choices, in establishing and enhancing China's strategic outreach into the Indian Ocean. Whatever be the case for China to project itself as the controller of the Indian Ocean these two countries (Pakistan and Myanmar) will play a pivotal role in fulfilling China's ambition. Their military strength and growth are of vital importance to understand on which side the focus of China.

REFERENCES

1. M. Chansoria, *China's arms sales to Pakistan unsettling South Asian Security*, Vol 25(4), Oct-Dec 2010, 19 Apr, 2013.

2. Pakistan modernisation feeds China's export growth, http://spearheadresearch.org/SR_CMS/index.php/economyenergy, assessed on 25 Apr 2014.
3. R.F. Grimmeti "US arms Sales to Pakistan" Pakistan's Issues and Developments, Nova Science Publishers 2012.
4. S. Chawla, Pakistan—"Modernisation of the PAF", Defence and Security Alert (DSA) Magazine, 27 Dec 2012.
5. T. Bell (30 October 2007), "Burmese army 'abducts thousands of children'," *The Daily Telegraph* (London).
6. http://www.myanmathadin.com/news/human-rights/243-army-using-civilians-as-minesweepers.html.
7. http://www.newint.org/issue280/heroin.html.
8. Ibid.
9. http://www.karenhumanrightsgroup.org/photoreports/2008photos/gallery2008/section5.html,http://www.atimes.com/atimes/Southeast_Asia/HK04Ae01.html
10. D.M. Seekins, Historical Dictionary of Burma (Myanmar), vol. 59 of Asian/Oceanian Historical Dictionaries 59 (Illustrated ed.). Sacredcrow Press. ISBN 978-0-8108-5476-5, 2006.
11. J. Sommer, *Myanmar's military: Money and guns* (Burma, Guest Publishing 2013), pp. 32-28
12. http://www.asiapacificms.com/articles/myanmar_chinese_connection/, assessed on 27 Apr 2014
13. "Managing Country Risk". http://www.huffingtonpost.com/giorgio-cafiero/can-china-and-india-coexi_b_4824140.html,13 Dec 2013, assessed on 27 Apr 2014.
14. As part of the "Twelfth Five Year Plan" launched in 2011, China formally introduced the national "bridgehead strategy," which proposes to turn Yun nan into a strategic corridor and a bridgehead for China's strategic engagement in the Indian Ocean.

6

The Future of Regional Security in South Asia

Rajpal Budania

'Regions' in Security Studies

There was a time when globalism dictated international relations and security studies. No more so. Today, we find increasing literature being devoted to the study of regions and sub-regions in security studies. The regional level of security has become more autonomous and more prominent in international politics, and the ending of the Cold War accelerated this process.[1] The growing number of regional organisations reflects the emergence of regionalism as a strong trend in international politics. The capacity and influence of these organisations have depended on the political dynamics of a region. It is the regions and sub-regions which are becoming referent points for formulation of policies. Globalism as a referent point of analysing international security or politics has been pushed to secondary level of variables. The Asian region or South Asian, Middle Eastern or Southeast Asian sub-regions have acquired critical importance in understanding international security as well as politics.

With the end of Cold War, the dynamics of power relationships between the regions and the major powers have changed. The international security system has transformed and has become multipolar in the military and security sense. Nuclear proliferation in Asia and its sub-regions has undermined the Cold War hegemony of P5 or the legitimate five nuclear weapon states. In other words, the primary system consisting of global major powers is being challenged by the sub-systems at the Asian or South Asian or Southeast Asian level and at other regions. It is opined that "a search for total, inclusive regions that encompass all factors of security, economic, identity, and integration characterised the first regionalist wave."[2] This is validated by areas where regionalism has become successful in achieving cooperation and interdependence. But it is also argued that there is multi-dimensionality to regions. For regions, it is aptly observed: "We build them as we need them intellectually or politically."[3] Regions may be termed as functional regions characterised by economic, environmental, and cultural cooperation and integration. Regions have been over the centuries known more for politico-security characteristics. South Asia as a region is important in international politics more for its politico-security or strategic characteristics rather than cooperation and interdependence.

The global powers have lost their capability to project power globally all alone. Regionalism and powerful regional states in the post Cold War period have acquired salience in international politics.[4] There is already a politico-strategic competition among the sub-systems in Asia. China wants Asian order to be China-centric; India wants it to be India-centric; and Southeast Asian counties want it to be ASEAN-centric. Similarly, South Asia is India-centric in terms of India's overwhelming superiority in economic resources, size of its territory and population and its military capabilities. India would continue to press for its superiority and pre-eminence in the region. South Asia has witnessed transformation of power dynamics and India has emerged as the most powerful actor in the region. The bipolar structure at the regional level is weakening as Pakistan loses ground in relation to India.[5]

It will be useful to take note of Barry Buzan's views on security complexes in Asia. Barry Buzan has explained security scenarios in Asia through his 'regional security complex theory' (RSCT).[6] During the Cold War there were three 'regional security complexes' (RSCs) in Asia, namely Northeast Asian RSC, Southeast Asian RSC, and South Asian RSC. The post-Cold War period has witnessed transformation of the RSCs in Asia. Now the boundaries between the Northeast Asian and Southeast Asian RSCs have blurred and the two have evolved into a larger East Asian RSC in which there are three dominant actors: China, Japan and ASEAN. In contrast, South Asia is unipolar with India being the dominant actor. Moreover, in the post-Cold War period the external intervention in these RSCs has come down sharply. That has given greater leverage to countries like India and China to assert autonomy and manoeuvrability in politico-strategic realms. After the end of Cold War, regional powers like India have gained more space and autonomy in international politics. India has acquired political, economic, military and institutional strengths to project power at the regional level and even beyond the region. The economic and politico-strategic agenda India has prepared for itself cannot be overlooked as it was during the Cold War.

South Asia is more known for competitive processes rather than cooperative processes. South Asia is one such critical sub-region or region which has become of pivotal importance in security studies for a range of issues, such as balance of power, nuclear proliferation, terrorism and extremism, failing states, internal turmoils, so on and so forth. South Asian security is affected by domestic, bilateral or regional and international dynamics.

Security Scenario in South Asia

The world is describing South Asia as the most dangerous area in the world. Both diplomacy and war have not resolved conflicts in the region. National and regional security is stained by several unending conflicts in the region. Cooperative regional institutions have not been evolved for managing conflicts. The countries of region have not benefited from the globalisation regimes as the region remains among the least globalised. The region is lagging far behind in adopting the processes of globalisation as compared to other regions. Economic cooperation and integration in the region is dismally low. So is the intra-regional trade. The states of the region have not yet realised the importance of regional cooperation and integration as a tool of conflict management and resolution.

During the Cold War, inter-state conflicts dominated the region. After the end of the Cold War, new sources of conflicts have come to the fore. The countries of the region are facing new challenges and vulnerabilities. The problems of terrorism, religious extremism, ethnic conflicts and nuclearisation have had the most profound impact on the regional security in South Asia. The end of the Cold War brought several worries for the countries of the region. The countries of the region have witnessed profound internal transition in social, economic, and political fields. Terrorism has become multi-faceted and has threatened internal and external security of the states in the region. Economic and ideological conflicts remain unresolved. Movements for political change have tended to make neighbouring countries insecure. Religious extremism, migration and refugees have concerned the nations of the region. Territorial disputes remain unresolved. There is a fear that some states have either failed or are failing. There is a new alignment of forces in the region.

A nuclear arms race has intensified with both India and Pakistan trying for strategic superiority resulting into increased number of nuclear warheads and their delivery systems, particularly missiles. Arms race has been an important factor in the origins of war in South Asia. The unrestrained defence preparations have generated fears of surprise attack, military escalation and even nuclear conflict. India-Pakistan arms race has entered a dangerous nuclear phase wherein both the countries are entangled in bolstering qualitative and quantitative aspects of arms race. It resembles the Cold War arms race dynamics between the United States and the Soviet Union.[7]

These patterns of inter-state and intra-state developments have affected the security environment in South Asia. States have become more insecure now than ever before. It is assumed that feelings of insecurity and heightened threat perception should logically compel states of the region to behave more responsibly and come out with pragmatic policies to counter these threats. There have been numerous peace initiatives between India and Pakistan—states which determine the nature of security environment in a decisive way.

One Chinese scholar has tried to understand the framework of South Asian security by emphasizing three levels or dimensions namely "power dimension" which includes physical indicators like land area, population, economy and military strength; "mechanism dimension" which includes both bilateral treaties and multilateral treaties such as the SAARC and the South Asian Free Trade Agreement, which reflect the degree of regional integration; and "idea dimension" which mainly refers to policy makers' judgments on the sources of security threats.[8]

South Asian security is undoubtedly India-centric. India constitutes the core of the regional security in South Asia because of its overwhelming political, territorial and economic superiority. Its role and policies will shape the patterns of security environment in South Asia. During the Cold War, India suffered from several limitations while defining its regional and global security role. Consequently, its responses were mostly defensive and reactive. Now both global and regional security dynamics have changed and become more favourable to India. Its domestic constraints have also transformed and its capabilities have increased. India has started to play a more assertive and proactive role to change the course of international politics. Now it is envisaging a role which overlooks Cold War mindset and goes beyond South Asia. It is now willing to participate in the new alignment of forces. India is becoming more conscious of its legitimate influence in the region and it expects that neighbours will not do something which undermines its security. India's concerns are "real, and not just theoretical. In this context, there is some substance in the demand by the Indian strategic community that smaller neighbours should share their security arrangement details with it, particularly if these involved powers from outside the region."[9]

There are ongoing bilateral disputes and issues in the region. India is facing problems from most of its neighbours. India-Pakistan relations remain hostile. Role of extra-regional powers has multiplied the threat perception. India is particularly concerned at China's growing military power and its strategic co-operation with Pakistan. The Kashmir issue remains unresolved. Sri Lanka's Tamil problem is attracting humanitarian or human rights pressures. Political transitions in Nepal and Pakistan tend to affect the bilateral relations as well as the security environment in the region. Situation in Afghanistan is alarming. The US led war on terrorism in Afghanistan and Pakistan has had only limited success.

Terrorists are regrouping and adopting new tactics. There has been a resurgence of the Taliban along Afghanistan-Pakistan border. Pakistan government has miserably failed in stemming their rise and regrouping. Terrorism continues to seriously threaten national, regional and international security.[10] The positive fall-out of these challenges is that the countries of the region as well as extra-regional powers are more inclined towards coordination of efforts and policies for combating these threats in a collective manner. Internal developments in Pakistan, Nepal, Bangladesh and Maldives have created concerns for India and overall security environment in South Asia. India has taken several policy initiatives to recast its relations with its neighbours and manage South Asian security peacefully.

South Asia has been at the forefront of globalising terrorism and proliferation of weapons of mass destruction (WMD). These two threats to the international security have acquired intensity because of the Pakistan's role in both the activities. There is an urgent need to take confidence building measures (CBMs) for strategic stability in the region. Strategic rivalry between India and Pakistan has remained alive and that is a great concern for regional security. India's perception of the emerging security scenario has been appropriately described thus: "In an environment where most conflicts will be "low intensity" regional affairs, the real change will be "winning peace," and marshalling and deploying soft power assets will be as important as "hard power" assets. Beyond regional instabilities and conflicts caused by failed or failing states, the greater problems are associated with the new set of transnational threats that grow in importance proportionately to the progress of the informative age and globalisation trends that fuel them just as they drive economic expansion."[11]

South Asian states are characterised by political, social, ethnic, religious and cultural diversities. In recent years, management of diversity in South Asia has deteriorated. States have witnessed movements, mostly violent, from diverse groups. Diversity has been manipulated and even suppressed for political gains. Discrimination has occurred against minority groups whether ethnic or religious. There are intra-religious conflicts building up. All this has caused instability at intra-state level and created irritants in inter-state relations. The absence of genuine democracy as in Pakistan has accentuated fears of using the ethnic, religious, or cultural plurality for political gains.

Globalisation in South Asia has coincided with the end of the Cold War. The South Asian regional conflicts, particularly the Indo-Pakistan conflict, have been associated with the Cold War geo-politics. Naturally, the end of the Cold War was believed to have a major impact on the existing conflicts. During the Cold War period, the security structures and international institutions were not effective in preventing and resolving conflicts in South Asia. The end of the Cold War required overhauling of the existing security structures and institutions and initiatives of new approaches to preventing, managing and resolving conflicts.

The UN Secretary General's report of 17 June 1992 to Security Council highlighted the importance of preventive diplomacy, peacemaking and peacekeeping for conflict prevention and resolution. *The Report of the Commission on Global Governance* underlined the importance of a long term programme, partially to demilitarise security policies. The new era called for the shaping of democratic institutions and civil societies, besides building political, military, humanitarian and economic structures for conflict prevention, management and resolution.

In the post-cold War period, humanitarian intervention as a tool of resolving conflicts is being seriously debated. During the Cold War, humanitarian intervention was neither considered a legitimate method nor did the bipolarity allow its practice. But perceptions have changed in the new age of the 21st century. Now the community of states is coming round to the perception that humanitarian intervention—forcible or non-forcible—must be tried as a legitimate method of resolving conflicts in the states where the state machinery has either failed to ensure safety and survival of people or the state itself is indulging in genocide or large scale human rights violation.

As we know, the traditional approach to humanitarian intervention puts primary focus on states and forcible intervention. Coercion and a breach of sovereignty are the main characteristics of intervention. It is also non-consensual. On the contrary, non-forcible humanitarian intervention is characterized by non-violent activities of states, international organizations and non-governmental organizations in humanitarian assistance. It promotes third party facilitating role in conflict resolution and reconstruction. It can be consensual or non-consensual. Both states and non-state actors are considered important actors in conflict management or resolution.

The Report of the High-level Panel on Threats, Challenges and Change (December 2004) spells out a new vision of collective security for the 21st century. It says that the UN Security Council has the authority to act preventively and there is a need for it to be prepared to be more active in the future for conflict resolution through humanitarian intervention. The report underlines the responsibility of states to protect civilians from large scale violence. It outlines its strategy thus: "When a State fails to protect its civilians, the international community then has a further responsibility to act, through humanitarian operations, monitoring missions and diplomatic pressure—and with force if necessary, though only as a last resort. And in case of conflict or use of force, this also implies a clear international commitment to rebuilding shattered societies." The report has also highlighted the need for new institutions to meet evolving threats and challenges. It has recommended the creation of a peace-building commission within the UN. This commission, working closely with regional organizations and international financial institutions, could fill a crucial gap by giving necessary attention to countries emerging from conflict.

In South Asia we find states either failing or too weak to handle a conflict. There are serious human rights violations in almost all states, particularly in non-democratic states. Involvement of states in abetting transnational terrorism is a well-known fact. The issue of humanitarian intervention is very complex, involving the questions of legality and legitimacy of such an intervention. In the South Asian context, forcible intervention may generate further conflicts. Non-forcible intervention is more pragmatic, but for such intervention the criterion developed by the Panel or otherwise must be carefully considered.

Globalisation has increased the importance of the non-statist perspectives of conflict formation and conflict prevention, management and resolution. Non-state actors are influencing policy-makers to adopt people-centric and problem-solving approaches.

The contemporary security debates focusing on human security have relevance for the South Asian region. While states in South Asia have continued to be guided by the traditional military and state-centric notions of security, states have faced large number of problems internally. This region remains underdeveloped, resulting in acute humanitarian crises. Law and order problems have remained highly critical. Human rights of the people have been violated throughout the region. States have witnessed oppressive regimes. Now the concept of security needs to be reassessed in the context of these humanitarian problems in South Asia.

The South Asian states have poor indicators on all the seven areas of human security as formulated in the UNDP 1994 report, namely, economic, food, health, environmental, personal, community and political security.[12] These problems are more acute in the least developed and failing states in the region. The observation in the CHS 2003 report, that the state has often failed to fulfil its security obligations and has even become a source of threat to its own people,[13] holds true about the South Asian states. These states have not adequately addressed the issues of 'freedom from fear' and 'freedom from want.'[14] The states of the region have been found wanting in addressing the three dimensions of human security, as envisaged by Amitav Acharya, namely, human needs, human costs and human rights. From human security perspective, states in South Asia have invariably caused human insecurities.

The Challenge of a Collective Future

It is well known that how states in South Asia have miserably failed in achieving their stated goals both in terms of securing themselves from the traditional threats and also from the non-traditional threats. The examples of other regions where regional cooperation and integration have successfully enhanced security of states have not inspired the conflict ridden region of South Asia. European Union (EU) and Association of Southeast Asian Nations (ASEAN) are two of the examples in this regard. What are the stumbling blocks and how the states of the region can overcome them?

First, regional cooperation all over the world has promoted development, peace and security. The EU, the ASEAN and the North America Free Trade Area are good examples of high level of regional integration and interdependence as a result of regional cooperation. People in these regions have witnessed rapid increase in their living standards and protection of their civil liberties. In comparison, South Asia has a unique distinction of having very poor levels of regional cooperation. The regional organisation, the South Asian Association for Regional Cooperation, has remained highly unsuccessful in realising developmental and welfare objectives. States in the region have deliberately put regional cooperation on the back burner. This has caused and furthered human insecurities in South Asia.

Second, states in South Asia have neglected developmental issues. They have even followed repressive strategies, resulting in structural violence and human rights violations. Many of the movements in the countries of the region are considered as the consequences of the state oppression. The Maoist movement in Nepal, the Naxalite movement in India, the Tamil problem in Sri Lanka, the Baloch problem in Pakistan are some examples of structural violence in the region. There are other numerous protests at the local levels in the countries of the region. Human rights activists have even questioned the rationale of counter-terrorism. They believe that counter-terrorism by states has resulted in curtailment of civil liberties of people and undermined human security.[15] That will generate more violence against the states.

Third, according to CHS 2003 report, security between states is a necessary condition for the security of the people.[16] On the contrary, states in the South Asian region have embarked on traditional military security and witnessed acute rivalry and arms races. States in the South Asian region have not only threatened the security of their own people but also the security of the people across the borders. India and Pakistan rivalry is probably the most dangerous in the 21st century. Both states are equipped with nuclear weapons. Their hostility has remained unabated even after four military clashes between the two. Both are spending huge amounts of money on defence, and development suffer. Both diplomacy and war have failed to resolve the disputes between the two countries. The policies of the two states are determined by the traditional thinking of state survival through military preparedness and strategic machinations.

Fourth, states in South Asia have pursued very aggressive and interventionist policies. This applies mainly to Pakistan. It will not be wrong to state that Pakistan has embarked on policies and strategies which have undermined the security of the people of Pakistan itself, the security of the people of other countries in the region, and even the security of the people of countries outside the region. Pakistan's territory is being used to unleash terrorism against other states. Pakistan's policies have been in promoting extremism and terrorism and terrorist organisations in Afghanistan, India and elsewhere.

Finally, states must have strong institutions to promote human security. South Asian states present a sorry example in this field. They have miserably failed to evolve strong political, economic and judicial institutions to protect and promote human security. Many states in the region have struggled to have a democratic system. Some states are even based on ideology of religious extremism. Governance has suffered as some regimes have strived to remain in power at any cost, by any means. Pakistan, Afghanistan and Nepal are being called failing states, if not already failed states. In fact, Afghanistan, Pakistan, Bangladesh, Bhutan, Sri Lanka along with India's eastern neighbour, Myanmar, have been described as failed states.[17] This is astonishingly a large number of failing or failed states in a single sub-region. They have struggled to be viable and stable states. Often these states have used military means to resolve internal strife, which violates the principles of human security.

Thus, states in South Asia have been a major cause of undermining human security and also generating new insecurities for the people. States in this region have miserably failed to evolve national strategies as well as regional cooperation and co-ordination for the pursuit of common security values.

Futuristic Perspectives

The world politics has witnessed profound changes after the end of the Cold War. Globalisation has brought about radical changes the way people live and the way states make their foreign and security policies. It has witnesses both integrative as well as disintegrative approaches for conflict management and resolution. The new regionalism has further integrated nations and unleashed cooperative regional policies. The experience all over the world has shown that democracy promotes friendly relations and democratic nations do not go to war for resolving disputes. In South Asia, India-Pakistan relations are at the core of the regional security. Moreover, extra-regional powers have played a key role in destabilising the regional security in South Asia. Without their constrictive role, South Asian states will not be able to evolve mechanisms to resolve disputes. States in South Asia have miserably failed in nation-building projects; consequently, state-building task also remains unachieved. Without viable states it is not likely that security threats will wither away. There are some key dynamics which will determine the future of South Asian regional security.[18] Let us discuss them.

Disintegration as Conflict Management

The post-Cold War period has witnessed integration and disintegration as instruments of conflict management and resolution. The integrative approach has established peace in several parts of the world. States have reunited and inter-governmental organizations (IGOs) have stepped up regionalism and integration. Unification of Germany and emergence of European Union (EU) have gone a long way in conflict management and resolution. Disintegration is seen as a lasting solution to the problems in Middle East, Iraq, Ukraine and elsewhere. In South Asia, disintegration was used as a method of resolving the communal conflict in the Indian sub-continent in 1947. In the same process, Bangladesh was created in 1972. At present, in India, Pakistan and Sri Lanka the separatist movements seek disintegration as a solution to the ongoing conflicts. However, no state would like to disintegrate for resolving a conflict. As a result, conflict management and resolution has become a very difficult task to achieve. Policy-makers believe that conflicts need to be resolved without violating territorial integrity and sovereignty. But in future the disintegrative forces are likely to multiply and affect not only the internal cohesion of a country but also generate serious inter-state tensions and even conflicts.

The process of globalisation has strengthened the belief that integration and interdependence as a result of increased functionalism will promote integrative approach for resolving or managing inter-state conflicts in the region. States of the region are trying to build institutional capabilities to manage conflicts. The boundaries between external and internal security threats or conflicts are getting eroded. Most of conflicts in South Asian countries have both internal and external dimensions. If they have to be resolved or even managed then both the dimensions need to be addressed. The definitional boundaries of external and internal conflict or threat have got blurred and intertwined. The process of globalisation has further helped this phenomenon. Globalisation is having serious impact on the nature of conflicts. A social, ethnic, economic, political or even environmental crisis in a country can easily transform into an inter-state or a regional conflict due to the interconnectedness and integrative processes unleashed by globalisation.

A Security Role for SAARC

A range of non-military approaches, such as regional cooperation as envisaged by the South Asian Association for Regional Cooperation (SAARC), can be useful in guarding not only against the non-military threats but also against military threats. It is well established by now from the functioning of the regional organisations that collective approach can transform the international politics of a region and resolve most of the conflicts in a peaceful manner. Moreover, regional cooperation can minimise the intrusive role of extra-regional powers and thus raise the level of individual or national security of the countries in the region. The SAARC can play a significant role in altering the prevailing competitive politics and security as existing between India and Pakistan and promote cooperative security. Interdependence among the countries of the region is logical given the fact that series of problems cannot be solved by an individual state on its own.

Experience has borne out that strengthening of regional cooperation and integration takes time, demands strong political commitment, and an adequate legal and institutional framework. It greatly depends on favourable political atmosphere, which, however, is often stirred by interacting internal and external pressures. The diversity of regional arrangements shows that they can be attuned to specific needs and features of regions, reflecting their political sensitivities, cultural traditions and models of society.

Regional cooperation in South Asia must be understood and analysed keeping in view two factors. First, South Asia provides a unique case where both military and non-military variables seriously threaten peace and security in the region. Moreover, historical variables still continue to be applied to the contemporary situations. This has hampered the process of regional cooperation and integration. Negative nationalism continues to thwart the ascendance of transnationalism, unlike what has happened in the case of the European Union. Second, it is believed that regional cooperation can transform both military and non-military threats to security. Security is understood not only as the ability to overcome the real threats to core national values but also as a psychology problem that these values will be attacked. Regional cooperation in South Asia can do away with both the real threats as well as the lurking fear that in future a country's security might be undermined by the external sources of threats. The hostility between India and Pakistan has created the pattern of such objective dangers and subjective fears that the core national values may be attacked. Regional cooperation and interdependence of shared interests provide an alternative to such threats and fears. Once interdependence is achieved, no one will think of threatening the other state. In a relationship of interdependence, states are sensitive to each other. Moreover, states try to adjust their policies in a coordinated manner so that the actions of each are less damaging to the other. Such a framework of interdependent relations in Such Asia will logically result into the transformation of conflict behaviour and increase cooperation for a peaceful resolution of all disputes.

SAARC has not been formally given a security role unlike many other regional organisations. But if it wishes to be a viable and dynamic organisation it cannot avoid tackling political and security matters which affect all the countries in a critical way, just as ASEAN and other regional organisations have been doing.

SAARC is the only regional grouping in Asia that has two acutely hostile nuclear powers as its members. It will be unrealistic for SAARC members if they do not consider evolving a framework in which the non-contentious and common security concerns could be addressed and means evolved to seek solutions.

Non-military threats to the security by South Asian countries can acquire dangerous proportions in the times ahead. Poverty, environmental degradation, extremism, terrorism, illegal migrants and refugees and so on are the issues and threats which can put the survival of the states at stake. Moreover, these are the security threats which cannot be resolved by the efforts of a single state. They require collective strategies and resolutions. Collective interests must precede particularistic or individualistic interests.

South Asian community cannot realistically succeed unless the behaviour patterns and stereotyped perceptions of the states of the region transform. The concerns for national security must be and they can be, reconciled with the regional common security perceptions. Progress towards the emergence of regional institutions must be stepped up and a regional outlook on a range of issues must be evolved.

State-building

Many of the states in South Asia have struggled to be viable and stable. As discussed above, many of the South-Asian states—Afghanistan, Pakistan, Bangladesh, Nepal, Bhutan, Sri Lanka along with India's eastern neighbour, Myanmar—have been described as failed states.[18] This is a large number of failing or failed states in a single sub-region. These states are facing serious problems of internal political strife or instability, economic strife, law and order problem, low-levels of human development, extremism and even terrorism. These states have very weak political, civil and financial institutions.

Many states in South Asia have failed to evolve as secular and modern viable states. States are being guided by extremism and religious fundamentalism. States based on theocracy or ideology of extremism and religious fundamentalism generate internal conflict and endanger the national security of neighbouring countries also. Such states create conflicts and never move forward on issues of mutual security. Pakistan is a theocratic state. Theocracy inherently promotes hatred and intolerance. It is the anti-thesis of secularism, liberalism and democracy. Therefore, in South Asia it is essential that fundamentalism and extremism do not become a basis for state-building.

Afghanistan is a typical example of the problem of 'statelessness' in a third world country. In this phenomenon of statelessness, the foundations of the state have come under threat from competing and divergent interests within the state and from outside. Apart from the undoubted role of the external factors, the domestic dynamics of Afghanistan society and polity have also undermined the very edifice of statehood and integrity in Afghanistan. The state-building project in Afghanistan has become very complicated. The coalition forces are facing more widespread Taliban and al-Qaeda terrorists all over Afghanistan and neighbouring Pakistan. The situation in Afghanistan has the potential to destabilise strategic and political environment in the region. Any regime in Afghanistan controlled by the Pakistan security forces will work against India's interests and aggravate India-Pakistan relations.[19]

Democratic Peace

The values of democracy, pluralism, and freedom have witnessed a slow growth in the South Asian region. These values are not prevalent in all the South Asian states. The region has asymmetrical political systems. Most of the states have failed to develop truly democratic and secular values. If democracy acquires roots in these states then that would create political system symmetry in the region. It is believed that if Pakistan adopts a democratic system then many of the conflicts with India can be resolved or managed peacefully. However, the process of democratization is not free from challenges and new conflicts. It is believed that democratization itself would generate new conflicts, and the inability of fragile states to manage this will be a cause for concern. In the absence of an institutionalized capability to manage such conflicts, it is quite likely that authoritarianism will reassert itself.

India is the only truly viable democratic state in South Asia. In recent times, India's neighbours have witnessed internal political transitions. At times these developments have tended to destabilise South Asian security. Changes in some countries have come through violence. Pakistan, Nepal and Bangladesh have witnessed political violence. On the other hand, Bhutan has peacefully managed its political transition to constitutional monarchy and democracy. Extremist and sectarian violence in Pakistan, Afghanistan, Bangladesh, and more recently in Sri Lanka has not only troubled the respective states but the entire region as well. India wants to promote democracy, stability and peace in its neighbourhood through non-interventionist approach. It does not want to achieve objectives through intervention. India believes that democratic ideology in South Asia can help in management and durable resolution of disputes.

Globalisation furthers the values of democracy, pluralism, and freedom. These values are not prevalent in all the South Asian states. The region has asymmetrical political systems. Most of the states are non-democratic and non-secular. In such states if democracy and secularism acquire roots then that will create political system symmetry. It is believed that if Pakistan adopts a robust democratic system then many of the conflicts with India can be resolved or managed peacefully. However, the process of democratization is not free from challenges and new conflicts. Kumar Rupesinghe rightly observes: "Democratization itself will generate new conflicts, and the inability of fragile states to manage this will be a cause for concern. In the absence of an institutionalized capability to manage conflicts, it is likely that authoritarianism will reassert itself."

India-Pakistan Cooperation

There may be some tactical cooperation in the economic field, but security cooperation is not to achieve any significant levels of cooperation between India and Pakistan. According to one observation there "are prospects for tactical cooperation on the economic front, intended primarily to boost narrow business interests. They are 'genuine' insofar as they potentially offer real and tangible benefits to those who are advocating them. However, at a strategic level, Pakistan has refused India's suggestion that political differences should not be allowed to impede trade relations. Islamabad insists that Kashmir be resolved before economic ties can be normalized."[20] Similarly, Pakistan-China strategic cooperation is a big riddle for the regional security of South Asia. China's support to Pakistan will not liberate India-Pakistan relations from conflicts. It would not be wrong to say that "Sino-Pakistani collaboration is the biggest structural cause of India's security deficit. Its contribution to regional instability tends to be underestimated."[21]

Negotiations and bilateral agreements are the most viable means of settling the core issues of state-sponsored terrorism and Kashmir. Such an approach is also bound to have a positive impact on other outstanding issues between India and Pakistan. Despite the ever lurking trust deficit, India and Pakistan have taken a number of initiatives for management and resolution of the bilateral issues and disputes. There is no possibility of Kashmir being resolved according to the wishes of Pakistan. India has made it clear to Pakistan and the international community that there is no religious or territorial solution to the Kashmir problem and the boundaries between India and Pakistan cannot be redrawn. Resolution of the Kashmir issue is considered key to South Asian stability. It is believed that Resolution of the Kashmir issue would go a long way towards making Pakistan a more normal state and reducing its preoccupation with India.[22] According CIA veteran Bruce Riedel, "Resolution of the Kashmir issue would also remove a major rationale for the army's disproportionate role in Pakistani national security affairs; that in turn would help to ensure survival of genuine civilian democratic rule in the country."[23] He further opines, "By eliminating Pakistan's desire to wage asymmetric warfare against India, it would also discourage Pakistan from making alliances with the Taliban, Lashkar-e-Taiba and al Qaeda."[24] Thus the resolution of the Kashmir issue is crucial to Pakistan's survival. Pakistan should, therefore, adopt rational and pragmatic approach to finding a viable solution to the issue.

India has consistently maintained that normalisation of relations between the two countries is greatly dependent on Pakistan completely discarding its policy of using terrorism as a state policy against India in all of its manifestations. India will not compromise on this stand and will put further pressure on Pakistan through new strategies. In fact, terrorism in South Asia cannot be defeated unless both India and Pakistan collaborate and cooperate not only for their bilateral gains but for the sake of eradicating a key threat to the existence of several states in the region. The situation in Afghanistan will also improve considerably as a consequence of India-Pakistan cooperation.[25]

Role of Extra-regional Powers

With the beginning of the 21st century, more so after 9/11 events, the India's relationship with the United States has acquired a new positive momentum. The US now considers India as a victim of terrorism, supported mainly by Pakistan. In fact, the U.S. State, Defense, and Commerce Departments have already started to formulate a new vision of relations with emerging powers, such as India, China, Brazil and South Africa, which are going to affect the distribution of power in the world in the near future.[26] It is in India's interest to have best of relations with the US and engage it in its goal of strategic stability in South Asia and also make it a factor in the balance of power at the Asian level. The US role on combating terrorism has to be supported more assertively by India, particularly, in Afghanistan. The Indo-US nuclear deal has can be termed as the most defining movement in the history of politico-strategic alignments in South Asia.

The US has started appreciating India's growing global and Asian stature. It no more sees India's threat perception and policy response through the prism of South Asian security alone. On the issues of terrorism, non-proliferation, and strategic cooperation among the democracies, the Indo-US relations have acquired definite South Asian and global contexts. The US should play a constructive role in promoting peace and stability in South Asia. Its global alliance against terrorism has brought about positive results for the South Asian security.

Russia considers India as an important player for promoting South Asian security. Russia has been supportive of India's stand on Kashmir and its resolution according to the Shimla Agreement. Russia has been supportive of strengthening peace process between India and Pakistan for the development of the region and resolution of the bilateral problems.[27] Both India and Russia have similarity of perceptions on transnational security threats like international terrorism and religious extremism. Apart from Russia, the U.S., China and other countries are also concerned on these issues, and hence they have a mutuality of interests. The convergence of interests between India and other major powers on these issues will put pressure on Pakistan for mending its policies on Kashmir and transnational terrorism.

Lasting peace in South Asia is possible only when China resolves its problems with India and does not cooperate with Pakistan on anti- or counter-India basis. China needs to rethink its strategy of aiding Pakistan to tie down India in the South Asian wrangle. The forces of globalization have compelled China to develop new understanding with India in the economic field and also take joint measures against terrorism, increase bilateral military cooperation and take new CBMs for resolving the border dispute. China has emerged as India's largest trading partner in its global trade. In such a situation, China's national interests would dictate normal relations with India. It is believed that India and China together can sustain peace and stability in the region. Both share the perception that "there could be no Asia-Pacific century or Asian century without India and China forming crucial elements of such architecture."[28]

Summing up

South Asia has witnessed transformation of power dynamics at the domestic level, inter-state level and in the relations of the individual states with global powers. India has emerged as the most powerful state in the region with consequences for the future of regional security in South Asia. Pakistan, the main challenger to India, is weakening day by day. Its internal problems have become a challenge to the security of the entire international community. Pakistan has also lost the trust of the US and its other friends. China is having strategic cooperation with Pakistan, but future of their relationship will be shaped by the increasing threat of Islamic extremism in China which is supported by elements in Pakistan. Pakistan's position in South Asia and international politics is undermined by the fact that its failure to deal with terrorism and religious extremism is posing a grave threat to all of its neighbours: India, China, Afghanistan and Iran.

The patterns of inter-state and intra-state developments have affected the security environment in South Asia. States in the region are facing new security vulnerabilities and have become more insecure now than ever before. The feelings of insecurity and heightened threat perception should compel states of the region to adopt rational policies to counter these threats through cooperative mechanisms.

After the end of Cold War, regional powers like India have gained more space and autonomy in international politics. India has acquired political, economic, military and institutional strengths to project power at the regional level and even beyond the region. The economic and politico-strategic agenda India has prepared for itself will have impact on the South Asian and Asian security architecture.

India has special responsibilities in the region's peace and stability. It has the political, economic and military wherewithal to play a proactive role in promoting all aspects of security in the region. India has promoted peaceful periphery and at the same time also promoted the welfare of the people in the neighbouring countries through humanitarian assistance. India has been reluctant in assertively playing a role in internal matters of the others. But such a policy cannot be sustained for all times to come. In grave situations of insecurity and humanitarian crisis India will have to do differently and play a proactive role. The future of South Asia will have to be largely shaped by India. India has to ponder over the question of humanitarian intervention in cases where states have failed or are unable to secure their own people and that situation is threatening India's as well as the region's security. India's national security cannot be enhanced in isolation from regional security.

REFERENCES

1. B. Buzan and O. Waever, *Regions and Powers: The Structure of International Security* (Cambridge: Cambridge University Press, 2003, p.3.
2. R.E. Kelly, "Security Theory in "New Regionalism," *International Studies Review* (9) 2007, p. 205.
3. *Ibid.*
4. *Ibid.*, pp. 197-229.
5. B. Buzan and Ole Waever, *Regions and Powers: The Structure of International Security*, pp. 101-127.
6. B. Buzan, "Security architecture in Asia: the interplay of regional and global levels," *The Pacific Review*, Vol. 16 No. 2, 2003, pp. 143-173.
7. R. Budania,"India-Pakistan Politico-strategic Rivalry in the 21st Century," *Indian Journal of Politics*, Vol. 47, Nos. 3-4, July-December 2013, p. 86.
8. Y. Xiaoping, "The Security Architecture of South Asia: Problems and Prospects," <http://indiachinainstitute.org/wp-content/uploads/2012/04/Yang-Xiaoping-Security-Architecture-of-SA.pdf>
9. S. Sathiya Murthy, "For an India-led security architecture in South Asia," *The Hindu*, January 8, 2013.
10. Speech by Indian Foreign Secretary Shivshankar Menon on "India and International Security" on 3 May 2007 at the International Institute of Strategic Studies, London. See *Strategic Digest*, 37:6, June 2007, p. 752.
11. *Ibid.*, p. 756
12. United Nations Development Programme (1994). *Human Development Report 1994* (Oxford: Oxford University Press, 1994), pp. 24-25.
13. Commission on Human Security. (2003). *Human Security Now* (New York: United Nations), p. 2.
14. D. Rizal, 2010. Faultering Footprints of Security in South Asia. Global Consortium on Security Transformation, *Policy Brief Series*, No. 4, January.
15. G. Shani, "Globalization, the 'War on Terror' and Human In/Security in South Asia," in Giorgio Shani, et al., eds., *Protecting Human Security in a Post 9/11 World: Critical and Global Insights* (New York: Palgrave Macmillan), 2007, pp. 115-130.
16. Commission on Human Security. (2003). *Human Security Now* (New York: United Nations), p. 3.
17. *Foreign Policy* (2013). The Failed States Index 2013. http://www.foreignpolicy.com/failedstates2013

18. *Foreign Policy* (2013). The Failed States Index 2013.
19. "Facets of the U.S. Strategy in Afghanistan Conflict: India's Concerns and Role," *South Asian Affairs,* Vol. 2, No. 1-2, January-December 2009.
20. P. Mahadevan, "Regional Security in South Asia—Future Tense," 12 January 2012, <http://www.isn.ethz.ch/Digital-Library/Articles/Special-Feature/Detail/?lng=en&id=143963&contextid774=143963&contextid775=143960&tabid=1452427331>
21. *Ibid.*
22. "Resolution of Kashmir issue will make Pakistan a normal state," *Indian Express*, July 4, 2013.
23. B. Riedel, *Avoiding Armageddon* (New Delhi: Harper Collins, 2013).
24. *Ibid.*
25. R. Budania, "The Spectre of Terrorism in South Asia: Taking Stock of India-Pakistan Cooperation," *Journal of Social and Political Studies*, Vol. IV (2), December 2013, p. 72.
26. According to Goldman Sachs and Deutsche, by 2010, the annual growth in combined national income from the BRIC countries (Brazil, Russia, India, and China) will be greater than that from the U.S., Japan, Germany, the United Kingdom, and Italy combined. By 2025, it will be twice that of the G-7. See Daniel Drezner, "The New World Order," *Foreign Affairs* 86:2 (March-April 2007), p. 36.
27. "Dangers to construct world on unipolar principles: Putin," *The Hindu*, December 4, 2006.
28. "India is a core state for Asian security: Pranab Mukherjee," *The Hindu*, June 4, 2006.

7

Nepal's Recent Experiment with Democracy

Rohit Kumar and Saurabh Sharma

Introduction

Peace process in Nepal began with the decade long political conflict nearing its end in 2006. Drafting of the constitution by the elected Constituent Assembly was the pivot of the peace process, with an initiative of social inclusion being taken by the people of Nepal with respect to equality, liberty and social justice in every sphere of life. After two postponements, Nepal's Constituent Assembly(CA) election took place on April 10, 2008. The elections were held on the basis of a mixed system of direct elections and top-up nominations (Thapa and Sharma 2009). From an electoral perspective, the result of the election was a surprise to many (Sharma et al. 2008). The results showed substantial support for the Maoists, who with 229 seats became the largest single party in the Constituent Assembly. The newly formed Constituent Assembly declared Nepal a federal democratic republic and abolished the monarchy at its first meeting (Nguyen 2014).

The Constituent Assembly election produced more inclusive outcomes. It increased the scope for power sharing and lowered the risk of conflict. The outcome of the Constituent Assembly election was accepted by political actors and the international community. After the election, results were declared and the Constituent Assembly was formed. The task of the Constituent Assembly was to draft a constitution within a stipulated time. But due to causes like orthodox parties tendency, unstable government, politics of power sharing and inter and intra party conflict the Constituent Assembly failed to deliver the constitution. The Constituent Assembly was one of the most important instruments which by adopting the new constitution could have eliminated the centralized and unitary form of governance. It was enshrined to disseminate a democratic constitution in 2008 as it was elected to deliver some of these important tasks. However, the democratic process of constitution making failed dismally (Bhandari 2012).

After the dissolution of Constituent Assembly, Prime Minister Baburam Bhattarai announced fresh elections in May 2012, for a new Constituent Assembly after four years of deadlock in which political parties of Nepal failed to agree to a new constitution for the country. Apparently, this has affected the public trust in democratic institutions. It has also affected public perception of the political class in Nepal. Another round of Constituent Assembly elections took place on November 19, 2013. In this election, Nepali Congress, the oldest political party of Nepal, got the maximum number of seats. Now the major concern is that whether the new Constituent Assembly will be able to successfully deliver a constitution to Nepal.

India as an international observer has played an important role in democratization in Nepal. India believes that all its neighbours are crucial for its economic growth and stability. Nepal is an important neighbour of India and occupies special significance because of its geographic location as well as historical, cultural and economic linkages (Nayak 2014). This paper tends to analyse the process of Constituent Assembly election and the underlying reasons behind its failure. It further probes the role of India in the peace and democratization process in Nepal.

Historical Context of the Constituent Assembly

Constituent Assembly is an assembly of elected representatives of people from all over the country for preparing a constitution and it is a process of eliminating concentration of power in the hands of the feudal elites. The Constituent Assembly is not a new phenomenon of discussion in Nepal. The demand for a Constituent Assembly in Nepal goes back to the Rana regime. In February 1947, Rana Prime Minister Padma Shamsher formed an unusual prototype of a Constituent Assembly consisting of twelve elected and twelve nominated members to initiate constitutional reforms in the country. It can be said that it was not complete, since it lacked four immensely necessary features of a Constituent Assembly: a fully representational institution, a forum which was independent of the constitutional discourses, an autonomous body to develop constitution on its own and the right to promulgate a constitution without the interference of any individual or institution. However, this act could not been implemented (Bhandari 2012).

For the first time, Nepal moved on the path of democracy in 1950. After that, in 1951 an Interim Constitution was formed which remained effective for eight years. Then, in 1959 Nepal succeeded in installing a western styled parliamentary democracy. But it could not be sustained for long. Declaring parliamentary democracy a failure eighteen months later, King Mahendra dismissed the Koirala government and promulgated a new constitution on December 16, 1962. The new constitution established a party less panchayat system. Nepal returned to the authoritarian rule of monarchy under the cover of democracy. This continued nearly for twenty eight years and was overthrown in the 1990 democratic movement. The 1990 movement for the democracy was a major landmark in the contemporary political history of Nepal. The post 1990 period of democracy was marked by political instability. The preliminary changeover was backed by the spirit of popular movement and restoration of multiparty system with the commissioning of a new constitution in November 1990. The 1990 constitution reinstalled constitutional monarchy in the country, so it was a semi-constitutional monarchy (Upreti 2010).

Gyanendra succeeded as the monarch, after the royal massacre of 2001 in which King Birendra and his family members were killed. After that, the 1990 Constitution was replaced by the Interim Constitution promulgated in January 2007. The basic objective of the Interim Constitution has been to provide a set of rules and regulations for the government of the country till it was replaced by a permanent constitution (Upreti 2010). The salient features of the Interim Constitution included: a constraint on the powers of the King, an outline of the Constituent Assembly's basic structure and a strong executive. In short, the Interim Constitution provided a suitable framework for the conduct of elections (ANFREL Report 2008).

After the election of first Constituent Assembly of Nepal, the Assembly members quickly voted to abolish the monarchy and declared Nepal as a federal democratic republic (World Election 2013). The primary task of the Constituent Assembly was to draft a constitution within a stipulated time in which it failed. Following the dissolution of the Constituent Assembly without adopting a constitution, then Prime Minister Baburam Bhattarai announced fresh elections for a new Constituent Assembly. Nepal went for another Constituent Assembly election on November 19, 2013. The result of the election was an eye opener for the world and the Maoists too. Nobody had imagined that the party which had emerged as the largest in the 2008 Constituent Assembly elections will move down to number three in 2013 and Nepali Congress would emerge as the winner (Shrestha 2014).

First Constituent Assembly Election–2008

The Interim Constitution laid a suitable framework to conduct elections. During the pre-election period the Election Commission (EC) had acted as a neutral body; which had been a responsible body for holding the Constituent Assembly elections. The Commission had also been able to maintain transparency while generating a positive relationship with all political actors (Carter Center Report, 2009). To initiate the process of election smoothly, election rules and a code of conduct was issued by the Election Commission (WPAF Report 2008). Overall the responses were good enough barring a few places like that of Lamjung, Banke, Madhesi in Tarai where there had been complaints raised by the Maoists.

The Election Commission became extensively active for voter registration during the beginning of 2007 which significantly increased the number of registered voters. The turning point in this was the modernization of secure national identification card scheme and public registry which proved to be an efficient and planned attempt (EUEOM September 2008).

Registration of Political Parties and Candidates

The political parties had been the main driving force for the democratic system and because of this there was no major hurdle for registration of either parties or candidates in Constituent Assembly election. The Election Commission in 2007 issued a regulation on 'Political Party Registration Rules' to allow for the registration of political parties on the basis of constitutional powers. The Commission's regulation details the procedures regarding what kind of documentation a party has to submit for registration. It has imposed certain mandatory conditions for party registration followed by the verification process and examination with the final decision of Election Commission to register the party. The regulation also contained provisions on non-eligibility and deregistration of parties (Franklin 2008).

To maintain transparency, political parties have to take the signature of at least 10,000 registered voters, supporting their application. But, there was no appeal mechanism and Election Commission's decision was taken as final. In addition to the 15 political parties represented in the Interim Parliament, the Election Commission registered 47 new parties in 2007. Following the decision to reschedule the Constituent Assembly election for April 10, 2008, party registration was reopened. This allowed an additional 13 parties, mostly groups from the Terai, to register, raising the total number of registered parties to 74 (EUEOM September 2008).

Adoption of Electoral System

The electoral system adopted for the 2008 Constituent Assembly election sought to elect a body of representative of all Nepalese, to cope with some specific issues such as a relatively high rate of illiteracy. It was a mixed member system (Sharma et. al. 2008). According to the Interim Constitution (as amended on December 28, 2007) Article 63 (3) the 601 member Constituent Assembly was to have the following composition:

(a) 240 members to be elected on the basis of First Past the Post (FPTP) from single member constituencies;
(b) 335 members to be elected on the basis of the party list based proportional electoral system considering the whole country as one single constituency;
(c) 26 members nominated by the Interim Council of Ministers on the basis of consensus from the distinguished persons and persons from ethnic and indigenous groups who fail to be represented under a) and b) and who have made significant contribution to national life (Vollan 2011). There was a provision for proper representation of women, dalits, janajatis, aadivasis, madhesis and backward regions (Bhattarai).

First Past the Post System (FPTP)

First Past the Post is a system in which candidate seeking the highest number of votes is declared as a winner. It is also known as plurality system. It means that there have to be a plural number of candidates for election and one of them is declared as a winner. This system of election has been quite popular in India, USA, U.K., Canada and New Zealand etc. In Nepal also, in 1959 and 1990 onwards, elections were held on the basis of this system. It is popularly known as the majority system. This election system has been quite popular and easy in operational terms.

Proportional Representation System (PR)

For the proportional election, the whole of Nepal is considered as one electoral constituency. Only political parties registered with the Election Commission can participate in election under the PR system. In the proportional representation a political party is given seats in the legislature in proportion to the votes secured by it in the election. The parties nominate their candidates in the election and then seats are allocated to them in proportion to the votes secured by those chosen candidates.

International Involvement in Nepal's Constituent Assembly Election

Many international communities rigorously supported the peace process and the Constituent Assembly election. The US, UK, India, Germany, China, South Korea, Switzerland, Norway and Denmark also supported Nepal in its peace initiative through development cooperation and electoral support. The presence of the international community in Nepal acted as a deterrent against excessive use of violence and abuse of human rights. The international community had placed Nepal in the category of a fragile state. United Nations Mission in Nepal (UNMIN) and European Union Election Observation Mission (EUEOM) played a crucial role in the election.

United Nations Mission in Nepal (UNMIN)

The UN had been engaged for several years in political efforts to end the hostilities in Nepal and it encouraged a negotiated political solution. In July 2006, following a request by the government of Nepal for UN assistance, the Secretary General dispatched a pre-assessment mission to the country. In August, the government and the Maoist sent a joint letter to the Secretary General requesting UN assistance in monitoring the ceasefire code of conduct and providing technical support for the planning, preparation and conducting the election of a Constituent Assembly as well as monitoring the Nepal Army to ensure that it remains within its barracks and that its weapons are not used (United Nations 1981).

UNMIN was established by the Secretary General resolution 1740 and was headed by Ian Martin. This mission was extended three times until July 23, 2009. In July, 2009 Ban Ki Moon recommended another extension, to last until January 2010. Nepal's political leaders have said that its presence was needed until the integration and rehabilitation of the Maoist army personnel was resolved. UNMIN maintained twenty four hour presence at main weapons storage areas of the seven main Maoist cantonment sites and the Chhauni barrack of the Nepal army. It was a political mission under the control of Department of Political Affairs (Eurich 2010).

As part of its mandate, UNMIN successfully registered and stored the weapons of the People's Liberation Army and contained Maoist fighting at various sites across the country. It was generally assumed that UNMIN would continue its monitoring activities until the political parties and Maoist reached a final agreement on the future of the former PLA combatant, including integration of at least a part of the Maoist force into Nepal's security force. Due to misunderstanding of its mandate or a mischievous interpretation of the same for partisan purposes, the arms monitoring part of UNMIN's engagement had drawn the most criticism from Nepali political actors (Einsiedel et al. 2012).

In April 2008, UNMIN played an important support role in successfully holding a historic Constituent Assembly election that was a major milestone in the peace process. As the first Constituent Assembly could not achieve its objective of framing a new constitution of Nepal the whole exercise of electing a new Assembly had to be repeated and the tenure of UNMIN had to be further extended.

European Union Election Observation Mission in Nepal

The European Union has deployed Election Observation Missions around the world to provide support for the development of democratic institutions and to assist partner countries in their objective to hold elections according to their international, regional and constitutional commitments and obligations. Following an invitation from the Interim Government of Nepal the European Union (EU) established an Election Observation Mission in Nepal to assess the election. The EUEOM opened on March 2, 2008 and remained in Nepal for the duration of the election process until May 10, 2008. The Chief Observer was Jan Mulder, Member of the European Parliament. The EUEOM deployed the largest international mission with 120 observers from Norway, Switzerland and 22 EU Member States present in 62 of the 75 districts (EUEOM April Report 2008).

The observers were deployed throughout Nepal to observe and assess the electoral process in accordance with international standards and best practices for elections as well as the laws of Nepal. The EUEOM was independent in its findings and conclusion and adhered to the Declaration of Principles for International Election Observation commemorated at the United Nations in October, 2005. The EUEOM was joined by a seven member delegation from the European Parliament, led by Josep Borrell Fontelles, Member of the European Parliament, who endorsed the views expressed in this statement. On the day of election, observers visited 517 polling stations in 83 constituencies to observe voting. The EUEOM observed the counting and remained in Nepal to observe post-election developments and the tabulation of results (EUEOM September Report 2008).

Result of Constituent Assembly Election 2008

Election for the formation of Constituent Assembly that was supposed to happen on June 7, 2007 and later on November 22, 2007 after being postponed twice finally took place on April 10, 2008. In this election 17.6 million citizens were entitled to vote, 10.9 million voters exercised their franchise, accounting for a 61% turnout. A total of 3,946 candidates from 54 political parties and independents contested for first-past-the-post seats, though 3,129 of them lost their deposits. 10 of the 54 political parties contesting the polls were communist factions. Altogether, 25 parties returned to the assembly, of which the Communist Party of Nepal-Maoist (CPN-Maoist) secured a total of 229 seats and became the largest party in parliament.

The Maoist won 120 constituency seats through first-past-the-post vote and 100 seats through proportional representation. They gained 9 of the 26 nominated seats and had 229 seats in the Constituent Assembly. Nepali Congress Party got second place with 115 seats; the Communist Party of Nepal-Unified Marxist Leninist (CPN-UML) had 108 seats and Madhesi Jana Adhikar Forum, Nepal (MJF-Nepal) got 54 seats. No other party had more than 21 seats. Twenty parties had representation in single figures, including the Rashtriya Prajatantra Party (RPP) and the Rashtriya Prajatantra Party-Nepal (RPP-N); both parties had to rely on the proportional representation section for seats. Only nine parties won seats in the first-past-the-post ballots (Sharma et al. 2008). The primary reason for the Maoist victory was the sheer electoral dominance of the Maoists across the breadth of Nepal. The electoral strategies of alliances with different sections of the population, the reach of the electoral campaign machinery and the wide support of the poorest were among the other significant reasons (Srinivasan 2008).

In the first-past-the-post system Communist Party of Nepal-Maoist (CPN-Maoist) had won 120 (50%) of the 240 seats. Nepali Congress (NC) received the second largest number of votes and won 37 seats (15.4%) while Communist Party of Nepal-Unified Marxist Leninist (CPN-UML) secured 33 seats (13.8%). Among the Terai-based Madhesi political parties, Madhesi Janadhikar Forum (MJF) won 30 seats, the Terai Madhes Loktantrik Party 9 seats and Nepal Sadbhavna Party 4 seats or collectively 43 seats.

After the counting of votes under the Proportional Representation (PR) system had been completed, it became evident that the CPN-Maoist led the number by attaining100seats (29.85%). The NC and the CPN-UML secured 73 (21.79%) and 70 (20.89%) seat share respectively. The Madhesi Janadhikar Forum (MJF) and Terai Madhes Loktantrik Party were in fourth and fifth positions, respectively, wining 22 (6.56%) and 11 (3.28%) seats. The Nepal Sadbhavna Party was in sixth position with 5 (1.51%) seats.

The first session of the Constituent Assembly declared the country as a federal democratic republic on May 28, 2008 abolishing the 239 year old monarchy and instructed the government to make sure that the King left the Narayanhiti palace within fifteen days (Dahal 2008). In fact, it was a step towards implementing the provision of a Republic enshrined in the Interim Constitution. 564 members of the CA voted on this proposal, with 560 in favour and 4 against. Of all the parties represented in the Constituent Assembly, only the Rastriya Prajatantra Party (Nepal) voted against the motion.

Causes of the Failure of Constituent Assembly

The termination of the Constituent Assembly of Nepal in May 2012 was a disappointing end to a promising process that began with the People's War from 1996 to 2006, the Comprehensive Peace Agreement (CPA), the 2008 Constituent Assembly election, the formation of the Constituent Assembly, proclamation of the republic and abolition of the monarchy. The Maoists might well have expected that the Communist Party of Nepal (Unified Marxist-Leninist) and Nepali Congress (NC) would pitch their tents on the side of the status quo and prevent the writing of a progressive constitution that would assure a truly federal democratic republic of Nepal. The central objective of the Constituent Assembly was to draft a new constitution for Nepal and adopt it through due process. The Interim Constitution of Nepal itself provided applicable adoptive procedures (Adhikari 2012).

The main declaration by the Prime Minister which brought an end to Constituent Assembly on May 28, 2012 has been one of the most hampering points in the setup of the constitution building process. The collapse of the Constituent Assembly without making the constitution meant that the job of writing a new constitution, as promised by the Interim Constitution of 2007, had become uncertain (Chautari 2009). There were several factors responsible for the failure of the Constituent Assembly which has been further discussed.

Inter and Intra Party Conflict

One of the major reasons, that the constitution could not be formulated as it was meant to be within a certain time period, was the lack of seriousness among the political parties. It is difficult to determine the exact cause for such non-seriousness on the part of the political parties. Possibly, conflicts and suspicions amongst the various political parties resulted in major setbacks while attempting to draft the constitution. The blame game that began amongst the major political parties regarding the Maoist party's monopoly in the operation of the government was seen as a factor for disunity amidst the parties. For instance, the CPN-Maoist, country's largest party—was internally divided. With two different road maps inside the party, a new revolution or a peaceful struggle, it was arduous for parties to work together and end the transition (Bhandari 2012).

After the dissolution of first Constituent Assembly when the campaign for fresh elections began; the three major parties UCPN-Maoist, NC and CPN-UML engaged themselves in blaming each other in their election manifestos. They never thought to search for the causes that have been responsible for the failure to prepare the new constitution by the Constituent Assembly. These three parties themselves got involved in blame-game, forgetting to bring up the draft of the constitution which had been prepared by experts on advice and consensus. The meeting which led to an agreement of May 15, 2012 was initiated to sort out the differences amongst the political parties, which turned out to be a war of words. The parties failed to reach a compromise for 117 disputed issues. The differences continued to persist, from Constitutional Committee to Constituent Assembly, particularly on the agenda of state restructuring, the formation of government and judiciary (Poudel 2012).

On May 19, 2012 the major political parties asked the parliament secretariat to finalize the draft constitution. This came into the knowledge of political parties through a report published by the Parliament Secretariat. The review process was done for three days by a team comprising of Madhav Poudel, Nilambar Acharya, Tirthaman Shakya, Bheshraj Sharma and Secretary of the Constitutional Committee, Tek Prasad Dhungana but the draft could not be finalised. The UCPN-Maoist blamed the "status-quoist forces", namely UML and NC, for the Constituent Assembly's incapability to accept the constitution (Bhandari 2013).

Contrary to this, the NC and the UML blamed UCPN-Maoist for not abiding by the agreement. There seemed to be an inner fragmentation among the parties. They did not seem to be bonded on the same lines as they were when they were up against monarchy. The allegations and blame game had started among the parties. UCPN-Maoist had agreed to extend the term of Constituent Assembly by three months. The then Deputy Prime Minister and Law Minister Krishna Prasad Sitaula registered a proposal on May 22, 2012 in this regard. But, the NC president opposed the extension proposal and eventually the term was not extended. The Nepali Congress blamed its weak strength in the Constituent Assembly, as well as CPN-UML's unpredictability and Madhes-centric party's lust for power as the reasons for Constituent Assembly's failure to adopt the constitution (ibid).

Politics of Power Sharing

The consolidation of the peace process in the post-election phase depended much on the working of the Maoist-led government. In a post-conflict political settlement, assenting on the share of power arrangement amongst the political parties is one of the main focus. However, in Nepal, this has been a flawed process from the beginning (Pandey and Delinic 2012). The way events and phenomena turned around have been quite contemplating; the politics of government formation, the way it took place raised a number of questions. This clearly points that even at a stage of critical political transformation, the manner and idioms of Nepal's politics have not changed much. The issue of the formation of the government was ultimately decided by the Constituent Assembly (Upreti 2009).

Prior to the formation of Constituent Assembly political parties agreed on the issue of power sharing arrangements. However, after the Constituent Assembly election and particularly after CPN-Maoist emerged as the single largest party in the Constituent Assembly, the issue of political arrangement over power sharing between them and other parties received a setback. The CPN-Maoist nominated Pushpa Kamal Dahal—Prachanda as its prime ministerial candidate and the Nepali Congress nominated Sher Bahadur Deuba. The Communist Party of Nepal Unified Marxist-Leninist—CPN (UML) and the Madhesi Jana Adhikar Forum (MJF) joined the government while the Nepali Congress decided to sit in opposition. There has been an accusation by Nepali Congress leaders on the Maoists for not reaching a consensus (ibid.). Particularly, these differences started to emerge among the three major parties; Nepali Congress, Unified Communist Party of Nepal (Maoist) earlier known as Communist Party of Nepal (Maoist) and Communist Party of Nepal Unified Marxist-Leninist over a number of issues as well as regarding the sharing of the ministerial portfolios (Pandey and Delinic 2012). This was also a major hurdle in making progress on both peace and constitution drafting processes (Upreti 2009).

In the power structure, the presidential seat had gone to the Nepali Congress, vice presidential seat to Madhesi Jana Adhikar Forum, prime ministership to Communist Party of Nepal (Maoist) and the post of speaker of the Constituent Assembly to Communist Party of Nepal Unified Marxist-Leninist.

Unstable Government

After the formation of Constituent Assembly, its 601 members began the extensive and strenuous process of drafting a new constitution for Nepal. UCPN-Maoist, which won 38% of the Constituent Assembly votes, was asked to form a government. The government formed was a multi-party coalition of political parties as no party has achieved the requisite majority. Government was led by UCPN-Maoist with Pushpa Kamal Dahal, Chairman of the party being elected as the Prime Minister.

Successfully drafting the constitution was an extremely difficult task for the transitional government of Nepal. Four governments came into power from 2008 to 2012 but none of them was able to meet the deadline for constitution drafting. According to the Constituent Assembly's schedule, the first draft of the constitution should have been released for public comment by January 2010 but this deadline could not be achieved and it was given four extensions of six month each time. The government led by Baburam Bhattarai since its formation from August 2011 tried its best to speed up the constitutional drafting process but it ended unproductively with the dissolution of the Constituent Assembly on May 28, 2012. Before the dissolution of the Constituent Assembly, the country was made to believe that there had been a breakthrough in resolving the contentious issue of state restructuring. But, it looked more like an illusion, because soon after that, the Constituent Assembly was dissolved. The four unstable governments formed after the formation of first Constituent Assembly election (2008–2012) were mainly responsible for its failure as they could not provide stability and suitable environment for writing the constitution of Nepal (Afful 2013).

Unstable Governments of Nepal from 2008–2013

Prime Minister	*Structure of Government*	*From*	*To*
Pushpa Kumar Dahal	Coalition Government led by UCPN-Maoist	August 2008	May 2009
Madhav Kumar Nepal	Coalition Government led by UML	May 2009	June 2010
Jhalanath Khanal	Coalition Government led by UML	February 2011	August 2011
Baburam Bhattarai	Coalition Government led by UCPN-Maoist	August 2011	March 2013

Source: Afful, Ken (2013), *Nepal's Transitional Governments: Issues of Governance*, Institute of Development Management Studies.

Ideological Conflict

In the beginning of Constituent Assembly elections, the core conflicts and contradictions were monarchy versus republican setup, unitary versus federal system of governance, settlement of weapons and armies, and electoral systems among diverse ideological and identity groups. But even after the Constituent Assembly election, the matter was not resolved between the Maoists and others in forming the constitution and concluding the issue of arrangement of arms and armies, design of federal states, mechanism of governance and modality of legislative body. The different perceptions for different issues became a cause of concern. The communist fringe and Nepali Congress wanted to establish peace first and then the constitution as a second preference. Their argument was that a fragile environment would not lead to a stable constitution. Therefore, peace was required to be established first, in order to make the environment free of terror and shadows of doubt. But Maoists had a view that peace and constitution-making could be brought about simultaneously as both were equally important. Nepali Congress rejected the idea of mass regularizing or mainstream induction of existing rebel armies by integrating them with the national military force without fulfilling norms, values and qualifications. These contradictory positions put twin goals under the shadow of ideological conflict (Chhetri 2011).

Conflicts and differences were continuing at both inter and intra party level. The major parties of Nepal were debating amongst themselves about how to complete the peace process and draft the constitution. The democracy of any country is governed by laws and rules of the land. Encounters and disputes emerge when political parties and actors violate the laws and rules of the land. The ideological conflict in Nepal was the consequence of violation of norms and elucidation of democracy by solely keeping the interest of the party in mind. During the earlier phase, both the parliamentary parties and the Maoists agreed to launch absolute democracy by ending autocratic monarchy, same being mentioned in the 12-points of understanding as well. It became the foundation for the fight against monarchy and prevalent political scenario.

After the success of the April Movement in 2006, the term 'absolute democracy' was used by the political parties. Different parties took it in different ways. Maoists took it as people's democracy while other parties took it as liberal democracy. Maoists were hesitant to accept liberal democracy after coming into power. They did not abide by the commitment and agreements that were forged by them with the government and other parties. The politics of consensus and coalition culture worked effectively until the Constituent Assembly election. After that it came to an end. Since then ideological struggle and structural ambiguity have been obstructing further political development (ibid). These ideological differences also became the bone of contention between the political parties resulting in the failure of drafting the new constitution.

Attendance Issue

In the four year period, the entire house of the Constituent Assembly met for a total of 122 meetings; 101 during the first two years (2008-2010), 8 in the third year (2010-2011) and 13 in the last year (2011-2012). The minimum average rates of attendance numbered around 62% over the four years, which is at par with the attendance average of the original two year tenure recorded at 63% and up from the 58% recorded for the third year. Nevertheless, it is immensely important to note the differences in number of meetings held. There were only 8 meetings in 2010-2011 period and 13 meetings in 2011-2012. Most importantly, during the entire period of the Constituent Assembly, merely two thirds of its members attended the meetings. In the other phase, over a third of the members elected by the people of Nepal to write a new constitution after a decade of civil war and a democratic movement, were absent (Chautari2013).

The average attendance rate of all the political parties in the Constituent Assembly was approximately 62%. The UCPN-Maoist had attendance rate of 61.29%, which was slightly below the average attendance rate; Nepali Congress (NC) and CPN-UML registered partially higher than the average rate at 63.54% and 67.00% respectively. Consequently, attendance rates of all political parties of Nepal importantly affected the Constituent Assembly and constitution making process (ibid).

Second Constituent Assembly Election–2013

After the expiry of the Constituent Assembly on May 28, 2012, the then government announced the election of the second Constituent Assembly (Citizen Survey 2013). The task of preparing the new constitution which was entrusted upon the first Constituent Assembly failed to reach on agreements on various key issues. Therefore, Supreme Court did not extend its mandate any further. The dissolution of the Constituent Assembly, failure to agree on the formation of new Constituent Assembly and the lack of consensus among political parties regarding which party would head the government during the election, led to protracted political and constitutional crisis (Carter Center Report 2013). After a period of political instability, the leaders of the major political parties agreed on the establishment of a High Level Political Committee (HLPC) in March 2013, and on a care-taker government, the Interim Election Council of Ministers (IECM), under the leadership of Chief Justice, Khil Raj Regmi, whose sole mandate was to hold the 2013 Constituent Assembly elections (EUEOM Report 2013).

On June 13, 2013, the Interim Constitution Council announced the election for Constituent Assembly which was to be held on November 19, 2013. Both the announcements one for the appointment of sitting Chief Justice and another for holding the election were opposed by smaller political parties and also by 33-party alliance led by the CPN–Maoist which initiated the boycott process of electoral system. It gradually became aggravated as the day for election came near. Fore-sighting the situation the IECM prepared and announced the security plan which included the deployment of armed police force and army for managing the security issues during the election (Carter Center Report 2013).

The process for the Constituent Assembly election restarted with the registration of new political parties under the political parties' registration rule, 2007. Gradually, all the registered political parties started their election campaign. Campaigning started with the nomination of first-past-the-post candidates on October 3, 2013. Election campaign activities were largely manifest through small meetings at a local level. Candidates and political parties focused on making close contact with voters through activities such as door-to-door campaigning, small meetings and processions with flags and slogans. According to EU observers, in the campaign events, the principal topics discussed were the content of party manifestos, with significant emphasis given to decentralization and issues of local governance, thus indicating the major concerns of voters (EUEOM Report 2013).

During the Constituent Assembly election 2013, the EUEOM had 112 observers present in Nepal. The Carter Center mission had deployed 80 observers and the Asian Network for free Elections (ANFREL) had about 60 observers. The Election Commission played a very proactive role by inviting special guests and members of embassies based in Kathmandu. Chief Election Commissioners from SAARC countries and governments officials as well as parliamentarians from Australia, Japan and the UK were also invited (EUEOM Report 2013).

The result, compared to 2008, was a defeat for the Maoists, who went down from being the single largest party to third largest party. This time Nepali Congress and Communist Party of Nepal (Unified Marxist Leninist) shared the lead with Congress Party ahead with slight margin (Gellner 2014). It was a surprise for Pushpa Kamal Dahal—Prachanda's Unified Communist Party of Nepal (Maoist) which could secure only 80 seats in both first-past-the post and in the proportional representation system, as compared to 2008 elections where they had a majority of 229 seats. Two of the most important parties, the Nepali Congress and the Communist Party of Nepal (Unified Marxist Leninist) which are considered as traditional parties and had a centric role in constitutional monarchy as political parties (1991-2005) of Nepal re-emerged as most important political actors (World Elections, 2013).

Role of India in Democratisation of Nepal

India is a role model for its neighbouring countries because it has stable democracy. It has played a crucial role as a neighbour of Nepal for promoting democracy. India has continued to work closely with Government of Nepal and the major political parties in the country with the view to support the country's transition to a democratic, stable, peaceful and prosperous State. India's Minister of External Affairs, S.M. Krishna visited Nepal in 2011. He assured the leadership of Nepal of India's strong commitment for a stable, prosperous and democratic Nepal and India's support to the constitution drafting process and strengthening of democratic institutions and creating an inclusive democratic process.

Indian diplomats have been actively involved in the the negotiations for smoothening the process of transition and conflict transformation. During 2004-05, India has facilitated a dialogue between Maoist leaders and the Seven Party Alliance (SPA). In February 2004, a secret meeting took place between Madhav Nepal, leader of the CPN-UML and representatives of the CPN-Maoist in Lucknow, India. Subsequent talks between the SPA and the Maoists ultimately led to the 12-point Agreement—also called the New Delhi Agreement because it was signed in the Indian capital in November 2005. It was with this agreement that the Maoists and the SPA agreed to cooperate in order to put an end to Gyanendra's authoritarian rule, to establish a democratic system and to conduct elections for a new Constituent Assembly (Destradi 2012).

During Jan Andolan II in April 2006, Nepal's political system was destabilized by the mass protests against the King. Then, India exercised diplomatic pressure on King Gyanendra by requesting the release of arrested political leaders, professionals and students. India welcomed King Gyanendra's decision since it implied the promise of a return to multiparty democracy. India has a policy of clear and open support for the successful establishment of democracy in Nepal. In addition to the use of praise and soft persuasion in diplomatic interactions, India contributed substantively to the democratic transition by facilitating further negotiations between the CPN-Maoist and the other political parties. Moreover, India had played an important role in promoting the early execution of elections, which had been repeatedly postponed. With donations of vehicles and food as well as of containers for the storage of arms under UN supervision, the Indian government supported the peace process, while more explicit support for democracy came with the adoption of 'classic' democracy assistance measures during the April 2008 elections. India contributed to the training of the Nepalese election observers and provided computers, electronic voting machines and vehicles to the government of Nepal (Destradi 2011).

India's Prime Minister Narendra Modi visited Nepal in August 2014. It is the first bilateral visit by an Indian PM to Nepal in 17 years. India has informed Nepal that it is ready to revise the 1950 India-Nepal friendship treaty. Prime Minister Narendra Modi discussed bilateral ties with Nepali President Ram Baran Yadav. Modi in his meeting with Yadav discussed how to further strengthen ties between the two countries (PTI 04 August 2014a). Along with this, India's PM also addressed the Nepalese Constituent Assembly. Simultaneously he also met its chairman Subhas Chandra Nembang and Maoist leader Prachanda. In the joint statement which was issued at the conclusion of the visit declared, "The two prime ministers expressed satisfaction over the excellent state of Nepal-India relations that encompass a broad spectrum of political, economic, social and cultural ties that are deep-rooted at both government and people's levels. They also agreed to review, adjust and update the Treaty of Peace and Friendship of 1950 and other bilateral agreements" (PTI 04 August 2014b).

Modi gifted a copy of "Samvidhaan—The making of the Constitution of India", a ten-part television mini-series based on the making of the Indian Constitution, directed by Shyam Benegal to the chairman of Nepal's Constituent Assembly. Nepal is in the middle of writing a constitution which has been delayed for years now, resulting in a kind of political and constitutional deadlock. It was a subtle way of reminding Nepal that while the writing of a constitution is not easy and it involves tough political manoeuvres, it is essential to go through this process if a modern nation is to be built (Bagchi 2014).

Conclusion

Nepal's recent experiment with democracy stands at a critical juncture. In recent years the nation ended its civil war, abolished the monarchy system and established a multi-party democratic republic. Nepal's journey from a constitutional monarchy to a republican state and constitutionalism has not been easy. Constituent Assembly election played an important role in constitution making process. This was the only way to overcome the political and constitutional impasse in Nepal. The election of the Constituent Assembly was an important step in sustaining democracy in Nepal and strengthening the peace process.

Due to its failure in drafting a new constitution the first Constituent Assembly was dissolved after its original and extended total tenure of four years.

The unfortunate failure of the Constituent Assembly was a result of political and ideological differences amongst the parties. The setback has been particularly painful because the Constituent Assembly missed the historic opportunity of defining and designing new institutions. Ultimately, Prime Minister Baburam Bhattarai announced fresh elections for a new Constituent Assembly. The next Nepalese Constituent Assembly elections initially slated for November 22, 2012 were held a year later on November 19, 2013 amidst a 10 day long nationwide bandh and transport strike called by the alliance of 33 political parties led CPN-Maoist—Baidya. However, more than 70% of Nepal's voters turned out in elections defying a boycott call by 33-party alliance. After the elections and several rounds of negotiations, leaders of Nepali Congress, Communist Party of Nepal (Unified Marxist Leninist) and Unified Communist Party of Nepal (Maoist) in their first meeting of the second Constituent Assembly on January 21, 2014 have pledged to draft a constitution of Nepal within a year.

India has played a crucial role as a neighbour of Nepal for promoting democracy. It is one of the top contributors among the list of international actors who have played the most important role in the transition. Democratisation process in Nepal has been full of violence and protest. During the period of democratisation there has been a shift from closed and centralized political system to open and decentralised democracy. There has also been an attempt to bring the marginalized groups into mainstream politics. Nepal has been unstable for over a decade and this period has also been used to destabilize the country internally and to function it, in the favour of the external forces to execute their own interest. However, now it can be expected that whatever has happened in the last decade will not be repeated and the parties involved in electoral process would accomplish the expectations of the people who want nothing more than constitution, peace and development of Nepal.

REFERENCES

Adhikari, Bipin (2012), "Some Initial Comment on the Failed Constitution Building Process", *Studies in Nepali History and Society*, 17(1): 143-153.

Afful, Ken (2013), *Nepal's Transitional Governments—Issues of Governance*, Institute of Development Management Studies, [Online: web] Accessed 04 February 2014, URL: http://www.odcincorp.com/pdf/Concept%20Paper%20Round%20Table%20on%20Transition_2013.pdf.

ANFREL (2008), *Nepal: Constituent Assembly Election 10th April 2008*, The Asian Network for Free Elections, Thailand.

Bagchi, Indrani (2014), "India Ready to Revise 1950 Friendship Treaty with Nepal", *The Times of India*, New Delhi, 04 August 2014.

Bhandari, Arjun (2013), "Parties in Blame-Game for CA failure", *The Himalayan Times*, Kathmandu, 20 October 2013.

Bhandari, Rajneesh (2012), *Five Reasons Why Nepal Won't Create a New Constitution*, [Online: web] Accessed 27 October 2013, URL: http://www.policymic.com/articles/5941/five-reasons-why-nepal-won-t-create-a-new-constitution.

Bhandari, Surendra (2012), "Constitution Making and the Failure of Constituent Assembly: The Case of Nepal", *Ritsumeikan Annual Review of International Studies*, 11: 1-40.

Bhattarai, Hari P. (2007), "*Inclusive and Participatory Constitution Making*", Kathmandu: Nepal South Asia Centre.

Carter Center (2009), *Observing the 2008 Nepal Constituent Assembly Election April 2008*, Atlanta: Carter Center.

Carter Center (2013), *Observing Nepal's 2013 Constituent Assembly Election*, Atlanta: Carter Center.

Chautari, Martin (2009), "Update on the Constituent Assembly", *Studies in Nepali History and Society,* 14(2): 405-422.

Chautari, Martin (2013), *The Debilitating Dynamics of Nepal's Constituent Assembly*, Kathmandu.

Chhetri, Than Bahadur (2011), "*Ideological Conflict in Nepal*", GRIN Verlag.

Citizen Survey 2013: *Nepal in Transition, Nepal Democracy Survey Round III*, Stockholm: International IDEA.

Dahal, Dev Raj (2008), "*Nepal: The Constituent Assembly Election and Challenges Ahead"*, Kathmandu: Friedrich-Ebert-Stiftung.

Destradi, Sandra (2012), "India as a Democracy Promoter? New Delhi Involvement in Nepal return's return to Democracy", *Democratization*, 19(2): 286-311.

Einsiedel, *et al.* (2012), *Nepal in Transition: From People's War to Fragile Peace,* New Delhi: Cambridge University Press.

Eurich, Hanja (2010), "*Factors of Success in UN Mission Communication Strategies in Post-conflict Settings: A Critical Assessment of the UN Missions in East Timor and Nepal*", Logos Verlag Berlin Gmbh.

EUEOM (2013), *Constituent Assembly Election Final Report 2013.*

EUEOM (April 2008), *Nepal Final Report on the Constituent Assembly Election 10 April, 2008.*

EUEOM (September 2008), *Largely successful election day despite tense campaign*, Kathmandu.

Franklin, Jeremy (2008), *Nepal: Constituent Assembly Election April 2008,* Norwegian Centre for Human Rights.

Gellner, David (2014), "The 2013 Elections in Nepal", *Asian Affairs*, 45 (2): 243-261.

Nayak, Nihar (2014), "*Strategic Himalayas: Republican Nepal and External Powers*", IDSA New Delhi: Pentagon Press.

Nguyen, Nam (2014), "*History of Each Country around the World*" Nam Nguyen.

Pandey, Nishchal and Tomislav Delinic (2012), "*Towards a More Cooperative South Asia*", Kathmandu: Centre for South Asian Studies.

Poudel, Keshab (2012), *May 27 Deadline Eleventh Hour Deal*, Spotlight News Magazine, [Online Web] Accessed 26 February 2013, URL: http://www.spotlightnepal.com/News/Article/MAY-27-DEADLINE-Eleventh-Hour-Deal-.

PTI (2014a), "Modi Discusses Bilateral Ties with Nepal President", *The Times of India*, Kathmandu, 04 August 2014.

PTI (2014b), "PM Modi Returns from Kathmandu; Nepal Asks for More FDI, Market Access", *The Times of India*, New Delhi, 04 August 2014.

Sharma, Bishnu et al. (2008), "Nepal—A Revolution Through the Ballot Box", *Australian Journal of International Affairs*, 62(4): 513-528.

Shrestha, Shyam (2014), *Maoist Defeat in Nepal—The Price of a Missed Opportunity*, [Online Web] Accessed 23 July 2014, URL: http://healthteamforneopal.wordpress.com/2014/04/09/maoist-defeat-in-nepal-the-price-of-a-missed-opportunity/.

Srinivasan, Ramani (2008), "Nepal Political Diary-I", *Economic and Political Weekly,*XLIII: 24.

Thapa, Ganga B. and Jan Sharma (2009), "From Insurgency to Democracy: The Challenges of Peace and Democracy-Building in Nepal", *International Political Science Review*, 30(2): 205-219.

United Nations (1981), "*United Nations Today*", United Nations Publications, [Online: web] Accessed 02 March 2014, URL: http://books.google.co.in/books?id=yzDEWkUpjo0C &pg=PA125&dq=unmin &hl=en&sa=X&ei=CPMJU47xIYSNrgftuoDoBQ&ved=0CFcQ6AEwCQ#v=twopage&q=unmin&f=false.

Upreti, Bhuwan Chandra (2009), "Challenges in the Post-Election Scenario in Nepal", *Economic & Political Weekly*, XLIV (11): 23-25.

Upreti, Bhuwan Chandra (2010), *Nepal: Transition to Democratic Republican State: 2008 Constituent Assembly*, New Delhi: Kalpaz Publications.

Vollan, Kare (2011), "Group Representation and the System of Representation in the Constituent Assembly and Future Parliaments of Nepal", *International Journal on Minority and Group Rights*, 343-368.

World Elections (2013), *Elections, referendums and electoral sociology around the world* [Online Web] Accessed 22 July 2014, URL: http://welections.wordpress.com/2013/12/08/nepal-2013/.

WPAF (2008), *Observation Report of Nepal's Constituent Assembly Elections-2008*, The Researcher, Pakistan [Online Web] Accessed 5 August 2014, URL: http://www.theresearchers.org/Publications/EleObser_MonReport/Nepal_Observation_Report.pdf.

8

Factoring Tibet Issue in India's National Security

Tseyang Lhamo

Tibet issue since PLA march into Tibet in 1950-1951 has been a matter of grave concern to India's security given that India is a sole nation bearing the brunt of Chinese consolidation in Tibet. China knew from the very beginning that India is the only power most intimately connected to Tibet through cultural, historical links and geographical proximity. Moreover in an event of any probable external intervention on Tibet issue, India would definitely play a crucial role. Thus, China attached great importance to India's role on Tibet issue. Having said that it is pertinent to delve into various aspects of Tibet issue which are directly linked to India's national security. The issue of Tibet has indeed been an irritant in the Sino-Indian bilateral relations.

Geo-strategic Importance of Tibet

Sheer location of Tibet at the heart of Asia speaks volume about Tibet's strategic location. For centuries, Tibet has acted as buffer keeping two Asian giants—India and China geographically apart. The strategic importance of Tibet is neither lost to China nor to India. As for India, strategically, Tibet must be denied vantage point and a mounting military base to any foreign power.[1] The main reason for Chinese takeover of Tibet was strategic rather than historical claims or ideological motives. Chinese have realized early the strategic importance of Tibet and decided to shut China's back door in 1950.[2] Tibet plays important role in the India-China rivalry for dominance in Asia. China's brutal occupation of Tibet not only changed power equation of the region but also it enabled China to exercise geo-strategic influence over much of South Asia thus challenging India's dominance in the region. Besides, loss of Tibet as a buffer zone crippled the security of its northern frontiers forcing it to maintain thousands of soldiers along the Himalayan frontier. Tibet constitutes approximately one-fourth of China's land mass. Tibetan plateau is situated at more than 4500 meters above the sea level hence commonly called as 'roof of the world'. It has total land area of 2.5 million square kilometres and sparsely populated. Tibetan plateau is endowed with rich and untouched around 132 different minerals out of which it has significant reserves of uranium, chromite, boron, lithium, borax and iron. It is no wonder that Chinese refer to Tibet as 'Xizang' which literally means Western Treasure House. Thus, Tibet has given immense leverages to China.[3]

India's primarily concern has been that a Tibetan ethnic area is a source of water for India and Asia at large. Tibet's vast glaciers and high altitude have endowed it with the world's greatest river systems. The Indian subcontinent is nourished by perennial flow of four major rivers originating from different directions of the Kailash range in western Tibet. Firstly, from the east flows the Yarlung Tsangpo as known in Tibet, becomes the Brahmaputra in India and joins the Ganges in Bangladesh before draining into the Bay of Bengal. Secondly, from the west flows the Sutlej, passing through Himachal Pradesh and Punjab in India and joins the Indus River in Pakistan. Thirdly, from the north flows the Sindhu/ Indus passing through Jammu and Kashmir in India and entering Pakistan before joining the Arabian Sea. Fourthly, from the south flows the Macha Khabab, entering western Nepal as a Karnali before becoming the Gaghara in India to join the holy Ganges. Other mighty rivers flowing from Tibet such as the Drichu (Yangtse), Machu (Yellow), Gyalmo Ngulchu (Salween) and Zachu (Mekong) sustain the lives of millions in China, Myanmar, Laos, Cambodia, Thailand and Vietnam.[4] Tibet's river waters are a lifeline not only to the world's two most populous states namely India and China but also to Bangladesh, Myanmar, Bhutan, Nepal, Cambodia, Pakistan, Laos, Thailand and Vietnam. These countries constitute 47% of the global population.[5]

Almost 65% of Asia's population and approximately 30% of the world's population receives fresh water from rivers originating in Tibet.[6] Tibetan plateau is called the Water Tower of Asia and also it is called Third Pole as Tibet holds third largest storehouse of ice. With establishment of China's rule over Tibet, China controls all of these rivers originating from Tibetan plateau thus wields enormous advantage over these rivers in terms of flow and utilization of rivers. China now enjoys advantages of being an upper riparian state which was once enjoyed by Tibet.

Tibetan Plateau is an area of incalculable geo-strategic importance and damage to the environment, climate and waters of Tibet will compel South and

Figure 1: Major Rivers Originating from Tibetan Plateau

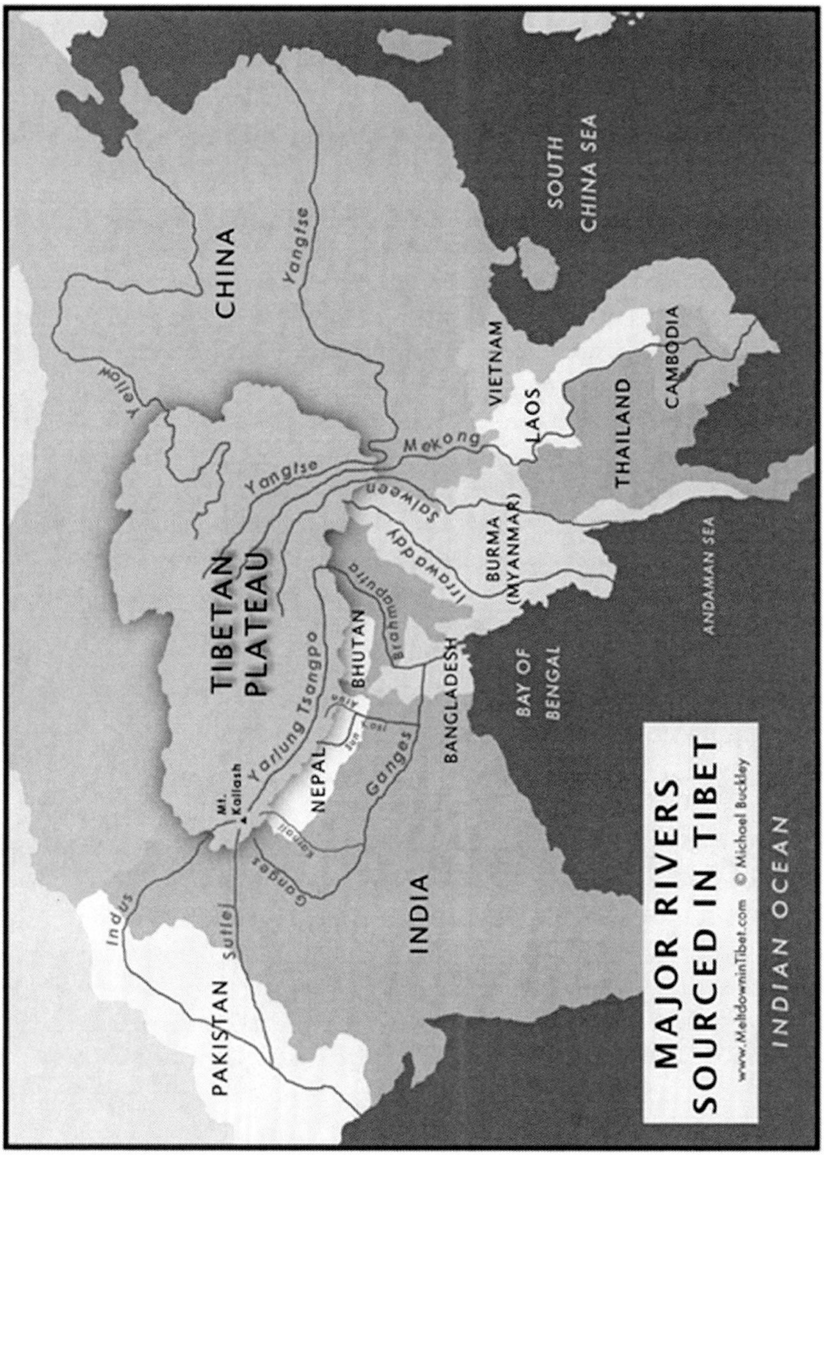

Source: http://www.meltdownintibet.com/f_riverbyriver.htm

South East to confront a potential existential threat.[7] At the backdrop of such immense geo-strategic significance of Tibet, it is a matter of grave concern for regions around it to take serious notice of China's actions in Tibet which have adverse effects on its environment and river system. No doubt, China is at advantageous position being an upper riparian state controlling Tibet enjoys dominant status and it has been said that China will use water as a strategic commodity and as a tool for energy and economic diplomacy with its neighbours and when required.[8]

China's unilateral act of damming and diverting rivers from south to north are major concerns for lower riparian states in South Asia and Southeast Asia. China's act of diverting Brahmaputra and construction of mega hydel project of 38 GW power station has potential for floods and has been great concern for India.[9] Chinese activities like damming, water diversion projects, extensive mining, nuclear waste dumping, industrial and other related activities might cause eco-disaster aggravate meltdown of Himalayan glaciers. Additionally China's reluctance to enter into institutionalized water sharing arrangement or any such mechanism with other downstream riparian states aggravates the problem. Thus, China's activities in Tibet causing adverse impact on its ecology and its river systems have repercussions to whole Asia including India. China's control over the riverhead of Asia's waters has major security implications for lower-riparian states like India.

Tibet and the Sino-Indian Border Dispute

China illegally occupies approximately 38000 sq km of Indian Territory in Aksai Chin area. The statement of the Indian Minister of Defence placed in Parliament on September 2012 notes that 'Indian territory under occupation by China in Jammu & Kashmir since 1962 is approximately 38000 sq. km. In addition under the so called China-Pakistan 'Boundary Agreement' of 1963, Pakistan illegally ceded 5180 sq. km of Indian Territory in Pakistan occupied Kashmir to China. On above that there are number of areas on the Line of Actual Control (LAC) at western sector, eastern sector and Central sector which are disputed.[10] China had laid claims to the Indian state of Arunachal Pradesh covering an area of approximately 90000 sq km, which China accords as part of Tibet or Southern Tibet.[11]

Now to bring out the relevance of Tibet issue to the long pending border disputes, it must be noted that when India and China are discussing border disputes they are actually discussing Indo-Tibetan lands. Indo-China border dispute cannot be resolved until and unless Tibet issue is resolved. To add on that, Jagat S. Mehta who was main representatives at the 1960 Indian and Chinese officials meeting on the boundary question stated that most of the items of evidence of presented by the Chinese side were official Tibetan documents.

Figure 2: Sino-Indian Border Dispute

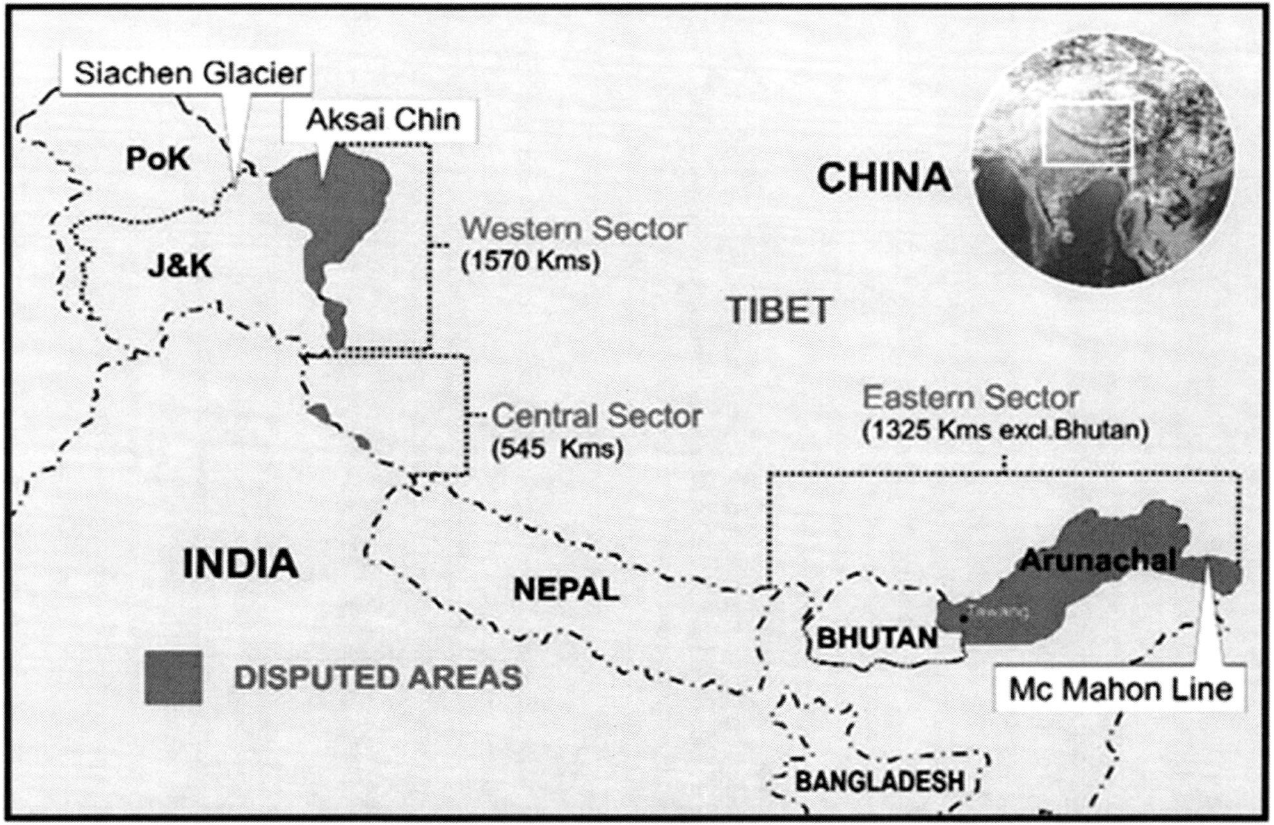

Source: Ashok Tureja, "Border Dispute with China Still Far From Settled" at http://www.tribuneindia.com/2012/20121023/edit.htm

Chinese claim over Aksai Chin by declaring it as once part of Tibet's Zinjiang and Ngari District.[12]

China's claim over Tawang on the basis of old Tibetan religious and monastic links again manifests relevance of Tibet issue to China-India border disputes. China has laid claims on Tawang in 1984 on the ground that it was the birth place of the 6th Dalai Lama and hence central to Tibetan Buddhism. Moreover non-acceptance of McMahon line as boundary in eastern sector by China again brings out relevance of Tibet issue in Sino-Indian border dispute. With regard to eastern sector, India and China have different perceptions of Simla Accord in 1914 where border was defined between India and Tibet according to McMahon Line. The McMahon line was drawn in tripartite conference between Indian, Chinese and Tibetan representatives in Simla in 1914. China had subsequently repudiated the Line. China refused to recognise this agreement arguing that Tibet was under its suzerainty hence it has no capacity to enter agreements with other nations. While Indian government claims the McMahon line as the eastern boundary. By recognising Simla Accord as valid India had recongnised Tibet has a treaty making power then thus makes India's position problematic. During Simla Accord of 1914 Tibet acted as independent nation evident from Tibet as one signatory to this agreement. Endorsing legality of McMahon Line by India utterly contradicts China's claim that Tibet is historically inalienable part of China because then independent Tibet fully exercised treaty making power in 1914 Simla Convention. Moreover such argument by India could be used to bolster Tibet's case for independence.[13] China is well aware that unless and until Tibet was recognised as inalienable part of China historically China's occupation of Tibet would lack legitimacy and would be considered as an imperial conquest. Thus, conflicting claims on border dispute eventually comes down to Tibet issue.

Irrespective of agreements on border peace and tranquillity and confidence building measures signed in 1993 and 1996 and sixteen rounds of meetings between India and China border disputes still persist. The Tibet issue is the one of the primary reasons precluding India and China to reach an understanding on their border dispute. It appears that China is deliberately keeping border issue alive and is following a 'go slow' policy. Some analysts had argued that an unsettled border provides China the strategic leverage to keep India uncertain about its intentions, and nervous about its capabilities, while exposing India's vulnerabilities and weaknesses, and encouraging New Delhi's "good behavior" on issues of vital concern.[14]

While some had pointed out that Chinese have persisted in their policy of keeping India under pressure.[15] This is well mirrored in numerous unfriendly gestures on part of China towards its border dispute with India. To elaborate further, on the eve of Hu Jintao's visit to India Chinese ambassador to India made a statement claiming the whole of Arunachal Pradesh as part of China, which was further confirmed by Chinese Foreign minister Yang Jiechi. Chinese walked the talk by denying visa to Indian dignitaries from Arunachal Pradesh on the grounds that since the state was part of China the official did not need a visa, numerous stapled visas to residents of Arunachal Pradesh and J&K then followed. Chinese blocked a loan from Asian Development Bank for a project in Arunachal Pradesh, and they engaged in military provocation including border intrusions and incursions along the LAC.

Not to forget, China's strongly objected the Dalai Lama's visit to Tawang monastery in Arunachal Pradesh however in spite of massive pressure from China the Dalai Lama was allowed to visit Tawang in 2009. China also put forward criticism against Manmohan Singh's visit to Arunachal Pradesh irrespective of which Manmohan Singh visited the State twice and he even had audience with the Dalai Lama in 2010. On above this Chinese adventurism at India-China disputed border continues as the Depsang incursion by Chinese on April 2013 and Chumar incursion on July 2013 reflect. According to one source, there were 228 cases of Chinese intrusions reported in 2010, 213 cases in 2011 and 64 in 2012 until April.[16] Some of intrusions are deliberate acts of provocation, which certainly aims at sustaining claims on Indian Territory. These incidents signal a message to India that India should be far more active on resolving Tibet issue on the ground that settlement of Tibet issue not only opens up greater prospect for resolving border disputes but also leads to the presence of friendly people across India-China border. Assuming that China's reluctance to solve border dispute with India is partly due to persistence of Tibet issue in which India is an important player, resolution of Tibet issue would certainly allay fear in Chinese mind about any probable India's aid or interference in Tibet issue, thus, China would be more willing and cooperative in resolving border dispute with India.

Infrastructure Developments in TAR and India's Concerns

India has always been concerned about infrastructure developments carried out by PRC in TAR region. No doubt such developments are driven by requirements such as growth and development of the region, integration of the region with mainland China and secure China's control over estranged ethnic minority. However, vital role infrastructure plays during conflicts in terms of facilitating troops movements has come under the purview of India as well as military strategists. Besides, dual use of infrastructure for civilian and military use further adds to India's concerns.

China's infrastructure development plan in TAR is laid down in 'Western Development Campaign Policy' strategy, it forms vital feature of 12th five year plan (2011-2015). A careful analysis of 'Go West' strategy reveals that it is primarily aimed at gaining strategic capability for China rather than removing economic backwardness of the region. China has developed 41000 km of road network in Tibet including five major highways and a number of subsidiary roads. The Central highway (Xining-Lhasa), Western highway (Kashgar-Lhasa) and Eastern highway (Chengdu-Linzhi) are major two way arteries across Tibet. Subsidiaries roads run from these main arteries connecting most of remote areas even up to Sino-Indian border in some cases.[17] In 12th five year plan, it is proposed to increase road network to 70,000 km. The road infrastructure in TAR has a combined capacity of 1, 15,000 metric tonnes, which facilitates easy, and swift movement of troops, war like materials and equipment. In addition all the major passes of military significance—eleven in Ladakh—Western Tibet, five in Uttar Pradesh-Central Tibet and fifteen Arunachal Pradesh-East Tibet are connected by roads.[18]

The Golmud-Lhasa Railway covering distance of 1142 km has been operating since 2006. The Chinese plan to extend this Railway Line to Shigatse which is situated near to Indian border. There are also plans to extend the Shigatse line to Nepal border and further to Chumbi Valley. The plans of extending Golmud-Lhasa Railway line further to Yadong and Nyingchi would bring railway line close to Sikkim and Arunachal Pradesh. This will be further extended to Dali in Yunnan Province. This line running parallel to Arunachal Pradesh will enable the PLA to rapidly relocate troops stationed in Kunming, Dali and Kaiyuanan to TAR.[19] The Railway line facilitating troops transport to Lhasa as early as 2007 clearly depicts its use for military purposes.[20]

Besides highways and railways, there are seven airports in TAR region: Lhasa Gonggar Airport, Ngari Gunsa Airport, Nyingchi Mainling Airpor, Qamdo Bamda Airport or Changdu Bangda Airport and Shigatse Peace Airport, Nagchu Dagring Airport and Daocheng Yading Airport. All these airports are operational and of strategic significance to India.[21] Thus China's massive infrastructure development in this region undoubtedly stands as serious security challenge to India and at the backdrop of border disputes with India such acts create doubts about China's intentions especially when such quantum of infrastructure development in the region far exceeds genuine needs of Tibet or Tibetan people. Additionally steady militarisation of Tibet has been perennial concern for India. With respect to PLA troop deployment in TAR, according to Central Tibetan Administration in Dharamsala the estimated number of troops deployed in Tibet stands about 500,000 in the form of People's Armed Police (PAP), the Chinese Frontier Guards and Garrison Duty Forces. The Chinese military arsenal on the larger Tibetan plateau including areas outside TAR, is reported to have eight missile bases, with at least eight inter-continental ballistic missiles, 70 medium range and 20 intermediate range missiles.[22] Infrastructure development in TAR coupled with enhanced military capability is not only a security concern for India but also facilitates China to approach border disputes from a position of greater strength.

Presence of the Dalai Lama, Tibetan Government in Exile and Tibetan Refugees in India

India's decision to provide asylum to the Dalai Lama and more than one lakh Tibetan refugees after the annexation of Tibet by China in 1959 was a landmark decision. India being a host nation to largest Tibetan refugees and their leader, the Dalai Lama and Tibetan government in exile clearly brings out India's concern over Tibet issue. Tibetan people living in India have utmost gratitude for India's acceptance of Tibetan refugees who escaped from China's oppression and occupation of their land. Regarding relation between the Tibetan government in exile and Government of India, the latter has been generous host and former has been extremely grateful guest. India's decision to grant asylum to the Dalai Lama and Tibetan refugees stemmed from long-standing spiritual and cultural links between Tibet and India and also Indian public's high regard for the Dalai Lama. However, India hosting the Dalai Lama and Tibetan refugees which China brands as a 'splittist' has been perceived by China as interfering in its internal matter or sort of conditional recognition of Tibet as part of China.

Even though India has never afforded formal or legal recognition to the government in exile yet at the same time India allowed establishment of Tibetan government in exile and currently Tibetan government in exile called as Central Tibetan Administration (CTA) based in Dharamsala functions as a de facto government with all the departments and also features of a free democratic government and over sees 35 Tibetan settlements across India. India has provided Tibetans a favourable environment to preserve their distinct culture, religion and identity and most importantly Tibetans are able to carry forward their struggle for Tibet's cause while in exile in India. Geographical proximity of India to Tibet has not only made Tibetans feel close to their home land but also helped in accommodating Tibetan fleeing from Chinese rule. Thus, India has indirectly played crucial role in keeping Tibet's cause alive much to the annoyance of China.

India's contradictory position should be seen in relation with India's interest in securing its northern border. Tibet has increasingly become a major security concern for India particularly with increased militarisation of the region and the presence of the Dalai Lama and Tibetan community in India is a leverage India holds against China. India not only hosts largest Tibetan refugees but also India acts as bedrock of activities and movements promoting Tibet's cause, in addition, presence of Tibetan government adds political colour to the Tibetan movement.[23]

China far from reconciling Tibetans under their rule has been very sceptical of India's role in Tibet issue, given that India is a sole nation having greatest say in Tibet issue due to aforesaid grounds. Irrespective of repeated statements from Indian government recognising Tibet as part of China, they remained insecure and suspicious of any covert Indian aid or involvement in Tibet cause.

Current State of Dialogue between the Dalai Lama's Envoys and the PRC's Representatives

It is pertinent to discuss about the current state of negotiation as this negotiation is the only existing mechanism for resolving ongoing Tibet issue. Unfortunately current state of dialogue process between the Dalai Lama's envoys and the PRC representatives seems to shatter any optimism regarding possible positive outcome from dialogue apart from some even questioning very efficacy of the dialogue or China's hidden intentions. The dialogue intended to bring amicable solution to the Tibet issue has its genesis in 1979 and nine rounds of dialogue were held so far and the latest dialogue was 9th dialogue held in 2010 which resulted in no breakthrough. The Dalai Lama's envoys presented 'Memorandum on Genuine Autonomy' for the Tibetan people and on 9th round of dialogue they presented a 'Note relating to the Memorandum on Genuine Autonomy for the Tibetan People'. The Note contained seven points that addressed the fundamental issues raised by the Chinese leadership during the eighth round and some constructive suggestions for a way forward in the dialogue process.[24] There has been no further dialogue since 2010.

To make matters worse Tibetan envoys who had participated in dialogue process resigned in June 2012 due to failure of dialogue to germinate any substantial solution and lack of positive response from Beijing amidst deteriorating conditions in Tibet with regard to self-immolations by Tibetans in Tibet. Nevertheless, Tibetan government in exile remains committed towards engaging with China through meaningful dialogue or negotiation process to find mutually agreeable solution to Tibet issue.

Thus dialogue process between the Dalai Lama's side and the PRC remains stalled today hence depicting bleak picture devoid of any positive developments relating to the ongoing Tibet issue in the near future. Government of India should be seen in support of the 'Dalai Lama's middle way' on the ground that it is only workable solution towards reconciliation between Tibet and China, particularly Dalai Lama's middle way policy safeguards China's territorial sovereignty and integrity.[25]

India's Concerns over Post-Dalai Lama Scenario

India's lingering concern over post-Dalai Lama Scenario again highlights that Tibet issue occupies important place in India's national security. Post-Dalai Lama scenario has been a matter of grave concern for India as it is filled with uncertainties. Regarding Beijing's perception on post-Dalai Lama Scenario, Beijing anticipates that Tibet issue would resolve itself soon after the passing away of the Dalai Lama. China also anticipates that they would have decisive say with regard to the next Dalai Lama as they did with the Panchen Lama. To substantiate further, Beijing had undertaken various acts which attempts to strengthen basis for Beijing's decisive say in the next Dalai Lama. These were firstly PRC's reincarnation law of 2007 was an act of preparing a legal basis for it, secondly in 2006 Beijing cautiously started describing Buddhism as a non-aggressive and old Chinese religion, thus officially endorsing Buddhism, thirdly they convened the first World Buddhist Forum in China in 2006 where Chinese nominated Panchen Lama was given international profile, and again second World Buddhist Forum was held in Wuxi, Jiangsu in 2009 along with increasing and internationalising their campaign against the Dalai lama hence attempting to claim leadership role in the Buddhist movement.[26]

The cloud of uncertainty hangs thick over the post-Dalai Lama scenario, where many questions were raised. This uncertainty could have its impact on India-China relations, as Tibet remains a live issue shaping them. There are opinions that passing away of the Dalai Lama could lead to a feeling of despair in Tibet which may trigger more serious problem or conflict in Tibet.[27]

India being host nation to Tibetan refugees including the Dalai Lama has been increasingly concerned about post-Dalai Lama scenarios. As it has been stated, there are two complex issues which concerns India, firstly who will be chosen successor and whether a chosen successor will be considered legitimate. This first issue needs to be addressed by giving due consideration to Tibetan in exile, Tibetans in TAR, Tibetans in traditional Tibetan areas falls out of TAR and the PRC. The second issue pertains to how does Tibetan movement as a whole play out in the absence of undisputed and utmost revered leader the 14th Dalai Lama.[28] Many scholars and analysts had anticipated that Tibetan Youth Congress (TYC) which seeks Tibet's independence as opposed to autonomy may drift away from non-violent and peaceful path of pursuing Tibet cause. However Tibetans believe that they have enough unity to continue with non-violent and peaceful path in the absence of the Dalai Lama. Furthermore, the Dalai Lama has warned that any shift towards a more radical position is filled with perils. Asymmetry of power, lack of international support, the small size of the Tibetan diasporas compared with the Tibetan population inside China makes struggle for independence not only impracticable but politically suicidal.[29]

The author envisage that Tibetan government in exile is a significant institution with well-established foundations with addition of elected Prime Minister would definitely play crucial role in leading Tibetan people in the event of the absence of the Dalai Lama. Thus, probability of Tibetan movement fizzling out is highly unlikely. However, such eventuality would test the real strength of Tibetan government to lead Tibetan people in unity along path of non-violence towards the goal of achieving genuine autonomy for Tibetan people. Likewise, it would equally test India's ability to face enhanced pressure from China while keeping intact India's support for Tibetan people and Tibetan government in exile. India should approach this eventuality by taking into consideration various factors like due care must be taken so as not to severely weaken India vis-a-vis China, border negotiations shouldn't get adversely impacted, significant dominance that India holds over international Buddhism which is referred as India's soft power shouldn't be lost in the eyes of international audience.[30] India should also facilitate transition and continuation of Tibetan movement.

Conclusion

Tibet issue has been and still remains significant for India's security. India's security is inextricably intertwined with the existence and survival of Tibet as a buffer state and the survival and strengthening of Tibetan culture and religion. China's role and policies in Tibet could be a threat to India as well as India could exploit such to its gain which India hasn't done so far. However, the presence of the Dalai Lama and largest Tibetan refugees in India sometimes gives leverage to India to indirectly apply pressure on Beijing just as China's policies towards Pakistan sometimes do to India. Moreover, it has been pointed out by some that the greatest threat to the India-China relation emanates firstly from widely differing views of the history and secondly from ultimate destiny of Tibet.[31]

Given stalled nature of dialogue process between Dalai Lama's representatives and Chinese government, Tibetans demands for genuine autonomy to all Tibetans living in China along with preservation and promotion of their distinct culture and identity still remains elusive. As mentioned earlier, India should be seen in support of Dalai Lama's genuine autonomy as it in no way threatens China's territorial integrity, doing so would set good example for other nations and there is high probability that other nations would follow India. This should be preceded by building favourable Indian public opinion for Tibetan's demand for genuine autonomy. This responsibility rests on Tibetan government in exile and Tibetan people to create awareness about middle way policy and subsequently generate their support. Some have proposed that India because of its unique position as the de facto protector of the Tibetan national identity for more than half century, to play a mediator role in breaking dialogue impasse and bringing about mutually acceptable solution for Tibetans in exile and the PRC if such role is accepted by PRC.[32] The author personally exhorts Indian government to play far more active role in facilitating early resolution of Tibet issue. Currently, New Delhi has been very cautious of Chinese sensitivity regarding Tibet issue while Beijing isn't reciprocating same on India's Kashmir issue.

Tibet issue continues to loom large in India's national security. At the backdrop of ongoing tragic and extremely unfortunate self-immolations[33] by Tibetans which sadly highlights the intensity of despair in the Tibetan plateau clearly reveals not only China's lack of legitimacy to rule Tibet but also its sensitivity over the Tibet issue and with addition of China's tendency to blame on outside hostile forces mainly hinting to India and US for any ethnic outburst in Tibet, further reinforces significant position that Tibet issue occupies under India's security calculations. Furthermore, China's activities in Tibet encompassing infrastructure developments in TAR, enhanced military capability of China, growing assertiveness and unilateralism in China's dealing with border disputes and China's control over major rivers including Brahmaputra have serious implications for India. Besides, China's insecurity about Tibet as the main driver of its approach towards India underlines the importance of ongoing or evolving Tibet issue. Thus, Tibet issue occupies crucial position in the India's national security and would continue to remain so.

REFERENCES

1. V.P. Malhotra Tibetan Conundrum, New Delhi, Knowledge World, 2006, p. 91.
2. D. Norbu, "Chinese Strategic Thinking on Tibet and the Himalayan Region", Strategic Analysis, Vol.32, No.4, 2008, pp.687-688.
3. A. Mazumdar, India-China Border Dispute: Centrality of Tibet, Economic and Political Weekly, Vol. 41, no. 41 Oct. 14-20, 2006, p. 4325.
4. V.P. Mallhotra, n 1, p. 89.
5. B. Chellaney, "China-India clash Over Chinese Claims to Tibetan Water", at http://www.japanfocus.org/site/view/2458, p. 1.
6. Malhotra V.P., n 1, p. 89.
7. J. Ranade, China Unveiled : Insights into Chinese Strategic Thinking New Delhi: Knowledge World, 2013, p. 299.
8. "Reappraisal of India's Tibet Policy", Foundation for Non-violent Alternatives, New Delhi, 2013, p. 27
9. Ibid, p. 28
10. "China's Strategic Posture in Tibet Autonomous Region and India's Response", Vivekananda International Foundation, New Delhi, 2012, p. 36.
11. D. Kapoor, "India's China Concern", Strategic Analysis, vol.36, no.4, 2012, p. 666.
12. D. Norbu, China's Tibet Policy, Great Britain : Curzon Press, 2001, p. 287.
13. S. Raghavan, The Case for Restraint on Tibet, *Economic and Political Weekly*, April 5, 2008, p.12.
14. M. Malik, "China and India Today: Diplomats Jostle, Militaries Prepare", http://www.worldaffairsjournal.org/article/china-and-india-today-diplomats-jostle-militaries-prepare
15. R. Sikri, "Tibet Factor in India-China Relations", *Journal of International Affairs*, Vol. 64, No. 2, Spring/Summer 2011, p. 64
16. n 10, p. 38
17. D. Kapoor, n 11, p. 672
18. n 10, p. 27
19. n 10, p. 25.
20. Ibid.
21. Ibid, p. 26
22. A. Bhattacharya, "Chinese Nationalism and the Fate of Tibet: Implications for India and Future Scenarios", Strategic Analysis, vol.31, no.2, 2007, p. 258
23. Ibid, p. 258
24. For details on "Memorandum on Geniune Autonomy for the Tibetan People", at http://

tibet.net/important-issues/sino-tibetan-dialogue/note-on-the-memorandum-on-genuine-autonomy-for-the-tibetan-people/

25. A talk on "Tibet and The Security Environment" By Ambassador Dalip Mehta at Dharamsala on 11th April 2012, http://tibetpolicy.net/multimedia/ambassador-dalip-mehta-tibet-and-the-security-environment/
26. J. Ranade, "The Dalai Lama and India-China Relations," Issue Brief, 17/09, December 2009, Centre for Air Power Studies, New Delhi; 'Tibet and India's Security: Himalayan Region, Refugees and Sino-Indian Relations", IDSA Task Force Report, May 2012, pp. 107,112
27. Ibid, p. 105
28. D. Anand, "China and Tibet: Tibet Matters", *The World Today*, Vol. 65, No. 4, April 2009, p. 31.
29. Ranade J., n. 26.
30. David M. Malone and Mukherjee R., "India and China: Conflict and Cooperation", Survival, vol. 52, no. 1, 2010, pp 146-153.
31. Ibid.
32. P.S. Jha, "India's Tibet Problem", *Air Power Journal*, Vol. 4, No.2, Summer 2009, p. 19.
33. The most recent incident of self-immolations was reported on 15th April 2014 from Tawu County, Kardze Tibetan Autonomous Prefecture, Sichuan Province, thereby touching 130 self-immolations out of which 112 have died. For details see, http://tibet.net/2014/04/15/self-immolation-at-tawu-county/

9

India and Sri Lanka: A Relationship Bound by Strategic Proximity but Separated by Tactical Issues

Utham Kumar Jamadhagni and Ramakrishnan Ramani

Introduction

India and Sri Lanka are located on the southern tip of the Asian continent. India is Sri Lanka's closest neighbour—geographically, separated by a narrow strait called the Palk Strait. This proximity has allowed both the countries to be historically and culturally close. For over two millennia both the nations have witnessed various levels of relationship became-from religious propagation, commercial and cultural exchanges to occasional war. Since the mid 20th century, bilateral relations between the two nations have been cordial. However, the relationship strained due to the Sri Lankan civil war (between the ethnic Sinhalese and Tamils) and India's lacklustre intervention and lack of strategic foresight. Later, the strain stretched over fishing issues. This article studies the relationship of both these countries and the dynamics between the two South Asian states.

India-Sri Lanka Relations: A Brief Historical Overview

Ancient Days

It does not take any great effort to hop over to the northern shores of Sri Lanka from the southern tip of India. This proximity has made both countries natural neighbours for centuries. Actually, the relations between India and Sri Lanka stretch back to over two millennia. There are legends about a prince from the western Indian state of Bengal who arrived at the island with hundreds of his retinue and settled here after marrying the queen. It is a fact that there are over 400 words in Sinhalese that have exactly the same meaning in Bengali. When it comes to religion, the ties are stronger. The great religion of Buddhism was introduced to the country by Mahendra, the son of Emperor Ashok the Great during the 4th century BC, as per traditional works like Dipavamsa. During this time, a sapling of the Bodhi Tree was brought to Sri Lanka and the first monasteries and Buddhist monuments were established. To the Buddhists of the island nation, India is Dharmadveepa or the land of the Dharma.[1]

Figure 1: Political Map of India and Sri Lanka[2]

Indian Epics

The island nation is an integral part of the world famous Indian Mahakavyas (epics)—the Ramayana and the Mahabharata. In the Ramayana, Sri Lanka and its capital 'Lankapuri' is the island kingdom of Ravana. Despite Ravana being the 'villain' of the epic, Lanka has been described in the most superb manner—

a land that is a veritable heaven on earth. The main citadel of the island was said to be a massive collection of several constructions that spanned over 13 kilometres in height. The island had a large mountain range known as the Trikuta Mountain on which was situated Ravana's capital that spanned 1288 kilometres and over 380 kilometres in breadth. The buildings were decked in gold and precious stones. According to the book 'Ravana, King of Lanka', the kingdom spread across today's regions of Nuwara Eliya, Badulla, Polonnaruwa, Anuradhapura, Kandy, Monaragula, Matale and Chilaw.[3] The citizens were beautiful to behold, rich and very civilized.

The Cholas

Many centuries later, the great Chola emperor Rajaraja invaded Sri Lanka in 993 AD. Records mention how his army crossed the seas and burnt Anuradhapura. In fact, the Chola armies occupied the northern half of the island and named the captured dominion 'Mummudi Chola Mandalam'. During their stay, the Cholas made the city of Polonnaruwa as their capital and renamed it Jananathamangalam. The emperor is known to have built a temple for Lord Shiva in Pollonaruwa.[4] Later, Rajendra Chola brought the entire island under Chola rule.[5] In 1070, Sri Lankan King Vijayabahu I allied with the common enemies of the Cholas—the Pandyas and the Cheras and drove out the Cholas, thus for the first time in many centuries reuniting the country.

The British

Very many centuries later, during the British Raj, both India and Sri Lanka were colonial territories and hence had a common master—the British Crown. A major phenomenon during the British period was the massive influx of cheap Indian labour in their multitudes to vast plantations across Sri Lanka. This was something that was to later on be a thorn in the relationship. Poor migrant workers from all over India went across the sea to serve in the British-owned plantations. Over the decades, these migrants have integrated with the Sinhalese. Only those from Tamil Nadu retained their language and cultural identity. Today the main ethnic groups of the island are as follows[6]:

- Sinhalese – 73%
- Sri Lankan Tamils (As a consequence of the war) – < 12%
- Tamils who were brought in from Tamil Nadu as indentured labour – 7%
- Muslims – 10%

Post-Independence

Immediately after its independence from Britain, one of the concerns of Sri Lanka was its security. The Sri Lankan government under its first Prime Minister D.S.

Senanayake signed a defence agreement with Britain enabling the latter to use the Trinconamalee harbour and other facilities that were built during the Second World War. This was arranged primarily to secure it from perceived Indian hegemonistic ambitions. The Sinhalese government felt that India wanted to fill the vacuum that the British had left on their departure. This fear was incorrectly accentuated by the Pannikar Doctrine.[7] Thus, they wanted the protection of the British.

Despite such fears, India and Sri Lanka continued to maintain cordial relations. The relationship between the heads of state and government representatives of both countries was both official and personal. Both Sri Lanka and India wanted to play pivotal roles in the regional politics and 'champion the rights of the new world emerging from colonial bondage. 'Both Prime Ministers—Kotelawala and Nehru firmly believed that their countries should not align themselves to any power bloc. They stood for regional solidarity. In this regard, Prime Minister Kotelawala called for a meeting of the 'Colombo Powers'—India, Pakistan, Burma, and Indonesia. The outcome of this meeting led to the Bandung Afro-Asian Conference in Indonesia. During those initial days after the exit of Britain, the close cooperation of both the Prime Ministers, despite their political differences, helped drive a unified Asian voice for peace and coexistence.

The 1960s

The 1962 Sino-Indian war was a speed breaker in the relatively smooth relationship. While India was at war with the Chinese, Sri Lanka continued to maintain cordial relations with them-something India disproved. However, the subsequent passing away of Prime Minister Nehru was considered a loss by the Sri Lankan government. Nehru was succeeded by Prime Minister Lal Bahadur Shastri who helped in trying to resolve the Indian immigrant problem. However, mutual agreements signed between Prime Ministers Sirimavo Bandaranaike, Lal Bahadur Shastri and later with Smt. Indira Gandhi were not implemented.

The 1970s

During the early 1970s, following the creation of Bangladesh, India emerged as the predominant power of South Asia. India's military operations were viewed not as a 'nation saving' action, but as a successful intelligence-military operation that dismembered Pakistan. Sri Lanka found India to be more assertive in the international forum. The Sri Lankan government was cognizant that for India its security was paramount—even over others. India seemed to show this through its efforts to strengthen its armed forces, which was perceived as a threat by the neighbours. The 1971 Bangladesh Liberation War also opened doors for the Super Powers—United States of America and the Union of Soviet Socialist Republic.

Despite an environment that was congenial for mistrust and alienation, Sri Lanka aligned itself with India's regional thoughts. It, in fact, took the initiative and declared the Indian Ocean as a Zone of Peace. During the mid 70s, Indira Gandhi's visit to the island nation helped to resolve the Kachchativu issue—at least for Sri Lanka. It is interesting to note that in 1977, Prime Minister Sirimavo Bandaranaike was defeated by JR Jayewardene, who was 70 years old. In India, Ms. Bandaranaike's friend and fellow Prime Minister Smt. Indira Gandhi was defeated by 80-year-old Morarji Desai. Morarji and Jayewardene shared close personal rapport. However, Jayewardene's progressive pro-West policies and actions were looked upon with suspicion by India. He was of the opinion that only two countries were truly non-aligned—USA and USSR. For him, the priority was domestic affairs and in improving Sri Lanka's image in the international marketplace. He sought to tilt towards the West and attract foreign investment and trade. The mutual dislike between Jayewardene and Indira Gandhi aggravated the relationship.

The 1980s

The 1980s was the beginning of a long and dismal period in the relationship. There were multiple factors for this. One, it was a period that India began to assertively exert its military influence in the region. It wanted the goodwill of all its neighbours. However, Foreign Policy experts and strategists believed that Sri Lanka, through its pro-West tilt, was inching towards the US camp. Second, domestically, the growth of Tamil nationalism during the 1960s and 70s took a more vociferous form during the 1980s. The DMK party, which was part of the Indira Gandhi coalition government, changed the centre's perception of the (till then) Sri Lankan domestic issue of the Tamil ethnic problem.

The Cold War protagonists too had a major hand—though invisible—in the relationship dynamics in South Asia. The United States had permission from the Jayewardene government to install a Voice of America (VoA) radio relay station in the country. This enabled its programs to reach the far interiors of the Soviet Union. The Soviet Union, which had won the friendship of India, couldn't be silent. It felt it was necessary to destabilize the Sri Lankan government to get them out of the 'hold' of the Americans. The environment in Sri Lanka was conducive. The heightening ethnic problem between Sinhala government in the centre and the ethnic Tamils in the north was beginning to flare up. The attitude of the government and that of the Sinhalese was anti-Tamil-they were not ready to concede to rights of the Tamil minority. As the insurgency intensified, India gave refuge to Tamil militants and helped them with arms, training and finance. Sri Lanka's perception of India's pro-militant involvement, which was correct, was that of assertive overt action. India, on its part, made no attempt to hide its support to the militants. India was playing a dangerous game-on the one hand, it supported militancy and, on the other, hand, it was negotiating on behalf of the Tamils. K Godage in 'Historical Continuities'[8] states, "*Matters came to a head in March 1987 when India, fearing that the insurgency would be put down by the Sri Lanka Army (the 'Vadamarachchi operation'), indulged in a crude act of intimidation of its small neighbour. India violated the country's air space and dropped some food to the population whom they claimed was starving and demanded that the military operation against the insurgents be called off. Lanka had no option but to do so. If the insurgency was put down it would also have ended India's hegemonic hopes of 'Bhutanizing' Lanka.*"

While the relations were bad during the period of Indira Gandhi, it improved somewhat under the Prime Ministership of Rajiv Gandhi. However, India under the new prime minister continued to support Tamil Insurgents. In 1987, an agreement was signed between the two countries. India was able to make Sri Lanka abstain from obtaining military and intelligence services from foreign countries other than itself. It also mandated that the Trincomalee be made unavailable for military use by any other country and that the oil tanks in the port be restored only through Indian Oil Corporation. The Sri Lankan government also had to review its contracts with foreign broadcasting organizations.

The relationship reached its nadir during the Presidency of Premadasa when he ordered the Indian Peace Keeping Force to leave the island. Indian army's misadventure in Sri Lanka not only alienated India in the eyes of Sri Lanka and the Tamils it was supposed to help, but directly led to the assassination of Prime Minister Rajiv Gandhi in 1991.

Post-1990

In tune with global changes, economically, politically and socially, India's strategic priorities in the region underwent a change during the past two decades. In Delhi and Colombo, the very term of security underwent a re-look. It encompassed economic security, energy security, and social security of the citizenry in addition to territorial integrity. The relationship between the two countries reflects the regional power dynamics.

The decade of the 90s, saw a sharp improvement in economic cooperation. This reflected in the maturing political relationship in both the countries that reflected the geo-political realities of the world order. Following the assassination of Prime Minister Rajiv Gandhi by the LTTE the PV Narasimha Rao government withdrew from intervening in the ethnic conflict in Sri Lanka.[9] It adopted a new policy of non-intervention in the ethnic strife in the island country, but projected an active interest on economic cooperation. This new stand contributed to removing the cultivated fear complex of Sri Lanka. The initial phase of the post-1990 period saw establishment of bilateral institutional networks so as to ensure sustained cooperation irrespective of domestic and external changes.

A noteworthy development during this period was the large legal framework that was provided by the Indo-Sri Lanka Free Trade Agreement (ISFTA) signed on December 1998. Its overall objective was to enhance trade and economic relations between the two countries and promote Foreign Direct Investment. Frequent contacts at the highest political levels—the President, Prime Minister and Foreign Ministers of both the countries—helped drive this initiative.[10] Both India and Sri Lanka understood that myopic restrictions on trade are detrimental to their larger interests. Following the success of FTA, both the governments are expected to sign the Comprehensive Economic Partnership Agreement (CEPA) in the near future.

Prime Minister Atal Behari Vajpayee visited Sri Lanka during the 10th SAARC Summit stressing home the point that India would be willing to enter into bilateral Free Trade Agreements with member countries as well.

The Relationship Today

Relationship after the LTTE Era

The end of the civil war in Sri Lanka ideally marks the beginning of a new era in bilateral relationship. The period focuses on humanitarian issues of relief, rehabilitation, resettlement and reconciliation of the masses due to the war—as well as a permanent political solution. This is also a good opportunity for the central government in India to appease Tamil sentiments in Tamil Nadu. This will enable a truly win-win situation for all interested parties—the Sri Lankan government, Tamils in India and Sri Lanka and the Indian government. It is very important for India to adopt a pro-active stance and help resolve the Tamils' cause now that the war is over. Economic aid would be a definitive and welcome approach.[11]

However, the end of the LTTE era is witnessing Sri Lanka inch closer to China, Pakistan and Israel—especially the former—as these countries supported Colombo during the war. It is discernible that China is quickly filling the vacuum created by India's reluctance to actively participate in Sri Lanka's war effort—and thus in the development of Sri Lanka. India did not provide any military aid, but China liberally supplied them with a wide range of equipment. This has enabled China to gain a strong foothold and credibility in the island. Today, China has constructed a commercial port in Hambantota in southern Sri Lanka. The future will definitely see a more assertive China in this part of the Indian Ocean—much to India's concern.

With the dawn of the second decade of the 21st century, political relations between the two counties have been marked by high-level visits. Cabinet ministers and heads of state of both countries frequently visit each other's countries. In January 2013, Prof. G.L. Peiris, the Sri Lankan Minister of External Affairs of Sri Lanka visited India for the India-Sri Lanka Joint Commission during when he met his Indian counterpart Salman Khurshid. Several important decisions were taken which included intensification of economic engagement, combating international terrorism and illicit drug trafficking, amongst others.

The end of the civil war saw a major humanitarian crisis—rehabilitation of those affected. Over 3,00,000 civilians-predominantly Tamils had to be housed, fed and provided a self-supportive rehabilitation plan for their future. In 2009, Prime Minister Dr. Manmohan Singh authorised Indian Rupees 5 billion for relief and rehabilitation. The Indian government developed an assistance programme of assistance to help the civilians return to normal life in their original regions as soon as possible. This included construction of houses, donation of work tools such as farmers' equipments.

In September 2012, President Mahinda Rajapaksa visited India and met President Pranab Mukherjee and Prime Minister Dr. Manmohan Singh. Former National Security Adviser Shivshankar Menon was invited to Sri Lanka in June 2012 where he met President Rajapaksa and other dignitaries and discussed security related issues. Former Speaker of Lok Sabha, Smt. Meira Kumar led a 60-member delegation consisting of Members of Parliaments, Speakers and Member of State Legislative Assemblies and Councils and accompanying officials for the 58th Commonwealth Parliamentary Association meeting in September 2012. Here, she met the heads of states and discussed many important issues.

Trade & Commerce

Since the turn of the new millennium, trade and commerce has especially received a lot of impetus from both the governments. Sri Lanka is India's largest trade partner in South Asia. Today India and Sri Lanka are engaged in robust trade and investment relationship with each other. A special India-Sri Lanka Free Trade Agreement came into force in March 2000. Since then bilateral trade has grown over five-fold. In real terms, in 2012 for example, bilateral trade between the neighbours was to a tune of US$ 4.002 billion. A Comprehensive Economic Partnership Agreement is on the anvil and is expected to be enacted soon.

In terms of FDI investments in Sri Lanka, India has made large investments in petroleum retail, hospitals, telecom, copper and other metal industries, real estate, telecommunication, hospitality and tourism, banking and financial services, and IT. Major Indian brands are present in the island nation—IOC, Tatas, Bharti Airtel, Piramal Glass, LIC, Ashok Leyland, L&T and Taj Hotels. India is amongst the top four investors with cumulative investments over US$ 800 million.

In reciprocation, Sri Lankan business entities too are making inroads into Indian markets, significantly, Ceylon Biscuits (Munchee brand), Carsons Cumberbatch (Carlsberg), Brandix, which plans to set up a garment city in Vishakapatnam in Andhra Pradesh, MAS holdings, John Keels, Hayleys, and Aitken Spence (Hotels).

Strategic Gaps in the Relationship

Despite strong one-to-one rapport between leaders, close cultural similarities and a closely knit destiny (being closely situated neighbours in South Asia), the relationship between India and Sri Lanka does have strategic gaps that need urgent attention and filling up. While most issues are tactical in nature, their impact plays a strategic role in shaping the relationship. The Tamil issue, for example, while concentrated along the north and north-eastern coast of the island—and the southern Indian state of Tamil Nadu, still continues to play a major role in shaping short term events that cumulatively leave a long-term impact.

The ghost of the Kachchativu issue does not seem to fade—at least for India as the regional government of the state of Tamil Nadu does not abide with the Central government's view of it being a settled matter.

The Issue of Sri Lankan Tamils Still Continues...

It is well known that indentured labour of Tamils was brought from the southern shores of India to work in the vast tea and rubber plantations during the British colonial rule. The issue became a major problem between the two countries in 1953 when India refuted from its earlier position that the immigrants were Indian nationals. Only what they did was that Sirimavo Bandaranaike and Lal Bahadur Shastri signed an agreement, which was further endorsed later by Indira Gandhi and Bandaranaike in 1974. India agreed to take back 6,00,000 of them while Sri Lanka agreed to grant citizenship to 3,73,000. However, the agreement was not fully implemented—and thus, this issue has been left to fester.

India continues to reiterate for reconciliation through transparent, negotiated political settlement between the government and the Tamils—acceptable to all stakeholders. The Sri Lankan government conveyed its assurance in the form of the 13th Amendment to the Constitution. The 13th Amendment to the Constitution of Sri Lanka has created Provincial Councils in Sri Lanka. The Amendment has also made both Sinhala and Tamil as the official languages of the country. English continues to be the link language.

The overall security scenario in Sri Lanka has improved with increasing signs of societal stability. Tamils aren't being targeted for special interrogation anymore and the wide-ranging security systems are being phased out. The Sri Lankan government has lifted Emergency and the number of arbitrary arrests and detainment of Tamils under the Prevention of Terrorism Act (PTA) has gone down. However, large presence of Sri Lankan military forces in the north continues to hamper resettlement, rehabilitation and re-establishment of a functioning civil society.

Resettlement continues to be a pressing problem. While most of the Internal Displaced Persons (IDPs) have left refugee camps and returned to their places of origin, problems continue to persist on issues such as infrastructure development and de-mining of former war zones. The Sri Lankan government is welcoming the return of Sri Lankan Tamils from refugee camps in Tamil Nadu. However, there are reports, especially by organizations such as the Human Rights Watch (HRW), that Tamils are being intimidated by torture and blackmail and are thus, desisted from returning.

India, on its part, is pushing the Sri Lankan government to resolve outstanding issues at the earliest and in as peaceful a manner as possible. Tactically, the Indian government is also trying to help in the cause of IDP. However, diplomatic and protocol issues do crop up, hampering goodwill initiatives.

Fishing in Troubled Waters

The waters of Palk Strait continue to be dangerous fishing grounds not only due to the presence of large numbers of sharks, but due to the absence of any clear demarcation of the border. The regional media are galore—on a daily basis—of allegations of the Sri Lankan Navy firing at Indian Tamil fishermen fishing in Palk Strait—a region that separates both the countries and only 12 nautical miles at its narrowest point. The same is the case of Sri Lankan fishermen straying into the Indian side. There have been reports of arrests too. Al Jazeera states that from January to June 2014, about 200 Indian fishermen have been arrested by the Sri Lankan authorities.[12]

Indian Government has time and again brought up the issue of Indian fishermen's safety to the Sinhalese government. A Joint Working Group was formed to look into this issue and to propose solutions for a variety of issues such as (a) prevention of use of force against Indian fishermen (b) early release of confiscated boats (c) bilateral arrangements for licensed fishing and so on. This problem has not only been a bone of contention between both the national governments, but also between the government of the state of Tamil Nadu and the central government of India.[13] Political leaders like Jayalalithaa, Vaiko and Karunanidhi constantly bring up this issue to the notice of New Delhi.[14]

Sri Lanka: A Base of Covert and Overt Anti-India Activities?

Sri Lanka is a strategic element in China's 'Contain India' policy and as such, it is proactively encouraging bilateral relations between itself and Sri Lanka. Its infrastructure development support for Sri Lanka can be translated to be strategic extensions for anti-India operations if and when the need arises. Sri Lanka is a 'major' pearl in China's string of pearls.[15]

For the Pakistan ISI, Sri Lanka has been a fertile recruitment ground for anti-India operatives. Sri Lanka has a sizable Muslim population, which has been tapped by fundamentalist elements too. In April 2014, Indian intelligence agencies and Tamil Nadu police gave statements to the local media claiming to have busted a major terror network with the arrest Sakir Hussein, an ISI suspect in Chennai. The arrested person is alleged to have links to a major Pakistani terror outfit.[16]

Sri Lanka, on its part has vociferously stated that it would not allow its soil to be used for terrorist activities targeting India. In a special interview to *The Hindustan Times*, President Mahinda Rajapaksa stated, "India's fears are unfounded. We will never allow any country to act against India in any way from our soil."[17]

Looking Ahead: The Way Forward

The bilateral relationship between the two countries is multifaceted and as such, it has enormous scope for significant expansion in scope and depth in the future. What must be essentially understood is that as both countries have strong roots in common values, share a common culture and adhere to the democratic political system—all of which are centred around the people of both the countries, the relationship is by far heavily dependent on people-centric initiatives.[18] While an immediate reconciliatory process between the ethnic groups in the island nation would have a salutary impact from India and will definitely on further strengthening bilateral relations, Sri Lanka has to actually open up to improving commercial and social ties with its neighbour. India, on its part too, must expand its scope of engagement, while not losing sight of the needs of the Tamils. However care should be taken so as to not allow Tamils and Tamil Nadu to hijack more strategic issues such as those of security, economy and international relations.[19]

Benefits of a Strong Relationship

Strategic Concerns: India and Sri Lanka's relations have existed for over two-and-a-half millennia intertwining religious, cultural and social ties that have helped to foster goodwill and friendship among both the nations. After independence, they have cooperated in facing the challenges of regional and global politics. In the coming years, both the countries will have to face and overcome more many more numerous challenges. The present geo-political realities offer great challenges, but also equally numerous opportunities to work together and lay a firm foundation for closer and mutually beneficial cooperation in many fields, such as security, trade, education, health, culture, and so on.

To enable this objective, stronger and more transparent confidence building measures should be put in place on the basis of trust, co-operation and mutual understanding across all areas of bilateral relations. To this end, the governments of both the countries, preferably under the auspices of the regional and international comity of nations, should identify important domains for greater action especially in economics, culture and political and strategic issues. In parallel, both governments should avoid making public statements on sensitive issues that erode efforts to maintain and enhance confidence and trust between the two countries.

While India should not be directed by the pressures of Tamil Nadu to direct its strategic plans and actions, the Sri Lankan government, on its part, should address the grievances of the people than that of groups with narrow vested interests. The authorities should commit to the effective devolution of small administrative units such as through provinces and should initiate a structured dialogue towards political consensus on the ethnic issue. In other words, Amendment 13 of the constitution should be enacted in letter and spirit at a multiparty forum and within a specified time-frame.

Bilateral dialogues should be instituted based on sovereign equality and mutual respect that addresses strategic interests of both countries. Political sensitivities, especially of internal issues and their security impact should to be considered completely to maintain mutual confidence. For this, institutional mechanism should be strengthened. Though not a recourse that is generally adhered, it would be in good stead if both countries refrain from raising issues in multinational fora, especially when they can be discussed bilaterally.

Terrorism, narcotics, human and people trafficking are the scourge of any nation—developed or developing. For Sri Lanka and India too, these issues pose a serious threat to the social and political fabric. Both the countries should strengthen mutual consultative arrangements to combat these problems. In this regard, both the countries should make efforts to further expand existing defence cooperation. This should also be directed to enhance maritime security cooperation and sea-lane protection.

Trade and Commerce: Economy is amongst the most focused areas of every government today as it is an issue concerning not only the financial status of the nation (at the macro level), but the quality of life of every citizen (at the micro level). Thus, despite its intricacies and the need for parity in relationship, trade and commerce should be amongst the top three agendas in the bilateral relationship.

This is the right time for India and Sri Lanka to focus and build on the success of the Free Trade Agreement (FTA). In fact, both countries should encourage the promotion of a Comprehensive Economic Partnership Agreement

(CEPA). With the new BJP government in New Delhi and a post-war Sri Lanka, both countries should now explore ways to expand bilateral trade and mutual investment. Private business partnership must be encouraged. Institutionalisation of business relationship between entities should be identified and entertained. Sri Lankan business entities can leverage India expertise in manufacturing and services, especially by building strong links with entities in South India. Both governments should create an institutional capacity to support the Sri Lankan private sector to enhance relationship with their Indian counterparts. Medium businesses should be encouraged to expand operational geographies. Special Foreign Direct Investments should allowed, especially in areas that require greater need for capital.

Economically, the northern and eastern regions of Sri Lanka (former LTTE controlled regions) should be the focus to identify reconstruction and development requirements. The populace of these regions should be given secure livelihood and opportunities to grow economically. India's experience in such developmental activities should be leveraged. The livelihood skills of victims and displaced people should be enhanced—vocational training on a large scale, especially for displaced people, including returnees from India can be provided.

Energy is a key driver of national economies and as such both India and Sri Lanka should analyse prospects for bilateral cooperation in depth. This should include opportunities in power generation, petroleum industries, and renewable energy sources.

Over the years, the relationship between the neighbours has matured. Both nations have overcome challenges to be in the status they are now in the comity of nations. With such understanding India and Sri Lanka should overcome mind blocks and ensure a level-playing field for business entities. Favoured nation status is a good and proven way forward.

People-to-People Engagement: With the LTTE era is a thing of the past and with the present need to resettle displaced people, Sri Lanka and India need to explore ways to settle the Tamil issue permanently. Expanding this view, both countries should significantly expand people-to-people contacts across multiple channels—travel and tourism, religious activities, medical tourism, arts and crafts, cultural exchanges, media, education, sports, and so on.

REFERENCES

1. K. Godage, 'Historical Continuities', Seminar India, Vol. 507, 2002 (Source: http://www.india-seminar.com/2002/517/517%20k.%20godage.htm) (Accessed on 30 June 2014)
2. http://www.mapsofindia.com/neighbouring-countries-maps/india-srilanka-map.html# (Accessed on 29 July 2014)
3. 'Ramayana's demon king Ravana was a great ruler, says a new book', IBNLive.com, Source: http://ibnlive.in.com/news/ramayanas-demon-king-ravana-was-a-great-ruler-says-a-new-book/406724-40-100.html (Accessed on 29 June 2014)

4. N. Sastri, 'A History of South India', Oxford University Press, New Delhi, 2000, ISBN 0195606868.
5. Indian History with Objective Questions and Historical Maps Twenty-Sixth Edition 2010, South India page 59 (As given in Wikipedia.com - http://en.wikipedia.org/wiki/Chola_occupation_of_Sri_Lanka_(993-1077) (Accessed on 1 July 2014)
6. K. Godage, 2002.
7. J. Perera, 'India's Panikkar 'Diplomacy' in Sri Lanka', 28 March 2011, Asian Tribune, Source: http://www.asiantribune.com/news/2011/03/27/india%E2%80%99s-panikkar-%E2%80%98diplomacy%E2%80%99-sri-lanka (Accessed on 12 June 2014)
8. K. Godage, 2002.
9. Gurnam Chand, India-Sri Lanka—Changing Political Relationship: Post-1990, Mainstream, Vol XLVIII, No 25, June 12, 2010 (www.mainstream.com)
10. Ibid
11. Ibid
12. http://www.aljazeera.com/indepth/features/2014/06/fishing-issue-clouds-india-sri-lanka-ties-2014691244367569.html (Accessed on 14 June 2014)
13. http://www.gktoday.in/india-sri-lanka-fishermen-issue-measures-to-resolve/ (Accessed on 05 July 2014)
14. http://timesofindia.indiatimes.com/India/Reclaim-Katchatheve-Island-from-Sri-Lanka-NFF-urges-PM/articleshow/37785376.cms (Accessed on 30 June 2014)
15. http://www.ipcs.org/pdf_file/issue/1445888596RP16-Brian-SriLanka.pdf (Accessed on 18 June 2014)
16. http://timesofindia.indiatimes.com/india/ISI-agent-linked-to-Pakistan-official-in-Sri-Lanka-held-in-Chennai/articleshow/34390661.cms (Accessed on 12 June 2014)
17. http://www.hindustantimes.com/world-news/won-t-allow-anti-india-acts-says-lankan-president/article1-1123050.aspx (Accessed on 25 June 2014)
18. http://www.ft.lk/2013/01/23/resetting-india-sri-lanka-relations-the-way-forward/ (Accessed on 1 July 2014)
19. http://www.ipcs.org/seminar/india/india-sri-lanka-relations-836.html (Accessed on 13 June 2014)

10

Maritime Security Challenges in South Asia and its Impact on India's Security

Sanjay Kumar

Introduction

The 21st century is going to be a maritime century. The globalization of the world economy and its profound effect on world sea-borne trade, energy imperatives and sea resources indicate the growing importance of the seas. India is an important maritime state. Since ancient times, India has been a seafaring and shipbuilding nations and had commercial and trade ties with neighbouring countries. Yet, at the same time, there seems to be that maritime interactions amongst countries have not been properly understood.

The Indian Ocean region, was considered an important Ocean Since 1946, the euphoria of independence was overshadowed by the turbulence of inter-state wars. During the cold war era, the two superpowers cultivated their maritime influence directly or indirectly through an impressive array of available port facilities in this region. History was repeating itself in an evolved form.

The post cold war era has seen a socio-politico-strategic shift in security policy. Globalization, specifically in economics, today dominates strategic considerations. This has led to considerable maritime security concerns, since most regional trade is sea-borne. Inspite of regional countries' wide dissimilarities and divergent interests, each country is free to pursue economic linkage with Europe or North America rather than with each other. This negative fallout has inevitably limited the region's economic growth.

Geo-Strategic Importance of Indian Ocean

The Indian Ocean is known for many choke points, such as Straits of Hormuz, Straits of Malacca, Lombok and the Sunda Straits. Any disruption in traffic flow through these points can have disastrous consequences. The disruption of energy flow in particular has become a security concern for littoral states, as majority of their energy resources are sea-based. Since energy is important in shaping the geopolitical strategies of a nation. Any disturbance in its supply has serious security consequences. Given the required demand of energy from India, China and Japan, it is inevitable that these countries are sensitive to the security of the Sea Lines of Communications (SLOCs) and choke points of the regions.

Due to a continental mindset, many countries do not consider the significance of the Indian Ocean, but regard it as a 'divisive character', southward of the 'well connected' Asian landmass. Admiral Mahan said in 1890: "Whoever controls the Indian Ocean will dominate Asia...in the 21st century, the destiny of the world would be decided on its waters".[1] The Indian Ocean has seen serious maritime activities for the past 600 years, primarily for trade. In ancient times, the motivation for trade was for silk and spices. Today, it is for oil, the primary source of energy which has influenced the economic-industrial sectors of major states and, hence has becomes the principal strategic determinant. West Asia contains 65 per cent of the world's proven reserves[2] and accounts for more than half of the world's oil exports and almost all of Asia-Pacific's imports. The demand for oil imports is likely to increase and despite efforts to diversify sources, disruption of supplies is bound to impact seriously, as in was the case of oil shocks on national economies which lead to inflation and widespread unemployment. Exports to the West through this route include large quantities of agricultural products such as tea, coffee, rubber and sesame. Not only this the Indian Ocean holds 65 per cent of strategic raw minerals and 31 per cent of gas, comprises 30 per cent of the world population and is characterised by fast-growing economies and a large consumer market.[3] This will result for collective desire for security and stability in the region.

The unrestricted use of sea-lanes of the ocean has become an imperative for economic security. The Strait of Hormuz is considered to be the world's most important energy route without an alternative. One-third of the world's trade and almost all of East Asia's oil pass through the eastern straits, Malacca, Sunda and Lombok-Makasser. Of the 14 states constituting East and Southeast Asia, 12 are highly dependent on West Asian oil.[4] In a sense, the sea-route extending from the North Arabian Sea to the Sea of Japan through the Indian Ocean is akin to the 'New Silk Route'.[5] Japan's need for energy compelled it to venture right till India's doorstep to seek cooperation with India.[6] China has vital trading interests transit through the Indian Ocean. It is also poised to become the second largest oil importing country, surpassing Japan.[7] Consequently, major power policies in Indian Ocean region may adversely affect its trade and energy flow. Straddling this new silk route, India's interests are linked to its maritime trade—95 per cent in volume. It is currently the world's seventh largest oil consumer and is expected to become the fifth largest by 2020.[8] Importing 65 per cent of its energy requirements from West Asia (expected to rise to 81 per cent by 2011-12), [9] the oil sea-route originating from the region will continue to be valued by India despite improvements in indigenous production, diversification and recourse to nuclear/non-conventional sources. The importance of energy to the 'demand of heartland' (India, China and Japan) is extensive. These countries view SLOCs as their very lifelines. At current levels of consumption, the oil import dependence of India is expected to reach 82.2% by 2010 and 91.6% by 2020. In case of consumption it will be 61%and 76.9%, while for rest of Asia it will be 95.1% respectively.[10] For India, almost 89% of its oil imports come from sea. It is important that the SLOCs should be secured. This security requirement has been increased many times. Most of oil originates in West Asia, and the SLOCs pass through areas India's primary adversary, Pakistan. Besides this, the political turbulence of areas in West Asia often holds hostage the supply of oil from the region. In the past, supplies from this region have been disarmed on various occasions, primarily because of political reason and which were not market driven.

Geographically, India lays astride the major Sea Lanes of Communication (SLOC) in the Indian Ocean-providing it with considerable strategic importance and potential. The vast proportion of our foreign trade—97% in volume and 76% in value terms—is sea-borne. According to World Bank estimates, in 1999 the world seaborne trade was pegged at 21,480 billion ton-miles, it is expected to reach 35,000 billion ton-miles in 2010 and 41.800 billion ton-miles in 2014.[11] The United Nations Conference on Trade and Development (UNCTAD) Report, "Review of Maritime Transport 2000", notes that world sea-based trade recorded its fourteenth consecutive annual increase, and Asia's share of import and export was 26.1%and 18.8% respectively. Thus, the prospects for sea-borne trade are set to rise dramatically.[12] The intensity of other threats, like maritime terrorism, drug trafficking, gunrunning, piracy, natural disasters and inter-state conflicts are also on proportional rise.

Maritime Threats to Indian Security

In such security environment, India's reliance on sea routes will, no doubt, increase trade, energy resources, shipping, sustainable exploitation of marine resources and ocean research and exploration. Its transportation routes has been hampered because of increasing vulnerable to disruption and a range of criminal and clandestine activities. The continuing militarisation of the Indian Ocean and the dynamic role of technology on naval warfare will also have great impact on the country. It is imperative, therefore, that maritime security issues will have to seen in a holistic, rather than compartmentalised, manner.

Maritime Terrorism

Maritime security has added a new dimension to overall security after 9/11 incident. Following the September 11 attacks, the possibility of maritime terrorism becomes a cause of real concern. The fight against maritime terrorism has received a boost with the backing of the international community, particularly the United States. The hijacking of the passenger ship, the *Achille Lauro,* in 1988 brought terrorism at sea to the forefront of international condemnation and resulted in the Rome Convention for the Suppression of Unlawful Acts against the Safety of Maritime Navigation (1988). A terrorist attack on ships carrying dangerous and hazardous cargo such as a liquified natural gas (LNG) tanker, especially in port, could result in considerable human and material damage as well as environmental destruction over a wide area of land and sea.

The Council for Security Cooperation in the Asia Pacific (CSCAP) Working Group has given a vast definition for maritime terrorism:

> "...the undertaking of terrorist acts and activities within the maritime environment, using or against vessels or fixed platforms at sea or in port, or against any one of their passengers or personnel, against coastal facilities or settlements, including tourist resorts, port areas and port towns or cities."

This definition, however, does not clearly state the meaning of terrorism. The question is whether it would only include maritime attacks against civilian (merchant) vessels or also attacks against military crafts. According to Akiva J. Lorenz, "the maritime terrorism is the use or threat of violence against a ship (civilian as well as military), its passengers or sailors, cargo, a port facility, or if the purpose is solely a platform for political ends."[13] In this definition, the use of the maritime transportation system to smuggle terrorists or terrorist materials into the targeted country can also be included.

Maritime terrorism is motivated by political goal. Piracy, according to article 101 of the 1982 United Nations Convention on the Law of the Sea (UNCLOS) is defined as[14]:

(a) "Any illegal acts of violence or detention, or any act of depredation, committed for private ends by the crew or the passengers of a private ship or a private aircraft, and directed:
   (i) On the high seas,[15] against another ship or aircraft against persons or property on board such ship or aircraft
   (ii) Against a ship, aircraft, persons or property in a place out of jurisdiction of any State;

(b) Any act of voluntary participation in the operation of a ship of an aircraft with knowledge of facts making it a pirate ship or aircraft;

(c) Any act inciting or of intentionally facilitating an act described in sub-paragraph (a) or (b)."

Given these definitions, the grey areas are cases of kidnap-for-ransom incidents, such as the May 2001 abduction of three American citizens and 17 Filipinos at the Dos Palmas resort on Palauan by Abu Sayyaf Group (ASG), an Al Qaeda affiliate.[16] This is done primarily for financial need to obtain their political aims. ASG has repeatedly perpetrated such acts of piracy. Their actions have given an indication of the distinction between terrorism and piracy.

A high degree of threat is being predicted from maritime terrorism to sea-lines and hub ports enclosed within the Hormuz and the Southeast Asian straits.[17] Insurgencies and terrorist activities with maritime traditions abound in the later sub-region, viz, several terrorists organisations in and around the Indian Ocean are known to possess merchant fleets of various types like—the Free Aceh Movement, the Moro Islamic Liberation Front, the Abu Sayyaff and LTTE. The established links of these regional groups with global terrorist groups like Jamaah Islamiyah (JI) and Al Qaeda, security concerns for the Indian Ocean littoral states are on rise. While the spillover effects of South Asian secessionism to the Bay of Bengal is a distinct possibility, the LTTE's activities equally pose a threat to littoral states as far away as in South Asia, given the Sri Lankan separatist group's claims that the Sea Tigers be recognized as a 'navy' in the region. The LTTE is known to indulge in piracy for its funding and material assets and hence, cannot claim insurgent/belligerents rights under international law, nor the status of a navy for the 'Sea Tigers'.[18] The LTTEs have an entire flotilla engaged in dubious maritime trade. The level of the threat posed by it, was exemplified by the incident in which it captured Maldives and the Indian forces were send their. Most of these are registered under Flag of Convenience (FOC) countries known as "pan-ho-lib," i.e. Panama, Honduras and Liberia,[19] and are difficult to track as they routinely change names and registry. Lloyds of London lists 11 merchant ships belonging to Asian front companies that are in reality managed by Kumaran Pathmanathan of the LTTE.[20]

Thus, Flag of Convenience (FOC) can be a cause of great concern to maritime security. Flying the flag of a state other than the country of ownership enables the owners to avoid high registration fees and taxes, and to employ cheap labour operating under sub-standard conditions. It is estimated that there are about 30 such registries (some in private hands operating on behalf of states) mainly run by small island or impoverished nations.[21] Since the checks and balances introduced by these registries are undeniably lax, there is no guarantee as to the type of crew or the type of cargo that these ships carry. Such ships are considered the safest bet for carrying out terrorist-related activities.

The attacks on USS Cole[22] in October 2000 at Aden and the French supertanker, MT Limburg off Yemen's coast in October 2002 are well known to the world to such realities of such a great threat. If a small explosive-ridden dinghy could cripple a state-of-the-art warship such as the Cole, replete with 'aegis' of 'various calibers', a similar attack on a defenceless cruise-liner or oil tanker would spell disaster. Limburg and Cole were both 'combatant vessels' involved in the 'War on Terror', but with the terrorists' aim of disrupting valuable and vulnerable sea-borne trade being evident, the threat to commercial ships, SLOCs and ports can be easily extrapolated. What emerges is the high probability of sinking an oil tanker in one of the vital choke points such as in the Malacca Straits or cruise a LNG carrier into a hub-port on a suicide mission.[23]

The Indian Ocean and its contiguous waters have always had a major share of global pirate attacks and armed robbery in territorial waters due to dense shipping, frail maritime policing and favourable hide-to-vanish environment. According to the 2003 IMB Report, the Indonesian waters were declared the world's most dangerous, followed by Bangladesh, Nigeria and India.[24] While such attacks declined worldwide by 22 per cent in the first six months of 2004, the Malacca Straits, however, recorded a 33 per cent increase.[25] Links between terrorism and piracy having being uncovered lately[26] and the likely possibility of WMDs falling in the hands of terrorists could further add to the threat.

Besides, one cannot ignore water as the medium to convey instruments of terror. Being the most inexpensive means of transportation, over 80 per cent of the world's trade involves ocean transit. Containerisation of sea-borne trade and resort to Flags of Convenience (FOC) shipping by non-state elements, compound the threat. Al Qaeda is known to maintain a secret shipping fleet flying such flags, allowing it to conceal ownership and covertly transport arms, drugs, recruits and maybe, even WMD material.[27]

Drug Trafficking and Gunrunning

Another important maritime security issue is drug trafficking. The drug trafficking has become the most incentive means of collecting funds to support terrorist activities and insurgencies around the Indian Ocean region. The terrorist groups often work hand-in-hand with drug mafia. While this symbiotic relationship provides established routes for drug and arms smuggling, it also provides terrorists with the logistical infrastructure to move people, arms and material according to their desires.[28] So far the geo-political setup of the Indian Ocean region is concerned, Pakistan, Iran and Afghanistan on the one hand, form a major portion of the "Golden Crescent," while on the other hand, Myanmar (Burma), Thailand and Laos form the "Golden Triangle." Both are famous for its illegal drug production. Narco-terrorism for the last few decades has become a major security concern for littoral states. Drug trafficking leads to money laundering. The sale of drugs promote gunrunning, insurgent and terrorist activities. Added to these, there is the transnational security problem. It is linked to human smuggling that has multiple effects. Furthermore human smuggling has promoted terrorism and illegal immigration. This in a big way has resulted in socio-political instability.

One is aware of the growing relationship between gunrunning and drug trafficking. It is rather difficult to control one without controlling the other. Gunrunning by sea is by far the safest means for transferring arms and ammunition around the world, while drug trafficking is most lucrative form of business. The LTTE has a vast and well-established network for gunrunning, with its reach extending as far as Japan. Their arms mostly comes from Cambodia, which are later loaded into small fishing trawlers from the port of Ranong in southern Thailand. This arms cargo is then send to bigger ships (often in mid-ocean), which transport the consignment to Sri Lanka.

The problem is also severe in Bangladesh. The various small fishing craft laden with arms during the last few years has led to the conclusion that a lot of these arms also make their way from Thailand to the Cox Bazaar in Bangladesh. Similarly, the Royal Thai Navy's seizure of arms meant for the People's Liberation Army (Manipur) off the port of Ranong clearly demonstrates the close nexus between arms trafficking and insurgent groups. The other major pipeline for Cambodian weapons is through Southern Thailand and from there across the Malacca Straits to Aceh.[29]

There has been clear linkages between the narcotics and illegal light weapons trade. It includes shared supply and transit routes, the use of weapons for protection amongst drug traffickers themselves and funding of gunrunning through drug trade and vice versa.

Piracy

Piracy has become the boon for the modern seafarer. The numerous cases of reported and unreported piracy have led to considerable concern and multinational efforts to control this violent menace. According to the International Maritime Organization Annual Report 2002,[30] the Malacca Straits, South China Sea and Indian Ocean are the areas that have been mostly affected by piracy.

Piracy has a lot to do with the geography of the area. But economic conditions and the mindset of the coastal people in the hundreds of minor islands that lace the Malacca Straits and South China Sea are significant factor for such developments. Recently, piracy-related incidents have become quite active in the Bay of Bengal and the Arabian Sea. Hence, the center of gravity of piracy may shift to the waters around India.

There seems to be much change in the functioning of piracy. Earlier so-called 'Asian Piracy' often involved mere stealing of valuables from ships with a negligible amount of associated violence. However, recent cases in the region have displayed a dramatic increase in brazen violence, and the methodology has made them akin to the South American or West African type of piracy.[31] In addition, the involvement of organized crime in hijacking ships was evident from the MV Alondra Rainbow case, from pirates in the Arabian Sea in late 1999 by the Navy and the Coast Guard. This case is also a modern example of various enforcement agencies acting together to fight piracy.[32] Today, there is a need for law enforcement agencies of various states to co-operate to bring piracy under control. If these activities are not curbed then it may go out of control. The problem lies in the fact that these entrenched gangs are well supported by states. Their links with narco–terrorism and human smuggling, is well-established and known to various governments.

Natural Disasters

Natural disasters are other maritime threats which are caused by collisions and accidents due to inclement weather or human errors. It causes environmental pollution. There are more than 150 collisions at sea on a yearly basis due to poor visibility, non-serviceability of radars, hull failure, boiler explosions and human errors.[33]

The natural perils of ocean transportation such as cyclones cause heavy disasters which are most common in the eastern Indian Ocean and adjoining seas. The possibility of a catastrophic oil spill, such as the one from the Tasman Spirit in August 2003 off the coast of Karachi, [34] became source of major concern. One cannot also forget environmental disaster in the form of tsunamis that killed well over two hundred thousand people in December 2004 in this region. In addition, environmental pollution not only affect land, water, and populations but can be a cause of tension or conflict within or between states. These beings the case, resource depletion and human degradation of the environment have been recognized as directly relevant to South Asia's security agenda.[35] Hydrocarbon resources are central factors in the strategic calculus in such conflicts and disputes as seen in Aceh and the South China Sea. The damage caused by tropical reefs, oil spills, overexploitation of fisheries, etc. have also severely affected the Asian environment and as such South Asian security is also affected.

Indian Concern for Maritime Security

In the 21st Century, the Indian Navy has developed a multi-dimensional force with lethal weaponry and sensors. It has emphasised the need of indigenisation of technology and production. Its modernisation is essential to keep pace with rapidly advancing technologies and doctrines of modern warfare. Hence, three elements become important for the development of the Indian Navy's doctrine;

rapid reaction manoeuvrability and concentration of firepower; land-attack capability to influence the war on land and naval diplomacy.

Today, naval battlefield environment has undergone major change. The information age has given further impetus to the 'Revolution in Military Affairs' (RMA) which is now producing more lethal weapon systems and facilitating the militarisation of outer space and cyber-related crime. The RMA, in turn, has influenced the 'Revolution in Naval Affairs' (RNA) which has greatly enhanced night capabilities, yielded precision weapons and seamless communication networks, and considerably reduced response time for naval forces. Stealth technology remains critical. The Indian Navy will need to incorporate these aspects in its war-fighting doctrine. India has to step up surveillance and protection of India's vast coastline of 7,516 km as well as its EEZ.[36] There are reports infiltration and arms drops by Pakistan have taken place in the State of Gujarat and Maharashtra coasts. Similarly, one can not ignore the problems created by the LTTE along the Tamil Nadu coast. The Arabian Sea and the Bay of Bengal have become vulnerable to a wide range of criminal, influx of refugees and Tamil terrorists. These include smuggling, arms and narcotics trafficking (hand maidens of terrorism), illegal fishery activities, piracy attacks, theft, fraud and other crimes and illegal activities at sea. Coastal security was one of the issues addressed by the Group of Ministers (GoM) in its report, Reforming the National Security System (2001).[37] Its recommended that the Coast Guard may be upgraded and specialised marine police in all coastal states and island territories may be established. These are currently under consideration.

Moreover, there are thousands of island territories and rocks in India which are largely uninhabited and lie at considerable distances from the mainland in proximity to other countries. The Andaman and Nicobar islands are particularly vulnerable to clandestine activities and illegal infiltration and occupation. Militant activities in both Myanmar and Indonesia have an adverse impact on these islands.

Since 70% of our energy requirements of crude oil are currently shipped from abroad, increased focus would be required on the ability to maintain the safety and security of energy shipments and the prevention of any disruption of supply. Special security provisions may be needed to protect our interests in the Gulf of Cambay and Kutch. 19% of Indian oil demands are generated by offshore basins. The defence of maritime assets and infrastructure are in critical stage. Protection of over 150 process and well platforms at sea, operating beyond the EEZ in the near future, would also be required. Some of the challenges to India's maritime security could include the surveillance and security of the extended maritime zone, an increase in domestic shipping tonnage, enhanced effectiveness of both major and minor ports and the strengthening of regulatory and enforcement mechanisms in India's maritime zones. India's maritime zones has certain rights and obligations, including a territorial sea up to 12 nm (22 km) from the baseline, a contiguous zone from 12 to 24 nm (22-44 km), an Exclusive Economic Zone (EEZ) from 12 to 200 nm (22-370 km) and a continental shelf up to 200 nm, as well as up to 350 nm if certain conditions apply. The latter is also called the Outer Continental Shelf (OCS). These zones currently comprise 2.013 million sq km area of sea which is the 12th largest in the world and equivalent to two-thirds of the total land area. With the inclusion of the deep seabed mining area in the central Indian Ocean, lying only 370 km from American naval and military facilities on Diego Garcia, and the formal delineation of the OCS by 2005, the total area of India's maritime zones could well be equivalent to India's total land area. In effect, this would provide India with sovereign rights over all non-living resources and sedimentary organisms within 650 km from the coast. This, indeed, is a vast "maritime space" and strategic space for India.[38]

Over the years, India has succeeded in demarcating its maritime boundaries with Indonesia, Maldives, Myanmar, Sri Lanka and Thailand. However, the problem lies with the demarcation of maritime boundaries with Pakistan and Bangladesh. The military build-up by Pakistan in the Kutch/Sir Creek area, the potential exploitation of oil and gas in these waters, as well as offensive patrolling at sea, could increase tensions. Harassment of Indian fishers takes place regularly.

Suggestions

To Upgrade the Regulatory Mechanisms

Today, in India, the regulatory mechanisms of maritime zones need to be upgraded through proper enactment of new legislation and then implemented in correct perspective. Hence, the promulgation of anti-piracy laws, legislation for the exploitation of mineral resources and the designation of Marine Protected Areas (MPA) become important for effective implementation. India is also carrying out scientific research in Antarctica, the ability to deal with dual-use scientific data and products, the protection and sustainable utilisation of the marine environment and the prevention. Immediate steps are been taken by the government to make the area free from pollution from land-based sources, shipping and oil slicks.

As such, a formal mechanism for coordination among the multiple users of the sea would be required. This would enable effective and time-urgent coordination between the Central Government and the concerned States and Union Territories. In this respect, the Group of Ministers' report has recommended the formation of "an apex body for management of maritime affairs".

To Promote Regional Co-operation

For maritime security, there is an urgency for the Indian government to work for diplomatic bilateral/multilateral relations with concerned countries. Regular maritime security dialogue with countries of the Indian Ocean Rim (IOR) is necessary in order to ensure the stability of sea lines of communication. Today, there is a need to make people aware of maritime security in the country in terms of both education and research. A specialised documentation division for the much neglected study of Indian maritime history and naval warfare also required.

The Indian Ocean in the 21st century will play a dominant role in international politics. The demand for key resources and markets, the privacy among regional and extra-regional maritime powers for influence in the region will continue. However, the altered complexion of security threats necessitates that states seek convergence to preserve the freedom of navigation. Moreover, military pacts or alliance are no longer valid today but bilateralism and multilateralism have acquired a fresh meaning in the management of security arrangements. Regional cooperation is one step to reduce inter-state tensions because it would lead to trust building and the maintenance of peace and stability. Beside this, among the countries concerned regional states should also develop marine technology and a joint strategy to ensure the safety of ports and harbours. Otherwise, it could have negative fallout. Earlier we have seen in the USS Cole bombing incident and recent attacks faced by the Sri Lankan Navy vessels, a small boat can unobtrusively collide with a larger vessel that can cause considerable loss of lives and equipment. On the positive side a state should pursue coordinated efforts on utilization and management of marine resources, both animal and mineral, in their respective Exclusive Economic Zones.

To Strengthen Naval Security Capabilities

There is a need to build certain capabilities which are essential to ensure maritime security of our nation. First, the entire region should be kept under surveillance. Secondly, the Navy must be in a position to meet threats ranging from maritime terrorism to high intensive warfare. It must have reach, staying power and adequate sea-lift capacity. There must be proper cooperation and coordination. It must be balanced in these capabilities in all the three dimensions of our armed forces. Integral air, anti submarine and anti missile defence must be built in with strong underwater defence and offensive capability.

To Counter Maritime Terrorism Mechanism

The threat of maritime terrorism has increased sharply and the system of management in the Indian Ocean is needed to face these challenges. Three areas of activities became important. First, the internal system of ocean management should be refined within the maritime nations by setting up Ocean Commissions. Secondly, greater maritime cooperation is necessary between maritime nations. And finally, the global maritime environment should be made more viable by replacing the system of Flags of Convenience with a more secure system to face the growing challenges of maritime terrorism.[39]

Addressing the 14th annual meeting of the ASEAN Regional Forum (ARF)[40] at Manila on August 2, 2007, Pranab Mukherjee, the then India's Minister for External Affairs, underlined the continued importance of 'India's Look East Policy' of its maritime security need. He said: "India will design and conduct a training module on maritime security especially for the ARF member-states, with themes of anti-piracy, search and rescue missions, off-shore and port security, anti-smuggling and narcotics control and anti-poaching operations. The nucleus of the module would be capacity-building for these and related aspects of maritime security."[41]

Conclusion

Sophisticated technological modes have direct influence on international and regional security at a time when the world has moved from unipolar world to multipolar order. In the face of technological change at an unprecedented rate, the ability to keep pace has seriously effected the different successful cultures of different hemispheres. In the last five decades, the world has amassed more scientific knowledge than it was generated in the past 5,000 years. Rapid changes in technology in the form of Information Age, however, have occurred since late 1980s. Today, scientific information has now increased two-fold every five years. It becomes important for India to stay ahead with technological developments to safeguard our security and decision-making power. There is a need to focuss on maritime dimensions of national security as they are linked to India's political stability and economic prosperity. To maintain our interests at sea and then manage the fast-paced technological developments there is a need to formulate a sophisticated proactive multi-pronged and long-term strategy.

A nation surrounded by water can become a great nation if it has adequate maritime capability. India is already a great maritime nation. The time has come to show capabilities and the will power to sustain effectively the ocean area which are of vital national interest. Hence, the role of Navy becomes important and it should work and coordinate with other forces so that these different kinds of threat can be dealt in a balanced manner. Maritime security threats include military and non-military dimensions. It is, therefore, necessary that both these dimensions are important for a proper understanding of the problem which might hamper our national security.

REFERENCES

1. See A.T. Mahan, The Influence of Sea Power Upon History 1660-1783, 1890, Scrivener; New York.

2. http://www.greekshares.com/global_energy.asp
3. K.K. Kohli, Maritime Power in Peace and War: An Indian View, African Security Review, 1996, 5(2).
4. K. Hashimoto, Excluding Myanmar and land-locked Laos, Asia's Energy Security and Role of Japan, PHP Research Institute, May 2000 at http://www.rice.edu/projects/baker/Pubs/workingpapers/jescgem /aesrj11/aesrj.html
5. U. Bhaskar, Regional Naval Cooperation, Strategic Analysis, November 1992, p. 736.
6. Raja Mohan, C., "After China, Fernandes Warms up to Japan", *The Hindu*, April 30, 2003 at http://www.worldpolicy.org/journal/articles/wpj03-2/menon.html
7. China People's Daily, November 20, 2003.
8. After US, China, Japan and Germany, *See Oil & Gas Journal*, January 20, 2004.
9. B.K. Singh, India's Energy Security, *The Hindu*, June 9, 2003.
10. P.K. Ghose, "The Maritime Dimension", in "Oil and Gas in India's Security" ed. J. Singh Knowledge World New Delhi, July 2001.
11. http://community.middlebury.edu/docs/ghose
12. http://community.middlebury.edu/docs/ghose
13. A.L. Lorenz, Al Qaeda's Maritime Threat, first published at http://www.ict.org.il/apage/11847.phpapril5,2007.
14. United Nations Convention on the Law of the Sea at http://www.un.org/Depts/los/convention_agreements/texts/unclos/closindx.htm
15. High Seas describes waters outside the common 12 nautical mile territorial (State) zone),
16. ICT Profile of ASG at http://fighel.com/organizations/org_frame.cfm?orgid=3
17. Holt, Andrew, Plugging the Holes in Maritime Security, Terrorism Monitor, May 6, 2004.
18. According to C. Fenwick, "...where a de facto political organization had been set up...and conducting military and naval operations in accordance with laws of war..., the situation must be recognized as one of public war (justifying it belligerent rights)." See, K.R. Singh, "Maritime Violence and Non-state Actors". *Dialogue*, Apr-Jun 2003, at http://www.asthabharati.org/Dia_Apr03/krs.htm
19. "Killing of Sea Bird Not A Big Blow to LTTE Shipping Operations", *The Sunday Times*, February 1996.
20. Ibid
21. "What are FOCs: A brief guide to flags of convenience", www.itf.org.uk/seafarers/foc/Body_foc.html
22. On October 12, 2000, the USS Cole, an Arleigh Burke class destroyer, was attacked by a small craft loaded with 270 kg of C-4 explosives while making a routine refill stop in the port of Aden, Yemen. Steered by two Saudi suicide 20, 11 terrorists, Hassan al Khamri and Ibrahim al-Thawar, the small craft exploded alongside the USS Cole 47 minutes after the refueling was initiated, killing 17 U. S. servicemen and injuring 37 more.21 The attack caused $250 million in damage to the warship taking 14 months to repair.
23. G.S. Khurana, Maritime Security in the Indian Ocean: Convergence plus Cooperation Equals Resonance, Strategic Analysis, Vol. 28, No.3, Jul-Sep 2004, p.415
24. http://news.scotsman.com/latest.cfm?id=2461349
25. http://www.alertnet.org/thenews/newsdesk/KLR2992.htm
26. Terrorists are known to indulge in piracy to obtain funds. Other links have also come to light, as in case of hijacking of the Indonesian tanker, Dewi Madrim off Indonesia in March 2003. Ten armed men seized the ship for learning how to steer it, may be equivalent to terrorists who took flying lessons at Florida flight school and a precursor to a 'maritime 9/11' at http://www.iags.org/n0524042.htm
27. http://www.military.com/content/morecontent/1, 12044, FL_ports_103001, 00.html
28. For a detailed treatment see B. Raman, "Control of Transnational Crime and War against Terrorism", Indian Defence Review, Apr-Jun 2002, vol. 17(2).

29. David, Capie. "Small Arms Production Transfers in South East Asia," Canberra Papers on Strategy and Defence, no.146, 2002, p.20.
30. International Maritime Organisation, "Reports on Acts of Piracy and Armed Robbery against Ships—Annual Report 2002," dated 17 April 2003, available in pdf at http//www.imi.org
31. http://community.middlebury.edu/docs/ghose
32. MV Alondra Rainbow, a 7,000-ton Panama-registered vessel belonging to Japanese owners was hijacked. The vessel was en route from Kuala Tan Jung, Indonesia to Milke in Japan. The Piracy Reporting Center of the International Maritime Bureau had announced through a worldwide broadcast that pirates had captured the vessel. After a high-speed chase and drama it was finally captured by Indian Naval ship INS Prahar.
33. M. Roy, "The Strategic Importance of Seaborne Trade and Shipping" April 2001 at http:/ /idun.its.adfa.edu.au /ADSC/Sloc/SlocRoy.htm
34. G.S. Khurana op.cit, p.416
35. Lorraine Elliot, "Regional Environmental Security: Pursuing a Non-Traditional Approach," in Non-Traditional Security Issue in Southeast Asia, ed. Tan and Boutin, p. 438. J. F. Bradford, The Growing Prospects for Maritime Security Cooperation in Southeast Asia, Naval War College Review,summer2005,Vol.58,No.3p.72. 36.
36. http://mod.nic.in/samachar/dec15-01/htm/ch2htm
37. Ibid.
38. Ibid.
39. Tribuneindia.com, Sunday, December, 4, 2005
40. The ARF comprises the United States, China, Russia, Japan, India and the European Union, besides the 10-member Association of Southeast Asian Nations (ASEAN). It also has among other countries Australia, Pakistan, Bangladesh, and Sri Lanka.
41. *The Hindu*, August 3, 2007.

11

Security Challenges in Indian Ocean Region; Maldives—A Strategic Pivot

Narender Kumar

> *Whoever controls the Indian Ocean dominates Asia. This ocean is the key to the seven seas in the twenty first century; the destiny of the world will be decided in these waters.*
>
> —**Alfred Thayer Mahan**

Indian Ocean is emerging as the centre stage for the 21st century "and it remains a stage for pursuit of the global strategic and regional military interests of regional and global powers.[1] Indian Ocean is the third largest ocean with approximately 73,556,000 square kilometres manoeuvre space with immense ocean wealth hidden in its belly. It is considered as heart of third world countries and an Ocean of South. It is a passage to prosperity for close to 2.6 billion people of the rim countries. Indian Ocean is a bridge between East and West Asia and links Europe with Asia. The region has seen explosion of population and mass relocation of demography from rural to urban and from one nation to another in search of better economic opportunities. Global economic power is shifting to the East, therefore, maintaining prosperity and stability across the Indian Ocean region becomes more important than ever.[2]

In spite of the opportunities it offers to the regional and extra regional nations, it has become an "incubator of terrorism" and home to the component of modern instability.[3] Majority of rim nations are in a state of political and economic transition. The continent itself is facing inter and intra state conflict due to territorial, cultural and competing claims for sovereignty. Due to these inherent contradictions the region has remained fragmented and in a state of power vacuum.

Indian Ocean Region Economic and Strategic Significance

Indian Ocean Region is a cradle of natural resources and diverse cultural entity. It has 55 % of proven oil reserves and 40 % of gas reserves. 33% of global trade and 50 % global container traffic transit through its sea lines of communication which are considered busiest in the world. Interestingly maritime trade in the region has been existing for the last 4000 years[4] making it one of the oldest trade routes only second to Silk Route. Therefore, it is correct to assume that, who so ever rules the Indian Ocean will rule the oceans since it connects Atlantic with Pacific and East with West. Rim nations are considered to be reservoir of human resource and industrial work force. Indian Ocean was declared an Ocean of Peace by UNGA in 1971 to avoid militarisation and interference by extra regional powers. With the rising economic and strategic interests of regional and extra regional powers, Indian Ocean Region has become an unstable plateau and has virtually become a nuclear ocean with the presence of largest number of regional and extra regional nuclear powers. In spite of the economic opportunities and availability of energy resources it continues to remain an arc of instability and comparatively poor.

The following factors what make Indian Ocean Region strategically significant are:

(a) IOR rim nations have abundance of oil and gas reserves which are important for economic growth of regional and extra regional nations.

(b) Indian Ocean is one of the busiest sea lines ‘of communication and trade corridor linking consumer markets of west with the industrial hub centres in the East.

(c) After the Pacific Ocean, the Indian Ocean is the richest in minerals, including oil and gas, polymetallic sulfides, cobalt-rich crusts, and other materials that are promising arenas for development and exploitation.[5] Developing and developed nations are queuing up for resource acquisition in Indian Ocean.

(d) Indian Ocean has large number of atolls and islands which makes it easy to extend sphere of influence and establishment of marine bases. That is the reason US, UK and France continues to occupy islands and atolls in Indian Ocean region.

Strategic significance of Indian Ocean to India can be summed by what former Prime Minister of India Mr Atal Vihari Bajpayee had said,

“As we grow in international stature, our defence strategies should naturally reflect our political, economic and security concerns, extending well beyond the geographical confines of South Asia". "Our security environment ranges from the Persian Gulf to the Straits of Malacca across the Indian Ocean, includes Central Asia and Afghanistan in the North West, China in the North East and South East Asia. Our strategic thinking has also to extend to these horizons".

Vulnerabilities and Challenges in IOR

Population Explosion and Bulging Youth Pressure: Indian Ocean Region is home to 39% of global population and bulging youth population. Resources are shrinking so is land to accommodate the population. This has resulted in relocation of masses from lesser opportune areas to those where economic survival is still possible. This is resulting in conflict between indigenous and relocated population. This scenario is fuelling insurgency and ethnic clashes. From Indonesia to West Asia the entire South Asia is finding it difficult to cope up with the conflict arising out of competing claims to secure resources and job opportunities. India which is still an island of peace and prosperity is facing insurgency and turbulence in North east India, the tribal belt of Central India and simmering problem of migrant population across the nation. Conflict arising out of the pressure of population has the potential of uncontrolled chaos.

Dominant Power Vacuum & Great Power Rivalries: There is a flux of power in the Indian Ocean Region; as a result there is conflict of interest between regional and extra regional powers. China advocates that Indian Ocean should be a "harmonious sea",[6] However, US has been more belligerent and hegemonic. India views it as a crisis situation in view of Chinese inroads in Indian Ocean region. Clash of strategic interests and aspirations for strategic autonomy has brought regional and global powers at a cross road with each other. Extra regional powers have exploited the power vacuum which has led to intervention in West Asia, Afghanistan and the Indian Ocean per se. There is a race for establishment of places and bases in IOR and the island territories. This scenario has polarised the entire region and smaller nations could be manipulated and exploited. This has brought non state actors and states in direct conflict with each other. Turbulence in Afghanistan, Iraq, North Africa including Sudan, Ethiopia & Eritrea, Somalia and the island nations is by product of this clash of interest. National and regional boundaries are becoming blurred and irrelevant as a result some of these nations are plunging in chaos and instability. Economic interests and strategic autonomy of the regional nations are waning and the overall situation is leading to high risk of conflict between states and state versus non- state actors.

Home to the Global Organised Crime and Terrorism: Indian Ocean rim nations have faced one of the highest incidences of transnational terrorism ranging from Jihad to narco terrorism. Al Qaeda and Islamic terror organisations have spread their foot prints from Turkey to Indonesia across the continental shelf and in the island nations. Somalia North African Nation is home to organised maritime crime and has foot prints of jihadi elements. Yemen has significant foot prints of Al Qaeda. Af-Pak region is in fact a Jihad factory. India is fighting Jihadi terror in J&K and across India. The presence of Huji and Al Qaeda is providing foot hold to Islamic terror organisations in Bangladesh and Indonesia. Irony is that non state actors have made national boundaries irrelevant. Nexus between terror organisations, drug warlords and criminals have become pronounced in the region and main source of funding to terror organisations is drug trafficking and arms smuggling. Golden triangle and Golden Crescent makes the region as one of the largest producer of narcotics. Global community must remember that the blowback phenomenon has returned to haunt the West, which supported jihadi and terrorism against the Soviets in Afghanistan.[7] Therefore, selective approach against terror will be catastrophic.

Global Population of Concerns 50% in IOR (Refugees and IDP): 50% of global population of concern lives in Indian Ocean Region. Displaced population is victim of interstate conflict, ethnic and cultural conflicts and natural disasters. Burden of rehabilitation and relief is on the regional countries with very little help from the international community. This population is most vulnerable to famine and disease at the same time a cannon fodder for terror organisations, which can be easily subverted and exploited.

Nations with Territorial and Maritime Dispute: Indian Ocean washes the shores of 37 Independent nations apart from the island territories still under the control of colonial rulers and US. Unresolved territorial disputes make this region vulnerable to conventional and sub-conventional conflicts between two states and state versus non-state actors. Territorial disputes between India- Pakistan and India- China have the potential of nuclear flashpoint. Similarly the desire to encroach upon the strategic space by US and China has raised the tension in the region. The biggest casualty of this competition is surrender of strategic space by the sovereign states in favour of their masters (in this case US or China).

Nuclearized and Militarized Zone: Most of the West Asian portion of the IOR has been characterised as "the global zone of percolating violence" and "is likely to be a major battlefield, both for wars among nation-states and state versus non-state actors, and protracted ethnic and religious violence"[8] The IOR is nuclearized and highly militarised zone with six nations having more than 400000 armed forces personals. According to a recent analysis of global conflicts by the Heidelberg Institute for International Conflict Research, altogether 42 per cent of world conflicts can be associated with Indian Ocean countries.[9]

Home to 8 Out of 20 Failed or Failing States: In the 21st century, geopolitically-constructed security threats have been ascribed by the West to the states in this region. Thus, "rogue states" and "failed states" have been portrayed by the West as being located outside the civilised world.[10] As per failed state index 2010, 8 out of 20 failed or failing states are in this region. Since these nations do not have complete control over their territories, thus non state actors, terror organisations, syndicates of organised crime and secessionist movement do get safe havens. As a result, these states create an atmosphere of insecurity and turbulence in the region and neighbourhood. North Africa, Af-Pak region, part of Myanmar and certain island nations are exploited by the state and non-state actors to unleash hybrid or irrational war against their adversaries. This phenomenon can destabilise the region which can give a licence to extra regional powers to interfere in the regional affairs.

Most Vulnerable to Climate Change: IOR will be worst affected by climate change. It is expected that if the global warming and environmental degradation continue at this rate, Maldives, Mauritius and 17% of Bangladesh is likely to be severely affected by the climate change. Some of the inhabited islands may be submerged and population will have to be relocated. India and other neighbouring nations are likely to face the problem of illegal migrants and perforce large population would be required to be accommodated if UN or international community do not take appropriate actions at this stage.

Home to "Component of Modern Instability": One of the main reasons for mass relocation of population, terrorism, secessionist movement and nations becoming failed or failing states is due to the existence of "component of modern instability" in IOR. Jerome Lauseig has described component of modern instability as poor governance, corruption, poverty, spread of disease, famine, drug trafficking, small arms proliferation and lack of development. South Asia is one of the worst affected regions within Asia. Irony is that it has the potential to cause turbulence in the entire Northern Indian Ocean region that may have serious implications on economic rise, governance, trade and internal security in rim nations.

Security Challenges to India: IOR is fragmented and completely polarised between US and China, and India- Pakistan and China. It is seriously impacting regional cooperation, maritime security and fight against terrorism. China is in the process of acquiring initially places which it would convert subsequently into maritime bases. So far China has only established trade related places in Myanmar, Bangladesh, Sri Lanka, Pakistan and Iran, however, some of these are likely to be developed as maritime bases and Gawadar port in Pakistan could be the first naval base of China in IOR followed by Marao in Maldives. Presence of Chinese naval fleet in close proximity to India has serious security implications for India. China has already stated that "Indian Ocean is not India's ocean" and that is a significant statement and indicative of China's intent to encroach upon the strategic space of India. India needs to take a decision to go alone or join a regional security construct since India, Australia and US share same security concern due to rising Chinese interests and forays in IOR. Options are limited and so is the time, a trilateral security architecture would allow the intensi?cation of defence ties among the three countries.[11] But the adverse impact is that India in that case will become front state of US, and that may erode India's strategic autonomy.

Maldives A Key for Maritime Security in IOR

Maldives is an island nation consisting of 1190 island out of which only 200 are inhabited. It has approximately 90,000 square kilometres territory with just about 300 square kilometre land mass. Maldives lie close to 6 and 9 degree channels which is considered busiest SLOC in the world.

Maldives has seen turbulence for quite some time now. Radicalisation and political instability has caused major turmoil which is detrimental to peace and stability in the region. Maldives is already on the radar of Al-Qaida and Islamic terror organisation, first terror attack on foreigners took place in Sep 2007 at Male where 12 foreigners were seriously injured. Maldives has 100% Muslim population and Wahhabi and Arabised Islam is finding its root in the island nation. As a result it is drifting away from India and becoming closer to Pakistan and China. There is a growing intolerance against other religion and some of the islands are now fully practicing Sharia and liberal Islam and Sufism is becoming extinct. Publically no religion other than Islam can be practiced in Maldives which is pushing it to be a radical Islamic nation.

Radicalisation of Maldives will have serious implications for India and Northern Indian Ocean Region. It will have impact on SLOCs and will give impetus to Islamic terror organisation. If not checked in time it can lead to proliferation of small arms to sustain subversive activities across the region including India. Presence of China and Pakistan just about 400 nautical miles away from Indian shore is a potential threat to India. India and regional allies can't afford an Afghanistan/Somalia in their backyard. Therefore, there is a need to work with natural allies such as Australia, Sri Lanka and US to keep Maldives isolated from China, Pakistan and non-state actors.

Maldives, Mauritius, Seychelles, Diego Garcia, Lakshadweep and Sri Lanka are strategically linked. These nations were favourably disposed towards India, however in the recent past there has been posturing and a tilt towards China and even Pakistan. 'China has engineered a coup by coaxing Maldives' Abdul Gayoom government to let it establish a base in Marao. Marao is one of the largest of the 1192 coral islands grouped into atolls that comprise Maldives and lies 40 km south of Male, the capital.[12] The biggest danger is that if India loses the control over these island nations, it will be near impossible to bring these island nations back to its fold. Therefore, India can no more neglect this significant turn of events.

Obligations and Responsibilities of India

India must assume leadership and be net security provider to the island neighbours in Indian Ocean Region. However, this is possible only if India without coercion towards regional countries, demonstrate through capabilities as a responsible and benevolent regional power. India needs to acquire capabilities to project power and that need not be military always, it could be economic, social, cultural and of course military. Military power projection should be aimed towards providing cooperative security as an umbrella against threats from non-traditional and non-state actors.

India must aim to build strategic partnership and cooperative security with the regional neighbours and extended neighbourhood. Isolation and big brother attitude may be counterproductive and thus, relationship should be built as equal partners for mutual benefits. India must develop the capability to maintain strategic partnership with a nation, irrespective of their internal politics and turbulence. Utopian and humanist stand in international diplomacy sans pragmatism. China has mastered the art of maintaining even quill relationship with its strategic partners and case in point is Pakistan. It has taken into account the larger national and geopolitical interests.

India needs to develop new set of responses in view of the changing nature of conflict and maritime threats from state and non- state actors. India should

Strategic Significance of Atolls and Island Nations in IOR

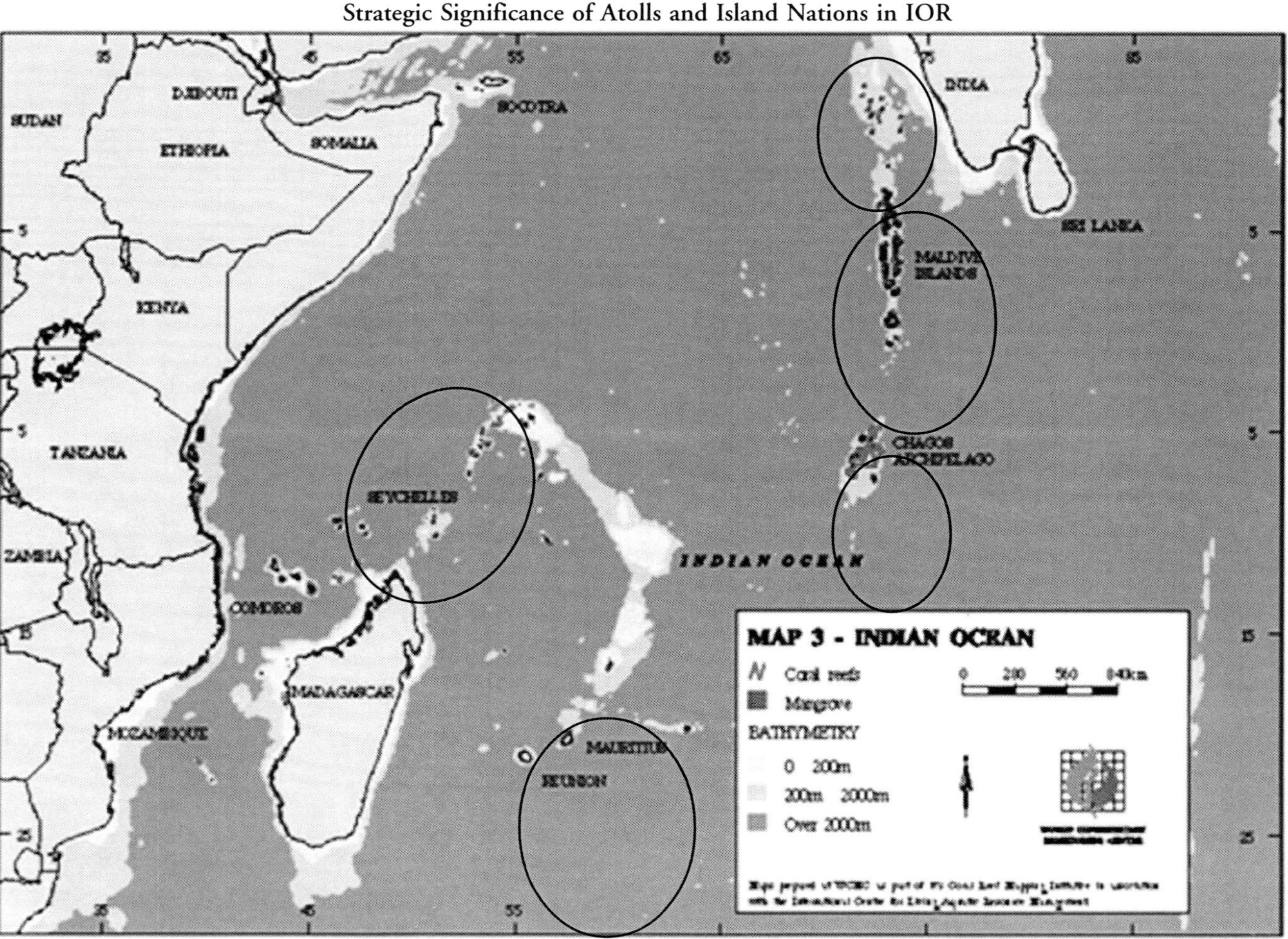

Source: www.ncdc.noaa.gov

be able to respond to the request of an island nation should there be any contingency due to internal or external threats. At the same time India should maintain its presence to prevent piracy and maritime violence in Northern Indian Ocean Region including Bay of Bengal and Arabian Sea. Regional and island nations may oppose or view it as a regional hegemony, but if put in correct perspective it would act as reassurance and confidence building measure for cooperative security.

Region is vulnerable to man made and natural disasters. Most of the rim countries are poor and neither have capabilities to prevent nor mitigate the disasters. India has huge responsibility to assist neighbours in the hour of need. This is one area where India can become a partner and guarantor to assist neighbouring countries.

Conclusion

"Those who disrespect the wealth of inheritance will find themselves homeless in their own backyard". India has an opportunity to assume leadership and be a net security provider to the regional partners. Maritime security challenges are multiplying and the options are shrinking. India has the opportunity to secure its strategic space, but this may be encroached upon if India does' not respond in time.

The challenge, today, is conventional and sub-conventional more so since the nature of conflict is changing fast. There is a danger that maritime shipping and container transhipment could be used by drug cartels, weapon traffickers, human traffickers and even the terror organisations to move men and material from hideouts to target nations. Some of the ships or fishing trawls floating in the high seas could be used to hide and protect the leadership and command elements of terror organisations cannot be ruled out. This calls for strict vigil and high sea policing and India can assume leadership in this field.

K.M. Pannikar, had stated: "The vital feature which differentiates the Indian Ocean from other oceans is the subcontinent of India, which juts out far into the sea for a thousand miles. It is the geographical position of India that changes the character of the Indian Ocean."[13] Sun Tzu had said, "Opportunities multiply as they are seized". If the opportunities are allowed to go past without having taken advantage, well, history will not forgive us for lack of strategic wisdom. In the light of the above fact, there is no alternative to capability building.

REFERENCES

1. A. Pandya, No Man's Sea: International Rules and Pragmatic Cooperation," in E. Laipson and A. Pandya (eds.) The Indian Ocean: Resource and Governance Challenges Washington DC: Henry Stimson Centre, 2009, p. 57.

2. S. Khurshid, J. Bishop, M. Natalegawa, Putting out to Sea a New Vision, *The Hindu*, November, 02, 2013.
3. N. Kumar, Challenges in Indian Ocean Region; Response Options, p 15.
4. V.L. Forbes, The Maritime Boundaries of the Indian Ocean Region, Chapter II- The Geographical and Political Setting, p.41.
5. S. Amjad, "Seabed Resources," in Maritime Threats and Opportunities in the 21st Century, Conference Proceedings Karachi: National Centre of Maritime Policy Research, Bahria University, 2007, pp. 42–45
6. C. Lou, Power Politics in the Indian Ocean: Don't Exaggerate the China Threat, East Asia Forum, October 24, 2013.
7. R. Thakur, Dismantling Terrorism's South Asian Front, CIGI, July, 28, 2008.
8. Z. Brezinski, The Grand Chessboard: American Primacy and its Geostrategic Imperatives, New York; Basic Books, 1997.
9. T.D. Potgieter, Maritime Security in the Indian Ocean: Strategic Setting and Features, Institute of Security Studies, Aug 2012, p.236.
10. D. Rumley, The Asia- Pacific Region and the New World Order, Ekistcs, Vol 70, No 422/ 423, 2003, pp 321-326.
11. R. Borah, India, Australia and the United States in the Indian Ocean Region: A Growing Strategic Convergence, Chapter-3, of Indian Ocean: A Sea of Uncertainty Future Directions International, p. 51.
12. Ibid., p 109.
13. A. D K Joshi, Maintaining Peace in the Indian Ocean Region, Asia Pacific Defence Forum, January, 01, 2014.

12

India's Nuclear Programme

Atul Mishra

Introduction

The general perception of India's political decision makers about their country's place in international politics in the immediate post independence era was that the emergence of a bipolar world where India wanted to play an independent role in international politics. Hence, Indian political leaders adopted the policy of non alignment to attain the foreign policy objective. The policy of non alignment also affected India's nuclear programme in at least two ways: Firstly, it protected India's nuclear programme from external interference. Earlier, India had vehemently opposed the idea of an international control of atomic minerals and nuclear plants (Baruch plan) proposed by the United States in the 1940s.[1] Besides this, India also opposed the idea of an international safeguards system on nuclear installations devised in the International Atomic Energy Agency (IAEA) in 1956. Secondly as noted above, India was able to extract technological assistance for its nuclear programme from both the east and the west by not aligning with either of the power blocs.

Perception of Indian Political Leaders

Indian leaders were sensitive about war and the use of force as a general problem in international relations. India had to fight a war with Pakistan at the beginning of independence in 1947-1948 and suffered a humiliating defeat in a border conflict with China in 1962. After the Sino Indian war and Nehru death, Shastri became Prime Minister. At this time, China conducted its first nuclear test on

16th Oct 1964. Indian Prime Minister Lal Bahadur Shastri quickly reacted by observing that "the Chinese blast has come to me and I think to the whole world as a shock and a danger to maintenance of peace".[2] On a radio broadcast three days later, Shastri indicated that India's nuclear policy would remain example of developing and testing nuclear bombs.

Notwithstanding Shastri's 'no policy change' stance, various political parties, the Indian media, many influential public opinion-makers and a majority of the Indian policy makers reacted sharply demanding the manufacturing of nuclear weapons for India. Jana Sangh spearheaded this demand by resolving at a working committee meeting on 9th Dec 1964 that it considers it imperative that an all out effort be made to build up an independent nuclear data set and urges the government of India to revise its stands accordingly.[3] "A majority within the Congress Party also favoured India's building of a nuclear arsenal in the aftermath of the Chinese nuclear test".

Giving reaction to Chinese nuclear test, the IAEA chairman Homi Bhabha claimed that Indian scientists could produce an atom bomb within eighteen months. This statement had been widely used by bomb advocates to build pressure on government. Anti bomb intellectuals in India argued that the economic cost of a weapons programme and its impacts on foreign policy and military implications would be unbearable for the country. Opponents pointed out that it would hamper economic and social development programmes, which should be the highest concern for the government. Opponents also claimed that building and maintaining a nuclear force would be an extra burden on the Indian economy since it was not a substitute for conventional defence. But the bomb advocates argued that national security should be give priority over other fiscal matters, Hence, the Indian government should not hesitate to build a nuclear arsenal.

Further, citing Homi Bhabha's estimate of an affordable figure to build an Indian nuclear arsenal, proponents estimated that a modest nuclear weapons programme could be accommodated within the government current level of expenditures. The Indian Institute of Defence Studies and Analyses conducted a study and concluded that "only an Indian nuclear arsenal could elevate India to position of equality with China.[4] It assured India that it would not be subject to nuclear blackmail and coercion by China. Therefore, it was clear that India must pursue a different course of action to counter the looming nuclear security dilemma emanating from China's possession of nuclear weapons.

A year later, in 1965 India and Pakistan fought a war which resulted in a cease fire agreement. For India the most disturbing aspect of this conflict was Beijing's diplomatic support to Islamabad and its threats to open a second front along India's Himalayan border. On 8th September 1965, China sent an open diplomatic note to India threatening grave consequences if India proceeded with military action against Pakistan. The Chinese army also increased aggressive troop movements along border areas raising the spectre of the PRC's military intervention. This Chinese move persuaded many Indian's, including bureaucrats and politicians, to conclude that that an independent Indian nuclear capability was the only means to prevent future Chinese nuclear blackmail and intimidation.

Indira Gandhi succeeded Prime Minister Shastri after his death. Upon assuming power, Mrs Gandhi clearly said that India would not make nuclear weapons. She even shelved her predecessor's sub-terranean Nuclear Explosive Project (SNEP). But her initial policy stance soon modified in view of strategic development. The first such development was Chinese test of a thermo nuclear weapon on May 9th 1966. In reaction to this, the Prime Minister announced in Lok Sabha that in addition to peaceful uses of atomic power, India would increase nuclear technological knowledge and other competence. It also indicated that she would pursue Shastri's policy of developing nuclear explosive technology.

In 1970 IAEC chairman Vikram Srabhai announced two important decisions that had far reaching implications for India's nuclear policy. The first was that India could not produce nuclear weapons but would retain the option of conducting underground nuclear explosions for peaceful purposes. The second decision concerned was the adoption of a ten year nuclear and space programme by the Indian government. India and Pakistan fought third war in 1971. The presence of the US enterprise in the Bay of Bengal during the war fueld Indian sensitivity of nuclear intimidation and created a feeling that even superpower could pose a nuclear threat to India. This war, therefore, prompted India to purse a more aggressive defence's annual budget. Defence Minister Jagjivan Ram informed the parliaments that "the atomic energy commission is studying the technology for conducting underground explosions for peaceful purposes".[5] Eventually, the explosion took place on 18th May 1974.

The Programme: The origin of India's nuclear programme, in fact, preceded its national independence. In March 1944 India physicist Homi Jahangir Bhabha started a nuclear research programme. His proposal to the Dorabji Tata trust to set up an institute to train nuclear scientists which paved the way to the establishment of Tata Institute of Fundamental Research (TIFR) in 1945. The primary objectives of the TIFR were to conduct fundamental research in theoretical and applied physics and to train scientists for the development of nuclear energy in India.

In order to focus attention on nuclear issues, one cannot ignore the contribution made by Homi J. Bhabha, Jawaharlal Nehru and VK Krishna Menon. Homi Jehangir Bhabha was undoubtedly the father of Indian nuclear research and the architect of India's nuclear strategy and diplomacy. In the 1930's, Bhabha studied with the eminent nuclear scientist Lord Ernest Rutherford. He also associated himself with other great experts in the field like Niels Bohr, James Franck, Erico Fermi and WB Lewis. On his return to India, Bhabha convinced the Tatas to finance the establishment of a centre for research to study nuclear physics. Thus, India's nuclear programme predates the dawn of independence. The Tata Institute of Fundamental Research (TIFR) was established in Bombay on 19 December 1945, four months after Hiroshima and months before India became independent Bhabha was already in command of India's nuclear future.

As a scientist, familiar with *realpolitik,* Bhabha was convinced that India's voice will be heard in international gatherings only if India became powerful and had nuclear weapons. Bhabha told Raja Ramanna, "We must have the capability. We should first prove ourselves and then talk of (Mahatma) Gandhi, non-violence and a world without nuclear weapons".[6]

Cooperation between Nehru and Bhabha on the scientific and nuclear field had also begun before independence. In 1946, they collaborated to set up the Atomic Energy Research Committee (AERC) to promote research in nuclear physics at Indian colleges and universities. On August 15th 1948, India passed the Atomic Energy Act (AEA) and established the Indian Atomic Energy Commission to begin work directly related to the exploitation of nuclear energy. The Atomic Energy Act provided that all research and development in the nuclear field would be conducted in secret and all uranium and thorium reserves would be placed under state control. The Chairman of Indian Atomic Energy Commission (IAEC) was responsible only to the Prime Minister. Indian Atomic Energy Commission set up the Rare Minerals Survey Unit in 1950 under Wadia. Wadia was responsible for locating the uranium deposits in Jaduguda, in 1952 and in Narwapahar in 1963.[7] In 1952 Indian Atomic Energy Commission established the Indian Rare Earths Limited (IREL). In January 1954, the Indian Atomic Energy Commission was created with Bhabha as its head responsible to the Prime Minister. All the scientists working related to nuclear power were transferred to Trombay.

During the early years of independence, India pursued what Nehru called "a peaceful nuclear programme" but Homi Bhabha, thought differently. Prof. Sumit Ganguly refers to a conversation between Homi Bhabha and the British Physicist Lord PMS Blackett about his interest in acquiring nuclear weapons.[8] In a paper delivered in the 12th Pugwash Conference in January-February 1964, Bhabha elaborated his views as follows: "Nuclear weapons coupled with an adequate delivery system can enable a state to destroy more or less totally the cities, industry and all important targets in another state. It is then largely irrelevant whether the state so attacked has greater destructive power at its command. With the help of nuclear weapons, therefore, a state can acquire what we may call a position of absolute deterrence even against another having a many times greater destructive power under its control".[9]

Following Eisenhower's 'Atom for Peace' initiative from 1954, the US Great Britain and several other major western nations liberalized earlier restrictions on nuclear technology transfer. Utilizing this favourable environment, Bhabha signed an agreement with the United Kingdom Atomic Authority in 1954, which provided India enriched uranium fuel element for building a swimming pool type reactor. Despite early cooperation with France and Great Britain, it was an assistance from Canada and the US that decisively contributed to the building of an Indian nuclear infrastructure.

In November 1954, Bhabha had informally asked Canada's atomic energy representatives for assistance in constructing a power reactor. The Canadian representatives agreed in principle to provide India with a research rector.[10] On 28th April 1956, the Canadian government signed an agreement with the Indian Government to supply a 40 megawatt thermal output reactor designed for research and isotope production. The Canadian India Reactor (CIR) was renamed CIRUS with the participation of the US in the project. Washington agreed to supply 21 tons of heavy water to be used in the reactor but former Rear Admiral Raja Menon said that "US supplied 20 tons of heavy water. Putting a side whatever the case was thc CIRUS went critical in 1960".[11]

However India's first real breakthrough was ASPARA (Water nymph) an indigenously built one megawatt thermal moderated and cooled swimming pool type research reactor. This reactor went critical on August 4th 1956.[12] It was the first nuclear reactor to be constructed not only in India but also in the whole of Asia outside the former Soviet Union. In 1958, India permitted Homi Sethna to start a chemical separation plant to separate plutonium. The project was called phoenix. It was to reprocess the 20 tons of fuel processed by CIRRUS to produce about 10 kg of plutonium a year.

Another indigenously designed and constructed research reactor ZERLINA (zero energy reactors for Lattice investigations and New Assemblies) was commissioned on January 14, 1961. Like APSARA, ZERLLINA also gave a technological boost and a confidence to Indian science to undertake larger reactor project.

On August, 8th 1963, India and US signed an agreement to establish the Tarapur Atomic Power Station (TAPS). Its construction started in 1964 and was completed in 1975. It had a production capacity of 125 tons of plutonium per year. In April 1964 New Delhi signed an agreement with Canada for building the heavy water moderated CANDU (Canada Deuterium Uranium) power reactor RAPS 1 in Rajasthan. The agreement provided that in addition to a financial loan of US$ 37 million by the Canadian Government Indian engineers would use technology and design assistance provided by the Atomic Energy of Canada Ltd to run the reactor. Furthermore, Canada agrees to supply half of the uranium fuel elements for the initial loading and subsequent fuel as requested in case India failed to produce it indigenously. Additionally, Canada agreed to share nuclear reactor related information and technology, such as blue prints.

Three factors were behind this American and Canadian willingness. First, the US atom for peace initiative, second, the commercial motives and third, despite substantial ambiguities in its nuclear activities India was able to convince these two countries that its atomic programme was intended to use nuclear energy only for peaceful purposes. It achieved this by accepting external safeguards on some of its nuclear facilities. For example, India accepted American safeguards on the Tarapur Reactor Project in 1963 and Canadian safeguards on the Rajasthan Atomic Power project (RAPP) I AND II in 1963 and 1968 respectively RAPP II was later converted into a tripartite safeguard agreement involving India, Canada and the International Atomic Energy Agency.

In 1967 Sethna sanctioned Purnima-I a reactor with higher neutron fluxes. Purnima was the school that led to both Pokharan-1 and the research reactor Dhruv. Purnima was followed by Purnima II, III and Kamini, all of which were made to explore the thorium route more scientifically. The Indian Nuclear Programme can be seen from the chart given below.

Reactor	*State*	*Type*	*MWe net, each*	*Commercial Operation*	*Safeguards status*
Tarapur 1 & 2	Maharashtra	BWR	150	1969	item-specific
Kaiga 1 & 2	Karnataka	PHWR	202	1999-2000	
Kaiga 3	Karnataka	PHWR	202	2007	
Kakrapar 1 & 2	Gujarat	PHWR	202	1993-95	in 2012 under new agreement
Kalpakkam 1 & 2 (MAPS)		Tamil Nadu	PHWR	202	1984-86
Narora 1 & 2	Uttar Pradesh	PHWR	202	1991-92	in 2014 under new agreement
Rajasthan 1	Rajasthan	PHWR	90	1973	item-specific
Rajasthan 2	Rajasthan	PHWR	187	1981	item-specific
Rajasthan 3 & 4	Rajasthan	PHWR	202	1999-2000	early 2010 under new agreement
Rajasthan 5 & 6	Rajasthan	PHWR	202	Feb & April 2010	Oct 2009 under new agreement
Tarapur 3 & 4	Maharashtra	PHWR	490	2006, 05	

To all these peaceful nuclear activities the biggest blow came from the nuclear explosion in 1974. The test seemed to defy the atom for peace premises at the heart of early U.S. and Canadian peaceful nuclear cooperation with India. Canadian tried for two years to persuade India to accept traditional non proliferation constraints and having failed broke off all nuclear cooperation. Although the USA did not end its Tarapur contractual relationship with India for the supply of low enriched uranium but voted against IDA aid to India. In August 1974, the London nuclear suppliers club made a trigger list drawn up by the Zangger Committee, consisting of certain items the import\ export of which would trigger IAEA safeguards.[13] In late 1960s India had decided to standardize its planned construction of a large number of indigenous power plants on the CANDU, PHWR design but it was found that implementing this plant after 1974 without continued Canadian technical support was both more expensive and technically difficult than expected. The sanction seemed to have spurred nuclear scientists who in late 1975, started work on DHRUVA. The significance of this cannot be understated not because work on DHRUVA began but starting work on a large research reactor in 1975 at the height of sanctions speaks for the determination of the scientists who took these decisions.[14]

India's nuclear technological capability substantially increased when the Dhruva nuclear reactor was commissioned in 1985. The Indian Atomic Energy Commission announced on 8th August that this reactor had gone critical and would become operational in November 1985.[15]

In the early 1990s, however, Indian discussions with Russia resumed on a tentative agreement dating back to 1987 in which the Soviet Union was prepared to sell India two light water reactors. The original Indian deal with the Soviet Union was to purchase two 440 Mwe VVERs but the revised deal calls for Russia to provide two 1,000 MWe VVERs on the turnkey basis. Russia intended that these reactors should come under IAEA safeguards safe guards to complete this deal.[16]

The Indian Atomic Commission (IAEA) began its breeder reactor programme with the pilot scale (15 mwe) Fast Breeder Test Reactor (FBTR) based on French cooperation and commissioned at Kalpakkam in South Indian in 1987. In early 1997 Raja Gopal Chidambaram Chairman in India's Atomic Energy Commission (IAEC) made an announcement of that the 500 Mwt prototype Fast Breeder Reactor (PFBR) He said that the PFBR would be used to breed plutonium not to burn it up.

The capacity of India's two uranium enrichment facilities one at the Tromboy (BARC) complex and the other at Rattehalli, near Mysore in Karnataka State have not been disclosed. However, these plants are presumed to be pilot rather than commercial in scale.[17] The semi commercial scale reprocessing plant at Kalpakkam India's third plutonium separation facility was completed rated with a capacity of 125 metric tons heavy metal (MTHM) per year. The Kalpakkam plant is to separate plutonium for India's PFBR as well as for the future commercial scale fast breeder reactor. The most recent reports indicate that the Kalpakkam plant became operational in 2008.

Indian Nuclear Power Industry Development: Nuclear power for civil use is well established in India. Its civil nuclear strategy has been directed towards complete independence in the nuclear fuel cycle, necessary because it is excluded from the 1970 Nuclear Non-Proliferation Treaty (NPT) due to it acquiring nuclear weapons capability after 1970. (Those five countries doing so before 1970 were accorded the status of Nuclear Weapons States under the NPT)

As a result, India's nuclear power programme has proceeded largely without fuel or technological assistance from other countries. Its power reactors to the mid 1990s had some of the world's lowest capacity factors, reflecting the technical difficulties of the country's isolation, but rose impressively from 60% in 1995 to 85% in 2001-02. Then in 2008-10 the load factors dropped due to shortage of uranium fuel.

India's nuclear energy self-sufficiency extended from uranium exploration and mining through fuel fabrication, heavy water production, reactor design and construction, to reprocessing and waste management. It has a small fast breeder reactor and is building a much larger one. It is also developing technology to utilize its abundant resources of thorium as a nuclear fuel.

The Nuclear Power Corporation of India Ltd (NPCIL) is responsible for design, construction, commissioning and operation of thermal nuclear power plants. At the start of 2010, it is said that it had enough cash on hand for 10,000 MWe of new plant. Its funding model is 70% equity and 30% debt financing. However, it is aimed to include other public sector and private corporations for nuclear power expansion, notably National Thermal Power Corporation (NTPC). NTPC is largely government-owned, and the 1962 Atomic Energy Act prohibits private control of nuclear power generation, though it allows minority investment. As of late 2010 the government had no intention of changing this to allow greater private equity in nuclear plants. Dates are for start of commercial operation.[18]

The two Tarapur 150 MWe Boiling Water Reactors (BWRs) built by GE on a turnkey contract before the advent of the Nuclear Non-Proliferation Treaty were originally 200 MWe. They were down-rated due to recurrent problems but have run well since. They have been using imported enriched uranium and are under International Atomic Energy Agency (IAEA) safeguards. However, late in 2004 Russia deferred to the Nuclear Suppliers' Group and declined to supply further uranium for them. They underwent six months refurbishment over 2005-06, and in March 2006 Russia agreed to resume fuel supply. In December 2008, a $700 million contract with Rosatom was announced for continued uranium supply to them.

The two small Canadian (Candu) PHWRs at Rajasthan nuclear power plant started up in 1972 & 1980, and are also under safeguards. Rajasthan-1 was down-rated early in its life and has operated very little since 2002 due to ongoing problems and has been shut down since 2004 as the government considers its future. Rajasthan-2 was restarted in September 2009 after major refurbishment, and running on imported uranium at full rated power.

The 220 MWe PHWRs (202 MWe net) were indigenously designed and constructed by NPCIL, based on a Canadian design. The Kalpakkam (MAPS) reactors were refurbished in 2002-03 and 2004-05 and their capacity restored to 220 MWe gross (from 170). Much of the core of each reactor was replaced, and the lifespans extended to 2033/36. Kakrapar unit 1 was repaired and upgraded in 2009, as was Narora-2.

More Recent Nuclear Power Developments in India

The new Tarapur 3&4 reactors of 540 MWe gross (490 MWe net) are developed indigenously from the 220 MWe (gross) model PHWR and were built by NPCIL.

The first—Tarapur 4 which started up in March 2005 was connected to the grid in June and began commercial operation in September. Tarapur-4's criticality came five years after pouring first concrete and seven months ahead of schedule. Its twin—unit 3—was about a year behind it and criticality was achieved in May 2006, with grid connection in June and commercial operation in August, five months ahead of schedule.

Future indigenous PHWR reactors will be 700 MWe gross (640 MWe net). The first four will be built at Kakrapar and Rajasthan. According to NPCIL in March 2010, work on all four has started and they are due on line by 2017 after 60 months construction from first concrete to criticality.

Russia's Atomstroyexport is building the country's first large nuclear power plant, comprising two VVER-1000 (V-392) reactors, under a Russian-financed US$ 3 billion contract. A long-term credit facility covers about half the cost of the plant. The AES-92 units at Kudankulam in Tamil Nadu state are being built by NPCIL and will be commissioned and operated by NPCIL under IAEA safeguards. The turbines are made by Leningrad Metal Works. Unlike other Atomstroyexport projects such as in Iran, there have been only about 80 Russian supervisory staff on the job.

Russia is supplying all the enriched fuel, though India will reprocess it and keep the plutonium. The first unit was to start supplying power in March 2008. It went into commercial operation late in 2008, but it took more time. The second unit is about 6-8 months behind it. While the first core load of fuel was delivered early in 2008 there have been delays in supply of some equipment and documentation. Control system documentation was delivered late, and when reviewed by NPCIL it showed up the need for significant refining and even reworking some aspects. Fuel loading of unit 1 will not now take place until late 2010, though in October 2009 NPCIL said the unit was 94% complete and that 99% of the equipment was on site.

Under plans for the India-specific safeguards to be administered by the IAEA in relation to the civil-military separation plan, eight further reactors will be safeguarded (beyond Tarapur 1&2, Rajasthan 1&2, and Kudankulam 1&2): Rajasthan 3&4 by 2010, Rajasthan 5&6 by 2008, Kakrapar 1&2 by 2012 and Narora 1&2 by 2014.

Kaiga 3 started up in February, was connected to the grid in April and went into commercial operation in May 2007. Unit 4 was scheduled about six months behind it, but is about 30 months behind original schedule due to shortage of uranium—it is not safeguarded so cannot use imported uranium. RAPP-5 started up in November 2009, using imported Russian fuel, and in December it was connected to the northern grid. RAPP-6 started up in January 2010 and was grid connected at the end of March. Both are now in commercial operation.

A 500 MWe prototype **fast breeder reactor** (FBR) is under construction at Kalpakkam by BHAVINI (Bharatiya Nabhikiya Vidyut Nigam Ltd), a government enterprise set up under DAE to focus on FBRs. It was expected to start up about the end of 2010 and produce power in 2011, but this schedule appears to be delayed about 12-15 months. Four further oxide-fuel fast reactors are envisaged but slightly redesigned by the Indira Gandhi Centre to reduce capital cost. One pair will be at Kalpakkam, two more elsewhere.

India's Nuclear Power Reactors Under Construction

Reactor	*Type*	*MWe net, each*	*Project control*	*Commercial Operation due*	*Safeguards Status*
Kaiga 4	PHWR	202 MWe	NPCIL	5/2010	
Kudankulam 1	PWR (VVER)	950 MWe	NPCIL	12/2010	item-specific
Kudankulam 2	PWR (VVER)	950 MWe	NPCIL	mid 2011	item-specific
Kalpakkam PFBR	FBR	470 MWe	Bhavini	9/2011, or 2012	
Total (4)		2572 MWe			

Nuclear Industry Developments in India Beyond the Trade Restrictions

Following the Nuclear Suppliers' Group agreement which was achieved in September 2008, the scope for supply of both reactors and fuel from suppliers in other countries opened up. Civil nuclear cooperation agreements have been signed with the USA, Russia, France, UK and Canada, as well as Argentina, Kazakhstan, Mongolia and Namibia.

India is now focusing on capacity addition through indigenisation" with progressively higher local content for imported designs, up to 80%. Looking further ahead its augmentation plan included construction of 25-30 light water reactors of at least 1000 MWe by 2030. The AEC has said that India now has "a significant technological capability in PWRs and NPCIL has worked out an Indian PWR design" which will be unveiled soon—perhaps 2010.

Other Indigenous Arrangements

The 87% state-owned National Aluminium Company (Nalco) has signed an agreement with NPCIL relevant to its hopes of building a 1000 MWe nuclear power plant on the east coast in Orissa's Ganjam district. It already has its own 1200 MWe coal-fired power plant in the state at Angul to serve its refinery and smelter of 345,000 tpa, being expanded to 460,000 tpa (requiring about 1 GWe of constant supply). A more specific agreement is expected in 2010.

India's national oil company, Indian Oil Corporation Ltd (IOC), in November 2009 joined with NPCIL in a memorandum of understanding "for partnership in setting up nuclear power plants in India." The initial plant envisaged is at least 1000 MWe, and NPCIL will be the operator and at least 51% owner. IOC will take a 26% stake in it. The cash-rich Oil and Natural Gas Corporation (ONGC) is having talks with AEC about becoming a minority partner with NPCIL on 700 MWe PHWR projects.

Indian Railways have also approached NPCIL to set up a joint venture to build two 500 MWe PHWR nuclear plants on railway land for their own power requirements. The Railways already have a joint venture with NTPC—Bhartiya Rail Bijlee Company—to build a 1000 MWe coal-fired power plant at Nabinagar in Aurangabad district of Bihar, with the 250 MWe units coming on line 2012-13. The Railways also plans to set up another 1320 MWe power plant at Adra in Purulia district of West Bengal for traction supply at economical tariff.

The government has announced that it intends to amend the law to allow private companies to be involved in nuclear power generation and possibly other aspects of the fuel cycle, but without direct foreign investment. In anticipation of this, Reliance Power Ltd, GVK Power & Infrastructure Ltd and GMR Energy Ltd are reported to be in discussion with overseas nuclear vendors including Areva, GE-Hitachi, Westinghouse and Atomstroyexport.

NTPC is reported to be establishing a joint venture with NPCIL and BHEL to sell India's largely indigenous 220 MWe heavy water power reactor units abroad, possibly in contra deals involving uranium supply from countries such as Namibia and Mongolia.

In September 2009 the AEC announced a version of its planned Advanced Heavy Water Reactor (AHWR) designed for export.

In August and September 2009 the AEC reaffirmed its commitment to the thorium fuel cycle, particularly thorium-based FBRs, to make the country a technological leader.

Uranium Resources in India

India's uranium resources are modest, with 54,000 tonnes U as reasonably assured resources and 23,500 tonnes as estimated additional resources in situ. Accordingly, from 2009 India is expecting to import an increasing proportion of its uranium fuel needs.

Mining and processing of uranium is carried out by Uranium Corporation of India Ltd, a subsidiary of the Department of Atomic Energy (DAE), at Jaduguda and Bhatin (since 1967), Narwapahar (since 1995) and Turamdih (since 2002)—all in Jharkhand. All are underground, the last two being modern. A common mill is located near Jaduguda, and processes 2090 tonnes per day of ore.

In 2005 and 2006 plans were announced to invest almost US$ 700 million to open further mines in Jharkand at Banduhurang, Bagjata and Mohuldih; in Meghalaya at Domiasiat-Mawthabah (with a mill) and in Andhra Pradesh at Lambapur-Peddagattu (with mill 50km away at Seripally), both in Nalgonda district.

In Jharkand, Banduhurang is India's first open cut mine and was commissioned in 2007. Bagjata is underground and was opened in December 2008, though there had been earlier small operations 1986-91. The Mohuldih underground mine is expected to operate from 2010. A new mill at Turamdih in Jharkhand, with 3000 t/day capacity, was commissioned in 2008.

In Andhra Pradesh there are three kinds of uranium mineralisation in the Cuddapah Basin, including unconformity-related deposits in the north of it. The northern Lambapur-Peddagattu project in Nalgonda district 110 km southeast of Hyderabad has environmental clearance for one open cut and three small underground mines (based on some 6000 tU resources at about 0.1%U) but faces local opposition. In August 2007 the government approved a new US$ 270 million underground mine and mill at Tummalapalle near Pulivendula in Kadapa district, at the south end of the Basin and 300 km south of Hyderabad, for commissioning in 2010. Its resources have been revised upwards to 40,000 tU and first production is expected early in 2011, using alkaline leaching for the first time in India. A further northern deposit near Lambapur-Peddagattu is Koppunuru, in Guntur district.

In Meghalaya, close to the Bangladesh border in the West Khasi Hills, the Domiasiat-Mawthabah mine project (near Nongbah-Jynrin) is in a high rainfall area and has also faced longstanding local opposition partly related to land acquisition issues but also fanned by a campaign of fearmongering. For this reason, and despite clear state government support in principle, UCIL does not yet have approval from the state government for the open cut mine at Kylleng-Pyndeng-Shahiong (also known as Kylleng-Pyndengshohiong-Mawthabah and formerly as Domiasiat) though pre-project development has been authorised on 422 ha. However, federal environmental approval in December 2007 for a proposed uranium mine and processing plant here and for the Nongstin mine has been reported. There is sometimes violent opposition by NGOs to uranium mine development in the West Khasi Hills, including at Domiasiat and Wakhyn, which have estimated resources of 9500 tU and 4000 tU respectively. Tyrnai is a smaller deposit in the area. The status and geography of all these is not known.

In Karnataka, UCIL is planning a small uranium mine at Gogi in Gulbarga area from about 2012, after undertaking a feasibility study. A mill is planned for Diggi nearby. Total cost is about $122 million. Resources are sufficient for 15 years mine life, but UCIL plans also to utilise the uranium deposits in the Bhima belt from Sedam in Gulbarga to Muddebihal in Bijapur. India's existing uranium mines and mills are mentioned as below:

State, district	*Mine*	*Mill*	*Operating from*	*tU per year*
Jharkhand	Jaduguda	Jaduguda	1967 (mine) 1968 (mill)	175 total from mill
	Bhatin	Jaduguda	1967	
	Narwapahar	Jaduguda	1995	
	Bagjata	Jaduguda	2009?	
Jharkhand, East Singhbum dist.	Turamdih	Turamdih	2003 (mine) 2008 (mill)	190 total from mill
	Banduhurang	Turamdih	2007	
	Mohuldih	Turamdih	2011	
Meghalaya	Kylleng-Pyndeng-Shahiong (Domiasiat), Mawthabah, Wakhyn	Mawthabah	2012, maybe 2010	340
Meghalaya	Kylleng-Pyndeng-Shahiong (Domiasiat), Mawthabah, Wakhyn	Mawthabah	2012, maybe 2010	340
Andhra Pradesh, Kadapa dist.	Tummalapalle	Tummalapalle	2011	220
Karnataka, Gulbarga dist.	Gogi	Diggi	2012?	

Uranium Fuel Cycle

DAE's Nuclear Fuel Complex at Hyderabad undertakes **refining and conversion** of uranium, which is received as magnesium diuranate (yellowcake). The main 400 t/yr plant fabricates PHWR fuel (which is unenriched). A small (25 t/yr) fabrication plant makes fuel for the Tarapur BWRs from imported enriched (2.66% U-235) uranium. Depleted uranium oxide fuel pellets (from reprocessed uranium) and thorium oxide pellets are also made for PHWR fuel bundles. Mixed carbide fuel for FBTR was first fabricated by Bhabha Atomic Research Centre (BARC) in 1979. Heavy water is supplied by DAE's Heavy Water Board, and the seven plants are working at capacity due to the current building program.

Fuel fabrication is by the Nuclear Fuel Complex in Hyderabad, which is setting up a new 500 t/yr PHWR fuel plant at Rawatbhata in Rajasthan, to serve the larger new reactors. Each 700 MWe reactor is said to need 125 t/yr of fuel. The company is proposing joint ventures with US, French and Russian companies to produce fuel for those reactors.

Reprocessing: Used fuel from the civil PHWRs is reprocessed by Bhabha Atomic Research Centre (BARC) at Trombay, Tarapur and Kalpakkam to extract reactor-grade plutonium for use in the fast breeder reactors. Small plants at each site were supplemented by a new Kalpakkam plant of some 100 t/yr commissioned in 1998, and this is being extended to reprocess FBTR carbide fuel. Apart from this, all reprocessing uses the Purex process. Further capacity is being built at Tarapur and Kalpakkam, to come on line by about 2010. India will reprocess the used fuel from the Kudankulam reactors and will keep the plutonium. In 2003, a facility was commissioned at Kalpakkam to reprocess mixed carbide fuel using an advanced Purex process. Future FBRs will also have these facilities co-located.

In April 2010, it was announced that 18 months of negotiations with the USA had resulted in agreement to build two new reprocessing plants to be under IAEA safeguards, likely located near Kalpakkam and near Mumbai—possibly Trombay. In July 2010, an agreement was signed with the USA to allow reprocessing of US-origin fuel at one of these facilities. Later in 2010, the AEC said that India has commenced engineering activities for setting up of an Integrated Nuclear Recycle Plant with facilities for both reprocessing of spent fuel and waste management. Under plans for the India-specific safeguards to be administered by the IAEA in relation to the civil-military separation plan several fuel fabrication facilities will come under safeguards.

Thorium Fuel Cycle Development in India

The long-term goal of India's nuclear programme has been to develop an advanced heavy-water cycle. The first stage of this employs the PHWRs fuelled by natural uranium, and light water reactors to produce plutonium.

Stage 2 uses fast neutron reactors burning the plutonium to breed U-233 from thorium. The blanket around the core will have uranium as well as thorium, so that further plutonium (ideally high-fissile Pu) is produced as well as the U-233.

Then in stage 3, Advanced Heavy Water Reactors (AHWRs) burn the U-233 from stage 2 and this plutonium with thorium, getting about two thirds of their power from the thorium.

In 2002 the regulatory authority issued approval to start construction of a 500 MWe prototype fast breeder reactor at Kalpakkam and this is now under construction by BHAVINI. The unit was expected to be operating in 2011, fuelled with uranium-plutonium oxide (the reactor-grade Pu being from its existing PHWRs). It will have a blanket with thorium and uranium to breed fissile U-233 and plutonium respectively. This will take India's ambitious thorium program to stage 2, and set the scene for eventual full utilisation of the country's abundant thorium to fuel reactors. Six more such 500 MWe fast reactors have been announced for construction, four of them by 2020.

So far about one tonne of thorium oxide fuel has been irradiated experimentally in PHWR reactors and has reprocessed and some of this has been reprocessed, according to BARC. A reprocessing centre for thorium fuels is being set up at Kalpakkam.

Design is largely complete for the first 300 MWe AHWR, intended to be built in the 11th plan period to 2012, though no site has yet been announced. It will have vertical pressure tubes in which the light water coolant under high pressure will boil, circulation being by convection. A large heat sink—"Gravity-driven water pool"—with 7000 cubic metres of water is near the top of the reactor building. In April 2008, an AHWR critical facility was commissioned at BARC "to conduct a wide range of experiments, to help validate the reactor physics of the AHWR through computer codes and in generating nuclear data about materials, such as thorium-uranium 233 based fuel, which have not been extensively used in the past." It has all the components of the AHWR's core including fuel and moderator, and can be operated in different modes with various kinds of fuel in different configurations.

In 2009, the AEC announced some features of the 300 MWe AHWR: It is mainly a thorium-fuelled reactor with several advanced passive safety features to enable meeting next generation safety requirements such as three days grace period for operator response, elimination of the need for exclusion zone beyond the plant boundary, 100-year design life, and high level of fault tolerance. The advanced safety characteristics have been verified in a series of experiments carried out in full-scale test facilities. Also, per unit of energy produced, the amount of long-lived minor actinides generated is nearly half of that produced in current generation Light Water Reactors. Importantly, a high level of radioactivity in the fissile and fertile materials recovered from the used fuel of AHWR, and their isotopic composition, preclude the use of these materials for nuclear weapons.

At the same time, the AEC announced an LEU version of the AHWR. This will use low-enriched uranium plus thorium as a fuel, dispensing with the plutonium input. About 39% of the power will come from thorium (via in situ conversion to U-233, cf two thirds in AHWR), and burn-up will be 64 GWd/t. Uranium enrichment level will be 19.75%, giving 4.21% average fissile content of the U-Th fuel. While designed for closed fuel cycle, this is not required. Plutonium production will be less than in light water reactors, and the fissile proportion will be less and the Pu-238 portion three times as high, giving inherent proliferation resistance. The design is intended for overseas sales, and the AEC says that "the reactor is manageable with modest industrial infrastructure within the reach of developing countries".

Conclusion

The journey that India took in the development of nuclear weapons have been a long and tedious one. India's nuclear programme is related to her security compulsion. Here, we have moved from idealism to realism in the conduct of foreign policy. India's nuclear policy and programme have taken its own time. This is not going to change in near future, inspite of international pressures to change or modify its nuclear policy. Over the next decade, it is expected that India will gradually increase the size of its arsenal, particularly ICBM and submarines capable of firing long range ballistic missiles. All these developments indicate that India's nuclear programme is security oriented and not prestige or status driven as we see in Pakistan's case.

REFERENCES

1. The Indian reaction of the Baruch plan, see the statement of India's ambassador to United Nations in UN General Assembly official records, 3rd Session, 156th Planning Meeting, 04 Nov 1998, pp. 422-424.
2. *The Hindustan Times*, 17 Oct. 1964.
3. B. Chakma, 'Strategic Dynamics and Nuclear Weapons Proliferation in South Asia: A Historical Analysis' European Academics Publisher Bern, 2004, p. 60.
4. Institute of Defence Studies and Analyses, 'A Strategy for India for A Credible Posture Against A Nuclear Adversary', New Delhi, 1968, p. 4.
5. B. Chakma, 'Strategic Dynamics and Nuclear Weapons Proliferation in South Asia: A Historical Analysis' European Academics Publisher Bern, 2004 p. 74.
6. For further details refer K Subrahmanyam, "Nehru and India China Conflict of 1962", B.R. Nanda (Ed.), Indian Foreign Policy: The Nehru Years (New Delhi, 1976), p. 113.
7. Short biography of D.N. Wadia, Atomic Energy in India (Govt. of India, DAF 1998), p. 238.
8. Quoted in Major David J Creasman, the Evolution of India's Nuclear Program: Implications for the United States (Fort Leavenworth, Kansas, 2008), p. 17.
9. R.S. Anderson and Baric M. Morrison Power from Power A new Scenario Emerges for India's Scientists Science Form, December 1974, p. 11.
10. R. Admiral Menon Raja, A Nuclear Strategy for India, Sage Publications, New Delhi, 2000, p. 72.
11. Economic Research Division BIRLA institute of Scientific Research India and the Atom New Delhi Allied Publisher PVT Ltd, 1982, p. 61
12. R.W. Jones & Mark G. McDonough with Toby F. Dolton and Gregory D. Koplentz, Tracking.
13. Nuclear Proliferation A Guide in Maps and Charts 1998, The Bookings Institution Press Washington D.C., USA, 1998, p. 113.
14. R. Admiral Menon Raja, A Nuclear Strategy for India, Sage Publications, New Delhi, 2000, p. 72.

15. B. Chakma, 'Strategic Dynamics and Nuclear Weapons Proliferation in South Asia: A Historical Analysis' European Academics Publisher Bern, 2004, pp. 103-104.
16. R.W. Jones & Mark G. McDonough with Toby F. Dolton and Gregory D. Koplentz, Tracking Nuclear Proliferation A Guide in Maps and Charts 1998, The Bookings Institution Press Washington D.C., USA, 1998, p 116.
17. Ibid, p. 112.
18. S Chandraskhar, Nuclear Policy of India, Murarilal and Sons, New Delhi, 2011, p. 225.

13

India's Borders and Cross-Border Issues: Problems and Prospects

Shreesh K. Pathak

From 'Frontier' to 'Border': Security of 'Space'

History of humanity begins with activities of geography and politics. 'Border', though is a geographical expression, but 'the idea of the border' cannot be separated with the essentiality of historical and political elements. Man evolved with the 'sense of space'. He develops a connection with the place where he lives. People always relate themselves with the land. The land, where they do various exercises for survival, hence, is deeply linked with their very existence. The affection of man towards territory is as old as the history of humankind. This attachment seems logical as territory is must for his existence. It is not possible to sequestrate the sense of place[1] from the people of a place. A civilised man wishes for his own space. This 'space' is quite attached to his personality which makes him a distinct one. Like an individual, a nation too has own personality which well rooted in 'collective sense of space' of the country. To secure the space and recognition of uniqueness, boundaries are carefully crafted around houses, so are the borders around the nation.

As spatial expressions of essential social and political organisations and territorial partitioning; frontier, boundary and border have been recognised and identified to be of prime importance as structural elements in the political geography of the state.[2] In the strict sense of the term, though frontier, boundary and border are not unique in their meaning and connotations, but they are the peripheral elements of politically organised space, often used commonly as interchangeably.

Frontier, Boundary and Border

It is very necessary to understand the clear distinction between the exact sense of the meaning of these three terms, *i.e.* frontier, boundary and border. These three terms show the consecutive development of definite understanding and authoritative establishment of recognised borders between states. This complex and cumbersome process begins with frontiers. With the development of necessary consensus between states on corresponding areas, boundary emerges. The borders are the final outcome of many essential procedures regarding boundary-settlements and finally, it is called Border or International Border.

Frontiers do not present an outline for the states but they represent the areas of influence between the states. Presence of frontiers means an absence of any border-settlement and also that there is no exclusive definition of the border settled out as of the moment due to lack of consensus. So, frontiers refer to a transition zone which is actually a foreland. Boundaries were often drawn through frontiers. In terms of national politics, boundaries are important because they mark the limits of sovereignty of a state. Boundaries appear on maps as thin lines, but in fact, a boundary is not a line but a vertical plane that cuts through the airspace, the soil, and the subsoil of adjacent states. The primary function of a boundary is to indicate certain well established limits (the bounds) of the given political unit, and all that which is within the boundary is bound together, it is fastened by an internal bond as the etymology of the word "boundary" immediately points. "Boundary" is a term appropriate to the present-day concept of the state, that is, the state as a sovereign (or autonomous) spatial unit, one among many. Kristof has written elaborately about the differences between frontier and boundary. "Frontiers", he writes, "are a characteristic of rudimentary socio-economic relations; relations which are marked by rebelliousness, lawlessness and or absence of laws. The presence of boundaries is a sign that the political community has reached a relative degree of maturity and orderliness, a state of law abidance".[3] Further he elaborates that, "the term boundary denotes a line such as may be defined from point to point in treaty, arbitral award or boundary commission report. A frontier is more properly a region or zone having width and as well as length".[4] According to him, the frontier is "outer-oriented", because life and interest of frontier men differ from those of the core-area of the state, while the boundary is "inner-oriented", as it is created and maintained by the State. The frontier, thus shows the presence of centrifugal forces, the boundary on the other hand, indicates the operation of centripetal forces. As the zone is liable to be integrated with the state, the frontier is "integrating factor", the boundary on the other hand, is a "separating factor". On the basis of the analysis of Ladis

Kristof, it can be stated that while the frontiers are "zonal", boundaries are "linear". Again frontiers are "natural and immovable", boundaries are however, defined and demarcated by man and thus prone to changeable.[5]

There are four formal steps which consequently form a 'Border':

(i) Description or establishment of a definition of a boundary,
(ii) Delimitation by cartographers,
(iii) Demarcation on ground, and
(iv) Regular administrative practices.

These four steps are very essential in forming the border. In South Asia, for most of the borders, this border-making process is yet to be completed; this is major reason behind many disputes and border-issues in the region.

'Emerging India' and its Security Concerns

Presence of emerging India is clearly visible at various global stages. India's voice is now listened by the world more profoundly. India is among the top ten most powerful countries in the world.[6] More than being a soft power, India's power is also evident in the global realm of economy, diplomacy, defence, science and technology. As the global prospects for India is emerging, various security concerns are also increasing for the country. India is situated at a very crucial location on the globe. India is at the centre of the great Asian arc stretching from Aden to Tokyo.[7] All the major air and sea routes of the world pass through India. India and Indian Ocean are an indispensable link in world trade and commerce. Hence, India naturally provides a connecting link among the geopolitical areas called West Asia and East Asia. This strategic location offers formidable geo-significance and it also poses deeper security challenges. As we know, in the era of globalisation, trade and terrorism both have become globalised. Global interconnectedness makes ample scope for greater opportunities and wide space for security vulnerabilities. As India is a frontrunner in the global war on terrorism, she has become softer target for terrorists.

Like many other countries in the region, India has its colonial past. After the colonial experience, major challenge for the country was to complete the processes of state-building and nation-building. These processes are yet to be completed. This situation has created the scope for anti-national insurgencies. Insurgencies in Jammu & Kashmir, in some states of North-East and in naxal affected red corridor of the country are potent enough to disturb the national unity and integrity of India. Though, India is trying hard to cope with these insurgencies, but they are very complex in nature and also get intensified and fuelled by hostile forces from outside the country.

The role of borders are very crucial to curtail this vicious link between insurgent groups and their external connection. Borders shape the nation. Borders provide access to various opportunities for cultural-social and dominantly economical interactions and at the same time it could also provide access to the people of ill-intentions. Hence, there are many problems arises on the borders, some are common to all borders and others are border-specific, but they also provide wide prospects for the betterment of the country. In order to leverage benefits from the borders and to contain ill-practices over there simultaneously a very efficient, comprehensive and integrated border management policy is needed. Border should work efficiently not only as a barrier and also as a bridge because borders bisect but they also blind.

Diverse Borders and Diverse Threats

India is a seventh largest country in area in the world, so the country possess not only lengthy borderline and but also the coastline. India shares 14,880 kms of boundary with Pakistan, China, Nepal, Bhutan, Myanmar and Bangladesh,[8] including a small segment with Afghanistan (106 kms) in northern Jammu and Kashmir (J&K), now part of the Northern Areas of Pakistan Occupied Kashmir, India's land borders exceed 15,000 kms sharing its borders with seven countries.[9] Out of 28 states of India, 17 states are bordering states. Jammu & Kashmir, Punjab, Rajasthan and Gujarat form the India's border with Pakistan. India's boundary with China includes the state boundaries of Jammu & Kashmir, Himachal Pradesh, Uttarakhand, Sikkim and Arunachal Pradesh. Bihar, Uttarakhand, Uttar Pradesh, Sikkim and West Bengal make the border of India with Nepal. Together with West Bengal, Mizoram, Meghalaya, Tripura and Assam, the International border of India-Bangladesh forms. Assam, Arunachal Pradesh, West Bengal and Sikkim share their boundaries with Bhutan. Myanmar is bordered with the state boundaries of Arunachal Pradesh, Nagaland, Manipur and Mizoram. India-Afghanistan boundary is small part of Jammu & Kashmir state boundary. All South Asian states, with the exception of Sri Lanka and the Maldives share land borders with India, but with the exception of Pakistan and Afghanistan, none shares them with each other.[10]

India is a peninsular country; its coastline (including island territories) of 7,516.6 kilometers is the 15th longest in the world[11] which includes 5,422 kilometers of coastline in the mainland and 2,094 kilometers of coastline bordering the islands.[12] The peninsular coastline of the country is shaped by the Bay of Bengal in the east, the Indian Ocean in the south and the Arabian Sea in the west, and is spread over nine states and four union territories, namely, Gujarat, Daman and Diu, Maharashtra, Goa, Karnataka, Kerala, Tamil Nadu, Puducherry, Andhra Pradesh, Odisha, West Bengal. In addition there are the two island groups: Lakshadweep and Minicoy in Arabian Sea and the Andaman and Nicobar in the Bay of Bengal.[13] India shares its maritime boundaries with seven countries namely; Pakistan, Maldives, Sri Lanka, Indonesia, Thailand, Myanmar and Bangladesh.[14]

India's borders are very much diverse in nature. India's international borders are a unique intermixes of mountains, plains, deserts, riverside and jungle terrain with varying degree of habitation and ethnic mix residing. Their social, historical, political and geographical profiles are having only few things in common. Almost each boundary and border of India has own distinct history of evolution. Every border wields a separate cultural individuality. Borderland areas and borderland people often belong to diverse social grouping. So each border really represents its unique identity which is constructed by respective surroundings and the people.

India's Border Distribution

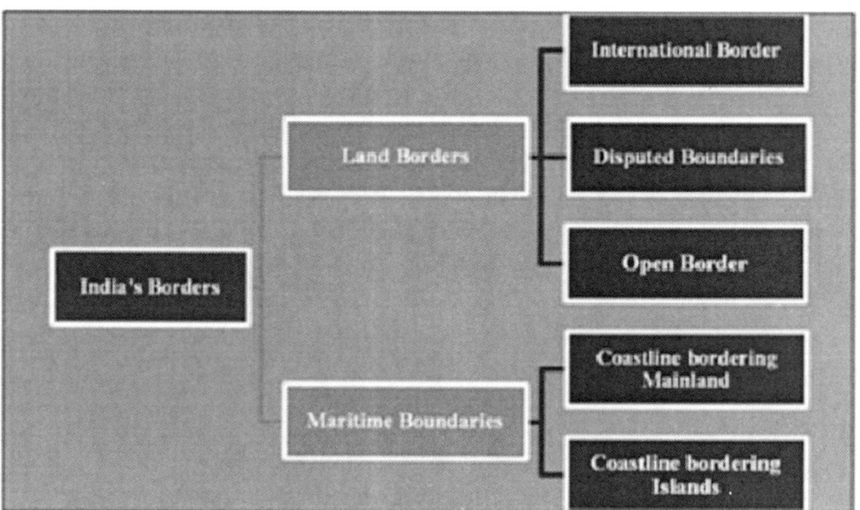

Looking over the diverse geographical scenario of India's borders, it is easily stated that, there is essentially nothing in common between the mountainous terrains of the high Himalayas, the marshlands of the Rann of Kutch, the Thar Desert, the 'Cold Desert' of Ladakh, the low land of the Tarai, the flat, river-crossed plains of the Punjab and the Sundarbans mangrove delta. The diverse borders of India can be classified according to their geo-political definition and circumstantial historical-military developments. India possesses both sorts of borders, *i.e.* Land borders and Maritime borders. There are three forms of boundaries included in India's land border classification. First one is International border. International borders are fully demarcated and delineated and also well recognised by sharing parties and others with a very few instances of exceptions. The second sort of land border can be called disputed boundary. They are generally outcome of ceasefire and aggression. Line of Control (LoC) and Actual Ground Position Line (AGPL) in Jammu & Kashmir are disputed boundaries of India with Pakistan. Both parties have own version of interpretation, reservation and justification regarding the disputes. With China, India has to bear another disputed boundary again in J&K, which is called Line of Actual Control (LAC), a ceasefire line, which came into being after India-China war in 1962.

There are two neighbouring countries, Bhutan and Nepal with whom India has a special kind of border-arrangement keeping in view the long historical and cultural connectedness. With both countries India shares virtually an open-border settlement. The bilateral 'Indian-Bhutan Group Border Management and Security' has been established to collaboratively assess and secure the open border between India and Bhutan.[15] Articles VI and VII of 'the Treaty of Peace and Friendship' which the two countries India and Nepal signed in 1950 specify that, citizens of both countries have equal rights in matters of residence, acquisition of property, employment and movement in each other's territory, thus providing for an open border between the two countries.[16]

A maritime boundary of India also has two sort of categorisation. About seventy-two per cent of India's coastlines are bordering around mainland and about twenty-eight per cent of coastlines are bordering around the islands of the country. India's coasts are characterised by a diverse range of topography such as creeks, small bays, back waters, rivulets, lagoons, estuaries, swamps, mudflats, as well as hills, rocky outcrops, sandbars, beaches and small islands.

Cross-Border Issues: Problems

Diversity of borders bring diversity of threats also. India is facing major security challenges in the region. India is growing and quite dominant in the region. This status attracts more security threats. Borders of any country are the first to face and feel any heat, generated from the source of another side. Due to lack of infrastructure and proper security and management policy for the borders, they are simply not strong enough to curtail the currency of anti-national activities. There are varieties of cross-border issues, which really pose a bundle of problems from the borders to the nation. Cross-border terrorism, illegal trade, smuggling of commodities, illegal migration, drug and human trafficking, forged currency and illegal arms and ammunition supply are major cross issues which make constant source of headache for security managers and strategic thinkers of the country.

Cross-Border Terrorism

India is facing direct threats of cross-border terrorism against the unity, integrity and sovereignty of the country. The recorded incidents of infiltrations on the borders with the vicious purpose to destabilise India as a state are increasing and increasing. Cross-border terrorism is planned, sponsored and backed by cross-border hostile centre of terrorism. They often use anti-national elements to perpetuate the terror around the country. An intelligence report says, there have been almost 200 ceasefire violations by Pakistan since January this year. Much more than the 117, last year and 61 in 2011. Of these about 130 have taken place after August, including some in Kargil, which had not seen such activity since the Indo-Pak conflict in the region in 1999.[17] The problem of cross-border terrorism in India is more severe especially in three regions—Punjab, Jammu & Kashmir and North-East. After independence, government of India could not able to deliver what was generally expected for the essential development. People of these areas got marginalised and often felt alienation. Across the border anti-Indian forces have exploited this situation in their favour to propagate destabilising activities in the country.

In the 1950s, India already experienced the problem of insurgency in the North-East in Nagaland, but the country faced the problem of sponsored cross-border terrorism and insurgency in 1980s when a separatist movement for Khalistan started. This period, which can be seen as a birth of modern terrorism in India, gradually initiated to evolve in other parts of the country like Jammu & Kashmir, the North-East and the red corridor—the central and eastern parts of India.[18] These insurgencies got intensified and have taken persistent momentum only due to external support which comes directly via from Pakistan, Bhutan Myanmar, Bangladesh and Nepal. As India shares land borders with all these countries, anti-Indian forces exploit the routes. Of these, undoubtedly, the groups from Pakistan have been the most active. The most unfortunate thing is the fact that some dominant state-structures of Pakistan not only support but design the programme of insurgencies and cross-border terrorism. It is the part of their 'New Generation Warfare (NGW)[19] which works actively in peace-time to wage a proxy war against India.

Cross-border terrorism is not confined to merely land boundaries, the security loop-holes of maritime boundaries are also exploited by terrorists and their masterminds. The 26/11 Mumbai attack was big example of it which clearly shows the equal vulnerability of country's maritime boundaries as well as land boundaries.

> "*When I say state actor, at the moment, I am not pointing finger at any particular agency. But clearly there was state support or state actors' support for the 26/11 massacre*".[20]—***P. Chidamaram***

The statement made by then Home Minister of India clearly stated the involvement of state machinery of Pakistan. There are two sorts of support system provided by external forces to sustain cross-border terrorism, firstly; to provide safe sanctuaries to terrorists and secondly they provide financial, logistic backing, conduct training and supply arms and ammunition.[21]

Illegal Migration

Illegal migration from across India's borders, particularly Bangladesh, has continued unabated for over five decades. India has yet to wake up to the implications of the unchecked immigration for the national security. Today, India has about 15 million Bangladeshi nationals, 70,000 Sri Lankan Tamils and about one lakh Tibetan migrants living in India.[22] Demographic changes have been brought about in the border belts of West Bengal. Even states like Delhi, Maharashtra and Rajasthan have been affected. Such large-scale migration has obvious social, economic, political and security implications. There is an all-round failure in India to deal with the problem of illegal migration. The massive illegal migration poses a grave danger to our security, social harmony and economic well-being.

Approximately 35 to 40 million people have moved across national boundaries in India, Pakistan, Bangladesh and Sri Lanka since 1947 as rejected people or unwanted migrants. The following are some of the major flows within South Asia. They can be categorized into three types—rejected peoples, political refugees from repressive regimes, and unwanted migrants:[23]

- **Indo-Pak Refugees flow (1947-48):** Estimated 6 to 7 million Muslims moved from India to Pakistan and nearly 8 million Hindus and Sikhs moved from Pakistan to India (Census of India 1951).
- **Exodus of Burmese Indians:** In 1948, 1949 and 1960 approximately 1, 50,000 Indians moved from Myanmar to India.[24]
- **Exodus of Sri Lankan Indians and Sri Lankan Tamils:** Approximately 1,25,000 persons had moved to India (Sri Lankan Tamils) by 1986.[25]
- **Flight of Chakmas from Bangladesh into India:** By the end of 1981, 40,000 Chakma refugees were settled in Tripura and Mizoram.[26]
- **Bangladeshis to India (Liberation of Bangladesh):** In 1971, nearly 9 million Bengalis crossed the border into West Bengal, Assam, Tripura. Most of them returned and a few stayed back.[27]
- **Tibetans to India:** By 1950 a little less than 1, 00,000 Tibetans fled to India.
- **Bangladeshis to India:** Approximately 15 million Bangladesh nationals have moved into India since independence and settled in different parts of India.
- **Nepal and India:** An estimated 25,000 Bhutanese of Nepali origin fled to West Bengal by 1990.
- **Bangladeshis to Assam:** An estimated 1 to 2 million Bangladesh nationals moved into Assam from 1971 to 1981.[28]

A major consequence of a porous border is the ease with which it is crossed illegally. Various "push" factors such as political upheavals, religious persecution, demographic pressures, and environmental crises and "pull" factors such as availability of land, employment opportunities, medical care, and education have contributed to the large-scale influx of Bangladeshis into India. Although there is an acknowledgement of this fact, there are no authoritative estimates of the number of such illegal migrants. Smuggling of cattle has become a serious concern. Truckloads of cattle from Haryana, Rajasthan, Uttar Pradesh and Madhya Pradesh are shipped to the India-Bangladesh border everyday ostensibly for grazing purposes. From here, these cattle are smuggled into Bangladesh. Along with cattle, smuggling of arms, and other essential items such as sugar, salt and diesel, human and narcotics trafficking, counterfeit Indian currency, kidnapping, and thefts are quite rampant along the India–Bangladesh border.

The Problems of Enclaves, Adverse Possession

The problems of enclaves, adverse possession and disputed land are prevalent on the Indo-Bangladesh border. Enclaves are independent states or exclaves of a neighbouring country that perforate the host country. These become convenient points for smuggling, avoiding customs and excise duties, for the importation of contraband, and as a point of entry for illegal aliens.[29] There are 111 Indian enclaves (17,158 acres) in Bangladesh and 51 Bangladeshi enclaves (7,110.02 acres) in India. Adverse possession means land belonging to one country under the control of another; e.g., Indian land under Bangladesh and vice-versa. There are 34 places (2,892.31 acres) of Indian land under adverse possession of Bangladesh and 40 places (2,251.66 acres) of Bangladesh land under adverse possession of India.[30] The Land Border Agreement of 1974 provides for the exchange of enclaves and settlement of the issue of adverse possession. A joint, working group has been constituted to solve the border related issues. India has been insisting on a joint census of the enclaves before these are exchanged, but Bangladesh has not agreed to the suggestion yet.[31]

Drug Trafficking, Smuggling and Informal Trade

Geographically, India lies between the world's two major opium producing regions—the Golden Crescent and the Golden Triangle. This has made it extremely vulnerable to trafficking in drugs.[32] The insurgency in Kashmir has been funded by Pakistan with the drugs money. The Geo-political Drug Despatch of July 1997 mentioned that the ISI used drug money to finance no less than ten fundamentalist organizations operating in Kashmir.[33] The Sikh terrorists in Punjab had struck an unholy alliance with the drug traffickers of South-West Asia.

The key elements of the drug trafficking situation in India with reference, particularly, to our land borders and coastline are:

- The smuggling of heroin across the Indo-Pak border in J&K, Punjab, Rajasthan and Gujarat.
- The smuggling of heroin from Myanmar into our north-eastern states, particularly Manipur and Mizoram.
- The movement of heroin across the Indo-Bangladesh border from India to Bangladesh.
- The smuggling of ephedrine arid pseudo-ephedrine from India across the Indo-Myanmar border.
- The trafficking of hashish and marijuana from Nepal into India through the Indo-Nepal border, in the states of Bihar and UP.
- Sri Lankan ports are increasingly being used as transit points for drug trafficking through India to other destinations.[34]

There were several instances of consignments on the Indo-Pak border containing narcotics as well as arms and ammunition being seized by the Border Security Force. The traffickers, in several cases, confessed that they were allowed to smuggle narcotics across the border on the specific condition that they would take a consignment of weapons to be delivered to the terrorists in India.[35] The economic and developmental disparity vis-a-vis countries bordering India have resulted in widespread smuggling of goods and items.

The location of India-Myanmar boundary at the edge of the "golden triangle" facilitates the unrestricted illegal flows of drugs into Indian Territory. Heroin is the main item of drug trafficking. The bulk of heroin enters India through the border town of Moreh in Manipur. It is reported that the local insurgent groups are actively involved in drug trafficking. The provision of allowing the tribal communities of both countries to travel up to 40 km across the border without any passport or visa has also contributed to increased smuggling in the region.

Heroin is again prime item for smuggling along the India-Pakistan border. Other items include saffron, textile, mercury, which are also smuggled from Pakistan. The villagers adjacent to the border are alleged to be involved in smuggling in a big way. Money laundering is also quite rampant along the border. A large scale hawala network is flourishing in Punjab, especially in Ludhiana.

Forged Currency

Fake Indian currency is printed by Pakistan and smuggled largely along the India-Pakistan border. Indian security agencies know it for a long time. Several arrested underworld and terror operatives have confirmed it repeatedly. Now the National Investigation Agency (NIA) has nailed the Pakistan government's imprint on fake Indian currency notes (FICN) pumped into the country. A detailed forensic analysis by the NIA has revealed that the paper used to print the counterfeit rupee notes is an excellent match with the legal tender of Pakistan. The NIA's explosive conclusion was recently revealed to Parliament's Standing Committee on Finance by the country's top intelligence agencies—the Research and Analysis Wing (R&AW), the Intelligence Bureau (IB), and the Department of Revenue Intelligence (DRI).[36] Earlier this year, arrested LeT operative Abdul Karim Tunda had told the Delhi Police that the ISI runs the entire network of Fake Indian Currency Notes (FICN) being smuggled into India.[37]

Besides, these cross-border issues, there are other important border related issues which can be dealt at diplomatic level and require policy level progress between the parties. Together with small and big cases, there are many **border-disputes** on almost every border. The colonial past of the region is the root cause in many disputed borders in South Asia. Demarcation of boundaries is yet to be completed. Border-disputes create a very tough situation for security managers to face day-to-day challenges and border-crimes on the border-spots. Border-disputes thwart the natural progress in the process of social-cultural and economic interaction across the borders. The people who reside on disputed borderland bear the brunt of unnecessary heat and edginess which stems and persists due to absence of understanding and negotiation between border-sharing neighbours. Both countries fail to leverage the usual benefits of mutual correspondence due to border-disputes.

Water-disputes on the question of water-sharing are another big issue which come on the way of better management of borders. Great Rivers are the cultural and economic backbone of South Asia. The Ganges, Indus and Brahmaputra have contributed to the rise and prosperity of some of the earliest civilizations in history and today are the source of livelihood for millions. The South Asian river basins, most of which have their source in the Himalayas, support rich ecosystems and irrigate millions of hectares of fields, thereby supporting some of the highest population densities in the world. Rivers are, however, also a source of conflict between countries and people in the region. Like border-disputes, water-disputes too, are very complex in nature and only concrete negotiation based on mutual trust can solve the problems.

Prospects for Better Borders

Management of India's Borders

The concept of the border security is not sufficient to deal with the modern challenges and so there is a need for a better mechanism which ensures the security of national borders and at the same time regulates the legitimate movements for essential interactions. Border management is the answer. Border management proposes such mechanisms which are necessary to adopt from the country in the era of global terrorism and global connectedness. Border management is a very new concept and it is evolving day by day. Border management is the package of various sorts of mechanisms; generally it depends on those sorts of needs of the nation which could be fulfilled through regulated and well-managed borders. Sometimes it seems that it is confined merely to secure the borders but gradually newer dimensions come to explore further advantages.

According to Prakash Singh, former Director-General, Border Security Force:

> "Border management is a fluid concept in the sense that the level of security arrangements along a particular border would depend upon the political relations, the economic linkages, the ethno-religious ties between people across the borders and the configuration of the border itself".[38]

The term "Border Management", is a wider term that denotes controlling the administrative affairs of the borders, including ensuring their sanctity. The most important players in border management are the people residing in border areas. It is these residents who would be the beneficiaries of proper border management. At the same time, it would be virtually impossible for any of the agencies involved in border management to successfully implement their agenda without the active participation of the border population.

Today, border management has acquired special significance. Globalization poses global opportunities with global challenges. While adopting a soft approach towards borders for global, economic, social and cultural activities is useful and important in a way, it could also pose serious threats to security and integrity of a nation in another way. This requires special sorts of mechanism for border regulation and this is the purpose behind whole idea of border management.

Cross-Border Cooperation for Cross-Border Issues

Variety of cross-border issues discussed earlier; make grave effect not only on security of borders but also on entire security complex of the region. These issues are fundamentally not country-centric. They belong to and affect each and every country of the region. To solve the cross border issues, the idea of 'smart borders'[39] can be borrowed from the US experience. 'Smart Borders' emphasises on cross-border cooperation to solve all sorts of cross border issues. Cross-border cooperation is definitely a key to unlock the border problems and border issues. But in the region like South Asia, cross-border cooperation is very much far-distant dream. The condition of South Asian Association for Regional Cooperation (SAARC) is known to all. As the member of the South Asia region, we have largely failed to foster consensus on shared issues with each-other and to make pledge and collective endeavour for development. But keeping in view the graveness of cross-border issues and to resolve, there is no other way-out. The leaders and diplomats of the member countries of the region have to show their political and diplomatic prowess and have to move on the path of cross-border cooperation. By nature, cross-border issues cannot be sorted out singlehandedly or in isolation. The problems of cross-border terrorism, illegal migration, drug, human and arms trafficking, forged currency and smuggling of goods can be only sorted out if serious and collective efforts would be made for joint mechanisms and cooperative connections.

Strengthening the Border-Guarding System

To deal with regular challenges and frequent border crimes on diverse borders of India, an effective system border-guarding is needed. The defence of national territory is the primary function of armed forces, with defence of the land borders being mainly the responsibility of the army, assisted by the air force and by para-military forces. It requires careful and constantly updated planning and preparation, including an appropriate defence policy. The repeated withdrawal, in large numbers, of paramilitary forces from border guarding duties for internal security and counter-insurgency duties has led to a neglect of the borders. All the organizations working in the border areas for the development and law enforcement should seek directions and be accountable to one nodal agency Ministry of Home Affairs (MHA) during peace and Ministry of Defence (MoD) during war. Multiplicity of forces on the same borders has inevitably led to the lack of accountability as well as problems of command and control. One border guarding force (Para-military) for the international borders and the army is required to remain deployed on the disputed borders till the final settlement. The border security system has to be augmented with technical monitoring systems, border fencing, floodlighting, border roads, etc. for effective border management. A better coordination in intelligence agencies to get updated information and involvement of local people in the process would bring effective result.

Due Importance to Geography over Politics

Border-disputes and water-disputes can only be sorted out by diplomatic endeavour and political will but without giving much emphasis on politics. Here, geographic approach would solve the purpose in more candid way. The simple reason behind this is that, negotiations are made for maximum period, but variables of politics are dynamic. Compare to political variables, geographical facts of the disputed boundary or water-distribution provide much more reliable basis for long-term beneficial negotiation. There are geographical compulsions which are true for both countries and those compulsions could be addressed only by the bilateral mechanisms. A country could not ever be able to overcome with geographical restraints individually.

Giving much importance on economic cooperation should be guiding force for every sort of negotiation. Economic cooperation across the borders is a necessity in the era of globalisation in which borders can play greater role as bridges more and as barriers lesser.

REFERENCES

1. There are two basic characteristics involved in the making of "the sense of place", the space and its uniqueness. The human experiences with the landscape, local knowledge and traditional tales make very deep contributions to these two characteristics, Cross, J. E. 2001, "What is Sense of Place?" [Online: web] Accessed 25 Aug. 2013, URL: http://www.western.edu/academics/headwaters/headwatersconference/archives/cros_headwatersXII.pdf.}
2. S. Adhikari, Political Geography, New Delhi: Rawat Publications, 1997 p.188.
3. L.K.D., "The Nature of Frontiers and Boundaries", Annals of the Association of American Geographers, Vol. 49(3), 1959, p.281.
4. Ibid.
5. R.L. Dwivedi, Fundamnetals of Political Geography, Allahabad: Chaitanya Publishing House, 2004, p.176.
6. I. Bagchi, 2013, "India ranks 8th among 27 most powerful nations in world", Online: web.
7. Accessed 25 Nov. 2013, URL: http://articles.timesofindia.indiatimes.com/2013-04-27/india/38861597_1_energy-security-india-technological-capability.
8. J. Bandyopadhyaya, "The Making of India's Foreign Policy of India", Allied Publishers, Mumbai, 2003, p.32.
9. P. Das, India's Border Management: Select Documents, New Delhi: Institute for Defence Studies, 2010 p.2.
10. G. Kanwal, "Indian Border Security: Poor Management in Evidence", IPCS Issue Brief, 2007, No. 55.
11. M. Chadda, "International Dimensions of Ethnic Conflicts" in D.T. Hagerty (ed.) South Asia in World Politics Lanham: Rowman & Littlefield Publishers, 2005, p.188.
12. Roy-Chaudhury, Rahul "Trends in the Delimitation of India's Maritime Boundaries",2009, [Online: web] Accessed 27 Nov. 2013, URL: http://www.idsa-india.org/an-jan9-5.html.
13. Government of India, Annual Report 2011-12, Union Ministry of Home Affairs, New Delhi, 2012, p.57.
14. Ibid.
15. Roy-Chaudhury, Rahul, "Trends in the Delimitation of India's Maritime Boundaries", 2009 [Online: web] Accessed 27 Nov. 2013, URL: http://www.idsa-india.org/an-jan9-5.html.
16. Government of India, Annual Report 2009, Union Ministry of Home Affairs, [Online: web] Accessed 27 Nov. 2013, URL: http://www.mha.nic.in/hindi/sites/upload_files/mhahindi/files/pdf/BM_MAN-IN-BHUTAN%28E%29.pdf.
17. P. Das, "Need to effectively manage the India-Nepal Border", [Online: web] 2009, Accessed 24 Nov., 2013, URL: http://www.idsa.in/idsacomments/ManagetheIndiaNepalBorder_pdas_190913.
18. N. Gokhle, "Infiltration attempts will increase as Lashkar, Jaish terrorists wait to enter India, warn intelligence agencies", [Online: web] Accessed 24 Nov. 2013, URL: http://www.ndtv.com/article/india/infiltration-attempts-will-increase-as-lashkar-jaish-terrorists-wait-to-enter-india-warn-intelligenc-433819.
19. S.V. Raghavan, and V. Balasubramaniyan "Terrorism in India-Cross Border Support Structures in India's Neighbourhood", Agni-Studies in International Strategic Issues, Vol. XIV, No. III, 2013 p. 66.
20. G. Das, "Securing India's Borders: Challenges and Policy Options", New Delhi: Centre for Land Warfare Studies, 2011, p.18.

——(2012), "Pakistan support for 26/11 confirmed: P Chidambaram", *The Economic Times*, New Delhi, 28 June, 2012.

21. S.V. Raghavan, and V. Balasubramaniyan, "Terrorism in India-Cross Border Support Structures in India's Neighbourhood", Agni-Studies in International Strategic Issues, Vol. XIV, No. III, 2013, p. 68.
22. M.A. Singh, "A Study on Illegal Immigration into North-East India: The Case of Nagaland", [Online: web] Accessed 17 Nov. 2013, URL: http://www.idsa.in/system/files/OccasionalPaper8_NagalandIllegalImmigrationl.pdf.
23. M. Weiner, "Rejected Peoples and Unwanted Migrants in South-Asia", *Economic and Political Weekly*, 30(1),1993, p.1543.
24. N.R. Chakravarti, *The Indian Minority in Burma*, Oxford University Press, New Delhi,1971.
25. H. Chattopadhyaya, *Indians in Sri Lanka*, Calcutta: O P S Publishers, 1979.
26. S.A.A. Ahsan, and B. Chakma "Problems of National Integration in Bangladesh: The Chittagong II ill Tracts", *Asian Survey*, 29(10), 1989.
27. R. Sisson, and L. E Rose "War and Secession: Pakistan, India, and the Creation of Bangladesh", Berkeley: University of California Press, 1990.
28. N.S. Jamwal, "Management of Land Borders", *Strategic Analysis*, 26(3):2002, 416.
29. R.A. Griggs, "Borders and Peace-building in Southern Africa: The Spatial Implications of the 'African Renaissance", *Boundary and Territory Briefings*, 3(2) 8, 2000.
30. C. Erkelens, (2007), "Improving the living conditions in the enclaves near the India-Bangladesh border" General Assembly, Special Political and Decolonisation (4th) Committee reports, [Online: Web] Accessed 15.03.2009, URL: http://lemun.org/reports/GA4_India_Pakistan.pdf.
31. P. Singh, "Border Management", *BSF Journal*, Gwalior: BSF Academy Tekanpur, 2001, p.12.
32. N.S. Jamwal, "Management of Land Borders", *Strategic Analysis*, 26(3), 2002, p. 418.
33. Ibid.
34. Ibid, p. 418.
35. Ibid, p. 419.
36. K. Sharma, "Pakistan prints fake Indian rupees: NIA finds counterfeit cash made from same paper as Pakistan's legal tender" [Online: web] Accessed 11 Nov. 2013, URL: http://www.dailymail.co.uk/indiahome/indianews/article-2488000/Pakistan-prints-fake-Indian-rupees-NIA-finds-counterfeit-cash-paper-Pakistans-legal-tender.html. 3
37. Ibid.
38. P. Singh (2001), "Border Management", *BSF Journal*, Gwalior: BSF Academy Tekanpur.
39. P. Das, "Managing India's Land Borders: Learning from the US Experience", *Strategic Analysis*, Vol. 36, No. 01, 2013, p.74.

14

Jammu and Kashmir: A View Point

Jaibans Singh

Those have visited Kashmir in happier times a few decades back would vouch for the modern texture of the Kashmiri society. Srinagar not only boasted of some very lovely theatres like the Broadway, it also had a few discos—something unheard of anywhere in North India other than New Delhi at that time. Five star hotels like the Oberoi Palace were standard destination for the rich honeymooners while those less fortunate would opt for more humble but equally vibrant dwellings.

Regardless of status or budget, Kashmir was the favourite destination of Indian honeymooners of yore. To put it succinctly, a holiday in Kashmir was a must for any youngster of substance and there was not one person who did not vow to get back at the earliest opportunity, such was the lure of the place.

What is it that made Kashmir such a favoured destination for fun and enjoyment? After all there are some equally beautiful locales in Himachal Pradesh, Darjeeling and many other hill stations in India, yet, it was only Kashmir that people had in their minds all the time. The answer is simple. It was not only the enthralling natural beauty of Kashmir which mesmerised people; it was the famed Kashmiri hospitality, the polite Shikara (Boat) riders, the warm houseboat owners, the beautiful Kashmiri women in their colourful attires, the haunting Kashmir music, the graceful and lilting Kashmiri folk songs, the sumptuous Kashmir food; overall, the sheer joy of being in the most beautiful place on earth which compelled film makers and tourists alike to visit the place in hordes.

The Concept of Kashmiriyat

The charm of Kashmir was due to the intrinsic culture and background of the Kashmiri civilisation. Kashmir is probably the only place in India which has a recorded history going back to 5000 years. The document is called the Rajatarangini.

By the 14 Century Islam had supplanted Hinduism as a dominant religion of the Kashmir Valley. The first to convert, in 1323, was Rincana a person of Ladakhi origin who set up a dynasty in Kashmir, his motivation came from a Sufi saint, Bulbul Shah. The second phase of Kashmir's history, known as "Salatini Kashmir", which dates back to the 14th century concerned itself with rule of native Muslims. Kashmir's switch over from Hindu to Muslim rule had a political dimension without any religious or cultural overtones. Even when the Mughals and Pathans invaded Kashmir they did not attempt to break the composite culture of the region, probably because their interest in this territory was restricted to enjoyment of its natural beauty. It is for these reasons that the composite culture of Kashmir popularly known as "Kasmiriyat", carried on for more than two millenniums.

The genre of Islam and Hinduism practiced in Kashmir is quite different from that found in the rest of the country or the world for that matter. Both are immersed in a unique brand of Sufism epitomised by a belief in common saints. This is the reason behind the common language, common customs, common dress, common food, even common religious practices that both communities have followed for centuries. It is also the reason behind the inherent secularism of Kashmiri society heralded today as "Kashmiriyat".

Kashmiris thrive on all such things that are graceful and elegant be it cinema, music, art, culture, cuisine or literature? Even today the biggest names in the field of art and culture are of Kashmiri origin. With such deep rooted traditions and culture, such liberal and emancipated beliefs, such modern and accommodative attitudes it is no wonder that the Kashmiri people are so well liked by those who visited their beautiful lands.

It was Kashmiriyat that came under the terrorist attack at the outset. The objective was to divide the communities, decrease their power and finally subjugate what was left behind.

The Pakistan Factor

Pakistan's romance with Kashmir is manifested with emotional platitudes like, 'Kashmir is the core issue and the root cause for tension with India', 'we feel for the people of Kashmir and will always provide to them emotional and diplomatic support'; 'Kashmir is not a part of India ethnically, culturally or in terms of religion' etc. With this philosophy in the background, the political agenda was supported by misadventures like the illegitimate Razakar incursions in 1947 and again in 1965 (Operation Gibraltar), General Zia-ul-Haq's policy of making India bleed with a thousand cuts, the Kargil incursion and above all the infiltration of hardened terrorists who created and continue attempts to create mayhem amongst the peace loving Kashmirs. In all this Pakistan succeeded, however marginally, because of a small right wing segment of Kashmiri politicians who supported these disruptive, violent and criminal elements.

Political disruption in Pakistan has, in a small period of time, bought about a volte-face in the so called highly ideological and moral Kashmir policy of Pakistan that was to withstand for a thousand years. Today, Pakistan—beset with problems of a manner similar to those that it wanted to perpetrate on Kashmir has literally withdrawn support to the cause of the Kashmiri's and has in the process, most ignominiously, dumped those nurtured to forward its unholy agenda.

Diplomatic efforts between India and Pakistan have been directed towards making the process of confidence building irreversible. Unfortunately, there seem to be certain forces which are bent upon derailing this peace process. The 26/11 terrorist attack in Mumbai happened just when the relationship between the two countries was looking up a bit. It is no coincidence that such Pakistan based terrorist organisations are normally responsible for derailing the peace process between the two countries which also have a stake in keeping terrorism alive in Kashmir—mainly the Lashkar-e-Toiba. This apart, some rigid and fundamentalist elements in the Pakistan Army also lose no opportunity in derailing the peace process.

Pakistan did and is doing what it can to keep the pot of dissent and disruption boiling in Kashmir. It attained success in the early stages to an extent that violence became so much a part of the psyche of the common Kashmiri that talking about it, witnessing it, experiencing it and even extolling it are things that he has begun to take in his stride. One may argue that this attitude is perhaps essential to survival in the extenuating circumstances that the Kashmiri's have been dwelling in during the last two decades of their life.

The Birth of Terrorism

Imagine what it would be like when millions of people simply vanish from the face of the earth. When prime land is grabbed and properties that have been in families for hundreds of years are pillaged and forcibly occupied. Imagine how it would feel when a particular community is subject to discrimination, loot, rape and arson.

Such is the story of the Kashmiri Pundits of Jammu and Kashmir who became the targets of one of the most savage ethnic cleansing pogroms ever to be inflicted on a body of people in the world. This also heralded an era of terrorist atrocity in a region well known for its old and secular civilization and peaceful disposition.

When Pakistan ignited the flames of insurgency in Kashmir its leadership realised that the movement will not be able to gain momentum unless the ethos of Kasmiriyat, which formed the roots of the socio-religious fabric of Kashmir, is dismantled.

The simmering discontent of the Kashmiri Muslim population as an off shoot of the partition was exploited by Pakistan with a grand design of disintegrating a larger and more powerful India through a policy of "slow bleed and death by a thousand cuts"; a low intensity conflict strategy evolved by the Pakistan dictator Zia-ul-Haq to pressurize India and Kashmir into submission. A religious sanction was obtained for this theory by pushing it into the ambit of "Islamic revolution".

The objective was to fracture a community that had coexisted with a dual religion concept for much more than 2000 years. The first and most critical facet of the whole strategy was to break the homogeneity of the Kashmiri people which was based on secular concepts of Kasmiriyat and Sufi culture.

The Pakistani leadership was well aware that even though Hindus formed a minority community in Kashmir they played an important role in the governance of the State. Due to higher education levels they constituted the intelligentsia and their flight would provoke a vacuum in the normal process of governance and economic development. The perpetrators of terrorism appreciated that in the absence of Kashmiri Pundits the State would be weakened due to breakdown of executive authority and would thus degrade into anarchy, lawlessness and pillage, a situation which was very close to their hearts.

Moreover, Kashmiri Pundits had offered stubborn resistance all through to the Pakistan sponsored secessionist movement in the State. They had also resisted Islamisation of the Kashmiri government and society. As such, their removal from the scene was considered imperative for giving the movement a much needed impetus. The Hindus, mainly Kashmiri Pundits were, consequently, marked for extermination as part of a deliberate and well conceived design.

The mercenary forces selected to inflame Kashmir were directed to ignite a cry for blood and gore that would inflame the fires of fundamentalism and bigoted Islamic idealism and in the long run pave the way for hard-line Islamic politicking. The killing of important government functionaries by terrorists would build the latter's stature in the eyes of the innocent, illiterate and impressionable rural population and give credence to the call for a Jihad. The terrorists would then gain the confidence of the people who would be more responsive to their diktats.

The forces of terror were well aware that acts of ethnic cleansing would bring instant media coverage and would thus assist in internationalizing the problem. The pressure from the displaced Kashmiri Pundits and the collective horror of the world would impel the Indian government towards emergent efforts to regain control of a situation supposedly going out of hand and would force it to the negotiating table.

Thus, ethnic extermination of Hindus became the first strategic objective of the terrorist rank and file. It formed the vanguard of the so-called Jihad for liberation of Jammu and Kashmir from India. In accordance with this strategy the minority Hindu community in general and Kashmiri Pundits in specific were targeted to be mercilessly killed and hounded. Having decided upon their evil design the terrorists went about fructifying their unholy agenda in a surgical manner. The terrorist assault on Hindus of Kashmir was perpetuated in 1989. In less than six months, more than seven hundred hapless and dumbstruck Kashmiri Pundits had been killed in the most brutal and savage manner. The killing was accompanied by torture and atrocities of a kind unheard of in the annals of history.

Religious sentiment was inflamed by foreign mercenaries to yield extraordinary results. Between 1989 and 1991 more than four lakh Kashmiri Pundits made a mass exodus from the Valley and settled down in the lower regions of the State, mainly Jammu. They became homeless refugees in their own State and country. They were forced to live in squalid camps, in an environment that did not suit their disposition as hill people. The deprivation that they faced cannot be described. With the passage of time the young ventured into other parts of India to seek a new life. However, even today the old continue to pine for everything that they held sacred including their affiliation with the Muslims of their area.

Terrorist Atrocity takes Muslims into its Fold

The success achieved in orchestrating a mass exodus of Kashmiri Pundits from the Valley did not produce the desired results for the perpetrators of terrorism in the State. The Indian Nation and the Indian government did not succumb to the pressure. On the other hand, vigorous counter terrorists operations were launched and necessary steps were taken to contain the menace. This defeat of their grand design caused Pakistan to change its strategy and target the population of the State without discrimination of caste and creed in order to keep the pot boiling and portray the region as a nuclear flash point. It was under these circumstances that the Muslims of the State also got a taste of foreign sponsored Jihad.

Terrorists threw ideology to the winds and became more self serving and epicurean in their beliefs. They escalated violence levels by indulging in heinous actions that exposed them as remorseless, fundamentalist and pathological killers who enjoyed inflicting misery for no logical purpose. They succumbed to the pursuit of a good life that in their limited sphere translated into good food, good wine and satiation of their carnal desires. There is no level of degradation to which they did not stoop to in pursuit of their pleasures. Exploitation of ethnic Muslims attained unprecedented proportions.

Lack of Local Support to Terrorism

Lack of local support for the terrorists was the single, most potent weapon that put a lid on terrorism. Terrorism in J&K had been sustained by recruitment of misguided youth through false propaganda, coercion, lure of money and a host of other blackmailing tactics. Taliban spill over's and other terrorists of foreign origin augmented the numbers tally. The metamorphoses of terrorists from a motivated cadre, fighting for what they perceived as a just fight, into a pack of unruly barbarians was to a great extent the undoing of the terrorist movement in Kashmir. The barbaric actions of terrorists against the innocent people were nothing more than acts of criminality which ultimately led to their alienation.

On being faced with extreme forms of exploitation the Muslims in Kashmir realised their mistake in being party either willingly or otherwise to the depredations inflicted upon their own families and their Hindu brethren of centuries by these foreign marauders. There were many questions which the locals started asking from those who professed to have their best interest in mind. Where is the brotherhood of this so called Jihadi movement? Where are the high sounding ideals of voluntary service in the name of the Ummah? Is raping young girls the concept of serving religion? The value of Kashmiriyat had been understood by the locals much before the political leaders started cutting party lines in inviting the Kashmiri Pundits back to their fold.

It was the poor villagers in remote areas who were the lifeline of terrorists; they took the lead in stopping support to the terrorists mainly on being given a sense of security and motivation by the army. Such was the disgust felt by the locals for the terrorists that in some instances even burial was refused to slain terrorists.

This popular awakening of the masses and their deep resolve to join the fight against terrorism had a far-reaching affect on its ultimate containment and near eradication. Terrorists started gasping for breath in an environment that became perceptibly anti-terrorism and all that it stood for.

The Ideology of Separatism

The separatist onslaught propagated by Pakistan in the Kashmir Valley is being played out as much on the political, administrative and economic machinery of the State as it is on the minds and psyche of the Kashmiri people dwelling both within the Valley and beyond. In fact, the poisoning of the minds of the Kashmiri's began much earlier than the instigation of acts of terror in the Valley. For Pakistan, to openly indulge in interference in the affairs of another Nation, some nature of legitimacy had to be created. The first step in this direction was taken by reducing Kashmiri's and the Pakistanis to a common denominator by playing the religious card. In other words the Kashmiri identity was equated with the Muslim identity.

Since Kashmir is essentially a cultural region with strong secular credentials, the first step was to discredit the cultural ethos of the region. This was achieved through organisations such as the Jama'at-e-Islaami. Established with the intent of dispensing the teachings of Islam and ensuring the spread of the religion, the organisation worked through a network of seminaries known as *dargahs* and *madrassas*. It endeared itself to the Muslim population of the Valley by denigrating what was termed as decadent social customs that involved unnecessary expenditure and effort on the part of the common man which he could ill-afford. Under the garb of simplification of lifestyles and spreading the teachings of Islam, this organisation channelised the fundamentalist principles of Islam and paddled anti-India sentiment. As a result, the Kashmiri Muslim was convinced that he was being hounded by India's basically Hindu entity and his future lay with the Muslim State of Pakistan. The claim of the organisation that it was a non-political and peaceful body was nullified when it acknowledged the existence of Hizbul Mujahedeen, its terrorist wing.

At the international level, Kashmir was projected as a Muslim issue wherein an alien force had forcibly occupied a territory and was committing a plethora of human rights violations on Muslims. This propaganda was expected to serve two purposes. The first was to ensure a regular flow of funds to Pakistan and onwards to Kashmir from a number of oil-rich Muslim Nations. That the funds were actually being used to create trouble through the perpetration of acts of terror against India, Pakistan's arch enemy and nemesis, was a thing that came to no one's notice or if it did, it was conveniently overlooked. The second purpose was to project India's efforts to counter the terrorist assault as a human rights issue, which afforded to the region and the propped up leadership of the separatist cause a lot of attention in the western world. Interestingly, the human rights violation of the Kashmiri Pundits and their resulting plight was not given the attention that was its due by anyone.

Even as a series of elections established Jammu and Kashmir as a functional and vibrant democracy, those leaders of the Kashmir Valley who wished to take their people along the suicidal path of secession from the Indian Union continued to stand unmoved in their political line of thought. The mainstream political parties went to the people with their manifestoes to get a mandate for their policies while the separatists, like feudal lords, maintained a haughty aloofness.

Separatists go about their work in a very systematic manner, they have a plan in place which runs with the weather and the circumstances, they know when to get going and when to lie dormant, they know who in the international arena can be exploited and to what extent, all this they do with utmost professionalism. In the application of their agenda they resort to some well established philosophies formulated and refined over years of political experience. An elucidation of these philosophies has been attempted purely on the basis of empirical suidies of the events and their manifestations.

Agitations and Stone Pelting: The Idea, the Process and its Manifestation

Stone pelting has become a lucrative business with the unemployed youth offering their service for a price. Committed cadre of organisations like the Hizbul Mujahideen, Lashkar-e-Toiba and the separatists give large sums of money to hire 'initiators' who start the process of stone pelting on pre-designated targets. The professionals mask their faces and know their escape routes. What is left behind to face the flak is the misguided youth in their teens who do it to show that they are brave and can hit the security forces. These factors, in themselves, question the claim being made that the agitation was and continues to be a homogeneous mass movement for 'Azadi' and 'Plebiscite'.

A political environment in some regions of the Valley is created whereby issues are picked up and blown out of proportion in order to derail the process of normalcy and to frustrate the government into inaction. This happens in accordance with the diabolic master plan of some disruptive elements functioning in the State with the financial assistance of foreign forces. The survival of these elements depends upon their capability to spread anarchy and force the government into inaction mainly because a prosperous society in Kashmir does not serve their purpose.

The destabilising potential of these protests needs to be viewed in the context of the geographic area to which they are confined and the number of people who respond to the call. What eludes the eye was that stone pelting is a spatially limited phenomenon which does not extend far beyond a few districts adjoining Srinagar. It was a phenomenon that has been created through orchestration of misguided youth and clever media management. Significantly, these disturbances, by and large, are concentrated in urban areas with very limited impact in the hinterland.

The average size of crowds ranges between 100-150 and not the 'thousands' as is repeatedly reported by the media. The approximate strength of the populace supporting the agitation varies between 20 to 25 percent. A majority of the people (70 to 80 percent) participating are the youth.

The long term ramification of this seemed to be that the Valley would move towards a rural-urban split which would add yet another security dimension to the already tense situation. Thus disruption of normal life due to stone pelting, though reprehensible, is not critical enough to be seen as a sentiment of the people as a whole, instead, it needs to be viewed as a law and order problem.

Evidently, the reasons for protest differed over the years but the methodology and the timing, from beginning May to July end, has remained more or less the same, This is the time when the summer holiday season is coming to an end and the Kashmiri tourist industry has earned its keep for the year. This is also the time for the sensitive and politically charged Armarnath Yatra to begin. The situation becomes ripe for some vested interests charged with the responsibility of keeping the Valley on the boil to strike.

The actions, including engagement with media were well coordinated and focused; loss of a human life in the resultant violence helped trigger more such protests. This was by all means an attempt to engineer a rebellion and those who are engineering it wished for a 1990 type of a situation as the end result. They wanted the process to attract an unacceptable number of misguided youth and escalate into a major security problem.

The Political Initiative

The successive Prime Ministers of the country have kept Kashmir in the forefront and have made concerted attempts to break the impasse. Since the beginning of this millennium the process of reconciliation, resolution and complete integration of Jammu and Kashmir with the Indian Union has been close to the hearts of two successive Prime Ministers of India Atal Behari Vajpayee and Manmohan Singh.

It was during the NDA rule and the premiership of Vajpayee that free and fair elections were held in the State for the second time in succession. The elections witnessed a regime change. The National Conference, which was seen as the unassailable regional party of the State, gave way to the Peoples Democratic Party-Congress coalition with Mufti Mohd Sayeed taking over as Chief Minister on November, 02, 2002.

In 2003, in the aftermath of the massive face off between India and Pakistan due to the attack on the Indian Parliament it was once again Prime Minister Vajpayee, who chose to walk the extra mile to announce ceasefire from Srinagar and extended a hand of friendship to Pakistan on November, 25, 2003. This he did at a public rally in Srinagar addressed by an Indian Prime Minister after 15 years. The ceasefire came as a massive jolt to the terrorists and was instrumental in turning the tide of terrorism in the Valley. It was Vajpayee who made the famous statement, "Jammu aur Kashmir ko insaniyat ke daire mein dekhna hai," which continues to resonate in most dialogues held with relation to the State.

It was the NDA government that attained success in getting the Hurriyat leadership on to the negotiating table. On January, 23, 2004, delegates of the All-Party Hurriyat Conference met with the Prime Minister in what was termed as a courtesy call. "We came to thank the Prime Minister on the initiatives taken vis-a-vis issues in the subcontinent, specially Kashmir... We are with these and the boldness shown by Musharraf," said Mirwaiz Umar Farooq. The Hurriyat went on to tell the Prime Minister that it supported the initiatives taken by him to solve the "issues in the subcontinent." A day earlier the team had met with Home Minister LK Advani.

Dr Manmohan Singh took over as Prime Minister from Atal Bihari Vajpayee on May, 22, 2004 when the peace and reconciliation process had been initiated and was progressing. Dr Manmohan Singh, over his two tenures as Prime Minister, made many valiant attempts to take forward the process and has met with mixed success. The silver lining is that each set back has strengthened his resolve to move forward more proactively towards finding a lasting solution.

As the security situation improved in Jammu and Kashmir and particularly so in the Valley the Indian government took a number of initiatives to get the political process also on track. Significant amongst them was one by Prime Minister Manmohan Singh in 2006, when he tried to engage the separatists in direct talks. The Prime Minister held discussions with a number of prominent separatist leaders like Mirwaiz Umer Farooq, Sajjad Lone and Mohammad Yasin Malik before initiating the political process of dialogue on the vexed issue of Kashmir through the forum of a Round Table Conference (RTC) in February 2006. It can be safely presumed that the confidence generated during these meetings motivated the Prime Minister to take this initiative. It was, therefore, a sad commentary on the political ideology of these leaders when, at a later stage, they consistently refused to share the table for discussion despite open invitations to do so. This became a classic example of the obscurantism which is seen as the bane of Kashmir politics.

A Case to Initiate Debate on Article 370

Prime Minister Narendra Modi, during an election rally at Jammu in December, 2013, sought debates and discussions on Article 370. The statement drew a stringent response from the Kashmir based political parties. Chief Minister Omar Abdullah led the charge with a vitriolic challenge to the then prime ministerial candidate of the BJP to hold an open debate on the subject. The debate did not come by due to the fog of election campaigning. The matter resurfaced after formation of the new government when Dr Jitendra Singh, member of parliament from Udhampur, Jammu and Kashmir and Minister of State, Prime Minister's Office, Department of Personnel and Training (DoPT), during his first interaction with the media on taking charge of DoPT reiterated the posture taken by his party leader in Jammu and elicited an equally stringent response from various quarters.

The fact that seminars on the subject are being arranged across the country indicates universal acceptance of the proposal mooted by Prime Minister Narendra Modi. People want more information and knowledge on the subject that has kept an entire region in isolation for decades since independence. They wish to learn beyond what is fed to them by micro-minute statements of politicians on television news channels. While highlighting the manner in which even a mention let alone a discussion on Article 370 has been suppressed over many decades all speakers expressed happiness at the prospect of the subject being openly and vigorously debated.

Many in Jammu and Kashmir feel that instead of connecting Jammu and Kashmir to India Article 370 is creating walls and barriers. The legislation has stalled development, negatively impacted important parameters like health and education and restricted political empowerment at the grass roots level of Sarpanches and Panches. Article 370 has been instrumental in restricting empowerment of the people and has denied to them the opportunity to stand on their own feet. The economic and political loss that the people of the state suffer due to continuation of the article far outweighs the preferential treatment that it assures. The common man in Jammu and Kashmir is convinced of not having benefited in any manner by the continuation of the statute in Jammu and Kashmir; the preferential treatment is limited to the crony circle of the family based feudal leadership that controls politics in the state, this forms the basis of the vested interest.

As things stand there are so many national schemes that cannot be extended to the state due to the limitations posed by Article 370. Business suffers because people from the rest of the country cannot establish infrastructure in the state. The socio-psychological divide created by the statute negates integration of the youth of the state in other parts of the country. The state is not accountable to the Nation despite looking for assistance all the time. These are only a few examples of many ways in which Article 370 negatively impacts the life of a common man in Jammu and Kashmir. The objective of every law and statute is betterment of the people; if such betterment is not coming by, then legality cannot be quoted as a reason for continuing with it.

Many legal luminaries and prominent citizens of the state are convinced that Article 370 was set up as a temporary measure to implement the Indian Constitution fully in Jammu and Kashmir. This line of thought logically concludes that Article 370 should have been repealed within six months after having completed the constitutional obligation. The country is already behind time by six plus decades in this regard! Many look upon the inability to do away with Article 370 as a failure of the political leadership at both the centre and the state levels.

There is a wide spread perception that those who misused the law and the constitutional situation to establish a feudal cult in the state of Jammu and Kashmir are now worried about their future as a more representative and aware character is seen to be emerging.

The Dialogue Process: Roadblocks and Imperatives

While addressing the matter of a dialogue to resolve this problem it is necessary to first identify those who are opposing the same. The premier position, naturally, goes to Pakistan. It is ironic how every time India makes a sincere generous effort to ease the tensions that prevail on the sub-continent, Pakistan manages to throw its efforts back in India's face. Whether it was the 'kheer' diplomacy of Prime Minister Gujral, Prime Minister Vajpayee's bus ride from Amritsar to Lahore or the Agra summit, Pakistan has always betrayed the trust that India has placed in it as its neighbour. Prime Minister Manmohan Singh has openly expressed a desire to visit Pakistan; sadly, the country has failed to create the climate where a high level visit of the nature would be feasible.

No two successive Pakistani governments have similar views on major policy decisions unless of course it is the anti-India rhetoric on the Kashmir issue. Today when Pakistan has a new government in place, one should pause and review the Indian Government's decision to go ahead with the process of dialogue with a positive frame of mind. It should depend solely on the capacity of Prime Minsiter Nawaz Sharif's ability to walk the talk so far as his conciliatory statements regarding relations with India are concerned.

The second set of players in the dialogue process are the separatists; for many years now the separatists have been insinuating that the centre is not serious about Kashmir; in actuality, it is they who are bent upon disrupting all sincere initiatives for dialogue taken by the centre because they are aware that an honest discussion will expose the hollowness of their positions. Take the example of the position taken by the Mirwaiz that the violence will stop only once concrete steps are taken. This statement can be inferred as a tacit admission that he can put a cap on the violence but will do so only when his conditions are met unconditionally. Does this not make him a perpetrator of the violence and an offender in the eyes of the law?

Despite these very potent roadblocks, if one has to move ahead then certain parameters for a lasting solution need to be worked out. The panel of interlocutors set by the centre was charged with this very mandate. In the discharge of their functions the interlocutors should have been sensitive to the manner in which the people and the events are being manipulated by vested interests.

The debate on Kashmir should involve a wider section of society. Jammu and Ladakh are also stake holders and their people need to be involved in the discussion process. Those entrusted with the security of the region and the territorial integrity of the Nation should definitely have been kept in the loop. Views of retired officers/bureaucrats who have served in Kashmir, intelligentsia, Kashmiri pundits, businessmen, scholars, analysts, journalists etc, need to be taken to bring about a holistic understanding of the problem. Presently, selected Kashmiri politicians and leaders are invited to express their views on pre decided agendas. They give one sided viewpoints which are mostly inconclusive.

Aspects of political aspirations and diverse shades of opinion can be dealt with after the basic issue of national security is addressed. It is often said that the most complex problems have simple solutions. Kashmir will emerge from the existing despondency through a simple, realistic, step by step approach based upon patience and self belief.

Talks are a welcome idea and must be encouraged. However, the Government of India and the State must not rush for them without a conducive climate and a hopeful agenda. A five point formula is worth consideration. First, talks should start once there is proper climate and representation of the people of Jammu and Kashmir. The climate can be called conducive only when the Kashmiri pundits feel safe to return to their homes voluntarily and with dignity. When forced migrants on both sides of the Pir Panjal ranges are given a voice in all matters that are vital to the destiny of their homeland. Secondly, talks have to be within the frame work of the Indian Constitution, by Indians who respect the Indian Constitution; nobody should be empowered to either compromise or even negotiate on a dilution of this aspect. Thirdly, the so-called representatives of the separatist agenda must prove their representation status duly authenticated by a democratic process. Nonsense value of causing public disorders (while holding public life to ransom) is no proof of real public representation which has to be gauged without such threats and pressures. Fourthly, these organisations have to come clean on their aims and objectives, show transparency about their financial support and be put through all the checks and measures applicable to political parties under the law of the land. Fifthly, the separatists have to admit that talks are not there to consider their individual demands emerging from a limited sphere of influence which is not the voice of Jammu and Kashmir as a whole. Lastly, Pakistan has to, at least theoretically, given up many of its inflammatory positions on Kashmir.

One is left wondering as to why the people, the peace loving citizens of Kashmir who are the centre of gravity of the whole issue, are choosing to remain silent? Is their silence not inviting "merchants of death" to kill their near and dear ones? Peace loving Kashmiris outnumber the handful of Pakistan-sponsored trouble creators. But their inaction has been encouraging terrorists and other handlers to wreck havoc in their homeland. They must launch a collective movement against militant atrocities. A collective will of this nature will thwart militant activities and ensure security and peace.

Role of the Army in Jammu and Kashmir

The Enduring Bond between the Army and the People of J&K

The Indian Army has an extraordinary relationship with the people of Jammu and Kashmir. The relationship is signified by the blood of thousands of its brave soldiers that has been and continues to be shed on the soil of the State to save it from the evil designs of inimical forces. The decades of conflict that witnessed three wars and a long period of terrorism has built a unique bond between the force and the people. Since the soldier and the common man have been partners in adversity they relate to each other on a very special plane.

Nonetheless, this relationship has borne more than its fair share of brickbats. It has, on many occasions, come under strain since operations cannot be conducted without some inconvenience and collateral damage to the common man. There have been some black sheep within the ranks of the army who have brought a bad name to the force and given an opportunity to the detractors to cast aspersions. Fortunately, such instances have been few and far between and have been handled by the Army with upmost strictness. Justice, where required, has been dispensed swiftly and without fear or favour.

There have been many attempts by vested interests to exploit this strain to their advantage, fortunately, they have not been successful. As of today the Army stands tall and shoulder to shoulder with those whom it affectionately terms as "Awaam". It has contained the challenging menace of cross border terrorism with more than two decades of relentless effort and the loss of many precious lives. This has been possible only due to the full and unstinted support of the civil population.

Those who are demanding a roll back of the security apparatus have so clouded their vision that the danger that is lurking in the shadows is not visible to them. They continue to parrot the demands of demilitarisation, revocation of the Armed Forces Special Powers Act (AFSPA) even as the security forces are losing precious lives to ensure that there is no resurrection of the terrorism that has plagued the Valley.

Whether the segment of the Kashmiri leadership which waxes eloquent on the issue of troop withdrawal deems itself to be absolutely secure or it is tired of existing in a peaceful environment is a question that the electorate of the State should put to it. Whatever may be its reasons, they definitely smack of a distinct lack of political and strategic acumen. With our "friendly" neighbourhood right across the border on the boil and the so-called Jihadi elements waiting for an opportunity to re-establish their foothold in J&K, one wonders how much of a service this leadership of the State are doing to its people by calling for a dilution of the security paradigm at this juncture.

Political and Legal Justification for AFSPA

AFSPA gives the security forces (Army, BSF, CRPF and ITBP) some special powers. These include powers to search premises and make arrests without warrants, use force even to the extent of causing death, destroy fortifications/ shelters/hideouts and to stop, search and seize vehicles. The provisions of AFSPA do not deviate too much from the norms of protection provided to government servants and police personnel through the Code of Criminal Procedure (CrPC) and other enabling legislations. Section 45 of the CrPC disallows arrest of public servants without prior sanction of the government; this section, however, is not valid in J&K where the Ranbir Penal Code is applicable and ipso facto, persons of Armed Forces can be arrested for any perceived excesses if AFSPA is not instituted. This fortifies the need for a protective umbrella for forces functioning in J&K.

The Supreme Court has also mandated a Government sanction prior to initiating prosecution against police personnel for excesses or killings committed during the maintenance of law and order. Thereby, police authorities still enjoy more encompassing and wider powers relating to arrest, search, seizure, summoning of witnesses, preventive detention etc than those vested upon the Army through AFSPA. The Act does offer protection to security persons acting in good faith in their official capacity, however, the Act also stipulates that arrested persons and seized property be made over to the police with least possible delay; a stipulation that is being followed most persistently.

Adequate checks and safeguards are inbuilt within AFSPA. The Army procedures ensure the use of minimum force during arrest/search of persons, opening of fire with due warning etc. Prompt disciplinary action is initiated against defaulters under Army Act 1950.

The Justice Jeevan Reddy Commission constituted in 2004 had, in its recommendations, stated that provisions of AFSPA should be incorporated in UAPA, 1967, which would be applicable to the whole country.

There is no denying that AFSPA gives some special powers to the security forces but it also has to be understood that extraordinary situations can be dealt with only through extraordinary measures. The Act is essential for the army to function proactively in counter terrorism and counter insurgency situations. When the enemy has penetrated within the civilian population it is he who has curbed the liberty of the people and not the security forces who are, in fact, trying to ensure that the right to life and dignity of the civilian population is not compromised by such mercenary and criminal elements.

No person on earth can function without the assurance that his actions will not draw punitive retribution by the State and the AFSPA ensures just that for the soldiers performing internal security functions. It also has to be ensured that terrorists do not misuse civil laws to get away with their nefarious activity, hence the need to fortify counter terrorist operations with special powers for search, arrest and detention.

The AFSPA does have provisions that curtail prosecution, suit or other legal proceeding against a person functioning under the Act except with the previous sanction of the central Government but this definitely does not imply that the soldier is placed above the law of the land. It only implies that he will function under a different set of laws. In any case the Indian Amy soldiers are subject to the Army Act 1950 which is invoked while investigating all cases of excesses committed in areas under the jurisdiction of the AFSPA and the Amy Act is by no means less stringent than the criminal procedure code of the Indian constitution, in fact, justice is both apt and timely when delivered under this Act.

While considering changes in the status quo, it has to be kept in mind that partial revocation of these legislations is not a very wise move. The Army cannot be amenable to any such suggestion since the areas that resultantly would not come under the purview of the legislations are likely to be used by terrorists and anti-National forces to recoup and re-launch operations. Politically also an action of this nature is fraught with danger since revocation of the legislations in some areas will trigger a chain reaction of demands for revocation in other areas and this will put the government on a totally unacceptable back foot.

Conclusion

In their tryst for peace the people of Kashmir have the unstinting support of the Indian people and the government of India. Successive Prime Minister's have exhibited statesmanship to make courageous attempts towards setting things right. This millennium has witnessed a spate of initiatives by both the UPA and the NDA government to understand the core issue and look for a lasting solution. Complete success may have been elusive but the process has won the hearts and minds of the Kashmiri populace who relate more to their nation now.

As in the case of all political disputes of long standing, in Jammu and Kashmir also many stake holders have mushroomed over the years. Most are interested to taking a piece of the pie and benefitting from it, some have nothing more than the good of Kashmir in mind but can do little to progress in this direction. The dispute and the people are sidelined in a mad rush for political, economic and social power.

A deep analysis would lead to a deduction that the politics are not in sync with the actual aspirations of the people; politics are being played without the public being the centre of gravity as is necessary in all vibrant democracies. Disruption holds a very hallowed place in the politics of the state, especially so, in the Kashmir valley. It is engineered and orchestrated with clockwork precision to garner preconceived results. It is timed, managed and applied to perfection.

Happily, the government seems to have cracked the process and is now in a position to pre-empt the same. However, the perpetrators still hold the capacity to spring surprises. Political and social disruption holds a prominent place in the contemporary affairs of the state.

The most critical element in the entire drama played out in Jammu and Kashmir over six decades is sadly also the most maligned, misunderstood and misrepresented security forces, the Indian Army being the most prominent. The Armed Forces of the nation have, right since independence, been called upon to defend Kashmir with sweat and blood. They have performed their duty with utmost courage and fortitude and that is the prime reason for the freedom that the region enjoys today. Yet, there are many detractors who project the force in a negative light. There are some vested foreign sponsored interests that wish to reduce the security umbrella so as to resurrect terrorism and insurgency.

The leadership of Kashmir should tread a path that uplifts their beleaguered people politically and economically. It does seem that Independence, United States of Kashmir or dispensations of this nature are as non viable today as they were historically. Resorting to these as a platform for political debate amounts to misguiding the people, it would be expedient to lead them on the path of progress and development that is today open for them, failing which, the Kashmiri leadership will be faced with the ignominy of going down as traitors to the cause of their people.

The journey to complete subjugation of the terrorist movement is long and arduous. The present circumstances, though a marked improvement from the times of peak terrorism, cannot be defined as totally normal. The slightest let down in pressure can give to the remnants the space to regroup and retaliate.

The very fact that things are improving in Kashmir today calls for a more honest and sustained effort to maintain the momentum till such time that peace is firmly embedded and the region moves on a self sustained and irreversible path of progress and prosperity. This is easier said than done because the complexity of the whole issue, the large number of stake holders and the psyche of a people bruised by decades of violence and abuse poses an omnipotent danger of the situation reversing in response to perhaps even a single innocuous catalyst. The situation requires deft and mature handling since one mistake can have disastrous consequences.

15

Significance of Warfare: A Historical Evolution from Early Period to the Present

P.S. Harish

Military has always acquired a significantly high status and it had played a crucial role in the past and continues to do so in the present. In the past many mighty empires sustained for a long time as vital attention was paid in building and maintaining a huge military apparatus. In the current scenario, we see that conflicts between nations have enormously increased and the feeling of constant fear of being attacked has become more widespread. The amount of money spent on strengthening the defence has come to a higher side and nations around the world have been allocating more funds for the purpose of enhancing their military power. To meet any eventuality, countries all over are making constant effort to raise huge armies. Modern weapons with maximum destructive capacity are also manufactured and in this regard the production of nuclear weapons has become the point of major focus.

In-depth studies are being carried out globally on safety, security and peace. Research is being focused on how wars were fought, technology used in weapons and other related aspects. Military history as an academic discipline has grown up widely in recent times and people have began to understand the ill-effects of war on civilization. For understanding the present day situation and setting a base for future technological innovations, the study of military history and warfare of the bygone years becomes significant and crucial. A study about the warfare of the past is also essential to understand the evolution of the weapons and military organization from time to time. Such studies also enable us to understand the social, political and commercial factors that led to the prevalence of wars among various nations or communities. Keeping this in background the present paper aims to bring about a historical evolution of warfare in different time periods and its increasing relevance with the progress of time. Further, it also examines India's growth and its development as a military entity in the post-Independence period which, in course of time highlighted its importance in the region of Southeast Asia.

The phenomenon of war has been a continuous activity with in human society. The alteration of war and peace had been the very process of the past. If we go along the socio-biologists view, it says that there is war because human being is innately aggressive.[1] In other words it can be said that the inherent tendency of human nature is to dominate others. There are various opinions expressed on the origin of war. One optimistic view considers the arising of war mainly due to material scarcity resulting in fierce competition for limited resources of land, food and wealth. Some pessimists on the other hand see violence as innate in human being. Freud in his book 'Civilization and Discontents' says that behind the veneer of civilization, there is a death wish in all individuals, which periodically leads to the release of savage destructive forces.[2]

In every civilization there have been wars and they had been instrumental in bringing about numerous changes politically, economically, socially etc in each historical period. The main aim of war is to subjugate the enemy and have a control over the resources. For example, Clausewitz considers war as an act of force to compel the enemy to do our will.[3] War can also be considered as 'dual on a larger scale,'[4] involving a huge armed force, more space and above all a bulky expenditure. A dual is between two persons or between two small groups of people and is smaller in scale, but the intentions of a war are huge and manifold.

Historical Evolution of Warfare

In every civilization there had been wars and military had always played a crucial role in every historical period. The foremost reason for its growing importance is due to the fear of being attacked. The first humans were big game hunters. They lived in small groups and each group hunted within a fairly well defined territory and rarely encountered strangers. Sometimes the whole group had to move over to another hunting ground in case of scarcity. At any moment, a sudden encounter with some wild animal might prove fatal or there was likelihood of strangers trying to occupy the hunting territory, forcing the group to make a choice between fighting back or trying to make peace.[5] Similarly, there is a reconstruction on the early beginnings of war by two contrasting views. One view had stressed on the point that the life of the early human being was of a continuous strife. It had also envisaged that the early man lived in antagonistic hordes which became a basis for generating conflicts.[6] In course of time as population increased, the number of hordes opposed to one another got reduced with the improved methods of procuring food and as a result relatively peaceful co-existence prevailed. The second view divides the history of human beings into two epochs: one when they were peaceful and innocent and a latter epoch when war came into their lives.[7]

Different methods of defence were adopted based on the availability of raw material. For example, branches of tree, bamboo etc, were employed for fencing as a means of protection and also were used as weapons for killing wild animals. The earliest tools were manufactured without employing any metal since it was unknown. These consisted of pebble tools, which included scrappers, choppers and hand axes. Scrapers were utilized for scraping bark of trees, bamboo shafts and skin of animals. Thus, the earliest weapons were derived from nature, which were conveniently used according to the need. An intrinsic part of the progress towards civilization was the evolution of technology based on working with fire. The main area where the earliest metal working appeared is the old world extending from Bulgaria in the west through Anatolia and into western Iran.

A vital step in the development of metallurgy was the discovery of smelting, a high temperature process by which pure metal could be procured from ore.[8] There is no exact evidence of when it started, but it certainly facilitated the production of metal weapons and goods. Iron played a crucial role in the growth of technology and technical knowledge. It led to the introduction of new agricultural techniques. The manufacture of large scale weapons rapidly transformed the field of military. In this context, the frequent conflicts between Aryans and Dasas can be mentioned, for numerous small to medium sized weapons might have been used. Even in the Indus valley, there is evidence of copper weapons, but of inferior quality compared to West Asiatic cultures.[9] Magadhan rulers like Bimbisara and Ajatasatru gave considerable importance to the aspect of defence. The Mauryas inherited a huge and powerful army from their predecessors. A huge war apparatus was formed during this period and the organization of army was very much developed and strengthened. The Kautilyan principles of warfare, diplomacy, ethics etc began to be followed by the rulers. The military system as a whole became systematic and practical.

The warfare as a whole became quicker and faster compared to the earlier times due to the use of chariots or *rathas* from this time i.e., the *Janapada* period. As a result the mobility of warriors became easier through the opponent ranks of the soldiers.[10] This provided the required safety and also ensured an easy victory. Hence the invention of chariot can be considered as a milestone in the history of warfare. There is not much reference to the army system of the Guptas, but certainly they would have maintained a formidable force, for it would have been impossible for Samudragupta to undertake numerous campaigns (including the *Aryavarta* campaign to the south) without the assistance of powerful military system. Similarly in South India, Pallava rulers took utmost care in maintaining a strong army as they had frequent conflicts with the Badami Chalukyas. Large number of elephants in the panels depicting warfare at *Vaikunta Perumal* temple at Kanchi suggests their knowledge of *Gajasastra*.[11] The Cholas of the later period who maintained a vast military force had different regiments. An interesting feature of Chola military apparatus was the prevalence of naval force which was utilized for the expeditions to the neighbouring Ceylon and to as far as Malaya (Indonesia).

By eighth century AD, the extreme northwest of the country (the region of Sindh) witnessed the first Arab invasion. From then onwards, there was a steady influx of invaders from the Middle Eastern region. But mostly their influence was confined to the north. It was only during the beginning of fourteenth century that the Deccan and South India faced the first external invasion from north under Alaudin Khilji. It is natural that they brought with them not only their customs and traditions but also the technology and scientific knowledge possessed by them. Many areas like agriculture, irrigation, spinning, sciences (including alchemy, metallurgy, engineering etc.), military etc underwent significant transformation due to the exchange of technical ideas and interaction between both the cultures. From the beginning the Arabs had a superior hand in the battles fought by them with the Indian rulers. Mohammed Kasim, who attacked the port of Daibal in Sindh, had a powerful engine known as *manjanik*. This was the most effective commonly employed siege engine which required the power of five hundred men to work on it. It hurled with great force huge pieces of rocks, stones, earthen, iron balls, naphtha or casks containing foul matter, scorpions and other poisonous reptiles.[12] This was done through a sling attached to a huge beam, which worked with the three different principles of torsion, counterpoise and tension.

One of the significant inventions that transformed the scenario of warfare drastically was the invention of gunpowder. It gave away to the manufacture of large scale firearms at a later period. Though there was a great deal of confusion and debate over the origin of gunpowder, it is generally now accepted that firearms originated in China. The earliest known formula for gunpowder can be found in a Chinese work dating probably to AD 800.[13] By AD 1200's gunpowder, which is an essential ingredient for manufacturing firearms seems to have been widely known. By 1300's Europeans certainly had firearms and the Turks, Iranians and Indians obtained the fire weapons not later than 1400's.[14]

In South India we come across the reference of sun dried missiles during Kakatiya period but we do not find any description of it.[15] In Vijayanagar time pyrotechnical devices were very much in use and Domingo Paes, the Portuguese traveler who visited Vijayanagar during sixteenth century describes the use of fireworks at the *Mahanavami* festival. He said that when the amusements ended many rockets and different sorts of fire were thrown.[16] Even at the time of the review of troops by the emperor, rockets were said to have been used. Hence it can be concluded by saying that though there was knowledge of gunpowder, it was initially utilized for non-war purposes even though in some regions of India crude forms of firearms were known. Firearms in contrast to fire weapons may have been used in the second half of fifteenth century. However, the use of firearms on a regular basis was introduced by the Portuguese initially in South India and by Babur in the north by sixteenth century.[17]

The influence of Europeans, especially Portuguese over the south-western coast of India from the beginning of sixteenth century gradually witnessed the diffusion of a new technology in the field of warfare. They used naval artillery, a technique that was entirely new to Indian rulers at that time. This can be considered as an achievement in the field of war technology after the invention of gunpowder. Of all the European powers, which had established their trade settlements in India, it was the British who finally got hold of the vast sub-continent and politically began to control the region. In course of time, India became the shinning jewel on the British crown as it contributed the most for the growth of the British Colonial Empire in the east. Similar to the earlier interactions that India had with various outsiders during ancient and medieval times, with Europeans too (particularly British), Indian rulers encountered a different set of culture which was entirely new to them. In course of time, the amalgamation of the two different cultures was to be found in various fields like literature, philosophy and military was no exception.

Influence of British Military Aspects over Indian Warfare

During the initial period of British entry into India, the formation of a body of armed men had its origin in the necessity of protecting factories in which valuable goods were stored. Hence the initial growth of small armies which later became the pillars for the British Empire was utilized for the security of commercial establishments. It was in course of time that these micro military units became huge with the expansion of British. Hence technically speaking, the roots of Indian army could be traced back to this period.

The British were the last colonizers who came to India but were able to firmly establish their roots in India by overpowering the other European powers and establishing themselves for more than two hundred years. During this period, there was considerable influence of British in various aspects including military and warfare. When the British became the masters, they began to take various measures to improve their military capabilities and especially after the creation of Presidencies, this process attained a great momentum. An essential basic ingredient for the operation of all the weapons was gunpowder. This began at Madras in AD 1639 and by the beginning of 18th century, all the Presidencies witnessed the manufacture of this chemical and other war materials. Before this, military supply to the Company's troops came directly from home country.

Military arms, equipment and stores were supplied in large quantities by the Board of Ordnance at England to the company's troops and Indian purchasers. In AD 1658, Cromwell granted license to one Mr. Bolt to export to India three mortars and two lakh twenty thousand rounds of shells for Aurangzeb.[18] The early Indian made guns were crude mostly of iron bars bound by iron rings or of iron cylinders with brass cast round them. They were clumsy and inefficient and Orme says that even in eighteenth century, Indian rulers thought of them as being efficient even if it could fire once.[19]

Numerous kinds of weapons were manufactured by the British in order to fight many wars with Indians as well as their European counterparts. The war weapons included different kinds of mortars, artillery, cannons, howitzers etc. There were three kinds of mortars—Land mortar, Sea mortar and Stone mortar. The land mortars were short cannon of a large bore and their use was to throw hollow balls filled with powder and known as shells.[20] When falling upon any building or into the works of a fortification, it bursts and its fragments destroy everything within its reach.

Mortars were distinguished chiefly by the diameter of the bore. For example, a ten inch mortar meant that the diameter of its bore was ten inches.[21] The sea mortars or those placed on board of ships were larger and heavier than the land ones. The stone mortars helped to fling stones on enemy's works. There was also another sort known as howitzer, which was a German invention that differs from the sea mortars in having their trunion placed nearly in the middle and being mounted upon carriages like traveling gun carriages.[22] It is noted that the use of howitzers differed from that of the common mortars as the howitzers were carried upon gun traveling carriages. They could be easily transported to the field and from one place to another and were more readily fired than others.

One of the major problems in this period was that many times the guns and mortars available would be unfit for use when deployed, as there was a major time lapse between the period of manufacture and use. Sometimes some defects could have occurred at the stage of manufacture itself. Therefore, the Europeans introduced strict inspections that were carried out regularly to check for their fitness before using them in battles. Although iron was generally used for making the body of the gun, gradually the superiority of bronze was realized and the Europeans developed procedures for producing bronze and other alloys.[23] Although these developments were taken up by the Europeans for their benefit, in course of time the weapon development activities in India also absorbed these advantages. Gradually the local people also began to get familiarize with the preparation of new alloys and inspection procedures for various arms.

The concept of drill was a very essential feature of a European army. Drill was performed for maintaining physical strength, discipline, for increasing concentration and instilling confidence in order to boldly face the enemy on the battlefield. In some cases there were night marches done in order to make soldiers alert in case of an emergency. Though in the Indian context there are references of Gupta rulers training their troops with exercises, this concept was almost absent in the Indian army. It is interesting to see that in European context; even the minute details like the timing of the march, the standing positions of soldiers with and without arms were aptly calculated. To some extent Tipu Sultan and his father Haider Ali were some of the rulers who introduced regular exercises to their troops in order to make their armed forces strong. They acquired this from the French with whom they had maintained cordial relations for a long time.

One of the important aspects that Europeans in general and British in particular followed was the preparation that went on before waging a battle. In order to undertake a military campaign, they took into consideration the nature of the country along with the quality of troops, the number of enemy troops and the plan of the campaign. The first requisite in the formation of an army was that it should be quick and rapid in its movements. Unlike the Indian armies in which we find heavy baggage with lot of commodities, the Europeans had restricted baggage in order to be free from any unnecessary encumbrance. For instance, when Nizam marched towards Arcot in AD 1742-43, a large number of people were said to have been employed to carry all the necessary items of the Sultan and the army.[24]

The armed forces of the west (i.e., Europe) placed a heavy reliance on superior technology. But along with technological greatness, various other factors played a crucial role for Europeans. As the Swiss military writer Antoine-Henry Jomini wrote in the early nineteenth century. 'The superiority of armament may increase the chances of success in war but it does not itself win battles.'[25] Even in the twentieth century, the outcome of wars has been determined less by technology than by better war plans, the achievement of surprise, greater economic strength and above all superior discipline. Western military practice had always exalted discipline rather than kinship, religion or patriotism. The crucial element in discipline had been the ability of a formation to stand fast in the face of the enemy, whether attacking or being attacked, without giving way for natural impulses or fear and panic.[26] These aspects certainly helped European powers to have an edge over Indian rulers and this in turn had helped them to build their Colonial base in the east.

Hence, it can be said that the European impact and British in particular had profound effect on the military aspect which, in course of time had set the base for the development of Indian army later. The kind of western exposure that the Indian rulers got certainly helped them to understand and borrow a few aspects that very well suited their needs in waging battles. Along with this, the various institutions set up by the British related to military and warfare and the kind of base that was established for catering their needs, also became the precursor for the defence build up later. By the time India attained its independence; Indian soldiers had considerable knowledge over western mode of warfare, as they had to fight for British during both the World Wars. It was for the first time that Indian army fought being a part of the European army during First World War. Though Indian soldiers were made to fight for the benefit of the British, Indian exposure in fighting a World War had definitely made them to understand the kind of tactics and technology used by British and other European powers.

India's Military Growth in the Post-Independence Period: Its Relevance in South and Southeast Asia

The period of 1940's witnessed the deepening of the anti-colonial struggle across African and Asian countries. In this regard, India too voiced its concerns and pressed the demand for the freedom from British. Even before India became independent, its leadership had foreseen the future of South and Southeast Asia and India's involvement in building up the unity among nations. In March 1947, India had convened the Asian Relations Conference with the main intention of supporting the freedom struggles spread across Asia. Similarly, the special conference on Indonesia in 1949, which was convened to express support to the armed struggle led by Sukarno against the Dutch certainly helped India in nurturing up its foreign policy in early 1950's.[27] By this time, the process of de-colonization which led to the gradual diminishing of the colonial authority over the east had profound impact. Now the prime concern of the newly independent countries, particularly in the South and Southeast Asian region, which consisted of India too was to maintain peace and concentrate on the development of their respective nations economically, socially, politically and also militarily (in order to defend themselves). This was necessary, as all these nations were in the yoke of colonial leadership for centuries and after that they had to develop and rise up as individual nations. In order to carry on with this long term process, co-operation, mutual trust and security were essential among the nations.

Indian army has been one of the largest military forces and right after independence; Indian military had many challenges and tasks to be performed, in which they could succeed in some of the occasions. These included wars with Pakistan, takeover of Goa from Portuguese in 1961 and intervention in Sri Lankan civil war etc.[28] Hence initially the strength of the Indian army was channelized in bringing in internal stability. Even in international sphere also, Indian army could excel on some assignments in 1950's during the crisis period in Korea and Congo. In these, the performance of Indian army was professional, which was very much complimented. Thereafter, India had to strike a strategic balance and develop cordial and friendly relations with its neighbours who were also liberated from colonial control on par with India. In this scenario, the aspect of security and defence and its development became the most crucial issue. The most important reason for this could be the threat of attacks from either outside or within the neighbours. In this background, Indian military had to be effectively trained and developed in order to meet any possible eventuality.

The military modernization got the required attention after its defeat against China in 1962 and India moved ahead to enhance its military capabilities in order to ensure sufficient defence and security. Due to this reason, defence expenditure was also on a higher side and additional emphasis was also laid on defence research and technology.[29] Along with this, there were other factors like leadership, security, national interest, internal and external conflicts and the international situation prevalent at that time had given required impact to reinforce and strengthen the safety and security.[30] With its neighbouring countries like China expanding in Southeast Asian region, India had to tighten its defence's around maritime zones and increase the surveillance across its waters in order to prevent the influence of Chinese military development. Globally too, the situation was volatile due to the escalation of the Cold War situation as the Cuban Missile crisis (1962) fuelled the tensions between the two power blocks. This naturally had an impact over the Asia, including India due to its proximity to Russia. These developments raised security concerns and more impetus was given for military sophistication. In addition to this, India's geographical location in Southeast Asia can also be considered as one of the reasons for its focus on defence build up. Being landlocked in the north and having a large coastline in south, the aspect of security has been a very key issue and hence naval development was one of the top priorities in India's military development. In this regard, it is also to be noted that the seas surrounding India had been prominent trade routes connecting Middle East in the west to Malaysia in the east from early period till the present, with forty percent of world's trade passing through Southeast Asia.[31] This in one way has been a positive factor in fostering India's bilateral relations and hence fruitful economic ties have been developed with its neighbours.

India's image as a rapidly growing military power trying to expand its influence beyond South Asia remained even after various changes in the global level. Even after the end of Cold war regime in early 1990's, India was looked upon as an effective policymaker to bring about a balance in South Asia and maintain a friendly atmosphere in the region. In a way, the economic reform programme during early 1990's enabled India to put in a new policy framework. Similarly the raising of the defence capability by undertaking various Confidence Building Measures (CBM's) by navy through different naval exercises and taking assistance from outside regarding import of certain defence equipments also highlighted India's position in the region.[32] Further, the upgradation of the Nuclear Programmes to meet the India's growing energy needs and security has heralded a new phase in the sphere of defence modernization, signaling a new era and more highlighting role for it in South Asia.

Conclusion

Hence it can be concluded that from the dawn of civilization, the aspect of defence or defending oneself was in vogue. Initially it was from wild animals and vagaries of nature, but with the passage of time, this aspect went on changing with new techniques of defence and weapons being adopted in every time period. With the increase in conflicts from early period to modern times, rapid development was seen in the field of military with sophisticated war apparatus being manufactured and effectively utilized on battlefields, especially after the advent of gunpowder. With the influence of the West, an altogether different military technology evolved which altered the war scenario. The process of colonization and the subsequent utilization of the manpower by Europeans from Afro-Asian countries in waging wars (including World Wars) against their enemies had exposed the armies to superior tactics and technology. This helped Indian army to tackle the post-Independence security threats effectively to some extent. The post-colonial phase, especially in Southeast Asian region had witnessed the emergence of India as the harbinger of peace and unity and its support for its neighbouring countries to get freedom from colonial authority was thoroughly acknowledged. Though most of the erstwhile European colonies had the imprints of their colonial masters including India, their internal development was necessary for their growth and sustenance. As Cold war situation arose in 1950's, the newly independent countries in the east were vulnerable to external as well as internal attacks and thus the aspect of security became a crucial aspect. Hence, defence sophistication was one of the prime concerns of India and in this regard, army, navy and weaponry had received considerable attention. The various Confidence Building Measures (CBM's) and periodical military exercises had made India to carve out a niche for itself in maintaining a cordial and friendly relations and striking out a between East and West.

REFERENCES

1. M. Howard, *The Causes of War and other Essays*, Temple Smith, London, 1983, p 7.
2. Freud, Civilizations and Discontents, in People, Science and Technology by Charles Boyle, Wheat Sheaf Books Ltd, London, 1984, p 151.
3. Karl Von Clausewitz, On War, Edited and Translated by M. Howard and P. Paret, Princeton University Press, Princeton, New Jersey, 1976, p 75.
4. Ibid.
5. H.W. McNeill, *A History of Human Community* (*Pre-History to Present*), Brill & Laiden, London, 1987, p 9.

6. J. Schneider, "On the Beginnings of Warfare", *Social Forces,* Vol 31, No. 1, October 1952, pp 68-69.
7. Ibid.
8. A.J. Gowlette, John, Accent to Civilization, Roxby Archaeological Limited, London, 1984, p 180.
9. Bridget, All chin, 'Substitute Stones', in Harappan Civilization, (a Contemporary Perspective), Edited by G.L. Possehl, Oxford & IBA Publishing Co, New Delhi, 1982, p 235.
10. S. Mishra, *Janapada State in Ancient India*, Bharatiya Vidhya Prakashan, Varanasi, 1973, p 194.
11. C. Minakshi, *Administration and Social Life under Pallavas*, University of Madras, Madras, 1977, p 80.
12. O.P. Jaggi, *History of Science and Technology in India*, Vol VII, Atma Ram & Sons, New Delhi, 1981, p 125.
13. K. Chase, Firearms, *A Global History to 1700*, Cambridge University Press, Cambridge, 2003, p 1.
14. Ibid.
15. G. Yazdani, *The Early History of Deccan*, Parts VII-XI, Oriental Books Reprint Corporation, New Delhi, 1982, p 667.
16. D. Paes, Chronicle of Domingo Paes, as quoted in 'The Forgotten Empire' by Robert Sewell, Asian Educational Services, New Delhi, 1980, p 271.
17. J. Qaisar, Ahsan, *Indian Response to European Technology and Culture, AD 1498-1707*, Oxford University Press, Delhi, 1982, pp 46-47.
18. H.S. Bhatia, *Military History of British India, AD 1607-1947*, Deep & Deep Publications, p.191.
19. R. Orme, *A History of Military Transactions of the British Nation in Indostan from the year MDCCXLV* (1745), Today and Tomorrow Publications, New Delhi, 1947, p 394.
20. J. Muller, J. Milan, *A Treatise on Artillery*, Whitehall, London, 1780, p 65.
21. Ibid, p 66.
22. Ibid.
23. Captain Thompson, A Treatise on Gunpowder—A Treatise on Firearms in the service of the Artillery in time of War, Translated from Italian of Alessandro Vittorio Papacino D'Antoni, T&J Egerton, London, 1789, pp 103-04.
24. R.A. Pillai, *The Private Diary of Ananda Ranga Pillai*, September 1736 AD to April 1746 AD, Translated from Tamil by the order of the Govt of Madras, Vol I, Government Press, Madras, 1908, p 214.
25. G. Parker, *The Illustrated History of Warfare, The Triumph of the West*, Cambridge University Press, Cambridge, 1995, p 2.
26. Ibid, p 3.
27. M. Ayoob, *India and Southeast Asia*, Routledge, London, pp 7-8.
28. R.P. Brass, *The Politics of India since Independence*, Cambridge University Press, Cambridge, 2001 (Reprint), 1990 (First Publication).
29. A. Gupta, "Determining India's Force Doctrine and Military Structure", *Asian Survey*, Vol 40, No. 5, 1995, p 443.
30. C. Smith, *India's Ad hoc Arsenal: Direction or Drift in the Defence Policy*, Oxford University Press, New York, 1994, p 8.
31. G.V.C. Naidu, *Looking East: India and Southeast Asia*, Paper presented at the Second Round Table Conference at Institute of Defence Studies and Analyses, October 27&28, Taipei, Taiwan, p 192.
32. Ibid.

Section II

NON-TRADITIONAL SECURITY THREATS

16

China's Water Diversion Projects: Analysis and Impact

R.N. Singh

Water, one of the most essential components for life is needed to ensure food security, feed livestock, progress industrial production and to conserve the biodiversity and environment. Growing human population, severe neglect coupled with over-exploitation of the resource and gross mismanagement, is making it a scarce commodity—forcing the world to gradually move towards potable water crisis. 'The 2030 Water Resources Group' in 2009 revealed that globally, the current withdrawals of water of about 4500 km^3 exceed the availability of about 4200 km[1]. By 2030 a global deficit of 40% is forecast[2]. Asian sub-continent being the driest continent considering its population density and availability of fresh water reserve would continue to witness intra-state and inter-state stresses to meet its water demands, leading to internal and external tensions, especially in case of trans border rivers.

S.No.	*Country*	*External flow Mn/m^3*	*Total Mn/m^3*	*External Dependency (%age)*
1.	China	17,169	28,40,000	0.90
2.	India	6,47,220	19,07,760	33.40
3.	Pakistan	1,70,300	2,25,300	75.59
4.	Bangladesh	11,05,644	12,10,644	91.30
5.	Vietnam	5,24,710	8,91,210	58.90

China is the biggest trans-border water provider in the world. Waters from China flow down to India, Pak, Kyrgyzstan, Kazakhstan, Russia, Bangladesh (BD) and the SE Asian nations upto Vietnam. The demand of water for economic and industrial growth is increasing every year; coupled with it is the rising pollution of existing water sources, resulting in reduction of per capita availability of fresh water. China being water abundant nation has minimal external water dependency unlike India which has 33.4% external dependency[3] being a lower riparian State. It is pertinent to mention that North and NE China is water scarce with 2/3rd of crop lands, in contrast to Southern China which is water abundant with 1/3rd of crop lands. It is in this context that China has embarked upon the biggest hydraulic initiative of diverting the waters from South to address the existing and foreseeable water crisis in its Northern regions.

All the lower riparian States and the related biodiversity would have an adverse impact if the waters of Indo-China trans border rivers were to be diverted to Northern China. It is, therefore, axiomatic that the major water diversion projects by China on its trans border river, Tsangpo/Brahmaputra, are analysed thoroughly to infer its impact on India and measures to be instituted to overcome the same, which this Paper attempts to.

Tibet and Trans Border Rivers

Tibet's high altitude, huge land mass and vast glaciers endow it with the greatest river system in the world. Tibetan plateau with 46,000 glaciers at an average altitude of 13000 ft is the earth's 3rd largest ice mass.[4] The net hydrological flows in Tibet are 627km^3/ yr out of which 577 km^3 flow into other countries (92%). Given the low precipitation in Tibet, higher proportion of river flows originates from the glaciers. The Tibetan Plateau is the greatest water system globally and is the primary fresh water resource to Northern India and China (Yellow river and Yangtse R) which are the most populous and fast growing economies in the region. China and India with eight other SE Asian nations and 47% of the world's population are heavily dependent on the Tibetan waters.[5]

Six major Asian river basins begin in the Tibetan Plateau: the Indus (India, Pakistan); the Ganges (Nepal, India, Bangladesh); the Brahmaputra (India, Bangladesh); the Salween (China, Burma, Thailand); the Mekong (China, Laos, Thailand, Cambodia, Vietnam); and the Yangtze (China)[6]—Tibet is without question "the most incredible water tank one can imagine".[7] Indus, Sutlej and Tsangpo/ Brahmaputra are the three major Indo-China trans-border rivers originating from the Chinese controlled Tibetan plateau. Additionally Karnali and Arun are the other two major rivers originating from Tibet which join the Ganges after draining through Nepal. Water discharge of Indus, Sutlej and the Brahmaputra, the three significant rivers, which originate in TAR, is a matter of

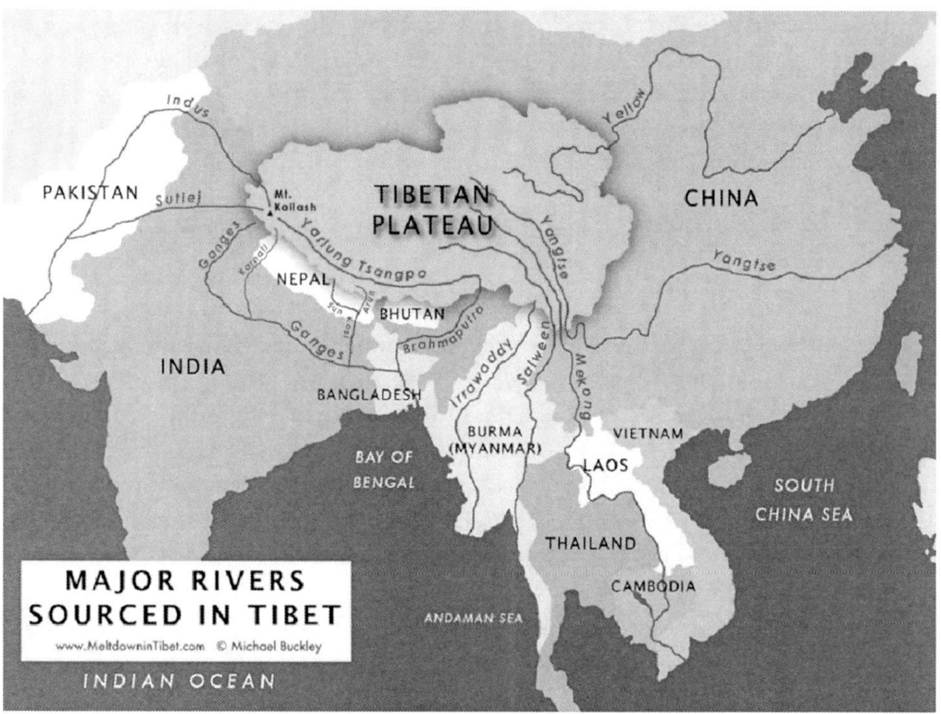

concern for India. While the waters of Indus and Sutlej drain into Arabian Sea through Pak, Brahmaputra transits its course through the North Eastern States and Bangladesh before draining into the Bay of Bengal.

	Origin	*Tibet*	*India*	*Pakistan/ Bangladesh*
Indus (3180 Km	Mt Kailash	358 Km	1114 Km	1708 Km (Pakistan)
Sutlej (1450 Km)	Raka Lake	240 Km	680 Km	526 Km (Pakistan)
Matsang Tsangpo Brahmaputra (2880 Km)	Angsi Glacier/ Mansarovar Lake	1625 Km	918 Km	337 Km (Bangladesh)

More than 60% of water in all the three rivers is added due to rainfall and other tributaries after they enter India. Most significantly 66.7% of the waters in Tsangpo are added post it enters India as Siang, while traversing 918 km with catchment area of 34%. This is primarily due to pattern in annual rainfall which in Tibet is 400mm and India is 3000mm, significantly increasing the water inflow into Brahmaputra. The data generated by Chinese writings depict annual flow of 168.9 BCM (Billion Cubic mtrs) of Tsangpo into India, whereas as per the Indian estimates it is 200 BCM. The Chinese plan of diverting 118 BCM of these waters towards Chinese main land would result in significant depletion in the waters of Brahmaputra, directly impacting the downstream navigation, ecology, irrigation patterns and fertility of land. The number of projects on Tsangpo has also increased significantly from 28 in 2008 to 39 in 2012. China claims that these projects are 'run of the river' with no major lakes being formed; still the effect on downstream India is significant to raise concerns.

China: Necessity of Water Diversion

Asia's Water Problem

The availability of freshwater in Asia is not even half of the global annual average of 6,380 m^3 per inhabitant making it the driest continent in the world.[8] When the estimated reserve of rivers, lakes, and aquifers are added up, Asia has less than one-tenth of the waters of South America, Australia and New Zealand, not even one-fourth of North America, almost one-third of Europe, and moderately less than Africa per inhabitant. Yet the world's fastest growing demand for water, for food, industrial production and for municipal support is in Asia, which now serves as the locomotive of the world economy.[9]

The world's global water demand is set to increase by 55% in next 30 years. Asia continues to draw on tomorrow's water to meet today's needs. Worse still, Asia has one of the lowest levels of water efficiency and productivity in the world. Against this background, it is no exaggeration to say that 'water scarcity is set to become the defining crisis of Asia by the mid century, creating obstacles in the path of its continued rapid development, economic growth and its environmental sustainability'.[10]

Chinese Water Crisis

Water Facts. China is one of the 13 countries that faces acute water crisis in the world. The per capita water share in China is 2300 m^3, which is 1/4th of the worlds average or 121st in the world. 70% of the rainfall in China precipitates in four months, and over 2/3rd of that water is wasted in floods and free flow. There has been five times increase in water usage in China since 1949,[11] further worsening the water situation. It also has a demographic problem—it hosts 20% of the world's population and holds 6% of the world's water resources. China is, thus, hard-pressed to implement the Brahmaputra project as an answer to its growing water woes arising from uneven distribution of water resources, demographic explosion, industrial upsurge, rapid expansion of cities, and greater demand for irrigated agriculture farming.[12]

Uneven Distribution of Water Resources The per capita water availability in Northern China is only 757 m^3/yr, less than 1/4th of Southern China. A study by UN pegs[13] countries and regions with water availability per capita below

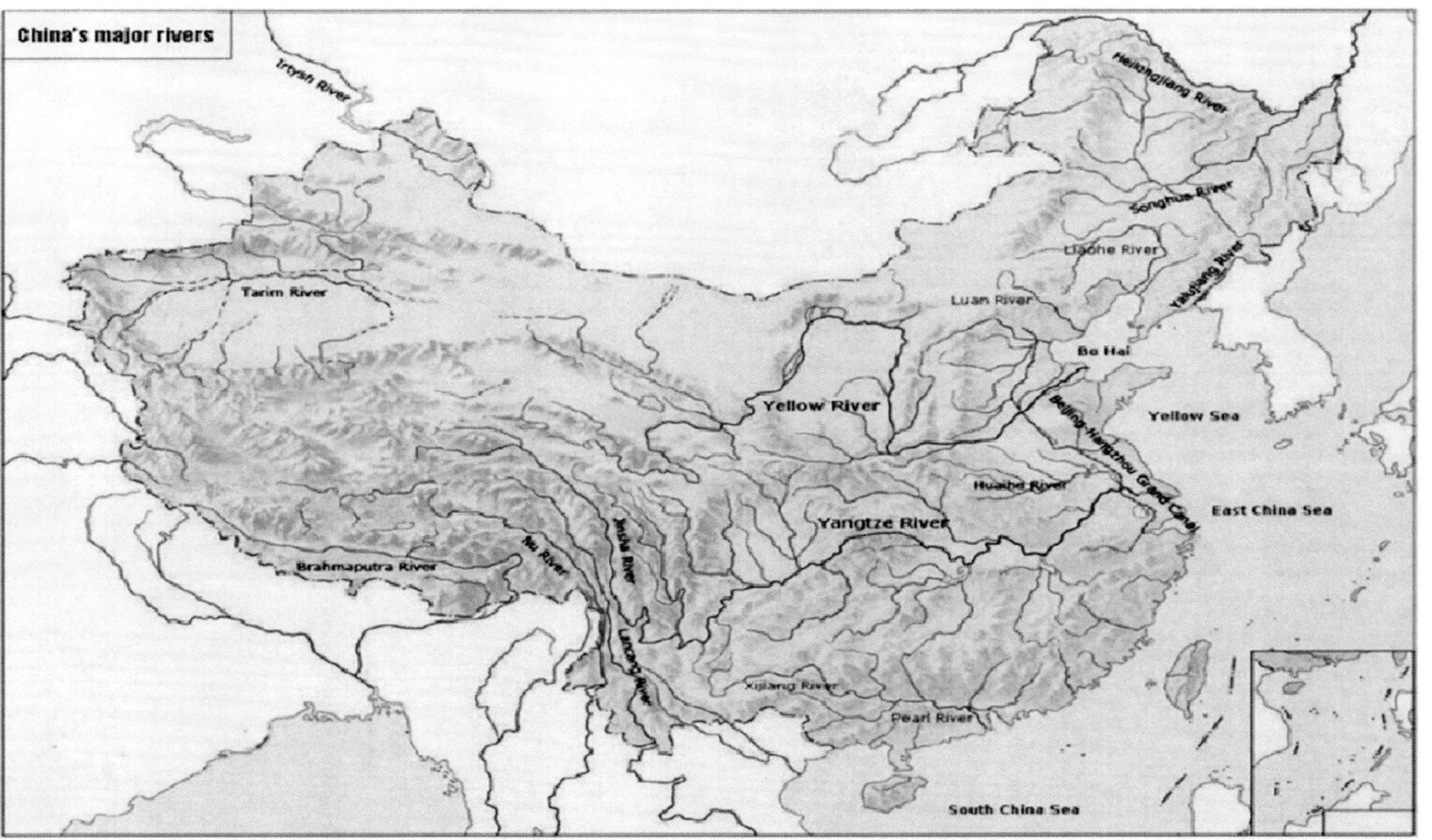
China's major rivers
Irtysh River
Heilongjiang River
Songhua River
Liaohe River
Yalujiang River
Tarim River
Luan River
Bo Hai
Yellow River
Yellow Sea
Beijing-Hangzhou Grand Canal
Huaihe River
East China Sea
Yangtze River
Nu River
Jinsha River
Brahmaputra River
Lancang River
Xijiang River
Pearl River
South China Sea

1,000 m^3/year as 'water scarce' regions. The average rainfall in South is 2000 mm/year in contrast to the average rainfall in North, i.e., 200-400 mm/yr. Resultantly, Yellow R550 mn people and 2/3rd of the crop lands, but has supply of only 1/5th of the water; whereas the Yangtse R (Southern China) supports 700 mn people, 1/3rd of the crop land and has supply of upto 4/5th of China's total water. On an average, 70% of the total water extractions in the world are to support agriculture, which explains the water scarcity in the Northern regions of China.

Primitive Irrigation Practices. The resource imbalance coupled with primitive irrigation practices of ponded water culture—main source of evaporation (wastage of fresh water) results in poor productivity. China uses 66% more water than any developed country for producing same amount of wheat. Over 1/5th of the China's crop land suffer from salineness (accumulation of highly soluble sodium, magnesium and potassium salts), which are left behind due to evaporation. Today only 5% of Chinese have adapted to modern irrigation practice of drip and sprinkler irrigation system, which ensure optimum utilization of water for grain productivity and nullifies salineness due to excessive evaporation.

Pollution. Currently, 45000 mn tons of untreated waste water enter China's rivers every year. Approx 700mn, more than half of China's population, consume drinking water contaminated with animal, industrial and human waste. 80% of domestic and industrial waste water is released untreated in the rivers in China which has badly polluted 88% rivers of PRC; many of them are biologically dead, unfit even for industrial and agricultural use. At an average 25 Km^3 of water in China becomes unfit for consumption every year[14] due to pollution thereby aggravating its water scarcity.

Desertification. Desertification has taken place at an alarming rate and has gobbled up almost 18% of China's landmass. Xinjiang province (16,60,000 sq km) is primarily dry land because of its distance from the ocean. It has 570 rivers that flow inland and surface water reserve available is 5800 crore m^3. Annual desertification rate has been registered at 350 sq km and if this desertification continues to spread eastwards; the most densely populated area in the world may turn into desert before arrival of the next century.

Living Standards. According to US Agricultural Department, Chinese consumption of meat has quadrupled in last 30 yrs. The production of same amount of meat protein is 10 times more water intensive than the plant protein, e.g., a kg of chicken requires 3,900 litres of water, a kg of pork 4,900 litres and a kg of beef 15,000 litres[15] Urbanization drive undertaken to propel the economy is set to increase the middle class having a multiplication effect on domestic water wastage due to washing machines and dish washers. It will also increase the number of high water consuming industries.

Effect : Water Shortage. The water resource usage is expected to peak in 2030 when the population peaks. This coupled with increase in pollution, poor discipline in management of potable water and effects of global warming would put undue strain on existing water resources which has forced the Chinese think tanks to consider the water diversion projects from South to North in an attempt to solve the problem. It is noteworthy that 92% water of the Tibetan rivers flow into South and South East Asia, hence firstly; it is logical to think of diverting the water resources of Tibet to quench the thirst of mainland China, secondly; any water diversion project amounting to reduction in the water flow of Tsangpo/ Brahmaputra, Mekong or Salween would affect the complete South Asian region and has a possibility of creating tensions between neighbours who share the waters of Tibetan trans-border rivers.

WATER DIVERSION PROJECTS IN CHINA: AN ANALYSIS

Historical Perspective

The Chinese psyche has historically laid great value in dreaming and commissioning grand schemes under their emperor of the time. Claude Arpi mentions that this mentality lead to creation of the Great Wall, the grand canal, Three Gorges dam, Gromo-Lhasa Railway Line and now the South-North Water Diversion Project and the Great Western Diversion.[16] China has been known to make canals and divert water historically. The Grand Canal, also known as the Beijing-Hangzhou Grand Canal, is the longest canal (1,776 km) or artificial river in the world. Starting at Beijing, it passes through Tianjin and the provinces of Hebei, Shandong, Jiangsu and Zhejiang to the city of Hangzhou linking the Yellow river and Yangtze R. The oldest parts of the canal date back to the 5th century BC, although the various sections were finally combined during the Sui Dynasty (581-618 AD).

South-North Water Project

The Project. The South-North Water Project has three routes—Western, Central and Eastern and is the biggest hydraulic initiative undertaken by China. It forms part of the 10 biggest construction projects costing above 27 bn in the world. The project is to link Yangtse R, Yellow R, Huaihe Rand Haihe R system with the overall aim to provide water to Beijing, Tianjin, Hebei, Henan and Shangdong with the cost of $ 62 bn.[17] It envisages diversion of 44.8 bn m^3 of water annually (Eastern—14.8 BCM, Central—13 BCM and Western—17 BCM).

- **Eastern Route.** Construction on the Eastern route officially began on December 27, 2002, and water was to reach Tianjin by 2012. It basically consists of an upgrade of the Grand Canal. Water from the Yangtze river is proposed to be drawn into the canal in Jiangdu, which has a giant

400 m³/s pumping station and then pumped up by stations along the Grand Canal and through two horizontal tunnels, 9.3 m diameter 70 m long,[18] under the Yellow river, from where it can flow downhill to reservoirs near Tianjin. The route is expected to initially provide water for the provinces of Shandong, Jaingsu and Anhui. The completed line will be slightly over 1,152 km long, equipped with 23 pumping stations with a power capacity of 454 MW taking 14.8 BCM of water to Tianjin.

- **Central Route.** The route is from Danjiangkou Reservoir on Han river (tributary of Yangtse river), to Beijing. This route is built on the North China plains and, once the Yellow river has been crossed, water would flow to Beijing by gravity. The construction on this route began in 2003/04 and by 2008, the 307 km long northern stretch of the Central Route was completed at a cost of US $ 2 bn. The whole project was expected to be completed around 2010; this has recently been set back to 2014 to allow for more environmental protections to be built. The completed line will be approx 1,267 km long, providing 9.5 BCM of water annually and subsequently 12 to 13 BCM annually.
- **Western Route.** The route is also called the Big Western Line which involves diversion of internal rivers of China. It aims to divert 17 BCM of water from the headwaters of the Yangtze river (the Tontian, Yalong and Dadu Rs) into the headwaters of the Yellow river. To move the water

through the drainage divide between these rivers, huge dams and long tunnels are needed to cross the Qinghai-Tibetan Plateau and Western Yunnan Plateaus. The Tongtian diversion line would be 289 km long, the Yalong 131 km, and the Dadu 30 km.

Project Controversy. Since the introduction of the South-North Project, it has created widespread controversy. Opponents object to it on the grounds that it is a waste of resources and would create large number of migrant people. It could waste massive quantity of water through evaporation and pollution and the project's huge cost would make the water prohibitively expensive for consumers.[19] The dry season could cause the Yangtze river to suffer from water shortages and would be detrimental to Yangtze river's inland transportation.

The Great Western Diversion

General. It is assessed by experts that Yangtse waters alone would not be adequate to flush out/rejuvenate the sluggish Yellow river and solve North China's water problem. This impelled the Chinese leadership to launch the gigantic inter connected scheme of damming Yarlung Tsangpo (Brahmaputra), Salween, Mekong and tributaries of Yangtse (as per Western Route) and transfer their waters to North China along the Great Western Route.[20] The project was the brain child of Gao Kai, a veteran hydrographer, who researched on the project for 17 years.[21] It was in 1988, the PLA got interested in the project and Zhang Jinong (Minister for Water Resources) established the Preparatory Committee. The first official survey was conducted in May-Jun 1999 in form of an expedition; its report was prepared and presented on 07 Oct 2000 which received support of the State Council, PRC's highest state institution and accorded its approval. The survey approved the feasibility and concluded the water source to be stable and secure.[22]

The Project. The project is named as Shoutian[23]—'Shou'—from SHOUMATAN (gorge near Tsethang in Central Tibet where the first dam to intercept Yarlung Tsangpo will be built) and 'Tian'—from TIANJIN, (terminal point where the Yellow river merges in the Yellow Sea). 'The Great Western Diversion Project' envisages diversion of the Tsangpo, Mekong and Salween trans-border rivers to Yellow river and the arid NW and Northern regions of China at an estimated cost of $ 125.4 bn. Out of this, 118.80 BCM is proposed to be drawn from Tsangpo, 48 BCM from Salween and 30 BCM from Mekong. The length of the route is likely to be 1339 km, with eight tunnels (longest—60 Km). If implemented, it would supply water to 65% of the Chinese territory.

Yellow river—Its Significance. This project will enable diversion of water to the Yellow R, which according to Mao Tse Tung is the most important waterway in China. The river has only 2% of the water flow of the rivers in China, but it irrigates 15% of the entire China's agricultural fields. Despite this, the Chinese have treated the river shabbily; approx 13 Crore Cubic m of waste is dumped into Yellow river annually. Sedimentation through sand deposition has seen lowering of its depth from 6 to 13 m in last 50 yrs.

The Plan. There are many versions of the plan to divert waters of Tsangpo/ Brahmaputra, the most logical is as under:

> **First,** to create a reservoir on Tsangpo by damming it to divert enough volume of water northwards and canalising water towards end of the Great Bend towards Medog, for generation of 40,000 MW of hydro power.
>
> **Second,** create a system of tunnels and canals and pump water from the reservoir with the help of the power generated to Yellow river through the Salween, Mekong, Jinsang and Dadu rivers.
>
> **Third,** create reservoir at Lajia Gorge (Yellow river) ; pump up water to Qinghai Lake making Lajia and Qinghai as major reservoirs.
>
> **Fourth,** canalise waters from Qinghai lake to East Turkestan towards Tarim Basin, Urmqi and Karamay; to Inner Mongolia towards Badian desert; and along the Yellow river to Tianjin.

Hydropower at the Great Bend—Concern for India. The project involves a tunnel to be created to divert the water before the Great Bend to the end of the bend which would be 15-20 km[24] (min distance as per google earth is 37 km) with a drop in altitude of 2500 m[25] reducing the distance of flow from 200 km (across the complete bend) to 37 km. The energy created by the water in such short distance would allow generation of 40,000 MW.[26] This power is proposed to pump water through the mountains up North into the Western Route of the diversion plan. Lake created as a result of the project would be more than 100 km upstream and would extend upto the Kongpo region. China has already connected Medog through a road to Eastern Highway and has clear intentions on embarking on this project as depicted in the National Power Grid Plan—China 2020.[27]

The Nuclear Angle. In 1995, the Chinese Academy for Engineers and Physics after study of the project concluded that tunnelling for diversion of Tsangpo waters for 'The Great Western Route' was possible only through nuclear explosions. It is may be recalled that the US and erstwhile USSR carried at least 155 Peaceful Nuclear explosions (PNEs) from 1961-1988,[28] and concluded that PNEs were the best for large scale excavations as the energy released by the lowest nuclear explosion was more beneficial than the largest conventional explosion. Though no PNE has been carried out across the world for the last 15 yrs, the precedent does give justification to China for use of nuclear explosion in their national interest.

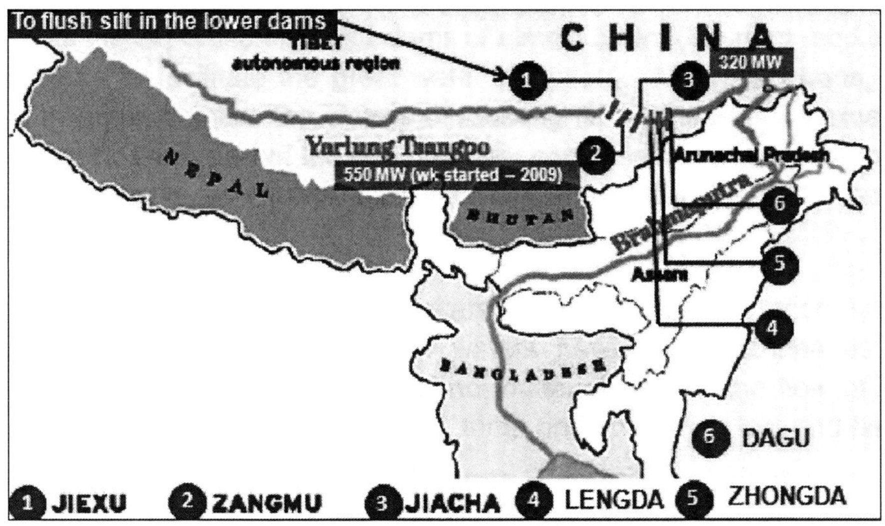

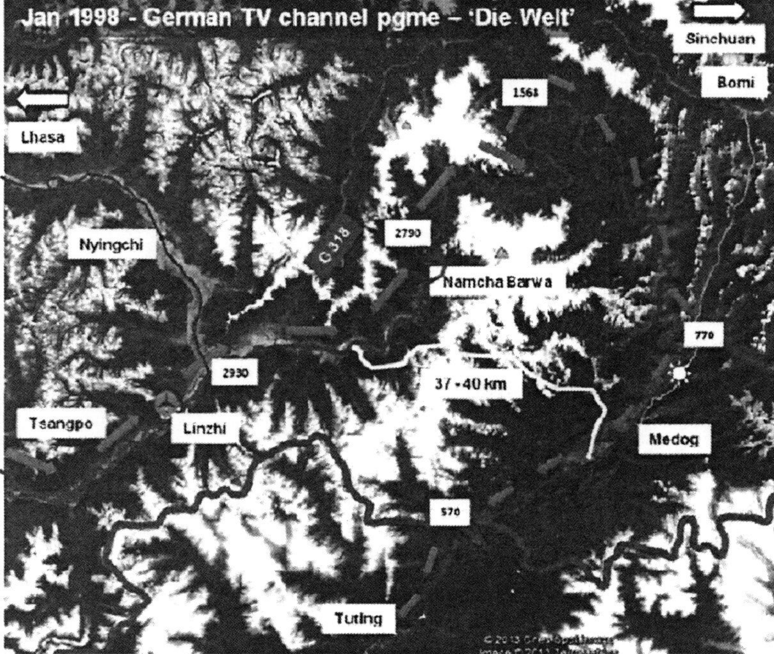

Chinese Behaviour on Trans-Border Rivers

Damming of Tsangpo/ Brahmaputra. China has already dammed various tributaries of Tsangpo; there are four projects above 1000 KW already functioning. China has planned six projects on the main stream with Jiexu being the upper most; waters of which will be used for flushing silt from the lower dams. The details are shown in the figure alongside.

Salween River: Salween is a free flowing trans border river into Myanmar from China which has not been dammed till now. China has been carrying out feasibility study for multiple power projects on the river. Myanmar also carried out the study and started rehabilitation of people from the project site; resentment and protests by the people and environmentalists forced the Chinese companies to halt the project. China finally has announced 13 projects on the river, five of which have been earmarked as priority in the 2001-15 five year plan.

Mekong River: The Mekong River originates in Tibet, flows through Myanmar (Burma), Laos, Thailand, Cambodia and Vietnam, before finally discharging into the South China Sea. China is engaged in an extensive programme of dam-building on the river and has already constructed five dams with varying capacities on the river. All countries on the Mekong River watershed, with the notable exceptions of China and Myanmar (Burma), belong to the Mekong River Commission (MRC). In developing the upper Mekong for navigation and hydropower projects, China has acted unilaterally and without consultation with downstream nations.[29]

Critical Analysis: Great Water Diversion Project

There are divergent views in the Chinese govt about the feasibility of the project; critics feel it may be impractical due to the u/m issues:

(a) Since Yellow river cannot receive such influx of water, a reservoir would have to be made on the river and a number of existing lakes would have to be connected (Qinghai lake and Erhai lake). Wang Hao (Engineer in Chief of China Institute of Water Resources and Hydropower Research) opined that—the 300 m high Dam would have to be constructed on the Qinghai-Tibet plateau (elevation over 4000 m) which is technically impossible.

(b) Chinese Academy of Engineering (CAE)[30] in its study on Sustainable Development of China's Water Resources in 21st century underscored two potential areas of error in the proposed project:

  (i) The project only plans to channel the water into Yellow river disregarding all the inland rivers of North and the NW China.

  (ii) The project violates the laws of nature and disturbs the adaptive ecological environments as it envisages natural arid zones of the NW China to be converted into wet lands.

(c) **Qian Zhengying:** former Minister of Water Resources (1979-82) informed the State Council that in near future there would be no feasibility—technical or economical for The Great Western Route.

(d) The bio-diversity along the Tsangpo river is an ecological marvel attained after millions of years; it won't be prudent to disturb it.

(e) **Wang Shuchang**, former Minister for Water Resources (1989-2007) felt that solution to China's water problem lay in building a water sustaining society instead of creating water diversion projects.
(f) It is estimated that cost involved in diverting Brahmaputra's water would be higher than alternative of desalination of sea water.

IMPACT ON INDIA AND OUR APPROACH

Exploitation of Brahmaputra in India

Whilst, it is true that the major water diversion projects by China would affect an approx reduction of 20% of Brahmaputra waters; however, it is pertinent to mention that out of total catchment area of 5.8 lac sq km of Brahmaputra, 50% is in Tibet, 34% in India and 16% in Bangladesh. India needs to exploit these catchment areas/drainage/tributaries—Siang, Lohit, Dibang, Subansiri, Kamala, Rong, Kameng and others, for generation of hydel power and other uses. These make the mighty Brahmaputra the size that is; not Chinese waters.[31] India's anxiety over Chinese overtures also stems from the fact that out of Arunachal Pradesh's estimated potential of 50,064MW of hydel power, less than 1% or 405 MW, has been harnessed so far.[32] Moreover, about 65% of the water is added to Brahmaputra in India, due to high precipitation as compared to the Tibetan Plateau; therefore the water loss to India may not be significant, notwithstanding the other bearing effects of the water diversion projects by China.

UN Provisions—Water Sharing

UN Convention on Shared Waters—1997. The law of the Non Navigation Uses of International Water Courses[33] was adopted in 1997 by the UN General Assembly. It concludes that cooperation rather than conflict has been the rule in international water relations and violence over water is rare. The u/m facts have been elucidated in the said convention:

(a) 145 countries are riparian to one or more of the world's 263 international basins.
(b) 1/3rd of the 263 basins (formal management institutions established in 117 basins) involve sharing by two countries and 19 involve five or more sovereign states.
(c) 40% of the world's population lives along these basins which contribute to estimated 60% of the global fresh water.
(d) Population growth has resulted in a near 80% decline in per capita water availability over past century.

Cooperation Management Network: The convention lays stress on cooperation management between the riparian states[34] and emphasizes an agreement to be reached by the States with certain safeguards. It must have an adaptable management structure—a flexible structure with scope for public participation and provision for extending benefit to non signatories. The clear and flexible criteria for water allocations and water quality management need to be ensured for equitable distribution of benefits. Concrete mechanism to enforce treaty provisions and detailed conflict resolution mechanism also need to be suitably factored in this cooperation management network. Apropos, last 50 years has seen 37 acute water disputes and 150 water treaties.[35]

Behaviour of Upper Riparian States Across the World

Effectiveness of Legal Provisions : Existing legal provisions for water sharing, at the international level, are characterised more by their weakness than their substance. In short, most agreements remain bilateral, monitored by joint commissions and the game is 'free for all', dominated by the upper riparian states. Chinese thinking on the issue is reflected in the native Chinese adage, 'upstream does not suffer' and supports the Chinese tendency to take unilateral action in matters of water exploitation.[36]

Getting this pre-eminent riparian power to accept water-sharing arrangements or other cooperative institutional mechanisms has proven unsuccessful in any basin. In fact, as epitomised by its planned or actual construction of a separate cascade of upstream dams on several major international rivers, including the Mekong, Salween and Brahmaputra, China is increasingly headed in the opposite direction—toward unilateralist actions impervious to the concerns of downstream nations.[37]

US: The US affected the diversion of Colorado river a trans border river with Mexico, by 1963 by diverting 9.3 BCM of water.[38] The interests of the lower riparian Mexico were not considered while planning and execution of the project. The Upper Basin—provides water to Wyoming, Colorado, Utah and New Mexico states. 90% of the supply water is spread into land irrigated for crops, 10% is for urban and other users. The Lower Basin provides water to California, Arizona, and Nevada and 85% is utilised for agricultural purposes.

Turkey. The country enjoys upper riparian advantage and is the nation with most dams after China. It has planned construction of 22 dams and 19 hydropower projects on Euphrates and Tigris and is working to get addl 1.8 mn hectares of land under irrigation. Syria and Iraq, the lower riparian are in no position to challenge.

Israel. It is the most water scarce country in the world. During the Six Day War in 1967, it captured the water rich Golan Heights and aquifer controlling waters of West Bank. It was also in control of Jordan river head works. Israel still controls the Golan Heights which provides water security and power of water diplomacy with its neighbours in the region.

Indo-China Water Sharing Arrangements

Existing Water Sharing Mechanisms: India and China have no water treaty, as signed by India and Pakistan (Indus Water Treaty) to formalise the sharing of the trans-border river waters. However, a MoU was signed between the two countries to share hydrographic data of Sutlej in 2002, post the Pare Chu flooding disaster and Brahmaputra in 2005[39] to facilitate preventive action to be undertaken downstream during monsoons in case of flash floods which in the past have resulted in massive loss to life and property. In May 13, a MoU was signed during the recent visit of Mr Li Keqiang, the Premier of China, on 'provision of information by China on water level, discharge and rainfall from its three hydroelectric projects upstream of Brahmaputra', which in the present scenario is not enough.

Complexities on Border Issues and Upper Riparian Status: China does not consider Arunachal Pradesh to be a part of India and considers it as Southern Tibet. India has been administering the State since the colonial era and it recognizes the Mac Mohan line as the boundary. China is the upper riparian State and according to basic principles of customary international law (not written but practiced) it has the first right to exploit the basin resources; Ripa in Latin means 'Bank of stream'. The Law of Riparian Nations states that 'Propriety of water rights go to the owner of land contiguous to the river with reasonable logic of sharing the waters with the lower riparian's'.[40] It allows China reasonable water share without defining reasonableness, hence the ambiguity on the water sharing issue.

Impact of Diversion on Lower Riparian Nation—India

The Indian concerns over plans to divert the Brahmaputra were not unwarranted. The two components of the diversion scheme would include the construction of the world's largest hydroelectric plant on the Great Bend of the river on the Tibetan plateau; the second is the diversion of the waters northwards across hundreds of km to China's north western provinces. Diverting Tsangpo would result in an overall reduction of minimum 20% in the water flow of Brahmaputra river. River morphology is the single most major casualty of damming and diversion of the river. The impact on the lower watercourse will broadly be in terms of reduced water channel and its related effects, biodiversity along the areas of lake formation and downstream, rehabilitation of local populace, disturbance of ecological fragility triggering landslides and earthquakes. The implications and impact of such project are being discussed in u/m paras.

Logistics Sustenance: Damming upstream has created capabilities with China to flood the downstream at will. Natural disasters and poor quality of workmanship may puncture the dams having catastrophic effects (major loss to life and property worth mns) on downstream India. This would trigger loss of revenue directed towards rehabilitation and reconstruction. All the roads follow valleys and water drained by the river will impact these roads due to flooding, having a direct impact on logistics sustenance and habitat in the region.

Reduced Water Channel: Reduced water flow would have an adverse impact on fresh water availability on the lower riparian States—India and Bangladesh. Threat to navigation in National Waterways of lower riparian States ie, National Waterway-2 on Brahmaputra river from Sadiya to Bangladesh border for 891 km would be affected. Irrigation channels, community pools downstream may dry up reducing the fish catch and crop yield in the region, directly impacting the food security. There is likely to be an increase in pollution as reduced flow would not be able to wash away the waste discharge fed into the river from habitation along it. Moreover, lowering of water table would reduce the fresh water availability.

Biodiversity/Ecology: Effect on bio-diversity would be further aggravated by loss of forests, plants, wildlife, birds—their migration patterns, fishes, insects and host of other rare living organisms. Rare species found in a part or section of the river owing to altitude, temperature and silt/ mineral pattern in the river would get destroyed and lost forever.

Year	*Population (Mn)*	*Per capita water availability (M^3/yr)*
1951	361	5177
1955	395	4732
1991	846	2209
2001	1027	1820
2025	1394	1341
2050	1640	1140

Seismic Zone: The Himalayas (including the Tibetan Plateau) were formed by the collision of Indian plate with the Eurasian plate and fall in the highly active seismic zone prone to intermittent earthquakes. Major changes to the river courses would have an adverse impact on the frequency of earthquakes and is likely to be a cause of mass scale destruction of life and material. The seismic hazard mapping shows the area to be falling in Seismic zone 5[41] (max chances of a calamity), hence the risks of massive flooding and loss to life and property if the dam is built on Tsangpo.

Effect on Water State in India: The per capita availability table India depicts a serious problem. One perspective of how water is likely to haunt us is report in

The Economist (2009)—citing official estimates—that India will run short of water by 2050 (when the population is expected to peak at 1.7 billion), unless massive improvements are made.[42] The land under irrigation is also going to expand and the water usage accordingly. We need to address the matter of water security seriously and devise policies to conserve water with efficient methods, as also to critically examine the Chinese plan to embark upon the project of diverting Tsangpo waters, and institute measures and undertake actions to ensure that our interests are not harmed and optimal utilisation is made of the Brahmaputra waters.

Recommendations

China being the biggest dam builder in the world[43] has built power projects on almost all the trans-border rivers except Salween river (which is being planned to be dammed by 2015). It has diverted waters to balance out water availability in its water parched Northern regions and has plans to build more water diversion projects. Water is essentially required by China to sustain its growth momentum and hence the likelihood of implementation of the project for diverting waters of the three trans-border rivers of Tsangpo, Salween and Mekong. Most severe impact of the reduced water availability would be to the lowest riparian States—India, Bangladesh, Myanmar, Thailand, Cambodia and Vietnam. This could strain relations, impact economic interdependencies, bilateral and multilateral trade and host of other issues. Hence a via media has to be found to resolve the water crises of China while the security interests of the lower riparian States i.e., India, amongst others, are preserved. *Inter alia*, politico-diplomatic efforts and efforts at the national level need to be initiated to arrive at an action plan to be periodically reviewed.

Rohini Nilekani in her well reasoned article, 'Is Water the Next Oil?' speaks of people's involvement, quoting a Chinese proverb ('Tell me, I forget. Show me, I remember. Involve me, I understand),[44] as the way forward to resolve the crisis. People must see themselves as not only part of the problem but also part of the solution. It is, therefore, incumbent on both the Chinese and Indian governments to make radical, science-based policy changes as soon as possible. Unless they do so, devastating water shortages will result within decades for billions of their citizens. Recommendations and engagement with China on the water diversion projects and actions to be undertaken are discussed in the succeeding paras.

Political and Diplomatic Efforts

(a) **Institution Building:** Institutions and forums by the water sharing nations need to be created in Asia. Regional cooperation water related mechanisms like—inclusive basin organisations; mechanism to expand rain fed agriculture; building Asian norms and rules; integrated planning to promote sustainable practice and careful balance between rights and responsibilities need to be initiated.

(b) **Lower Riparian Partnership**: India must take the lead in building lower riparian partnership in Asia. We need to conduct and publicise joint studies on adverse impact of water diversion and to quantify water requirement by each of the riparian State and its effect.

(c) **Joint Studies:** Joint studies may be initiated to quantify the impact of extensive damming on Brahmaputra waterways. Since generation of hydro power is also a necessity, quantification on the number and type (dam height, reservoir capacity and surface area of the lake) of dams which can be built with suggested locations, without major impact on the river morphology, should be spelt out.

(d) **Data Base:** The world water data base is not authenticated and acceptable to all. We should jointly initiate hydrographic data base for trans border water systems which holds as an authority for all future interactions. The data base must include—sourcing, discharge, degradation, siltation to the impact that water related infrastructure would have on the environment.

(e) **Diplomatic Intervention:** Seek UN intervention for violation of the UN Convention on Shared Water Basins of 1997 by China and sensitise the region and world community to stop funding the Great Western Diversion for the adverse impact it has on India.

(f) **Joint Monitoring Mechanism**: India must push to establish joint monitoring mechanism on river basins on all trans border rivers (Indus, Sutlej and Brahmaputra), for its equitable and justifiable use amongst riparian states.

(g) **PNEs:** Ensure that China is not allowed to carry out PNEs to construct tunnels for the water diversion projects.

National Level

(a) **Water Conservation:** We need to carve out effective policies for optimal use of available fresh water and to mitigate the wastage. National policy on water conservation should be enforced.

(b) **Recycling of Water**: Recycling of waste water should be the norm in every modern house hold and water harvesting especially rain harvesting should be encouraged.

(c) **Precedent:** We have an excellent precedent in negotiating treaties and implementing international norms on trans-border waterways; these need to be underscored to garner international support and to influence change in attitude of the Chinese. Poor water sharing resolution record within

Indian States needs to be addressed and justified water sharing arrangements be put into place at the earliest. Examples of fair treatment by India (upper riparian) to lower riparian states in the region, which need to be appropriately leveraged, are as under:

(i) Indus Water Treaty with Pakistan.

(ii) Treaties with Bangladesh on sharing of Ganges waters.

(iii) The project of 'Interlinking of Rivers' has been shelved by India on concerns raised by Bangladesh and environmental issues.

(iv) India's acceptance of award by UN based arbitrator on Baglihar project in J&K.

CONCLUSION

The Himalayan waters have been a major source of life and prosperity in China and the Indian sub-continent. The envisaged increase in population, industrialisation, global warming—resultant receding glaciers and depleting ground water levels would increase the stress on fresh water availability in the trans-border rivers. Any reduction in flow caused by the water diversion projects will be a cause of dispute between the higher and lower riparian countries in 21st century. Focussed efforts also need to be undertaken to exploit the large catchment areas of Brahmaputra in India for hydel power generation, as the loss/ reduction of Brahmaputra waters entering India is about 20% as result of water diversion projects by China.

Whilst, a 'water war' in the near term seems quite unlikely,[45] the core issue of the declining availability of water and the increasing demand for it is, nevertheless, a very serious, as well as complex and interlinked issue. Quite to the contrary, there is a realisation at both ends that territorial and other differences in perception need to be set aside, to enhance mutual trust and cooperation between China and India to tackle the various challenges they face. Any solution that is found well, therefore, have to be networked and international, rather than stand-alone. The dependence on water from the high Himalayas is such that China, and the South and Southeast Asian countries (the so-called lower riparian states), especially India have to collaborate instead of getting involving in conflict.

The current concern of dam construction activity over Tsangpo and its likely diversion by China have already involved India in worrisome tussle on control of waters. India as a nation will have to protect its rights over waters of trans-border rivers for a sustained economic growth. Sustained diplomatic efforts by India need to be initiated to influence the Chinese thought and conduct on the trans-border river issue. As the study is on the current dynamic subject, it needs to progressively collate data on balance of the trans-border rivers and study the Chinese behaviour on all these rivers continuously to formalise our action plan.

REFERENCES

1. Y.N. Roy, Diversion of Brahmaputra Waters to North China, Dialogue, April-June 2010, Vol II, No. 4.
2. Ibid.
3. B. Chellaney, Water: Asia's New Battleground; Georgetown University Press, Sep 13, 2010.
4. L. Brown, 'Tibet and China: Climate Crisis at the Earth's Third Pole'.
5. K. Layton, 'Tibetan Waters: Coming Conflict?', Institute of Peace and Conflict Studies, July 2009.
6. Ibid.
7. C. Arpi, 'Born In Sin: The Panchsheel Agreement. The Sacrifice of Tibet,' Mittal Publications, August 2004.
8. B. Chellaney, Asia's Water Crisis and the New Security Risks, *Journal of USI*, Vol. CXLI, No 587, Jan-Mar 12.
9. Ibid.
10. B. Chellaney, Water: Asia's New Battleground, Introduction.
11. Study Report by Organisation for Economic Cooperation & Development OECD, 2006.
12. P Stobdan,: 'China Should Not Use Water as a Threat Multiplier', IDSA Comment October 23, 2009.
13. http://www.un.org.ezp2.lib.umn.edu/waterforlifedecade/scarcity.shtml, May, 2012.
14. Food and Agriculture Organisation of the UN, Information System on water and agriculture, China 2010.
15. N. Matthews, China's water crisis needs better farming, not the South-North Water Transfer, Jun 13; www.thethirdpole.net.
16. C. Arpi, Water War in South Asia? Brahmaputra: Dam & Diversion, October 2003.
17. R. Mehta, Re-plumbing China: Leading to the World's First Water War?, *CLAWS Journal*, Summer 2010.
18. South to North Water Diversion Project, Article in www.water-technology.net/projects/south-north/, Sep 2008
19. The Inquirer, Philadelphia: China to resettle 330,000 people, 19 October 2010.
20. Y.N. Roy, Diversion of Brahmaputra Waters to North China, Dialogue April-June 2010, Vol II, No. 4.
21. Controversial Plan to Tap Tibetan Waters, Southern Weekend, translated by Shao Da for China.org.cn, 8 Aug 2006.
22. Ibid.
23. C. Arpi, 'Himalayan Rivers: Geopolitics and Strategic Perspectives,' Vol 23.2, June 23.
24. German TV channel ZDF programme—'Die Welt'—'The World', in Jan 1998—blog of Claude Arpi, 31 Aug 2013.
25. Y.N. Roy, Diversion of Brahmaputra Waters to North China, Dialogue April-June 2010, Vol. II, No 4.
26. B.L. Seth, 'Passive Neighbour', comment on www.downtoearth.org.in, Nov 2011.
27. National Power Grid Plan—China 2020; Practical Steps for Developing Renewable Energy in China's 12th Five-Year Plan' Haibing Ma, 02 Jul 2011.
28. M.D. Nordyke, The Soviet Program for Peaceful Uses of Nuclear Explosions, UCRL-ID-124410 Rev 2, Sep 2000.
29. R. Mehta, Re-plumbing China: Leading to the World's First Water War?, *CLAWS Journal*, Summer 2010.
30. Study—Chinese Academy of Engineering (CAE) on Sustainable Development of China's Water Resources in 21st Century, 2000.

31. P. Stobdan, 'China Should Not Use Water as a Threat Multiplier', IDSA Comment October 23, 2009.
32. U. Bhaskar, 'India firms up its strategy on Brahmaputra water diversion'; www.livemint.com/politics, 20 Nov 2013. Convention on the Law of the Non-Navigational Uses of International Watercourses New York, 21 May 1997; http://legal.un.org/avl//ha/clnuiw/clnuiw.html
33. Ibid.
34. Trans boundary waters. http://www.un.org/waterforlifedecade/transboundary_waters.shtml
35. V. Joshi, 'China's Water Crisis, its Management and Implications for India', published in an Indian Army Service magazine, 2009.
36. B. Chellaney, Asia's Water Crisis and New Security Risks, *Journal of USI*, Vol. CXLI, No. 587, Jan-Mar 12.
37. P.S. Kibel, J.R. Schutz, 'Rio Grande Designs: Texans' NAFTA Water Claim against Mexico', *Berkeley Journal of International Law*, Vol 25, Issue 2 Article 5, 2007.
38. Ibid.
39. G. Eckstein, 'Application of International Water Law to Trans boundary Groundwater Resources, and the Slovak-Hungarian Dispute Over Gabcikovo-Nagymaros', Suffolk Transnational Law Review, Vol 19, at page 67,Winter 1995.
40. Y.N. Roy, Diversion of Brahmaputra Waters to North China, Dialogue April-June 2010, Vol II, No 4.
41. B. Shantanu, 'Nightmare at Noon—What if I Had No Water to Drink?' December 1 2009, http://satyameva-jayate.org.
42. B. Chellaney, Asia's Water Crisis and New Security Risks, *Journal of USI*, Vol CXLI, No 587, Jan-Mar 12.
43. R. Nilekani, 'Is Water the Next Oil?', *Yale Global Online Magazine*, May 31, 2007.
44. B. Chellaney, Asia's Water Crisis and New Security Risks, *Journal of USI*, Vol CXLI, No 587, Jan-Mar 12.
45. R. Mehta, Re-plumbing China: Leading to the World's First Water War?, *CLAWS Journal*, Summer 2010.

17

Evolving a Theoretical Perspective on Human Security and Development

Raj Kumar Upadhyaya

Introduction

There is an urgency to examine the term human security[1] and development in the changed security situation. Development and human security are the two most frequently used terms during the end of the 20th century and the first decade of the 21st century. Since then, both the terms have acquired great meaning and scope in fulfilling the needs of the state. These terms are relevant not only in sociological, political, economic, environmental but are now focused on the studies undertaken by various social sciences. Both the terms indicate a state associated with the well-being of an individual. The performance of an individual well-being is related to such social environment and cultural structure to which he belongs. Both the terms have acquired a comprehensiveness that has a humanitarian aspect.

Development means a progressive enhancement. Today, it is looked upon as a physical and monetary factors which are important for national security. The physical factor include the area of physical feature and material resource. The monetary progressive enhancement is related with economic development. Generally, the term human security means the protection of state in the physical boundary. But now, the scope is far more wide as it covers individual areas of political, economic, environmental, education, healthcare and infrastructural surroundings. It is required that these are free from corruption as well as pollution.

Human Development Index (HDI) is now being considered as the standard of measurement of the development of a country. It is the yardstick of the security of a nation state.[2] Both are connected with the well-being of both the individual and state.

Development and human security are interdependent. Without human security, development is impossible. Development and human security is like the two sides of a coin. For development, human security is necessary and similarly for human security, development is essential. The terms development and human security are well related to the notions of the well-being of the individual in a broader framework of socially relevant matrix. Development and human security are inseparable just as form and content are inseparable. Both the terms are seen in a positive and progressive sense. Both strive towards increasing enhancement of the physical, material and human resources. Both the terms mean improvement in literacy, health, income, environmental awareness and cultural well-being. They include the elimination and reduction of negative indicators like disease, pollution, violence, corruption and ignorance. Both development and human security seek to establish the relationship between good and bad. Hence, both prefer that goodness should prevail and evils from society should be eliminated.

Development

Development is the one such concept in which is generally seen usually as user-friendly term. It assumes progress and moving onwards as well as forward. Development means progressive enhancement and material uplift. It may be diffusion of the values and life style. It is diffusion of whatever is universally desired. Today technology has given a new meaning to the concept of development. The third world countries could not make rapid stride because of past colonialism and poverty. Moreover, the inequality of land distribution resulted in poor land use. Farming technology remained traditional. Social and political organizations were fragmented. Subsistence farming and handcrafting of consumer goods generated no surplus for investment. The basic elements of infrastructure such roads, bridges and dams were primitive. The lack of health care and education affected adversely. The obvious solution appeared to be the adoption of the superior technology, institutions and habits and values. The diffusion was through the new modes of production that introduced the industrialization and consequently urbanization. Modern technology and medicine have become a part of the changed life style. Industrialisation and urbanisation make a country great or small. Urbanization has also facilitated the spread of the communication media and thereby enhanced the distribution of information.

The people tends to treat development as top-down process. It implies the assumption of trickle down of material benefits. There are certain sections of theoreticians and practitioners who do not refuse see to socio-economic changes as development. They desired that these changes should be nurturing, liberating and even energizing to the poor and powerless. The change should focus on human rather than on material resources. The resources of enhanced value is related to the quality of life. This includes not only comforts, productive and creative capacity but also self-reliance and capacity to interact effectively with one's physical and social environment. The bottom-up approach is the approach of empowerment. Hence, health and education become important and give a new dimensions to the proper development of nation-states. For the promotion of these basic amenities, community development through self-help is one big step towards development. It lays greater emphasis on the process itself rather than on the projects.

The approaches of development can be divided into two broad categories. The categories had the common assumption that progress or development is possible and desirable. The first broad category of this approach of development focus on harmonic interests. The author of The Wealth of Nations (1776) Adam Smith developed reaction to modernism. His school called for the minimum governments' intervention in economic transition. Smith's laissez–fair principle has reinforced David Ricardo's theory of comparative advantage. Their school is liberal of tariffs and other barriers to trade. The second approach lays emphasis on development through modernization. Its proponents Walt Rostow believed in the stage of "take off". The revolution of rising expectations was expected to accelerate social mobility. Samuel Huntington believed in the third world of cultural causation. In the 1980s Robert O. Keohane and Joseph S. Nye proposed the model of interdependence. Economic issues and tools have become as important as national security issues.

The second broad category development leads to different approach. The first approach is the Marxist-Leninist approach to development. Marx theorized that any mode of production is built on the theory of contradictions. Lenin believed that it was the responsibility of the professional revolutionaries to organize and lead the proletariat so that they can assume their historic role. The second model is of dependency theory. The Latin American theorists Raul Prebisch (Argentina) Cardoso and Santos (Brazil) and Sunkel (Chile) views are opposed to the modernization-development approach. Johan Galtung has advocated the center-periphery model. World system theory is proposed by Immanuel Wallerstein. International Political Economy (IPE) constitutes a combination of modernization and dependency approaches. The measurements tools are aggregate data and the law of the instrument. The concept of empowerment has gained popularity in 1980s.

Human Security

Human security is a non-traditional dimension of national security. The emphasis is more on the individual. In this age of globalization, human security puts emphasis more on the individual rather than on the security of the state. As such, the concept challenges the notion of traditional security. The concept of traditional security seeks to defend states from external aggression and to protect a state's boundaries, institutions and values. Thus, it focuses on the development of military capabilities. After the Second World War we have seen how the developed countries have enhanced their military capabilities. This was possible only where the state enjoyed economic and social stability. This perspective does not fulfil the ambition of developing state because these countries lack national unity and socially cohesive society. Within the state, there are different groups operating for different goals and their security issues are not the same. Such countries lack effective institutional capacities to provide peace and order.

After the fall of the Soviet Union, it became clear that military security was not the sole guarantor of protecting the territorial integrity of the state. Hence, economic power became more important as it could fulfil the requirements of common men, women, children and workers. Hence, the state territorial sovereignty cannot solely depend upon the traditional national security such as military aggression. For individuals in self-preservation and economic well being are important for survival. Therefore, it is necessary to take the holistic view of the security. Both traditional and non-traditional threats have to be addressed by the state. In view of this, traditional national security or comprehensive national security based on the development of political, economic, and military capabilities has to be complemented by social, technological and environmental strands. As such, in the year 1994 the concept of human security was first advanced in **Human Development Report** of the United Nations Development Programme (UNDP). The 1994 UNDP's Human Development Report is milestone document in the field of human security.

Mahbub ul Haq first drew global attention to the concept of human security in the 1994 UNDP's *Human Development Report.* This report is of vital significance that sought to influence the United Nations (UN) 1995 World Summit on Social Development in Copenhagen. The 1994 UNDP's human development report has defined human security as "safety from such chronic threats as hunger, disease and repression. Human security is protection from sudden and hurtful disruptions in the patterns of daily life. It is an assurance of protection in jobs, in homes, or in communities."[3] It is argued that the scope of global security should be expanded to include threats in seven areas:

- **Economic Security:** The real security issue is economic. Economic security needs an assured basic income for individuals. This income should come usually from productive and remunerative work. It is expected that the government should form a publicly financed safety net. In this sense, only about a quarter of the world's people are presently economically secure. The economic security is a serious problem in developing countries. The concern for economic security also affects the developed countries. Weak economy causes unemployment and it ultimately leads to political tensions and ethnic violence. Today, unemployment is the biggest threat. Creating job prospects will bring in real economic security.

- **Food Security:** Food security assures that all people at all times have access to food. People should have both physical and economic access to basic requirements of food. According to the United Nations, the overall availability of food is not a problem. The problem arises because of the poor public distribution of food and a lack of purchasing power. The past record shows that the food security problems have been dealt with both at national and global levels. However, their impacts has been limited. According to UN, the key is to tackle the problems relating to access to assets, work and assured income which is related to economic security. The key to food security lies in economic security.[4]
- **Health Security:** Health security aims to guarantee a minimum protection from diseases and unhealthy lifestyles. In developing countries, the major causes of death are infections and parasitic diseases. These kill approximately 17 million people annually. In an industrialized country, the major killers are diseases of the circulatory system, killing 5.5 million every year. The United Nations report shows that in both developing and developed countries, threats to health security are usually greater for poor people in rural areas, particularly children. The causes of ill-health are malnutrition and insufficient supply of medicine, lack of clean water or other necessary factors that are conducive to sound health.[5]
- **Environmental Security:** Environmental security aims to protect people from the short and long-term ravages of nature. Pollution is caused by man-made threats in nature. Pollution results from degradation of the natural environment. In developing countries, lack of access to clean drinking water resources is the greatest of all environmental threats. In industrially developed countries, major threat is air pollution. Global warming, caused by the emission of greenhouse gases, is another environmental security issue. Efforts are being made all over the globe to secure the planet from pollution.[6]
- **Personal Security:** Personal security aims to protect people from physical violence, whether from the state or external states. It protects them from violent individuals and sub-state actors. It is necessary to protect the young and the female from domestic abuse, and the young in particular from predatory adults. For many people, the greatest source of anxiety

is crime, particularly violent crime. Industrialization and urbanization have led to the increase in violent criminal activities in many ways.[7]

- **Community Security:** The aim of community security is to protect people from the loss of traditional relationships and values. It is to protect people from sectarian and ethnic violence. Traditional communities, particularly minority ethnic groups, are often threatened. Fifty per cent of the countries of the world's states have experienced some inter-ethnic strife. The United Nations declared 1993 as the Year of Indigenous People. The aim was to highlight the continuing vulnerability of the 300 million aboriginal people in 70 countries. Most of these groups face a widening spate of violence.[8]
- **Political Security:** Political security is concerned with whether people live in a society that honours their basic human rights. The recent survey conducted by Amnesty International points out political repression, systematic torture, ill treatment or disappearance is still practised in 110 countries. Human rights violations are most frequent during periods of political unrest. These violations continue repressing individuals and groups. It has been observed that governments, too, try to exercise control over ideas and information. Terrorism has assumed global proportions in the recent decades.[9]

These seven core areas of security has been merge into two categories of freedom: freedom from fear and freedom from want. Food, health, pollution, free atmosphere are the wants of humanity. Violence against individuals and groups from different forces, disparity and organized crime and violence are the fears from which namely needs to be liberated. In an ideal world, each of the UNDP's seven categories of threats need adequate global attention and resources. Yet attempts to implement this human security agenda have led to the emergence of two major schools of thought on how to best practice human security- "Freedom from Fear" and "Freedom from Want". The UNDP 1994 report has originally argued that human security requires attention to both freedoms from fear and freedom from want. Recently, divisions have gradually emerged over the proper scope of that protection. The differences are mainly over what threats from which individuals should be protected, and over which are the appropriate mechanisms for responding to these threats. Besides securing the territorial integrity of the state, security of the people is today's need.

(i) **Freedom from Fear***:* This school seeks to limit the practice of human security to protecting individuals from violent conflicts while recognizing that these violent threats are strongly associated with poverty, lack of state capacity and other forms of inequities.[10] This approach believes that limiting violence is a realistic and manageable approach towards human security. Thus, emergency assistance, conflict prevention and resolution and peace-building are the main concerns of this approach.

(ii) **Freedom from Want:** This school advocates a holistic approach in achieving human security and argues that the threat agenda should be broadened to include hunger, disease and natural disasters. The threats to hunger, diseases and natural disaster are inseparable concepts in addressing the root of human insecurity.[11] They kill far more people than war, genocide and terrorism combined.[12] Different from "Freedom from Fear", it is focus on development and security goals.

The theme of human security is to insure "freedom from want" and "freedom from fear" for all human beings. In recent years, the concept has gained significance in policy-making and research fields. This concept was included in the development studies, international relations, strategic studies, and human rights documents. Thus, human security is an emerging paradigm for understanding global vulnerabilities. The exponents of human security does not confine themselves to the analysis of traditional concept of national security but look beyond it. They argue that the security in modern context is more individualistic rather than the state oriented. The people-centric approach, hence, become more important of human security becomes more important for national, regional and global integration and also for promoting stability. Human security is necessary for development. Without human security the development becomes a stagnating process as it affects nation's progress. In other word, no development is possible without the proper base of human security. Today, the terms development and human security have become almost synonymous. The distinction between development and human security has no meaning. The relationship between the two is the means and end relationship. Human security is the mean. Development is its end. Human security is the condition that is conducive to development. Human security is the foundation. The process of development builds up its procedural action plan on this foundation of human security. In this way, human security is the basic condition which promotes the process of development.

Despite their differences, these two approaches to human security can be considered complementary rather than contradictory.[13] Expressions to this effect include: Franklin D. Roosevelt's famous Four Freedoms speech of 1941,[14] in which "Freedom from Want" is characterized as the third and "Freedom from Fear" is the fourth such fundamental universal freedom. The Government of Japan also considers Freedom from Fear and Freedom from Want to be equal in developing Japan's foreign policy. As Japan's Director-General, Yukio Takasu, in his speech at the International Conference on Human Security in a Globalized World in Ulaanbaatar on 8 May 2000 stated that "There are two basic aspects to human security-freedom from fear and freedom from want... We believe that freedom from want is no less critical than freedom from fear. So long as its objectives are to ensure the survival and dignity of individuals as human beings, it is necessary to go beyond thinking of human security solely in terms of protecting human life in conflict situations."[15]

The report also identified the following four essential characteristics of human security:[16]

- Human security is a universal concern. It is relevant to people everywhere, whether a nation is rich or poor;
- The components of human security are interdependent;
- Human security is easier to ensure through early prevention than later intervention. It is less costly to meet these threats upstream than downstream; and
- Human security is based on people centric approach. It is concerned with different style of living people's live in a society. It is also concerned with their choices, and their access to market and social opportunities, i.e. whether they live in conflict or in peace.

The key premises of the 1994 UNDP's human development report are: (a) joint focus on "freedom from fear" and "freedom from want", and; (b) emphases on universality, interdependence, prevention, and people centeredness. These formed, and continue to shape, human security debates. For example, Kofi Annan, the then UN Secretary General, in his address on "International Workshop on Human Security in Mongolia" at Ulaanbaatar in 2000 gave a comprehensive definition of human security:

> "Human security, in its broadest sense, embraces far more than the absence of violent conflict. It encompasses human rights, good governance, access to education and health care and ensuring that each individual has opportunities and choices to fulfil his or her potential. Every step in this direction is also a step towards reducing poverty, achieving economic growth and preventing conflict. Freedom from want, freedom from fear, and the freedom of future generations to inherit a healthy natural environment—these are the interrelated building blocks of human—and, therefore, national—security".[17]

UNHDP Report on Globalisation 1999: The 1999 UNDP Human Development Report on Globalisation stresses on the theme of human security. It was in the context of the 1998 Asian financial crisis. The report argued for deliberate actions to provide human security during economic crises. It demanded appropriate steps to reduce the causes of human insecurity. The causes of insecurity are global crime, environmental degradation, and communication that threaten cultural diversity.[18] It called for a strengthening of the United Nations System, "giving it greater coherence to respond to broader needs of human security."[19] Since the 1994 UNDP report, human security has also been receiving more attention from the key global development institutions, such as the World

Bank. S. Tadjbakhsh has traced the evolution of human security in international organizations. He concludes that the concept has been manipulated and transformed considerably since 1994 to fit organizational interests.[20]

World Bank World Development Report (WDR) on Poverty: The World Bank has produced a very constructive contribution to the human security debate. It uses the term security rather than human security. The World Bank's World Development Report 2000-2001 on poverty identifies three pillars of poverty reduction efforts such as (i) facilitating empowerment, (ii) enhancing security, and (iii) promoting opportunities. The "security" pillar is described as "Reducing vulnerability-to economic shocks, natural disasters, ill health, disability, and personal violence. It is an intrinsic part of enhancing well being. It encourages investment in human capital and in higher-risk, higher-return activities." In substance, the report uses security to refer to economic security for vulnerable populations. It refers to conflict prevention and resolution. It identifies priority areas for international cooperation, which include international financial stability. Other priority areas for cooperation are eradication of HIV/AIDS, tuberculosis and malaria. The areas like agricultural advances and environmental protection need international cooperation. All nations are required to come together and attempts for a reduction in arms trade, and post-conflict reconstruction.[21]

The Commission on Human Security 2003: The Commission on Human Security (CHS), co-chaired by Amartya Sen and Sadako Ogata clarified the concept of human security. It was convened to identify a concrete programme of action. It was required to communicate these findings widely. They defined human security as the protection of "the vital core of all human lives in a way that enhance human freedoms and fulfilment".[22] The report elaborated the definition of human security as protecting fundamental freedoms. It means protecting people from critical threats and situations. It means using processes that build on people's strengths and aspirations. It means creating political, social, environmental, economic, military and cultural systems. It means giving people the building blocks for survival, livelihood and dignity.[23] The report further pointed out that human security is far more than the absence of violent conflict. It encompasses human rights. It includes good governance. It gives access to economic opportunity. It brings to all education and health care. It is a concept that comprehensively addresses both "freedom from fear" and "freedom from want", rather then choosing one out of the two. To attain the goals of human security, the Commission proposed a framework based on the protection and empowerment of people.

Empowerment aims at developing the capabilities of individuals and communities so that they can act accordingly to their interests. Protection refers to the norms, processes and institutions. These will have to shield people from critical and pervasive threats. It implies a "top-down" approach. States have the primary responsibility to implement such a protective structure. However, international and regional organizations will have to carry it out. The enlightened, the civil society and the active non-governmental actors will put it in place. The private sector will play a pivotal role in shielding people from menaces. Neither protection nor empowerment can be dealt with in isolation as they are mutually reinforcing.[24]

Security for Whom	*What is the source of security Threat?*	
	Military	*Military, Non-military, or Both*
States	National security (Conventional realist approach to security studies)	Redefined Security (e.g., Environmental and Economic [Cooperative or Comprehensive] security)
Societies, Groups, and Individuals	Intrastate security (e.g., Civil war, Ethnic conflict, and Democide)	Human security (e.g., Environmental and Economic Threats to the Survival of Societies, Groups, and Individuals)

Source: Roland Paris ' Human Security: Paradigm Shift or Hot Air?", International Security, Vol. 26, No. 2, 2001.

Hence, the security threats are not only military threats but are also non-military threats such as poverty, disease pollution and illiteracy. These also include economic, health, environment and social threats. It is necessary that these kind of threat need to be eliminated because they cause and increase insecurity of the individual and the state.

Human Security as Concept of Development

The concept of development was earlier associated with just economic growth emphasizing on National Income Growth. Pursuing this old fashioned development, traditional security concept was suitable. But after 1970, it was observed by development thinkers that only growing national income was not only the factor that could bring prosperity to all citizens with equity and justice. It is now widely believed that this is a very inadequate characterization of development. Though, average per capita incomes are one important means to achieve such progress, but is not the criteria. Not only does average income fail to capture distribution across households, but it also may not be a good indicator of many important aspects of human well-being, such as people's health, education or their security. A series of alternative objectives have been put forward, one of the earliest being the PQLI (Physical Quality of Life Index). Prof. Amartya Sen has suggested that the development objective should be the enhancement of people's capabilities, or the opportunities open to people of being and doing a variety of things.[25] UNDP's *Human Development Report* defined the objective succinctly as enlarging people's choices in a way which enables them to lead longer, healthier and fuller lives.[26]

Therefore, there is need for humanistic approach to development. The human security approach not only focuses on equitable and pro-poor economic growth but also highlights the importance of human rights and the provision of adequate social services that together give people the building blocks of survival, livelihood, and dignity. The demands of human security are only partly addressed by improving economic growth, which usually benefits the most able or the better placed. People who cannot achieve the lowest level of security are the ones who survive in abject poverty, who fall victim to sudden crisis, or who are caught in the middle of violent conflicts. For these reasons, they are excluded from development. The losses of human capital to these horrible situations are increasing at alarming speed.[27]

According to **Amartya Sen**, "Human security is concerned with reducing and—when possible—removing the insecurities that plague human lives".[28] The definition has been expanded by the Commission on Human Security as:

> Human security in its broadest sense embraces far more than the absence of violent conflict. It encompasses human rights, good governance, access to education and health care, and ensuring that each individual has opportunities and choices to fulfil his or her own potential....Freedom from want, freedom from fear and the freedom of the future generations to inherit a healthy natural environment—these are the interrelated building blocks of human and therefore national security.[29]

This definition of security covers much of what is normally included in human development, i.e., levels of achievement as well as risks,[30] and also economic sources of insecurity as well as those arising from violence. The human security, therefore, is concerned with protecting people from various threats in social, economic, and political life, as well as threats from natural disasters. The human development concept, on the other hand, empowers people so that they do not fall into a difficult situation. If they do, they are able to get out of it with minimum damage done to their ability to get back on their feet. Both of these concepts focus on people and their lives. Security aims to protect them. Development aims to empower them. Each concept is dependent on the other. Both of them together can bring about a sustained improvement in human lives.[31]

Conclusion

People can live in security and dignity and is free from poverty and despair when they are well protected by the state is still a dream for many. But, in such a world, every individual would be guaranteed "freedom from fear" and "freedom from want", with an equal opportunity to fully develop their human potential. Building human security is essential to achieving this goal. In essence, human security means freedom from pervasive threats to people's rights, their safety or even their lives. Human security has now become a global phenomenon. Safety is the hallmark of freedom from fear, while well-being is the target of freedom from want. Human security and human development are, thus, two sides of the same coin, mutually reinforcing and leading to a conducive environment for each other.[32]

Development is an evaluative concept. It is not static but a dynamic concept which believes in progress. It has a definite positive connotation. Enhancement, progress value addition, economic and transformation welfare, due to modernization and urbanization are the hallmark of the development. The developmental change is nurturing, liberating and energizing.

Thus, Human security and development are the most frequently used terms of the contemporary times because of the following factors that shaped human society:

- Human security and development are interdependent. Without human security development is impossible. In the same manner for human security, development is essential.
- The interconnected concept of human security and development has undergone changes in meaning through the extension and comprehensive inclusion.
- The concept of security was introduced as security of territory from external aggressions. It was a protection of national interests. It was more related to the nation.
- Human security is concerned with the security of individuals.
- Human security is concerned with the two catch phrases 'Freedom from fear' and 'Freedom from want.' It is a people centred security. It is security with a human face.

REFERENCES

1. Human Security is currently being used to describe a peoples' sense of inclusion, of being valued, of being safe from perniciousness (by other individuals, organized crime elements, or from corrupted governmental or corporate impositions), basic comfort (as opposed to "luxury") and freedom.
2. Ul Haq Mahbub, "Reflections on Human Development", Oxford University Press, New Delhi, 1995, pp.46-48.
3. United Nations Development Programme, "Human Development Report", Oxford University Press, New Delhi, 1994, p. 22.
4. United Nations Development Programme, "Human Development Report", 1994, op.cit; pp.23.26.
5. Ibid.
6. Ibid., pp.23-26.
7. Ibid.
8. United Nations Development Programme, "Human Development Report", 1994, op.cit;

9. Ibid.
10. Human Security Centre, "What is Human Security?" [available at http://www.humansecurityreport.info/index.php?option=content&task=view&id=24&itemid=59]
11. C. Schitteccatte, "Toward a More Inclusive Global Governance and Enhanced Human Security, in A Decade of Human Security", Global Governance and New Multilateralism's edited by: S.J. Maclean, D.R. Black and Timothy M.Shaw, A Sage Publishing Limited, New Delhi, 2006, p.131.
12. C. Schitteccatte, "Toward a More Inclusive Global Governance and Enhanced Human Security, in A Decade of Human Security"; op.cit.
13. Ibid.
14. In his annual address to Congress on 6 January 1941, Franklin Roosevelt presented his reasons for American involvement in the World War II, making the case for continued aid to Great Britain and greater production of war industries at home. In helping Britain, President Roosevelt stated, the United States was fighting for the universal freedoms that all people possessed. As America entered the war these "four freedoms"– the freedom of speech, the freedom of worship, the freedom from want, and the freedom from fear—symbolized Americans war aims and gave hope in the following years to a war-wearied people because they knew the were fighting for freedom. "Four essential human freedoms" that he pointed out in his address are: "The first is freedom of speech and expression-everywhere in the world. The second is freedom of every person to worship God in his own way—everywhere in the world. The third is freedom from want—which, translated into world terms, means economic understandings which will secure to every nation a healthy peacetime life for its inhabitants-everywhere in the world. The fourth is freedom from fear—which, translated into world terms, means a world-wide reduction of armaments to such a point and in such a thorough fashion that no nation will be in a position to commit an act of physical aggression against any neighbour—anywhere in the world." Franklin D. Roosevelt Presidential Library and Museum, "Our Documents: Franklin Roosevelt's Annual Address to Congress—The "Four Freedoms", January 6, 1941," New York, [available at http://www.fdrlibrary.marist.edu/od4freed.html.
15. "Statement by Director-General Yukio Takasu, at the International Conference on Human Security in a Globalized World, Ulaanbaatar, 8 May 2000", Ministry of Foreign Affairs of Japan, Tokyo, [available at http://www.mofa.go.jp/POLICY/human_secu/speech0005.html.]
16. United Nations Development Programme, Human Development Report 1994, op.cit; pp. 22-23.
17. Annan, Kofi, "Secretary-General Salutes International Workshop on Human Security in Mongol", Two-Day Session in Ulaanbaatar, 8-10 May 2000. Press Release SG/SM/7382, [available at http://www.un.org/News/Press/docs/2000/20000508.sgsm7382.doc.html].
18. United National Development Programme, "Human Development Report 1999", Oxford University Press, New York, 1999, pp. 102-104.
19. United National Development Programme, "Human Development Report 1999", op.cit; p. 111.
20. S. Tadjbakhsh, "Human Security in International Organizations: Blessing or Scourge?" *Human Security Journal*, Vol. 4, 2007, pp. 8-16.
21. World Bank, "World Development Report 2000/2001: Attacking Poverty", New York: Published for the World Bank by Oxford University Press.
22. Commission on Human Security (CHS), "Human Security Now", New York: Commission on Human Security, 2003, p. 4. Alternate phrasings of this definition include: (i) The objective of human security is to protect the vital core of all human lives. (instead of protect: shield, guarantee, defend, maintain, uphold, preserve, secure, safeguard, ensure that...are shielded); (ii) The objective of human security is to protect the vital core of all human

lives from critical pervasive threats in a way that is consistent with long-term human fulfilment. (initial definition was this); (iii) The objective of human security is to guarantee a set of vital rights and freedoms to all people, without unduly compromising their ability to pursue other goals; (iv) The objective of human security is to create political, economic, social, cultural, and environmental conditions in which people live knowing that their vital rights and freedoms are secure; and (v) The objective of human security is to keep critical pervasive threats from invading the vital core of human lives. Sabina Alkire, "Conceptual Framework for Human Security", 16 February 2002, available at http://www.humansecurity-chs.org/activities/outreach/frame.pdf. [16 February 2002]

23. Ibid.
24. Commission on Human Security, "Human Security Now", op.cit; p.10. Also see Sadako Ogata, Johan Cels, "Human Security-Protecting and Empowering the People", *Journal of Article Excerpt*, Vol. 9, No. 5, 2003, p. 67-75
25. A.Sen, "Development as Freedom," Oxford University Press, New Delhi, 1999.
26. The first UNDP Human Development Report stated that "The basic objective of development is to create an enabling environment for people to enjoy long, healthy, and creative and defined human development as a process of enlarging people's choices." See UNDP, Human Development Report, Oxford University Press, Delhi, 1990.
27. F. Fouinat, "A Comprehensive Framework for Human Security," in R. Picciotto and R. Weaving (eds.), Security and Development: Investing in Peace and Prosperity, Routledge, New York, 2006, pp. 74-75
28. A.Sen, "Development as Freedom", op.cit., p. 8.
29. Commission on Human Security, "Human Security Now, 2003", op.cit; p. 4.
30. Although Sen suggests that, in comparison with Human Development, it focuses more on the downside risks. See Commission on Human Security (CHS) 2003, p. 8.
31. Human Development in South Asia 2005, op.cit., p. 9.
32. A Perspective on Human Security: Chairman's Summary 1st Ministerial Meeting of the Human Security Network, Lysøen, Norway, [available at: http://www.humansecuritynetwork.org/menu-e.php, Date of accessed 20 May 1999.]

18

Environmental Security Challenges to India

Dhirendra Dwivedi

Introduction

On our planet, nature embraces various forms of life inhabiting air, soil and water. As such human beings form an integral component of life. The environmental balance is related to the product of the evolution of life. The origin of organism, in the form of their life systems, diseases, lighting and erosion, form complex nature in which the equilibrium between living and non-living is maintained through natural selection. Man himself being a product of evolution has created his own environment. This man-made environment has been well shaped by his cultural evolution, and this cultural progress has become more important than his biological evolution. His inventive genius, still and efforts have given him protection against natural calamities and provided him freedom for his creative ideas. With the help of tools and techniques of science and technology, he has fashioned an environment suited to his own purpose and satisfaction.[1]

Environment, as a comprehensive term, refers to our surroundings and belongings. It includes all components-living and non-living (lithosphere, atmosphere and hydrosphere) that are present on the earth. Further, environment is sub-divided into natural and social environment. By natural environment, we mean land, water and air and social environment includes man, society and their interaction with the natural environment. The relationship between the two is called ecology. The study of all components of environment is known as environmental studies. In recent years, increase in human population raises high expectation of economic life. The natural environment has degraded to a great extent. The environmental and social factors like environmental pollution, exploitation of natural resources and environmental degradation and health hazards have enabled nations for the regulation of laws for conserving environment. Environmental security has attracted the alteration of the world communicators—governments, administrators, policy institution, academicians and local people.

Environmental security has become a well known concept since the end of the cold war but there is a lack of clarity in defining the term. The work on the concept has been evolved in an *ad-hoc* manner amounting to various interpretations. Hence, antiquity and different approaches are characteristics of this concept. The concept is made of divergent words like, 'environment' and 'security' which are important in any society for two issues: (i) who has been secured, and (ii) from what contingencies have they been saved?

The relationship between environment and security is said to take three forms:

(a) Destructive effect on the environment through military activity including weapon training, firing and testing;
(b) Environmental warfare or destruction and manipulation of the environment for hostile purposes;
(c) Environmental degradation or resource depletion causing social instability and violence.[2]

Environmental security as a concept encompassing non-military aspects of security was officially mentioned for the first time in the international conference on the Relationship between Disarmament and Development convened by the UN General Assembly in New York from 24 August to 11 September 1987. The final document was adopted by states on consensus basis. "Recently non-military threats to security have moved to the forefront of global concern. Underdevelopment and declining prospects for development as well as mismanagement and waste of resources, constitute challenges to security. The degradation of the environment presents a threat to sustainable development...... Mass poverty, illiteracy, diseases, squalor and malnutrition affecting a large proportion of world's population often become the cause of social strain, tension and strife."[3]

According to A. Goudie, "environment is the representative of physical components of the earth wherein man is an important factor affecting the environment. "Douglas and Holland has opined that "the term 'environment' is used to describe, in the aggregate, all the external forces, influences and conditions, which affect the life, nature, behaviour and the growth, development and maturity of living organism.[4] Environment has been defined most aptly by the Chinese as "the air, land, water, mineral, resources, forests, grasslands, wild plants and animals, aquatic life, places of historical interest, science spots, hot springs, resorts and natural areas under special protection as well as inhabited areas of the country." This wide definition of environment perhaps underlines the broad spectrum of the security space that is implied in it.[5]

Interpretations of environmental security are available in the various literatures. A 1998 survey by the Millennium Project of the American Council for the United Nations University deems ecological security to include the following: safety of the general public from environmental dangers caused by natural or human processes due to ignorance, accident, mismanagement or design; amelioration of natural resource scarcity; maintenance of healthy environment; amelioration of environmental degradation; and causatary effect of all these factors. Prevention of social disorder and conflict and, thus, promotion of stability.[6]

Furthermore, there are seven major areas which comprise the environmental security agenda. These are efforts to redefine security; theories about environmental factors in violent conflict; the environmental security of the nation; the linkages between the military and environmental issues; the ecological security agenda; the environmental security of the people; and the issues of securitization.[7]

Despite different meaning of environmental security, a policy discourse has emerged in the United States. Even this discourses is ambiguous about the meaning of environmental security. Hence, it is assumed, there is a need for further examination of the concept. In addition alternative to existing approaches, such as sustainable development, to assist in the comprehension and resolution through theoretically coherent and well intended, have failed to lead to the resolution of most environmental problem. At present, environmental security does not offer much scope. But a critical examination, and more coherent reformulation may be helpful in explaining the concept of environmental security problems in India.

Environmental Challenges in India: The problem of environmental problems goes back to the evolution of Homo Sapiens on this planet. The development of science and technology and the ever increasing world population brought tremendous changes in the earth's environment.[8] The idea of right to environment was founded in the ancient India texts and the protection was available under moral codes. Manusmriti prescribed different punishments for causing injury to plants and advised people not to disrupt the quality of water and not to contaminate the same by urine, stool and coughing, impious objects, blood and poison. Kautilya's Artashastra is said to have gone a step further and determined punishments on the basis of the importance of a particular part of a tree.[9] Yajnavalkya Smriti, a historic Indian text on statecraft and jurisprudence, prohibited the cutting of trees and prescribed punishments for such acts. Ashoka went further, and his Pillar Edicts expressed his view about the welfare of environment and biodiversity. Some important trees were even equated to a divine position. Thus, India had an ancient tradition of protecting the environment. History is full of sacred writings which prove that in India every individual had the right to practice the dharma to protect and worship nature. In one such old Hindu jurisprudence, "earth was considered as mother and we as her children".

During the British period in India, we have seen that in India several laws were made to protect the environment. Amongst the earliest ones were Shore Nuisance (Bombay and Kolaba) Act of 1853 and Oriental Gas Company Act of 1857. The Indian Penal Code of 1860 imposed a fine on anyone who voluntarily fouls the water of any public spring or reservoir. In additional, the code penalized negligent acts. The British India also enacted laws aimed at controlling air pollution. Prominent amongst these were the Bengal Smoke Nuisance Act of 1905 and the Bombay Smoke Nuisance Act of 1912. While these laws failed in having the intended effect, British-enacted legislation pioneered the growth of environmental regulation in India.[10]

After gaining independence from Britain, India adopted a constitution and numerous British enacted laws. But it was the Forty Second Amendment Act of 1976 which incorporated environmental protection and improvement. Article 48 A was added to the Directive Principles of the State Policy. It stated: "The State shall endeavour to protect and improve the environment and to safeguard the forests and wildlife of the country".[11] Similarly, under article 51g of the "Fundamental Duties," it is expected that the citizens "would protect" and improve the natural environment including forests, lakes, rivers and wild life."[12]

In the second half of the 20th century in India, numerous laws such as Prevention and Control of Pollution Act of 1974, the Forest (Conservation) Act of 1980, and the Air Prevention and Control of Pollution Act of 1981 were enacted. The Air act was inspired by the decisions made at Stockholm Conference. The Bhopal gas tragedy triggered the Government of India to enact the Environmental Protection Act of 1986. India has also enacted a set of Noise Pollution Rules in 2000. In 1985, Indian government created the Ministry of Environment and Forest. This Ministry is the central administrative organization in India for regulating and ensuring environmental protection. The Supreme Court and the High Courts of Mumbai, Kolkata, Chennai and Gujarat have a "green" bench. It has been observed by judges of many High Courts that environmental degradation violates the fundamental right to life. In many instances, the courts have behaved like administrators and have come down heavily on the polluters.[13]

Environmental Issues

Environmental issues like air pollution, water pollution, garbage and pollution of the natural environment pose major challenges for India. The situation was worse from 1947 to 1995. According to data collection and environment assessment studies of World Bank experts between 1995 and 2010, India has made one of the fastest progresses in the world in addressing its environmental issues and improving its quality.[14]

The causes of environmental degradation were mainly due to stresses from development and stresses from lack of development. In the 1970s, poverty was the sole cause of all problems. The most classic case of environmental degradation was mentioned in the Gazetteer of India, Vol III of 1973. It mentioned that "Civilizations of Babylon and Assyria and ruins of Taxcila and Harappa, Kutch and Rajasthan were due to wind erosion and abuse of land. The Rajasthan desert of 20,00,000 sq-km is advancing towards Ganga plains at a rate of 800 meters per year over a front of 1600 kms".[15] The 8th plan document (1992-1997) mentioned pollution, over-use and destruction of the natural environment and urged that it has to be protected and restored. The 9th plan also identified the following causes of environmental degradation. These causes are: deforestation; industrialization; urban transport; input intensive agriculture; and poverty-the problem of a huge population with limited resources.

These problems were discussed in the 88th Science Congress which was held in the year 2001. The theme of the Congress was the "Vision on Food, Nutrition and Environmental Security". The objective was to eliminate poverty and make India environmentally safe by 2020. Still, there is a vast difference between India and developed economies in terms of environmental quality because in India pollution remains a major challenge for India. Environmental issues like diseases, health and long term livelihood have become a cause of major concern for our country.

It is also important to mention that environmental issues such as human population growth, rising energy consumption, global warming and climate change, stratospheric ozone depletion, land degradation and crop land scarcity, desertification, deforestation, fresh water scarcity, loss of biodiversity, degradation of coastal areas and marine environment, decline in fish stock and degradation of mountain ecosystems like the Himalayas have become grave problems that India faces today.

Human Population growth: The increase in population growth and economic development in our country have degraded the environment through the uncontrolled growth of urbanization and industrialization, expansion and intensification of agriculture, and the destruction of natural habitats. Populations growth has adversely affected the natural resources and environment. These problems, no doubt, affected sustained development without environmental damage. The presence or the absence of favourable natural resources can either increase or decrease the process of economic development. Demographic factors like births, deaths and migration can produce changes in population size, composition, distribution and these changes can raise a number of important questions of means and end. India has approximately 18 percent of the world population but the geographical area is merely 2 percent.[16] The country's population growth can be assessed from the table 1.

The United Nations and World Bank Report projects, "that around the year 2026 India's population will be about 1.35 billion, and that by 2051 it will be about 1.57 billion." Of course, changes in fertility and mortality rates could drastically alter this projection.[17]

Table 1: Population: India and the States

(Numbers)

Sl. No.	States/U.Ts.	1981		1991		2001		2011	
		Male	Female	Male	Female	Male	Female	Male	Female
1	2	3	4	5	6	7	8	9	10
1	Andhra Pradesh	27,109,616	26,441,410	33,724,581	32,783,427	38,527,413	37,682,594	42442146	42138631
2	Arunachal Pradesh	339,322	292,517	465,004	399,554	579,941	518,027	713912	669815
3	Assam	9,444,037	8,597,211	11,657,989	10,756,333	13,777,037	12,878,491	15939443	15266133
4	Bihar	35,930,560	33,984,174	33,838,238	30,692,316	43,243,795	39,754,714	54278157	49821295
5	Chhattisgarh++		..	8,872,620	8,742,308	10,474,218	10,359,585	12832895	12712303
6	Goa	510,152	497,597	594,790	575,003	687,248	660,420	739140	719405
7	Gujarat	17,552,640	16,533,159	21,355,209	19,954,373	26,385,577	24,285,440	31491260	28948432
8	Haryana	6,909,679	6,012,440	8,827,474	7,636,174	11,363,953	9,780,611	13494734	11856728
9	Himachal Pradesh	2,169,931	2,110,887	2,617,467	2,553,410	3,087,940	2,989,960	3481873	3382729
10	Jammu & Kashmir+	3,164,660	2,822,729	4,142,082	3,694,969	5,360,926	4,782,774	6640662	5900640
11	Jharkhand++	..	..	11,363,853	10,480,058	13,885,037	13,060,792	16930315	16057819
12	Karnataka	18,922,627	18,213,087	22,951,917	22,025,284	26,898,918	25,951,644	30966657	30128640
13	Kerala	12,527,767	12,925,913	14,288,995	14,809,523	15,468,614	16,372,760	16027412	17378649
14	Madhya Pradesh	26,886,305	25,292,539	25,394,673	23,171,569	31,443,652	28,904,371	37612306	35014503
15	Maharashtra	32,414,432	30,368,386	40,825,618	38,111,569	50,400,596	46,478,031	58243056	54131277
16	Manipur[1]	721,006	699,947	938,359	898,790	1,161,952	1,131,944	1290171	1280219
17	Meghalaya	683,710	652,109	907,687	867,091	1,176,087	1,142,735	1491832	1475057
18	Mizoram	257,239	236,518	358,978	330,778	459,109	429,464	555339	541867
19	Nagaland	415,910	359,020	641,282	568,264	1,047,141	942,895	1024649	953853
20	Odisha	13,309,786	13,060,485	16,064,146	15,595,590	18,660,570	18,144,090	21212136	20762082
21	Punjab	8,937,210	7,851,705	10,778,034	9,503,935	12,985,045	11,373,954	14639465	13103873
22	Rajasthan	17,854,154	16,407,708	23,042,780	20,963,210	29,420,011	27,087,177	35550997	32997440
23	Sikkim	172,440	143,945	216,427	190,030	288,484	252,367	323070	287507
24	Tamil Nadu	24,487,624	23,920,453	28,298,975	27,559,971	31,400,909	31,004,770	36137975	36009055
25	Tripura	1,054,846	998,212	1,417,930	1,339,275	1,642,225	1,556,978	1874376	1799541
26	Uttarakhand++	..	..	3,674,540	3,438,943	4,325,924	4,163,425	5137773	4948519
27	Uttar Pradesh	58,819,535	52,042,977	70,362,417	61,636,387	87,565,369	78,632,552	104480510	95331831
28	West Bengal	28,560,901	26,019,746	35,510,633	32,567,332	41,465,985	38,710,212	46809027	44467088
	Union Territories								
1	A&N Islands	107,261	81,480	154,369	126,292	192,972	163,180	202871	177710
2	Chandigarh	255,278	196,332	358,614	283,401	506,938	393,697	580663	474787
3	D&N Haveli	52,515	51,161	70,953	67,524	121,666	98,824	193760	149949
4	Daman & Diu	38,298	40,683	51,595	49,991	92,512	65,692	150301	92946
5	Delhi	3,440,081	2,780,325	5,155,512	4,265,132	7,607,234	6,243,273	8987326	7800615
6	Lakshadweep	20,377	19,872	26,618	25,089	31,131	29,519	33123	31350
7	Puducherry	304,561	299,910	408,081	399,704	486,961	487,384	612511	635442
	All India[* & 1]	**353,374,460**	**329,954,637**	**439,358,440**	**407,062,599**	**532,223,090**	**496,514,346**	**623121843**	**587447730**

Source : Office of the Registrar General, India

+ : The 1991 Census was not held in Jammu & Kashmir. 1991 Census figures include interpolated Population of Jammu & Kashmir.

++ : The States of Uttarakhand, Jharkhand and Chhattisgarh are carved out from Uttar Pradesh,Bihar, and Madhya Pradesh respectivly, in 2001 Census. In 1991 the recasted figures for these States are given as per jurisdiction of 2001 Census.

1 - : India and Manipur figures include estimated figures for those of the three sub-divisions viz. Mao Maram, Paomata and Purul of Senapati district of Manipur as population Census 2001 in these three sub-divisions were cancelled due to technical and administrative reasons.

* : The figures for India and Manipur, exclude the population of Mao Maram, Paomata and Purul sub-divisions of Senapati district of Manipur for Census 2011 due to administrative reasons.

Fresh Water Scarcity: Fresh water scarcity is another important environmental problem that affects almost all countries, particularly those living in the resource scare and populated areas of the developing countries. Water is the very basis of life and is the foundation for human survival and development. Sustainable and equitable use of water over millenia have been ensured by cultural adaptation to water availability through water conservation technologies, agricultural systems and cropping pattern adapted to different climate zones, and conservation based life styles. But in the last few decades, the consequences of population growth, industrialization and urbanization, and the associated consumerist culture, have interfered with the natural hydrological cycle of rainfall, soil moisture, groundwater, surface water and storage of all sizes. This has led to overuse, abuse and pollution of our vital water resources and has disturbed the quality and the natural cleaning capacity of water. Water is one of the most crucial elements in our national developmental planning for the 21st century.

Access to safe drinking water remains an urgent need. Only 70.6 percent of occupied housing unit in urban areas receive organized piped water supply and rest have to depend on surface or ground water which is untreated. The situation in rural areas is much worse with only 30.8 percent households water sources come through tap water. In India, almost all surface water sources are contaminated and unfit for human consumption. The disease commonly caused due to contaminated water are diarrhea trachoma, intestine worms, hepatitis. Inadequate access to safe drinking water and sanitation facilities leads to infant mortality and intestinal diseases. As per census of 2011, 69.3 percent rural households and 18.6 percent urban households are still without toilet of any type.[18] This could be seen from Tables 2 and 3.

Table 2: Households Classified by Supply of Water and Toilet Installation by Rural and Urban

Year	*Total No. of Households*	*Households with Water Supply though Tap Water*			*Toilet Installation*	
		Total	*Inside*	*Outside*	*With Toilet of Any Type*	*Without Toilet of Any Type*
			2011			
Total	246692667	107,417,176	78,873,488	28,533,688	115,737,458	130,955,209
%age	100	43.5	32.0	11.6	46.9	53.1
Rural	167826730	51,705,165	29,969,145	21,736,020	51,575,339	116,251,391
%age	100	30.8	17.9	13.0	30.7	69.3
Urban	78865937	55,702,011	48,904,343	6,797,668	64,162,119	14,703,818
%age	100	70.8	62.0	8.6	81.4	18.6

Source: Office of the Registrar General of India (Census 2011).

Table 3: Distribution of Households by Availability of Drinking Water Facility

Sl.No	India/ State/ Union Territory[#]	Distribution of households by availability of drinking water facility													Availability of Drinking Water Source		
		Total No. of Households (Excluding institutional households)	Tap water			Well			Handpump	Tubewell	Spring	River, Canal	Tank, Pond, Lake	Any other source	Within the premises	Near the premises	Away
			Total	From treated source	From un-treated source	Total	Covered well	Un-covered well									
1	2	3	4	5	6	7	8	9	10	11	12	13	14	15	16	17	18
1	A & N Islands *	93,376	85.0	68.9	16.2	7.3	0.7	6.6	0.0	0.5	1.2	2.6	1.5	1.9	60.6	27.0	12.4
2	Andhra Pradesh	21,024,534	69.9	49.0	20.9	6.4	0.5	5.9	13.7	6.9	0.5	0.3	0.3	2.1	43.2	37.3	19.5
3	Arunachal Pradesh	261,614	65.5	26.4	39.1	5.7	1.4	4.3	10.7	2.4	5.7	6.0	0.9	3.2	41.1	37.4	21.6
4	Assam	6,367,295	10.5	9.2	1.3	18.9	1.7	17.2	50.2	9.2	1.3	3.4	4.6	2.0	54.8	26.7	18.5
5	Bihar	18,940,629	4.4	3.1	1.3	4.3	0.7	3.7	86.6	3.0	0.0	0.2	0.1	1.4	50.1	37.9	12.0
6	Chandigarh *	235,061	96.7	93.7	3.0	0.1	0.1	0.0	1.8	0.9	0.0	0.0	0.1	0.5	86.2	11.7	2.2
7	Chhattisgarh	5,622,850	20.7	12.3	8.4	11.4	0.8	10.6	58.4	7.2	0.7	0.9	0.2	0.5	19.0	54.5	26.5
8	Dadra & Nagar Haveli *	73,063	46.5	26.0	20.5	7.2	1.5	5.7	24.5	20.6	0.6	0.3	0.0	0.4	52.6	36.4	11.0
9	Daman & Diu *	60,381	75.2	54.6	20.6	0.7	0.5	0.2	5.5	18.1	0.0	0.0	0.0	0.5	76.4	22.1	1.5
10	Delhi *	3,340,538	81.3	75.2	6.1	0.1	0.1	0.0	5.3	8.4	0.0	0.0	1.2	3.6	78.4	15.4	6.2
11	Goa	322,813	85.4	82.1	3.4	11.1	4.0	7.1	0.1	0.3	1.2	0.3	0.4	1.3	79.7	15.5	4.8
12	Gujarat	12,181,718	69.0	39.9	29.2	7.1	2.3	4.8	11.6	9.6	0.1	0.3	0.2	2.0	64.0	23.5	12.4
13	Haryana	4,717,954	68.8	55.9	12.9	3.0	0.7	2.3	12.0	12.9	0.0	0.3	0.9	1.9	66.5	21.4	12.1
14	Himachal Pradesh	1,476,581	89.5	83.9	5.6	2.9	1.6	1.3	3.6	0.7	0.7	0.3	0.5	1.9	55.5	35.0	9.5
15	Jammu & Kashmir	2,015,088	63.9	34.7	29.2	6.5	1.9	4.7	11.4	1.5	6.2	6.7	0.7	3.1	48.2	28.7	23.1
16	Jharkhand	6,181,607	12.9	10.0	2.9	36.5	1.9	34.6	43.8	3.5	0.8	1.6	0.2	0.8	23.2	44.9	31.9
17	Karnataka	13,179,911	66.1	41.2	24.8	9.0	1.0	8.0	5.5	16.0	0.3	0.8	1.0	1.4	44.5	37.3	18.2
18	Kerala	7,716,370	29.3	23.4	6.0	62.0	14.6	47.4	0.5	3.7	1.4	0.2	0.7	2.1	77.7	14.1	8.2
19	Lakshadweep *	10,703	20.3	9.1	11.1	71.7	6.9	64.9	2.5	0.1	0.0	0.0	0.4	5.1	83.7	14.3	2.0
20	Madhya Pradesh	14,967,597	23.4	16.5	6.9	20.0	1.1	18.9	47.1	7.6	0.3	0.7	0.4	0.6	23.9	45.6	30.5
21	Maharashtra	23,830,580	67.9	56.3	11.6	14.4	2.2	12.2	9.9	5.7	0.4	0.4	0.4	1.0	59.4	27.6	13.1
22	Manipur	507,152	38.6	25.6	13.0	7.5	2.8	4.7	6.5	0.4	5.6	15.0	23.2	3.4	16.1	46.2	37.8
23	Meghalaya	538,299	39.3	27.8	11.5	25.4	6.9	18.5	2.8	2.6	19.0	2.6	5.7	2.6	24.1	43.2	32.7
24	Mizoram	221,077	58.7	39.4	19.3	4.7	2.0	2.7	0.8	0.9	18.4	7.7	1.8	6.9	31.2	46.7	22.2
25	Nagaland	399,965	47.2	6.1	41.1	25.7	6.6	19.1	2.2	4.5	5.6	2.0	10.3	2.7	29.3	42.4	28.3
26	Odisha	9,661,085	13.8	10.0	3.9	19.5	2.2	17.3	41.5	20.0	1.8	1.7	0.9	0.8	22.4	42.2	35.4
27	Puducherry *	301,276	95.3	90.8	4.5	1.9	0.1	1.8	1.2	1.4	0.0	0.0	0.0	0.3	77.4	21.5	1.1
28	Punjab	5,409,699	51.0	41.1	9.9	0.5	0.2	0.2	24.7	21.9	0.0	0.2	0.1	1.7	85.9	10.0	4.1
29	Rajasthan	12,581,303	40.6	32.0	8.5	10.8	1.2	9.6	25.3	12.2	0.1	0.8	5.9	4.3	35.0	39.0	25.9
30	Sikkim	128,131	85.3	29.2	56.1	0.6	0.5	0.2	0.0	0.0	11.1	0.4	0.6	2.0	52.6	29.7	17.7
31	Tamil Nadu	18,493,003	79.8	55.8	24.0	5.1	1.2	3.8	4.6	8.2	0.2	0.2	0.5	1.5	34.9	58.1	7.0
32	Tripura	842,781	33.2	20.3	12.9	27.4	2.9	24.5	18.1	16.3	1.9	1.8	0.5	0.9	37.1	30.5	32.4
33	Uttar Pradesh	32,924,266	27.3	20.2	7.1	4.0	0.6	3.4	64.9	2.9	0.0	0.1	0.1	0.7	51.9	36.0	12.1
34	Uttarakhand	1,997,068	68.2	53.9	14.3	1.1	0.7	0.4	22.0	2.0	1.1	0.9	0.7	4.0	58.3	26.6	15.2
35	West Bengal	20,067,299	25.4	21.0	4.4	6.0	0.7	5.4	50.1	16.7	0.5	0.3	0.2	0.8	38.6	34.7	26.6
	INDIA	**246,692,667**	**43.5**	**32.0**	**11.6**	**11.0**	**1.6**	**9.4**	**33.5**	**8.5**	**0.5**	**0.6**	**0.8**	**1.5**	**46.6**	**35.8**	**17.6**

Source: Registrar General of India, 2011

Water pollution, thus, has become a major environmental issue in India. The largest source of water pollution in India is untreated sewage. Other sources of pollution include agricultural run off and unregulated small scale industry. In India, rivers, lakes and surface water are mostly polluted and have also become a dumping ground for sewage, solid and liquid water. The proper management of our limited water resources is essential to ensure food security for our growing population and to eliminate poverty. In order to avoid the growing conflicts and the possibility of social unrest in the country in future, much attention has to be given to water scarcity problem.

Global Warming and Climate Change: The greenhouse effect has also resulted in altering the balance in fair elements-carbon, nitrogen, phosphorus and sulphur. These shape the planetary environment, particularly carbon and nitrogen. Increased emission of carbon gases cause global warming leading to violent storms. This has caused in depletion of the ozone layer around the earth's atmosphere, which absorbed radiation from the sun resulting in global warming. Some scientists have predicted that serious climatic changes have occurred in the past and the same could happen in future. As a result, it has, thereby, caused great environmental upheavals such as the break up of the Antarctic ice sheets, deglaciation and rise in sea levels, causing ecological havoc. If this continues for a longer period at the global level then it is necessary to take certain measures to check and adopt to the radical environmental changes.

India is one such country which is affected by these challenges. For instance, deglaciation can reduce the water in the sub continental rivers, particularly which flow into Pakistan. Since Pakistan's economy is an agrarian one, the reduction of water level in rivers in Pakistan could lead to social and political disputes over water between India and Pakistan. Similarly, the rise of coastal water will reduce the land mass of Bangladesh and will increase the influx of refugees in North-East states of India. It is difficult to contain this and would lead to conflict of interests with Bangladesh.

As global warming grows, receding glaciers in the north of the Indian Peninsula implies reduction in the water flowing in the river that feed the subcontinent. A geological Survey of India Report has shown that the Uttaranchal glaciers of Gangotri, Pindari and Milam have retreated at an alarming rate of 24.6, 23.4 and 12.5 meters every year, while the Bara Shigri glacier in Himachal Pradesh is retreating by 31.2 meters annually. [19]

Land Degradation: The cause of land degradation is due to loss of intrinsic qualities, decline in its capabilities or loss in its productive capacity. Land degradation may be due to natural causes or human causes or it may be due to combination of both. Land degradation is a global phenomenon which is related to agricultural productivity. The major causes include land clearance such as deforestation; agricultural depletion of soil nutrients through poor farming practices; livestock including overgrazing; inappropriate irrigation; urban sprawl and commercial development; land pollution including industrial waste; vehicle off roading; and quarrying of stone, sand ore and minerals. This has been well shown in Table 4.

Table 4 : State-wise Information on Degraded Land in the Districts

Upto March 2013 (hectare)

Sl. No.	*State/UT*	*District*	*Total Area*	*Total Degraded Land Area*	*% Degraded Land Area*
1	Andhra Pradesh	1 Chittor	1492644	127725	8.56
		2 Kurnool	1761393	309412	17.57
		3 Nellore	1307600	169808	12.99
2	Bihar	1 Banka	278768	29294	10.51
		2 Bhagalpur	255822	32589	12.74
		3 Gaya	473659	7727	1.63
		4 Munger	634594	144617	22.79
		5 Siwan	221900	22611	10.10
3	Goa	North Goa	175592	24634	14.03
		South Goa	194608	19639	10.09
4	Gujarat	1 Bharuch	776430	192841	24.84
		2 Bhavnagar	1115500	271337	24.32
		3 Surat	776161	85469	11.01
5	Himachal Pradesh	1 Chamba	671500	74238	11.06
		2 Kullu	566604	259127	45.73
6	Jharkhand	1 East Singhbhum	337155	27783	8.24
		2 Palamau	802291	50363	6.28
		3 Sarailela - Kharsawan	272340	37050	13.60
		4 West Singhbhoom	529021	58539	11.07
7	Karnataka	1 Bagalkot	658877	135145	20.51
		2 Bijapur	1053471	256010	24.30
		3 Chickmagalur	722072	16038	2.22
		4 Gulbarga	1610208	313347	19.46
		5 Tumkur	1055090	68808	5.57
8	Kerala	1 Palghat	448000	16204	3.62
9	Madhya Pradesh	1 Balaghat	924500	112941	12.22
		2 Chattarpur	863120	191511	22.19
		3 Gwalior	458449	144079	31.57
		4 Jhabua	646912	322601	49.87
		5 Morena	1168336	373553	31.97
		6 Ratlam	486007	160244	32.97
		7 Sidhi	1039194	226736	22.01
		8 Ujjain	609874	129700	21.27
10	Maharashtra	1 Bhandara	934716	49933	5.34
		2 Nasik	1527764	647462	42.38
		3 Wardha	630900	69308	10.99

Sl. No.	State/UT	District	Total Area	Total Degraded Land Area	% Degraded Land Area
11	Manipur	1 East Impal	57800	10238	17.71
		2 West Impal	51900	15098	29.09
12	Meghalaya	1 East Garohills	260300	34201	13.14
		2 Jaintia Hills	381900	178666	46.78
		3 South Garohills	185700	8003	4.31
		4 West Garohills	370700	42516	11.47
13	Mizoram	1 Aizawl	357631	109184	30.53
		2 Champhai	318583	184795	58.01
		3 Kolasib	138251	16865	12.20
		4 Lawngtlai	199119	95965	48.19
		5 Lunglei	453800	59913	13.20
		6 Mamit	302575	50986	16.85
		7 Saiha	196581	29416	14.96
		8 Serchhip	142160	70702	49.73
14	Nagaland	1 Kohima, Phek, Wokha, Zunheboto, Tuensang, Mokokchung, Mon	1657900	441339	26.62
15	Rajasthan	1 Ajmer	842388	398913	47.36
		2 Jhunjhunu	591681	81478	13.77
		3 Nagaur	1764504	361120	20.47
		4 Rajsamand	455093	136908	30.08
16	Sikkim	East	95400	5922	6.21
		West	116600	17274	14.81
		North	422600	94963	22.47
		South	75000	5323	7.10
17	Tamilnadu	1 Coimbatore	746128	19566	2.62
		2 Dhamapuri	962247	194532	20.22
		3 Erode	825997	5579	0.63
		4 Thirunelveli	682309	36240	5.31
		5 Tuticorin	459054	78213	17.04
18	Tripura	1 West	303300	21385	7.05
		2 South	314000	33396	10.64
		3 North	210070	60732	28.91
		4 Dhalai	221230	47323	21.39
19	Uttar Pradesh	1 Agra	400369	92650	23.14
		2 Bijnor	454057	37732	8.31
		3 Lalitpur	504149	95450	18.93
		4 Mahura	376432	22975	6.10
		5 Sitapur	570633	88717	15.55
20	West Bengal	1 North 24 Pargana	378090	64062	16.94
		2 Puruliya	625100	198619	31.77
		3 South 24 Paragana	96617	263635	27.29
	Grand Total		45916573	8980987	19.56

Soil is the non-renewable natural resource which supports life on earth. It is estimated that one-sixth of the world's soils have already been degraded by water and wind erosion. In India, about 130 million hectares of land (45 percent of total geographical area) is affected by serious soil erosion through ravine and gully, shifting cultivation, cultivated wastelands, sandy areas, deserts and water logging.[20]

Deforestation and Loss in Biodiversity: Industrialization, agricultural expansion and large dependence on forest products for meeting the energy needs have resulted in large scale deforestation in India. In order to increase agricultural production, farmers have encroached forests and other environmentally fragile areas. Before 1980's India deployed a bureaucrat method to estimate forest coverage. A land was notified as covered under Indian Forest Act, and then official's deemed this land area as recorded forest even if it was devoid of vegetation. According to Indian official data, the amount of recorded forest was 71.8 million hectares. The participation of people in the protection and management of forests have been emphasized in the National Forest Policy, 1988. Pursuant to this policy, Government of India through its resolution dated Ist June 1990 formalized the Joint Forest Management (JFM) Programme. The JFM is being practiced through constitution of forest protection committees.[21] This has been shown in the table given below.

Table 5: Diversion of Forest Land for Non-Forest Use Since the Enforcement of Forest Conversion Act, 1980

Sl. No.	*Year*	*Forest Area Diverted*	*Cumulative Area Diverted*
1	1981	1331.70	1331.70
2	1982	3674.32	5006.02
3	1983	5100.51	10106.53
4	1984	9348.90	19455.43
5	1985	7676.83	27132.26
6	1986	9310.45	36442.71
7	1987	25925.97	62368.39
8	1988	4868.71	67237.39
9	1989	66768.09	134005.48
10	1990	127361.79	261367.27
11	1991	5065.35	266432.62
12	1992	21756.77	288189.39
13	1993	16182.51	304371.90
14	1994	59962.02	364333.92
15	1995	51428.98	415762.90
16	1996	32863.55	448625.45
17	1997	24738.43	473363.88
18	1998	18425.21	491789.09
19	1999	45784.41	537573.50
20	2000	22386.43	559959.93
21	2001	267897.61	827857.54
22	2002	51172.31	879029.85
23	2003	42729.68	921759.53
24	2004	33079.50	954839.03

Source: Forests & Wildlife Statistics, India, 2004, MOEF.

Deforestation has also resulted in the loss in biodiversity in both in the terrestrial and coastal ecosystems. Biodiversity losses have also resulted from trade in forest products, introduction of non-native species, improper use of agro-chemicals and uncontrolled tourism. Loss in the coastal habitats includes a substantial loss in mangrove forests, largely as a result of shrimp ponds and paddy cultivation, with adverse impact on commercial fisheries that rely on the mangroves as nurseries for fish breeding.[22]

India with is varied climatic zones and tropical climates are blessed with rich resources and wealth of biodiversity like the Himalayas, the Western Ghats and the rainforest of the North East. A unique feature of biodiversity is that the developing countries or the so-called poor South is rich in biodiversity while the North or the developed countries are poor in the resource. From 1975 to 2000, 250 new species of flowering plants were discovered in Kerala. During the same period, none could be discovered in Europe. But the developed or the North are advanced in technologies.[23]

Though Prevention of biodiversity is important for mankind but more important is that human being depend on food, energy and raw materials for survival. Clean air and clean water make life possible that drive economies and societies. As such, a reduction or loss of biodiversity has not only undermine the natural environment but also the challenges related to preserving biodiversity have become an international issue.

Natural Disasters: Natural Disaster is deeply related to ecological factors. Rapid economic and population growth lead to the concentration of more and more people, capital and infrastructure in disaster prone areas. It is generally agreed that poverty, disaster, vulnerability and environmental degradation are closely intertwined. As coastal flooding due to global warming increase, the disasters are likely to disturb the living conditions of the people. Similarly melting of Himalayan glaciers may lead to sudden floods downstream and thereby create more and more havoc. Natural drainage congestion and construction in Indo-Gangetic over a period of time also make the area vulnerable disasters. This calls for a fresh and deeper rethink on the stages of disaster, namely, prevention, preparation, mitigation and recovery.

Many of the natural disaster occurring in India are related to the climate of the country. They cause massive losses of India life and property. Droughts, flash floods, cyclones, avalanches, landslides, brought on by torrential rains, and snowstorms pose the greatest threats, other damages include frequent summer dust storms, which usually track from north to South; they cause extensive property damage in North India and deposit large amounts of dust from arid regions Hail is also common in parts of India, causing serve damage to standing crops such as rice and wheat.

Ozone Depletion

Today, the reality is that rapid Ozone depletion is taking place in various parts of the earth. Indian Scientists are closely monitoring the Ozone layer and its effects: Opinions are many and varied. According to S.K. Srivastava, Head of the National Ozone Center in New Delhi, there is no trend to show total ozone depletion over India. V. Thaphyal and S.M. Kulshresta of the Indian Meteorological Department also point out that from the period 1956 to 1986 "ozone measurements exhibits year to year variability, but do not show any increasing or decreasing trend over India" However, former director of the National Ozone Centre, K. Chatterje, now with development alternatives, warns that there is no case for complacency. He asserts that his calculations exhibit an ozone depletion trend in upper layers of the stratosphere over New Delhi and Pune from 1980 to 1983 in the month of October when the Antarctic ozone hole is at its maximum. Since India already receives high doses of ultraviolet radiation, effects of ozone layer depletion could be have more disastrous impact on India. Total column ozone data has been recorded over India for a long time. A network of stations using Dobson Spectro photometers to measure total ozone, some six times a day, covers Srinagar, New Delhi, Varanasi, Ahmedabad, Pune and Kodaikanal. Ozone profiles are also regularly recorded using balloons.[24]

Hence, this grave threat to human security is often overlooked in India. Already too many lives have been lost in floods, industrial tragedies and natural calamities, which have been caused by gross ecological neglect. The author has touched some of the major issues in this survey of environmental challenges to our security. Many more have been identified and are literally permeating the air we breathe and the water we drink every day. To fight, against ecological threats then it should start at the individual level. Every human being can be a soldier in this struggle for survival. The time is ripe that we take note of the dangers surroundings us through our negligence over the grave issue that has made the life more vulnerable.

Conclusion

Environmental security is an important and rapidly growing subject for national security policy makers. Its growth is due to mainly humankind's sixth sense with regard to danger. Even in animals there is a change in behavior prior to an earthquake. Similarly, social, physical and natural scientists now have enough proof of the link of a mismanaged ecology with human poverty, suffering and violent conflicts. Political scientists are in the process of studying this new cause of conflict which in all likelihood is going to be more volatile due to resource scarcity.

Environmental degradation and resource depletion are long-term and results in a slow death. Many of the natural disasters occurring in India are related to the change in climate. They cause massive losses of life and property. Droughts, flash floods, cyclones, avalanches, landslides, brought on by torrential rains, and snowstorms cause extensive property damage in entire India and deposit large amounts of dust from arid regions. Hail is also common in parts of India, causing severe damage to standing crops such as rice and wheat.

For the protection and conservation of natural ecosystems, and to provide clean air for breathing, pure water for drinking, uncontaminated food for consumption, suitable drugs for medical care habitat with proper sanitation facilities, the following remedial measures may be recommended;

- Immediate legislation and implementation of acts for air and water pollution control.
- There is a need for stringent laws. Such acts like Factories Act (1976), Drug Control Act (1955), Food Adulteration Act (1976) and Insecticide Act require further modification with the introduction of several new chemicals in industry. Any violation of the set standards should be met with heavy penalty and rigorous imprisonment.
- Today environment protection has become such a grave problem that it should be included in the concurrent list of a constitution.
- Collaborative programme and researches should be initiated for the control of air and water pollution with the other industrialized countries, and from time to time appraisal may be made of the measure adopted by them.
- In order to foster awareness and understanding of the impact of ecological interdependent environment education should be made compulsory in the curricula of schools and colleges. The students should be imparted with the knowledge of preserving and improving the quality of the environment.
- Similarly, scientific societies, associations and academics, including the national committees should come out with concrete solutions in order to create a temper of science and generate awareness of environmental problems in the rural and urban sectors.
- Planting of trees properly suited to the climate is to be adopted as a routine measure through Forest Department and Educational Institutions. Deforestation should be legally prohibited.
- Reclamation of land to its original state should be left to the industries which are involved in mining in the area. Tough legislation and severe punishment for violation are necessary.
- Incentives are to be provided at the state level for such voluntary movements comparable to "Chipko" movement for the protection of plants.

- A large number of Biosphere Reserves containing endangered, rare or commercially important species should be established as early as possible on the basis of the Directory of flora and fauna. Adequate legislative measures are necessary for management of such reserves and such reserves are to be converted into national heritage.
- Cleaning of chocked lakes and rivers should be undertaken for all states.
- A suitable agency is necessary for the protection of our marine resource against pollution hazard. The Department of Environment may have a special cell for that purpose.
- At all levels of planning, including urban and rural, the involvement of ecologists are essential. Ecology is to be treated not as a luxury or option but a necessity for the very existence of life.

With the adoption of these measures severe enforcement of laws undeterred by any consideration, political or otherwise, one can then, look forward with great hope of keeping the environment safe from the evils of pollution. A polluted environment is not suitable for creative ideas, innovative skills or brilliant scientific discoveries. Not only the aesthetic value of society is hampered but efforts made in this direction will strengthen the national will of the nation.

REFERENCES

1. A.K. Sharma, 'Impact of the Development of Science and Technology on Environment', in Everyman's Science, Vol. XLVIII No.2, June 13-July13, published by the Indian Science Congress Association, Kolkata, p.89.
2. G. D. Foster, "Environment Security: The Search for Strategic Legitimacy", Armed Forces and Society, Spring 2001, p. 381.
3. N. Gaan, 'Environmental Security, Concept and Dimensions', Kalpaz Publications, Delhi, 2004, p.32.
4. V.P. Sati, 'An Introduction to Environment', Rawat Publications, New Delhi, 2012, p.3.
5. See n. 2, p.376.
6. See n. 2, p.381.
7. J. Barnett, 'The Meaning of Environmental Security,' Ecological Politics and Policy in the New Security Era,' Zed Books, London and New York, 2001, pp.7-8.
8. C.M. Jariwala, Changing Dimensions of Indian Environmental Law," in P. Leelakrishna, ed, Law and Environment, 1992, p.2.
9. M. Sharifuddin, 'Human Rights to Environment in India; Mittal Publications, New Delhi, 2011, p.41).
10. Environmental Issues in India-Wikipedia, the Free Encyclopedia, p.2.
11. See Article 48A of the Constitution of India.
12. See Article 51g of the Constitution of India.
13. Colonel P.K. Gautam (retd.), 'Environmental Security, Internal and External Dimensions and Response', Knowledge World, New Delhi; 2003, p.29.
14. "The Little Green Data Book "(http:// web. Worldbank.org/WEBSITE/EXTERNAL/ TOPICS/EXTSDNET and Environmental Assessment, Country Data: India (http//data. Wordbank.org/country/India, The World Bank, 2011.
15. Gazette of India, Vol. 111, 1973.

16. Environmental Statistics, Govt. of India, p. 7.1.
17. E. Goffman, India and path to Environmental Sustainability in Discovering Guides, Proquest, Released February 2008, p.4.
18. See n. 15, p.7.3.
19. S. Jain "Bad News; Ice is Breaking," *Indian Express*, 28 April 2002, p.11.
20. Environmental Statistics, Govt. of India, p. 5.4.
21. Energy Statistics, Govt. of India, p.3.7.3.
22. G. Vashudeva 'Environmental Security: A South Asian Perspective, Tata Energy and Research Institute, Arlington, p.11.
23. www. Biodiv.org/doc/publication/guide; Down to Earth, 15 January 2002.
24. A Review, *International Journal of Environmental Science and Development*, Vol. 2, No. 1, February 2011, p.31.

19

Natural Disasters in India

Jaspal Singh

Introduction

The concise Oxford Dictionary defines disaster as "sudden or great misfortune; calamity or complete failure". To take a simple example, the sudden loss of four family members in a road accident, would probably be described by that family as a disaster, but professionals involved in a counter disaster activities would probably describe this as an 'accident', 'incident', 'occurrence', or 'emergency'. Therefore, a 'disaster'[1] occurs when there is a serious disruption to community life arising with little or no warning; which threatens to or causes injury in that community and/or damage to property, which is beyond the day-to-day capacity of the prescribed government or statutory authorities and which requires the special mobilization and organisation of resources, other than those readily (normally) available to these authorities.

When a country faces such kind of disaster then the following measures become important.

Disaster Management: The claim, deliberate, judicious and controlled mechanisms instituted by a government to avert, if possible and if not isolate and prevent further escalation and thereafter adopt measures to restore normalcy in available time frame.[2]

Disaster Preparedness: It may be described as action designed to minimize loss of life and damage, and to organize and facilitate timely and effective rescue, relief and rehabilitating in cases of disaster. Preparedness, is supported by the necessary legislation and means a readiness to cope with disaster situations.[3]

Disaster Prevention: It may be described as measures designed to prevent natural phenomenon from causing or resulting in disaster or other related emergency situations. Prevention concerns the formulation and implementation of long-range policies and programs to prevent or eliminate the occurrence of disasters.[4]

Types of Disasters: The term 'disaster' evokes extraordinary response from outside their community or affected area. The disaster agent is a catalyst, which has a potential to create or produce disasters. For example earthquakes, cyclone, floods are disaster agents. Disaster is basically about vulnerability, susceptibility of a potential victim to the life threatening impact of disaster agent. For example, a drought or an earthquake in uninhabited land will not necessarily cause a disaster. It is only when an agent exposes the vulnerability of people that the disaster agent can lead to a disaster. This portion deals with general feature of some of the common disaster situations, which frequently occur in India. A wide variety of forces can cause disasters. These forces may be either natural or artificial or combination of both.

Manmade Disaster: Within this category of disasters, there are a variety of conditions resulting in disaster:

(i) **Civil Disturbances:** Riots e.g. 1984 Riots, Bombay and Ayodhya Riots of 1992 and the more recent Gujarat Riots and Muzzafarnagar Riots.
(ii) **Warfare:** Conventional, NBC Warfare, LICO (Low intensity conflict operation) and Terrorism.
(iii) **Refugees:** Forced movements of large numbers of people, usually across frontiers example: refugees of Rwanda, Zaire and Congo.
(iv) **Accident**: Collapse of buildings, mine disasters, chemical disasters, rail accident and Bhopal Gas Tragedy of 1984 in India.

Natural Disaster: Within this category of disasters, a variety of forces that may result in disaster:

Meteorological Disasters. These could be cyclones, tsunamis, hurricanes, cold wave, heat wave and droughts (possibly causing famines) **Topological Disasters are in the form of** Earthquakes, avalanches, landslides, and floods. **Biological Disaster could be** Epidemics of communicable diseases; example: Surat Plague, Mad Cow Disease in Europe and Bird Flu in SE Asia. The division between natural and man-made is to some extent an over simplification, as many disasters are actually caused by more than one or combination of various forces. Some disasters set a chain reaction of disasters. For example; a flood, which may eventually result in an epidemic of cholera. It is difficult to predict precisely where and when a man-made disaster will occur, therefore, it is difficult to prepare for one. It is possible however, with varying degrees of accuracy to predict the occurrences of a natural disaster.

India's Physical Geography

India's physical geography and climate, pattern of rainfall make it prone to a range of natural disasters such as floods, storm, cyclones, earthquakes and cloud bursts. Damage due to natural disasters has been given in detail in subsequent parts of the paper. Being densely populated and industrialized it is liable to experience a variety of manmade disasters. These could include industrial accidents such as Bhopal Gas Tragedy, major fire, transportation accidents such as Railway Accidents in 1995, or even hostile acts either in peace or war.

India has a highly diversified range of natural features. Its unique geo-climate conditions make the country among the most vulnerable to natural disasters in the world. Disasters occur with amazing frequency in India and while the society at large has adapted itself to these regular occurrences, the economic and social costs continue to mount year after year. It is highly vulnerable to floods, drought, cyclones, earthquakes, landslides, violence, etc. Almost all parts of India experience one or more of these events.[5]

Many regions in India are highly vulnerable to natural and other disasters on account of geological conditions. About 60 percent of the total area of the country is vulnerable to seismic damage of buildings in varying degrees. The most vulnerable areas, according to the present a seismic zone map of India, are located in the Himalayan and sub-Himalayan regions. Kutch and the Andaman and Nicobar Islands, which are particularly earthquake hazard prone. In India out 40 million hectares 8 percent is prone to floods, and the averaged area affected by floods annually is about 8 million hectares. Of the nearly 7,500 kilometers long coastline, approximately 5,700 kilometers is prone to cyclones, and 68 percent areas is susceptible to drought.[2] Disasters are no longer limited to natural catastrophes. Man-made emergencies also cause disasters in terms of fatalities and economic losses.

With urbanization and concentration of population in metropolitan cities, more and more people are becoming vulnerable to vocational disasters.[6] For instance, a quarter of India population lives within 50 km of the coastal line. The population within 1 km of the coast is 1.6 million, and 3.4 million within 2 km of the coast. These people are vulnerable to river flooding and coastal surges following cyclone or tsunami.[7]

The percentage of the population below the official poverty line was 28 percent in 2004-2005. The absolute number of poor people was 302 million in 2004-2005. Corruption is wide speared and the literacy rate has steadily gone up to 64.8 percent in 2001. The number of illiterate persons sill exceeds 304 million making India the country with the highest number of illiterate persons in the world.[8] Some parts of India still do not have electricity and telephone connectivity. All of these factors-from illiteracy and poverty to infrastructure inadequacy and aparthy, indicate that India is highly vulnerable to disasters.

Despite everyone's concern for disaster and technological developments in the world, the response to disasters has been knee jerk; uncoordinated at international, national and state levels. The problem is more acute in developing countries rather than in developed ones. The United Nations and its specialized agencies have always had an interest in and commitment to disaster relief. Therefore, there are now disaster relief, preparedness, prevention and mitigation programmes being carried out by various United Nations Organisations. However, most of the brunt and co-ordination for disaster relief is carried out by the national and state governments. It is in this area at India needs improvement in its approach and handling of disasters like situations.

The History of Disasters in India

With the Bengal famine. Orissa Super Cyclone, Latur earthquakes, Bhopal chemical disaster, Andhra cyclone, Gujarat earthquakes, recurring floods, Mumbai 2008 bomb blasts and many other disasters there is no foyer in the world with space large enough to exhibit the collective pain on the face of India has ranked at the top or near top in almost all type of disasters with number of deaths and people affected. India does not appear in the world tally of damages in financial terms due to disasters because of poverty and lack of infrastructure. Indian history is dappled with so many disasters that it is difficult to cover in a section of the chapter in a book. Therefore, only a sample of disasters is given in this chapter. Some type of disasters and some of the disasters need to be excluded due to space limitations. The data in this chapter are sourced from Universite catholique de Louvain, Brussels EM-DRT International Disaster Database (2009).[9]

Historically India has suffered from droughts and famine. The world's top 2nd to 5th droughts, according to number of people killed, occurred in India. And, the world's top 1st to 5th and 8th drought, according to number of people affected, also occurred in India.[10]

Earthquake Hazards in India

Earthquakes continue to be one of the nature's most devastating furies known to mankind since time memorial. India has a very long history of earthquake occurrences. About 56 percent of the total area is vulnerable to seismic damage of building in varying degrees. The most vulnerable areas according to the present seismic zone map of India are located in Himalayan and sub-Himalayan regions, Kutch and the Andaman and Nicobar Islands. Depending on varying degrees of seismicity, the entire country can be divided into the following seismic regions:

Kashmir and Western Himalayan: The region covers the states of the Jammu and Kashmir, Himachal Pradesh and sub-mountainous areas of Punjab.

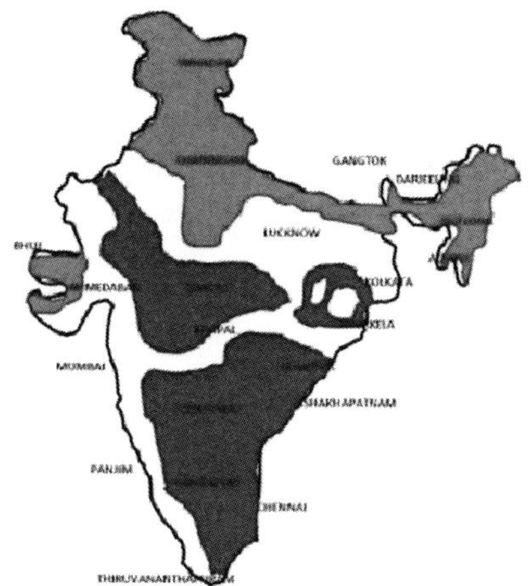

Central Himalayas: This region includes the mountainous and sub-mountainous regions of Uttar Pradesh.

Northeast India: This region comprises the whole of Indian Territory to the east of North Bengal.

Indo-Gangetic Basin and Rajasthan: This region comprise of Rajasthan plains of Punjab, Haryana, Uttar Pradesh and West Bengal.

Cambay of Rann of Kutch

Peninsular India including the Islands of Lakhsadweep.

The Andaman and Nicobar Islands.

Earthquakes: Some of the earthquakes in India were[11]:

- There was a earthquakes in 1618 in Mumbai in which 2,000 people lost lives.
- The loss of lives is estimated to be 300,000 in the Bengal earthquake of 1737 (that time Bangladesh was part of Bengal).
- The January 16, 1819 Kutch earthquake was of 8.0 on the Richer scale (XI intensity on Modified Mercalli scale) razed to the ground chief towns of Tera, Kathara and Mothala.
- An area of 250,000 square miles was affected by January 10, 1869 earthquake of 7.5 Richer scale in Assam.
- In the neighbouring Sillong there was wide spread destruction when 8.7 Richer scale and XII modified Mercalli scale earthquake struck on June 12, 1897.
- Kanga, in Himachal Pradesh had an 8.0 on Richer scale earthquake on April 4, 1905, killing 20,000 people.
- In Bihar, India (near the Nepal border) there was 8.3 Richer scale and XI Modified Mercalli intensity earthquakes in 1934 in which 6,000 people were killed.
- In the following year, at Quetta (now part of Pakistan), there was an earthquake of 7.5 and IX Modified Mercalli intensity, killing 25,000 people.
- In the year 1941, in the Andaman Islands there was 8.1 on the Richer scale (X on Modified Mercalli scale) earthquake causing very heavy damage. It is contemplated that survivors passed on the earthquake survival knowledge by oral tradition, which saved many local inhabitants in the 2004 Indian Ocean Tsunami.

- Assam faced yet another huge earthquake of 8.6 Richer/XII Modified Mercalli scale in 1950 (earlier earthquake in Assam were in 1869, neighbouring Shillong in 1897, and 1918) killing 1,500 people.
- On August 21, 1988, Assam, once again, had an earthquake. This time it was 7.2 on Riche scale (IX Modified Mercalli scale intensity) killing people. Twenty million people were affected from this earthquake, which is the 2nd largest number of people affected by any earthquake.
- Anjur in Gujarat had a 7.0 Richer or XII Modified Mercalli intensity earthquake in 1956 killing hundreds of people. Anjur is very near to the epicenter of 2001 Gujarat earthquake.
- The Latur, Marthawada region of the Maharashtra state, had a 6.4 on the Richer Scale (or VIII Modified Mercalli intensity) earthquake struck on September 30, 1993 affecting primarily Latur and Osmanabad districts of Maharashtra. Approximately 7, 928 people died and another 30,000 were injured. A reconstruction projects was launched with the help of the World Bank and the victims were given structurally safe constructed houses.
- The 2001 Gujarat earthquake struck India at about 08:14 AM when India was celebrating its republic day on January 26, 2001. It was 7.6 to 8.1 Richer scale earthquake, which was felt widely in India and Pakistan. In the aftermath of the earthquake, about 25,000 people died in different parts of Gujarat, including Bhuj, Bachao, Anjur, Ahmadabad, and Surat. There were 6.3 million people affected, which is the third largest number of people affected by any earthquake in the world immediately after the earthquake there was a total failure of command and control system, but afterwards many innovative changes and institutional mechanism were initiated. One of the important innovations was the training of people and their involvement with labour along with professional mason in rebuilding their own houses.
- The December 26, 2004 earthquake of magnitude 9.3 on the Richer scale off the coast of Sumatra in the Indonesian archipelago generated tsunami that affected nearly 2,260 kilometers of the mainland coastline of Tamil Nadu, Kerala, Andhra Pradesh and Pondicherry, as well as the Andaman and Nicobar Islands, with tidal waves upto 10 meters high penetrating up to 3 kilometers inland. This tsunami took at least 10,749 lives, and resulted in 5,640 persons missing. It affected more than 2.79 million people across 1,089 villages. It is estimated that 11,827 hectares of crops are damaged and that about 300,000 fisher folk have lost their livelihoods.
- On October 8, 2005 there was an earthquake of 7.6 richer scale intensity near the Muzaffarabad city of Pakistan killing 79,000 people in Pakistan,

1,309 in Kashmir of India; and 4 in Afghanistan. The serves cold weather conditions increased the sufferings of the evacuees sheltered in tents.

Based on the available data and excepted maximum intensity of earthquake related seismo-tectonic features in different parts of the country, a seismic zone map of India was standardized. Earthquakes are hazards that strike without warning and cause widespread damage to various man-made structures and systems. These can neither be prevented nor predicted in terms of their magnitude, place and time of occurrence. Therefore, the most effective measures of risk reduction are pre-disaster mitigation, preparedness and preventive measures for reducing the vulnerability of the built environment and expeditious effective rescue and relief actions immediately after the occurrence of the earthquake. The measures can also be divided into long-term, medium-term and short term. The long-term measures require five to fifteen years, the medium-term one to five years and the short-term to be taken up immediately in high-risk areas.

Floods: The country receives an annual precipitation of 400 million-hectares meters of the annual rainfall. 75 percent is received during four months of monsoon (June-September) and as a result, almost all the rivers carry heavy discharge during this period. The flood hazard is compounded by the problem of sediment deposition, drainage congestion and synchronization of river floods with sea tides in the coastal plains. The area vulnerable to floods is 4 million-hectares and the average area affected by floods annually is about 8 million hectares. The average annual total damage to crops, houses, and the public utilities during the period 1953-1995 was about Rs 9720 millions.[12]

Floods: Floods recur every year during the monsoon season in India. On an average every year, 1,588 lives are lost, 7.5 million hectares of land is affected, and the damage caused to crops, houses and public utilities is 18 billion Indian Rupees (Rs.) due to the floods. Between 1953 to 2005 a total of 84,207 lives were lost due to the floods in India, with maximum of 11,316 in 1977, and a minimum of 37 in 1953. The only other year that had less than 100 deaths was 1965. The data regarding each year's floods damage, with totals, averages, and maximum losses from 1953 to 2005 in terms of human live lost, cattle lost, population affected, monetary value of damage to public

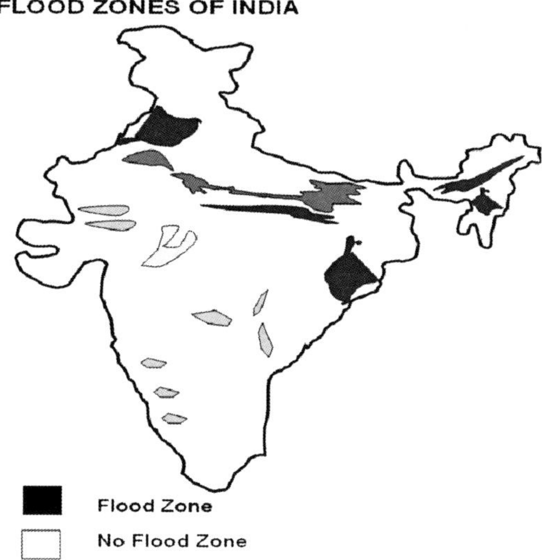

utilities, and total monetary damage loss, area affected, crops damaged, and houses damaged could be seen in National Disaster Management Guidelines:

- Management of Floods[13] On average, 32 million people are affected due to flooding. The maximum people affected were in 70 million in 1978. The total damage due to the floods during the 1953 to 2005 period of half a century was Rs 977 billion, a staggering figure for a poor country. The maximum damage was Rs 88 billion in 2000, and the average damage during 1953 to 2005 was Rs 18 billion. Heavy flood damages have occurred during the monsoon years of 1955, 1971, 1973, 1978, 1980,1984,1988,1989,1998,2004,2005 and 2008.
- There were wide spread floods in Gujarat in the beginning of July 2005, taking away lives and disrupting many lives. This was followed by the eight heaviest ever recorded 24-hour rainfall figure of 994 mm (39.1 inches) which lashed the Mumbai metropolis on July 26, 2005, and intermittently continued for the next day. That day 644 mm (25.4 inches) rain was received within the 12 hour period between 8 am and 8 pm. Apart from Mumbai, many parts of Maharashtra state open their car doors to escape and dies. Due to disruption of the transport system people could not reach their homes in the night. A least 1,000 people were feared to have passed away.
- In 2008 there were floods in many parts of India. There was diversion of water by Nepal near the India-Nepal border which lead to the flooding of the Koshi (is a Hindi word that literally meaning angry) river in Bihar. The severe floods made it difficult to reach the marooned people due to logistic difficulties. Many people remain trapped in flood waters for days. Approximately 1,500 people died due to Koshi river flooding.

Flood Disaster Management: The various measures adopted for flood mitigation may be categorized into two groups (a) as structural and (b) non-structural

The general approach has been aimed at preventing floodwaters from reaching the potential damage centers, as a result of which a large number of embankments came up along the various flood prone rivers. The main thrust of the flood protection programme undertaken in the country so far in the form of structural measures may be grouped into the following:

- Dams and reservoirs.
- Embankments, floodwalls and sea walls.
- Natural detention basin.
- Channel improvement.
- Drainage improvement.
- Diversion of flood waters.

The non-structural measure, on the other hand, aim at modifying the various susceptibility to flood damage as well as modifying the loss burden. The various non-structural measures being implemented in the country are:

- Modifying the susceptibility to flood damage through:
- Flood plain management.
- Flood proofing including disaster preparedness, and response planning.
- Flood forecasting and warning.
- Modifying the flood loss burden through.
- Disaster relief.
- Flood fighting including public health measures.

Tropical Cyclone: While cyclones in India generally strike the east coast, some of the Arabian Sea Cyclones strike the west coast of India as well, mainly the Gujarat and North Maharashtra. Out of the storm that develop in the Bay of Bengal, over 58 percent approach or cross the east coast in October and November. Only 25 percent of the storms that develop over the Arabian Sea approach west coast. In the pre-monsoon seasons, corresponding figures are 25 percent over the Arabian Sea and 30 percent over the Bay of Bengal. India has a very long coastline of 8041 km, large parts of which are vulnerable to cyclones.

Cyclones[14]: India also has history of suffering from cyclones. The imp ones are as follows:

- The 1935 tropical cyclone killed 30,000 people.
- In 1942, tropical storm in Orissa and West Bengal killed 40,000 people.
- In 1943, Rajputana tropical storm, killed 5,000 people.
- In eastern coast of Orissa, 1971 tropical storm killed 9,658.
- In 1977 cyclone, in Tamil Nadu, Andhra Pradesh and Kerala 14,204 people were killed.
- The biggest cyclone disaster is the Orissa super cyclone. It hit the Orissa coast of India on October 29, 1999 accompanied with 155 mph (250 km/h) cyclone winds and water surge from the sea. It caused the deaths of over 10,000 people, and heavy to extreme damage in its path of destruction.

Possible Risk Reduction Measures: The evaluation of risk for a tropical cyclone is relatively straight forward process. A hazard map should be prepared for any given area. Specific preventive measures will include an integrated warning/ response system, public warning system, training and community participation. The post disaster assistance could include evacuation, emergency shelter, search and rescue, medical assistance, provision of food and water, water purification, epidemiological surveillance, reopening of roads, reestablishment of disaster assessment and provision of seeds for re-planting.

Drought: The Indian subcontinent experiences an average rainfall of around 1200 mm and as such its water resources are enormous and are well comparable to any other country of its size and magnitude. However, the problem lies in its distribution across the country, ranging from over 10,000 mm at Cherrapunji and 8500 mm in parts of Western Rajasthan and Gujarat at the other. Looking at the picture as a whole, the distribution of the area sown for the country as a whole under various ranges of rainfall is as under:

- 33 Percent-Low Rainfall Region—750mm
- 35 Percent—Medium Rainfall Region—751-1125mm
- 24 percent—High Rainfall Region—125-2000mm
- 8 percent—Very High Rainfall Region—more than 2000m.

Drought[15]**:** The main droughts were:

- Drought of 1900, killing 1.25 million people.
- Drought of 1942, killing 1.5 million people.
- Drought of 1943, in Easter part of Bengal (now part of Bangladesh) killing 1.9 million people.
- Drought of 1965, killing 1.5 million and affecting 100 million people.
- Drought of 1972, affecting 200 million people.
- Drought of June 1982, affecting 100 million people.
- Drought of May 1987, affecting 300 million people.
- Drought of April 2000, affecting 50 million people.
- Drought of July 2002, affecting 310 million people.

Drought Management: The success of drought management depends on one's ability first to predict and then to control. The strategy for this management is basically three-fold:

(a) close monitoring of emerging drought scenario as to as develop an advance warning system;
(b) relief measures required for providing immediate occur to the affected population and the up keep of cattle wealth, and if possible to integrate with long-term objectives;
(c) hammering out an alternative crop strategy for maximum possible retrieval of the Kharif crop and a better ensuing Rabi crop;

Three other aspects that call for urgent attention in a drought situation are employment generation, drinking water supply and fodder availability. Public health measures also assume importance in an event of drought like situation. The nutritional requirement of all the children, expectant mothers and nursing mothers should be taken care of. Care has to be taken to disinfect drinking water sources to prevent the spread of water born diseases and plans need to drawn to cope with likely epidemics. There is a need for constant surveillance of public health measures including immunization. The upkeep of the cattle also assumes importance in such a situation.

Landslides: In the hilly terrain of India including the Himalayas, landslides have been a major natural disaster. The two regions most vulnerable to the landslides are the Himalayan and the Western Ghats. The Himalayas mountain belt comprise of tectonically unstable younger geological formations subjected to severe seismic activity. The Western Ghats and Nilgiris are geologically stable but have uplifted plateau margins influenced by neotectonic activity. Thus, the two regions have different geological setting leading to characteristic types of landslides. Compared to the Western Ghats region, the slides in the Himalayan region are huge and massive and in most cases the overburden along with the underlying lithely is displaced during sliding, particularly due to seismic factor. In contrast, landslide events in the Western Ghats are confined to the overburden without affecting the bedrock beneath and are generally in the nature of debris flow occurring mainly during monsoons. The effect, of course, is felt much more astutely because of comparatively high density of population.[16]

- Landslide zone mapping is a modern method to identify the landslide prone areas and has been in use in India since 1980s. Broadly the country has been divided into the following regions in terms of incidents and severity of landslides—

Region		*Incidences of landslides*
Himalayas	-	High to Very High
North-Eastern Hills	-	High
Western Ghats and Nilgiris		Moderate to High
Eastern Ghats	-	Low
Vindhayanchal	-	Low.

Mitigatory Measures: In general the chief mitigatory measures to be adopted for such areas are: drainage correction; proper land use measures; reforestation of the area; occupied by degraded vegetation; creation of awareness among local population; and policy for settlement in such areas to be spelt out;

- **Avalanches:** On mountain roads in heavy snow regions, there is always a danger of snow avalanches, because of site conditions and topographic conditions. It not only affects roads and corrective actions are required to cope with such disruptions. The Himalayas are well known for the occurrence of snow avalanches particularly Western Himalayas that is the snowy regions of Jammu and Kashmir, Himachal Pradesh and West Uttar Pradesh. There are three types of snow avalanches zones. They are:

Red Zone: The most dangerous zone, where snow avalanches are most frequent and have impact pressures of more than three tones per square meters.

Blue Zone: Where the avalanche force is less than three tones per square meter and where living and other activities may be permitted with connection of safe designs but such areas may have to be vacated on warning.

Yellow Zone: Where snow avalanches occur only occasionally.

Avalanches Control Measure: Avalanche control measures can roughly be classified into hardware and software types. Hardware measures are for the purpose of preventing of avalanches or for blocking of deflecting avalanches with protective structures. Software measures provided safety by eliminating the probability of avalanches by removing snow deposits on slope with blasting and by predicting the occurrences of avalanches and recommending evacuation from hazardous areas.

Avalanches Control Structure: There are two type of the avalanche control structures; they are preventive and protective structures. The preventive structures are provided to prevent the occurrence of avalanches such as avalanches prevention forests, stepped terraces, avalanche control piles, avalanche control fence, suspended fence etc. Whereas protection structure are structures that are installed in the avalanches path or in snow deposit area to change the flow direction of avalanches (deflecting structures), to attenuate their energy (regarding structures), to block their flow or to allow their passage (protective structure) these could be protective fences, retaining walls, deflecting structures, snow shades, retarding structures. Other avalanches control measures are predition and forecasting and disposal of avalanche potential snow packs.

Uttarakhand Disaster: The Tragedy

Disaster stuck on the night of June 15, 2013. Rudraprayag (Kedar Valley), Chamoli, Uttarkashi, Pithoragarh and Bageshwar were the worst-hit districts. 10,000 number of people estimated death according to the National Disaster Management Authority (NDMA). There were 4,521 number of deaths and 1,497 people missing as per government records. An estimated 9,200 livestock were lost in the flash floods. 9,000 km is the total length of roads damaged. 85 motorable bridges and 140 small bridges, which provide pedestrian connectivity were damaged and 140 small bridges, which provide pedestrian connectivity, were damaged.

As Uttarakhand marks the first anniversary of the devastating floods, thousands of survivors continue to struggle to pick up the pieces, hoping the government will eventually come good on its promise to provide jobs and new homes. The authorities say the road to recovery is long and painful but that they are making steady progress in putting the state back on its feet, including reopening the route for this year's Char Dham pilgrimage that is so vital for the local tourism industry. For the floods victims, two issues appear paramount housing and livelihood. While the governments' focus has been on quickly rebuilding roads and bridges, many say the authorities have been slow in helping people, rebuilding, their homes and finding jobs. After the disaster, the government announce an immediate compensations of 2 lakh to every affected family. It also promised to pay Rs. 3,000 a month for a period of two years towards payment of rent for each of 3,320 families which had lost their houses. Most victims say government disbursement of the rent amount has been at best erratic. And the condition attached to the compensation for building houses means that hundreds of people who lost their lands to the floods don't qualify. Also, land sharks seeking to exploit the situation have driven real estate prices up. In Chamoli, one of the five worst affected districts, dozens of people continue to live in makeshift camps in absence of any financial help from the government. As business and job dried up, thousands of people have left for the cities, traveling as far as Delhi and Mumbai to find work. The government is banking on grants and loans to get the state back on track, spending most of the money on rebuilding infra structure. Flood survivors says building roads and bridges was fine but the government needs to look at creating employment opportunities of them. There is still a long way to go to recover from the natural catastrophe which hit the state almost a year ago.[17]

Conclusion

India's relief and natural terrain features, combined with under developed infrastructure in certain regions, make it one of the most disaster prone countries. We may have learnt lesson from the recent disasters but the administration may still not be fully prepared for similar disaster in the future. All government, NGOs and other local organization need to be synchronized to provide suitable relief in acceptable time frame.

The magic mantra for the effective Disaster Management plan would be Prevention, Preparedness, Response and Recovery. In the case of Uttrakhand disaster, while the response was graduated with the time and the rescue teams worked tirelessly to move people to safer places, the "Recovery" phase have not been up to the mark. The government is yet to complete the rehabilitation of the affected population. People have lost fortunes and have been compensated with very merge amount. The tourism industry has suffered major losses and the clientele has been very thin in this year. The Centre and State government have to evolve an effective 'Disaster Management' plan learning from the experimental and knee jerk response to the disaster in Uttrakhand. The disaster planning Workshops and preparedness exercises should be regular feature of the administrative activities of civil bodies like municipal committees, block and panchayats, thereby involving the mass in this initiative.

REFERENCES

1. Australian Counter Disaster Handbook. p.1.
2. H. Prasad, Crisis Management Trishul. magazine.
3. B.J. Brown Disaster Preparedness and United Nations.p3.
4. Ibid.
5. K. Gupta, Disaster Management and India: Responding Internally and Simultaneously in Neighbouring Countries,2011, p. 3
6. Planning Commission Report, vol. 2008, p. 207.
7. Planning Commission Report, vol. 2008, p. 208.
8. Planning Commission Report, vol. 2008, p. 209.
9. Brussels EM–DRT International Disaster, 2009.
10. *The Hindu*, Coping with Natural Calamities, 25 May, 2001.
11. K. Gupta, Disaster Management and India: Responding internally and Simultaneously in Neghbouring Countries, 2011, p.6.
12. B.L. Bose, Statement-Ordeal by Floods, 30 Sep., 1989.
13. National Disaster Management Authority Report, 2008, pp 89-90.
14. K. Gupta, Disaster Management and India: Responding internally and Simultaneously in Neghbouring Countries, 2011, p.11.
15. K. Gupta, Disaster Management and India: Responding internally and Simultaneously in Neghbouring Countries, 2011, p.6.
16. Asian Survey, Feb. 2002.
17. A Trivedi, 'It's a long Road to Recovery', *Hindustan Times*, 16 January, 2014.

20

Population Growth and Population Policy of India, Pakistan and Bangladesh

Amar Singh

The debate on the growth of population among states is not a recent phenomenon but it has a long history. Of course, it may have divergent views, especially when it is related to the size and growth of human population. On the one hand, large population has sometimes been considered to be desirable as a source of the nation's strength and wealth and as an essential useful factor underlying technological development. But, on the other hand, over population has led to poverty and such catastrophes as famines and epidemics. The size and the growth of population is, therefore, an important element of national security.

The world has seen unprecedented change. In the growth of population, the most obvious and best-known example is the number game. The world population reached the 7 billion in 2011 and the same time resource limits and environment degradation are becoming more apparent every day. Resource scarcities especially food, water and energy, are likely to limit future economic growth and development.

South Asia has the highest population growth rate in the world. By 2050, even if fertility rates decline, the population of the region is projected to more than double. Food production depends on croplands and water supply and these are under strain as human populations increase. This often involves destruction of vital forest resources or overexploitation of arable land. Population growth appears today as the major factor determining food security. An effort has been made to examine the trend of population increase and to discuss the various constraints adopted to control the population growth in India, Pakistan and Bangladesh, so it does not have much negative impact on these countries.

Trends in Population Growth of India

India is at the turning point in its population development. India, being the second populated country after China (with 1.43 billion inhabitants in 2011), it is a home of 16 percent of the world population, although it occupies only 2.4 percent the earth surface.[1] From the first census (1871) the population of India has risen from 203 million to 683 million in 1981 and 845 million in 1991. The population of the country as per the figures of Census 2011 is 1210.19 million of which 623.7 million (51.54%) are males and 586.46 million (48.46%) are females.[2]

Table 1

Year	*Population (crore)*	*Decadal Growth rate (%)*	*Average annual exponential growth rate (%)*	*Progressive Growth Rate over 1901(%)*
1911	252,100,000	+.75	0.56	5.75
1921	252,321,213	-0.31	-0.03	5.42
1931	278,977,238	11.00	1.04	17.02
1941	318,660,580	14.22	1.33	33.67
1951	361,088,090	13.31	1.25	51.47
1961	439,235,771	21.6	1.96	84.25
1971	548,160,652	24.8	2.20	129.94
1981	683,329,097	24.8	2.22	186.64
1991	846,387,888	23.9	2.14	255.03
2001	1,028,737,436	21.5	1.93	330.80
2011	1,210,193,422	17.6	1.64	407.64

Source: Census of India, Govt. of India—Ministry of Home Affairs, 2012.

According to a report of UN, India will become the most populous country in the world by 2028, surpassing China. At 1.2 billion in 2011, India's population will touch 1.4 billion in 2025; 1.6 billion by 2050 before it starts declining by the year 2100, at which point India will have 1.5 billion people.[3]

The demographic transition model of the pre independence period can be regarded as the first stage of transition. This phase was characterized by the British imperial health service which showed a strong fluctuating course. It indicated an altogether medium-sized population increases. High birth rates were counterbalanced by high death rates, along with periodic famines, outbreaks of lethal diseases such as cholera and smallpox, and endemic parasitic diseases such as malaria. But epidemics and famines receded in the first half of the 20th century. The high values of both of these demographic indicators were perfectly in line with those of the Third World especially in the case of the death rate. The reasons of high death rate were famines, diseases and epidemics with heavy toll of lives. The two census periods 1891/1901 and 1911/1921 even had the effect of bringing about a population decrease amounting to no less than 41 million. The devastating influenza epidemic of 1918 cost 18.5 million lives. The British imperial governments improved public health services, controlled infectious tropical diseases and provided better access to medicine and medical care.[4]

The year 1921 is often referred to as the "Year of the Great Divide" because it marked the shift from a pattern of relatively static population size to one of steady and often rapid increase. As the mid-20th century approached, growth began to accelerate as the more serious threats to public health waned. Death rates fell but birth rates remained high. This marked the second phase of demographic transition. India's population growth rate was at peaked between the 1971 and 1981 censuses, but growth in absolute numbers has not yet peaked. The country added 16 million people annually in the 1980s and 18 million annually in the 1990s. This rapid population growth led to the sudden increase in the population which became known as the "population explosion" on account of its very magnitude. India's population growth slowed as the birth rate gradually declined beginning in the late 1960s. Since the early 1970s, the birth rate has fallen from just under 40 births per 1,000 populations to 20.97 births/1,000 population according to 2011 census. This decline reflected the concerted effort of the Government support for policies and programmes to slow the population.

India at present is at stage three of four stage model of demographic transition from stable population with high mortality and fertility to stable population with low mortality and fertility, with some of the states/UTs already into stage four. 2001-2011 is the first decade (with the exception of 1911-1921) which has actually added lesser population compared to the previous decade. The percentage decade growth during 2001-2011 has registered the sharpest decline since independence—a decrease of 3.90 percentage points from 21.54 (2001) to 17.64 percent (2011).[5]

Demographic Indicators (India): Fertility Trends

Since 1950, fertility in India has decreased by about half, from just under six children per woman to about three. The total fertility rate (TFR),[6] or average total number of children has declined from 5.9(1950) to 2.5 during (2010).[7] During the 1960s, especially the late 1960s, some fall in fertility was evident. Fairly reliable direct estimates of fertility from the Sample Registration System (SRS) are available since the 1970s allowing a detailed assessment of trends. The decade of 1970s saw perceptible fall in fertility, the child birth rate (CBR) fell below 40 and the TFR below 5. Fertility stagnated in the early 80s, but the decline resumed soon with the TFR falling below 4 points by the end of the decade.

Table 2: TFR of India (1950–2010)

Period	*Births per year*	*Deaths per year*	*Natural change per year*	*CBR*	*CDR*	*NC*	*TFR*	*IMR*
1950–55	16,832,000	9,928,000	6,904,000	43.3	25.5	17.7	5.9	165
1990–95	27,566,000	9,400,000	18,166,000	30	10.2	19.8	3.72	76.4
1995–00	27,443,000	9,458,000	17,985,000	27.2	9.4	17.8	3.31	68.9
2000–05	27,158,000	9,545,000	17,614,000	24.8	8.7	16.1	2.96	60.7
2005–10	27,271,000	9,757,000	17,514,000	23.1	8.3	14.8	2.73	52.9

Note: CDR (chide death rate), NC (Natural change), IMR (infant mortality rate)
Source: GOI (2011), "National Health Profile 2010"/ "National Health Profile 2011".

Further it declined from 5.2 to 4.5 during 1971 to 1981 and from 3.6 to 2.4 during 1991 to 2011. The TFR in rural areas has declined from 5.4 to 2.7, from 1971 to 2011 whereas the corresponding decline in urban areas has been from 4.1 to 1.9 during the same period. In 2011, around 67 per cent of the deliveries were institutional which includes government as well as private hospitals. The percentage of institutional deliveries in urban areas is 87.9 as against about 60.7 percent recorded in rural areas.[8] Contribution to fertility decline came from both a rise in age at marriage and fall in marital fertility. But the latter has made a greater impact on fertility than the former. The chart presents the level of TFR by residence for India and some of its bigger States as follows:[9]

Table 3: TFR of Bigger States and India, 2010

Year	*Total*	*Rural*	*Urban*
India	2.5	2.8	1.9
Andhra Pradesh	1.8	1.9	1.6
Assam	2.5	2.7	1.6
Bihar	3.7	3.8	2.7
Chhattisgarh	2.8	3	1.9
Delhi	1.9	2.1	1.9
Gujarat	2.5	2.7	2.1
Haryana	2.3	2.5	2
Himachal Pradesh	1.8	1.9	1.3
Jammu & Kashmir	2	2.2	1.4
Jharkhand	3	3.2	2.1
Karnataka	2	2.1	1.7
Kerala	1.8	1.8	1.8
Madhya Pradesh	3.2	3.5	2.2
Maharashtra	1.9	2	1.7
Odisha	2.3	2.4	1.6
Punjab	1.8	1.8	1.7
Rajasthan	3.1	3.3	2.4
Tamil Nadu	1.7	1.8	1.6
Uttar Pradesh	3.5	3.7	2.7
West Bengal	1.8	2	1.3

Source: GOI (2013), Chapter No. 2: Population, the Ministry of Statistics and Programme Implementation.

Although there are still considerable differences in state-level TFRs, the rate has declined by just over 2 children per woman in most of the states. In percentage terms, however, the declines were greatest in Kerala.[10] As a population transitions from high to low fertility, fertility often declines rapidly to a moderately low rate, then the pace of decline slows as the TFR approaches the replacement level of two children per woman. But the pattern of decline can vary significantly within countries, as illustrated by the trends in the birth rate from low-fertility states to high-fertility states in the above table.[11]

Contraceptive Use

The family planning programme was introduced in India in 1951 when free contraception was provided but acceptance was uncommon. The programme was strengthened in the 1960s, with the introduction of the extension approach, sterilization camps, incentives for contraceptive acceptance, and enhanced availability of contraceptive services through a large network of health centres. Yet, in 1970, only about 10 percent of couples of reproductive age used any contraception. The programme intensified during 1976, coinciding with the national emergency, and the acceptance increased. This raised contraceptive prevalence to over 20 percent. However, the backlash due to the emergency period excesses in family planning caused stagnation in contraceptive prevalence for some time. But after the mid-1980s, the upward trend in contraceptive prevalence resumed. According to the three rounds of the National Family Health Survey (NFHS-1, NFHS-2 and NFHS-3) the prevalence of modern contraception rose from 37 percent in 1992-93, to 43 in 1998-99, and 49 in 2005-06. According to UNICEF prevalence of contraceptive has increased to 54.85 in 2008-11.[12] The use of contraceptive has been dominated by sterilization.

Population Policy

Human development and improvement in quality of life are the ultimate objectives of all planning and policies. India justifiably claims to be the first country to adopt an official policy to slow population growth and was the first to initiate a government policy of promoting a family planning programme in 1952.[13] In the 1950s, the country saw accelerated population growth created by declining death rates and high birth rates—a situation shared by many developing countries in that period. Death rates had fallen as these countries gained better public sanitation, widespread immunization of children, and expanded medical care. But birth rates remained high, pushing population growth to unprecedented heights. Initial efforts to implement a family planning program were rather limited, with a budget of US$1.35 million.[14] The program began by setting up family planning clinics with the expectation that people would seek out the clinics on their own.[15] The objective of checking birth rates through family planning was hampered both by old traditions that favoured larger families and by the enormous challenge of bringing services to a large rural population.

The effective date of the adoption and implementation of a clear family planning programme is often put at 1966, when the 'extension approach' to the promotion of family planning throughout the country replaced the earlier clinic-oriented approach. Around the same time, a 'time-bound' target of reducing the crude birth rate from about 39 to 25 per 1000 population in 10 to 12 years was adopted. In practice, it has been a moving target and was not achieved even by 1999. Home visits by family planning workers were expanded in the 1960s to reach even more people. The population program gained status when a separate Department of Family Planning was set up in the Ministry of Health in 1966. Government's concern about the country's population growth was heightened in the 1970s when successive censuses had shown that the rate was rising, despite the policies and investments in family planning. It was one of the most controversial period for the family planning programme because for political reason. The National Emergency was declared by Prime Minister Indira Gandhi in 1975. Financial support from the central government and the political backing of Mrs. Gandhi's popular son Sanjay, many states adopted coercive measures along with quota systems that resulted in the forcible sterilization camps. In the 1976–1977 program years, 8.3 million sterilizations and primarily vasectomies were performed. The negative publicity generated by the emergency compromised the reputation of the government family planning program, and family planning services were suspended. By the 1977–1978 program year, the number of sterilizations had plummeted to 0.9 million.[16]

The involuntary sterilization was, to a great extent, responsible for the defeat of Mrs. Gandhi's party in the next elections. Successive governments—including Mrs. Gandhi herself, who returned to power in 1980 and served until her assassination in 1984—have been careful to emphasize the voluntary nature of the program.[17] The International Conference on Population and Development (ICPD), was held in Cairo in 1994. It was a major turning point in the history of population policies. At the ICPD, the consensus was developed among the countries for the advancement and protection of women's human rights. It was necessary that the efforts may be made to address population and development issues. The resultant ICPD Programme of Action focused unprecedented attention on gender equality, equity, and women's empowerment. The document also affirmed that coercive practices in the provision of family planning services constitute a violation of reproductive rights and should be eliminated. Today, most population policies continue to implicate women's reproductive health and rights, The major paradigm shifts from the earlier target oriented to a target-free approach (TFA) was adopted in 1996 and then to a client centered and demand driven Community Needs Assessment (CNA) approach, which was later renamed as Reproductive and Child Health (RCH) approach in 1997. This was initiated to translate the promises made at Cairo into policy and programme actions in India.[18]

The National Health Policy was then designed in 1983. It stressed the need for 'securing the small family norm, through voluntary efforts and moving towards the goal of population stabilization'. While adopting the Health Policy, Parliament emphasized the need for a separate National Population Policy. This came into reality in 2000 as a national population policy 2000. The NPP 2000 has distinguished between immediate, medium-term and long-term policy objectives. It was soon realised by the government that to address the unmet needs for contraception, health care infrastructure, and health personnel, and to provide integrated service delivery for basic reproductive and child health care.[19] The medium-term objective was to bring the TFR to replacement levels by 2010, through vigorous implementation of inter-sectoral operational strategies. The long term objective is to achieve a stable population by 2045, at a level consistent with the requirements of sustainable economic growth, social development, and environmental protection.

Given the diverse nature of Indian population, it was more often recommended that region-specific solutions need to be put forward towards the achievement of these national goals. There is need to prioritize alternate aspects of the RCH and the socio-economic development programme to suit the local needs and requirements. The prioritization of alternate strategic elements in the RCH programme would influence cost-effective policy and in turn would lead to the achievement of our country's socio-economic and demographic goals.

PAKISTAN

The size of Pakistan's population, which was 33 million at the time of partition and independence in 1947, has increased fivefold. Since then it has reached 180 million in 2011.[20] High population growth is compounded by continued, although declining, high levels of fertility. Pakistan is the sixth most populous country and, according to United Nations estimates, is one of two countries with a population in excess of 100 million and with total fertility exceeding four births per woman.[21] According to the PDHS 2006–07 survey, the TFR of the lowest wealth quintile was 5.8 births, while that of the richest was 3.0: a difference of 2.8 births. Women in the youngest reproductive age group of 15–19 had a fertility rate of 51 births per 1,000 women, illustrating that early marriage and childbearing persist. In fact, about 50 percent of girls marry before their 20th birthday.[22] The continued high population growth will amount to Pakistan's population to 220 million by the year 2020. Coupled with poor human development indicators such as low literacy, high infant mortality and low economic growth rates, such a large population will undermine efforts being undertaken to reduce poverty and to improve the standards of living of the populace.[23]

Pakistan is in the grip of population explosion of severe intensity, and has experienced a greater population growth compared to other developing countries. The population of Pakistan grew, on average, at a rate of 3 percent per year from 1951 until the middle of the 1980's decade. From the mid 1980's until the year 2000, the growth of the population slowed down to about 2.6 percent per year; and from 2000 to 2012, to about 2 percent per year.[24] This growth rate remains high compared to almost all neighbouring countries in South Asia. Moreover, government projections show some correction in the growth rate, which has slightly increased to 2.05 in 2010 from previous estimates of 2 percent per year. It is expected that Pakistan will attain fifth position in the world in terms of total population in 2050.[25]

Table 4: Population Growth of Pakistan

Census	*Population*
1951	33,816,000
1961	42,978,000
1972	65,321,000
1981	84,254,000
1991	112.61000
1995	124.49000
1997	130.56000
1999	136.41000
2000	146,404,914
2005	158 645.000
2008	172,800,000
2011	173 593,000

Source: "Social indicators of Pakistan 2007",[Online: web]Accessed 22 June 2009, URL: http:/ /www.statpak.gov.pk/depts/fbs/publications/social_indicators_of_pakistan2007/ sip2007.pdf

Fertility Trends in Pakistan

Pakistan's total fertility rate has declined in the past few decades. As per the UNICEF estimate, the total fertility rate was at 6.3 in 1990, this came down to 3.65 in 2011.[26] It is important to mention that family planning knowledge is high in Pakistan .96% of married women were aware of at least one contraceptive method in 2000-2001. However, with the highest fertility rate in South Asia, it is evident that women are not sufficiently using them. One reason for this is women perceive contraceptives as culturally or socially and religiously inappropriate.[27]

Past Record

The main factor contributing to rapid population growth in Pakistan in the recent past is high fertility, demographers have struggled to reach consensus on the exact levels over the last 50 years. Fertility in Pakistan has shown a widely acknowledged resistance to change. Because of sharp declines in mortality in the post-independence period, the population of Pakistan was growing at the rate of 2.7 percent per annum around 1960. In response to this, a program of family planning services was launched in the 1960s. However, it had hardly any impact on fertility, "The Population Growth Estimation (PGE) data established fertility levels of between 6 and 7 births per woman (1960s), the Pakistan Fertility Survey of 1975, placed fertility at 6.3 births per woman for the mid-1970s.[28] For the 1970s and 1980s, two major surveys were used to establish the trends in fertility: the Pakistan Demographic surveys (PDS) of 1984-1990 and the Pakistan Demographic and Health Survey (PDHS) of 1990-1991. There is considerable divergence in the fertility rates presented by these surveys. The surveys estimates for the late 1980s vary from 5.4 births per woman reported by the PDHS and 6.5 births per woman reported by the PDS in 1988. A more careful assessment of the PDHS (1990-1991) data, with scrutiny of its reproductive histories and adjustments for data errors, provides a fertility rate of 6.1 births per woman for the period 1986-1991".[29] The Pakistan Integrated Household Survey 1991 also estimated a TFR of more than six births per woman for the five years preceding the survey, thereby supporting the argument that the TFR reported by the PDHS report was a significant underestimation of actual fertility levels. Demographers agree that fertility levels in Pakistan began to decline by late 1980s or early 1990s, remaining above six births per woman between the 1960s and 1980s.[30] Finally at the turn of the century, there is definite evidence of fertility decline in Pakistan. Significantly, all estimates for the 1990s for the first time fall below 6.0 births per woman to a little less than 5. Furthermore the latest census held finally in 1998, indicates that the average population growth rate for the period 1981-98 was 2.6 percent per annum.[31]

Fertility Decline: Period I (1990-1999)

The Pakistan Fertility and Family Planning Survey (PFFPS) of 1996-1997 provided an estimate of 5.4 births per woman for the period 1992-1996. The Pakistan Reproductive Health and Family Planning Survey of 2000-2001 estimated a fertility rate of 4.8 births per woman for 1997-2000. Collective estimates imply a considerable decline of around 1.5 births per woman between the late 1980s and 1990s. The speed and timing of the decline, however, was not similar for urban and rural areas. Urban areas experienced the fertility transition earlier and at a much faster speed. The TFR in urban areas declined by almost two births, from 5.6 births per woman at the end of the 1980s to 3.8

births per woman by 1997. On the other hand, rural fertility remained above 6 births per woman until the mid-1990s at which point it declined from 6.3 births per woman (PCPS 1994-1995) to 5.4 births per woman by the end of the decade.[32]

Table 5: TFR (Total fertility rate) of Pakistan (1950–2010)

Year	*Live births per year*	*Deaths per year*	*Natural change per year*	*CBR*	*CDR*	*TFR*	*IMR*
1990–1995	4,566,000	1,166,000	3,400,000	38.2	9.7	5.67	90.1
1995–2000	4,674,000	1,201,000	3,473,000	34.4	8.8	5	83.2
2000–2005	4,387,000	1,213,000	3,175,000	28.9	8	4	76.8
2005–2010	4,666,000	1,277,000	3,390,000	28.1	7.7	3.65	70.9

Source: Sathar 2001: 23.

Fertility Decline: Period II (2000-present)

Given the considerable decline in fertility experienced in the 1990s, the demographers were optimistic about the speed of the fertility decline in Pakistan. The Status of Women, Reproductive Health and Family Planning Survey (SWRHFPS) of 2003 shows a TFR of 4.4 births per woman, while the TFR from the Pakistan Demographic Survey (PDS) 2003 is 3.9 births per woman. The PDHS 2006-2007 shows TFR stagnating at 4.1 births per woman for the period 2004-2006.[33] Rural-urban fertility decline since the turn of the century continued to follow the trends experienced at the end of the 1990s. However, rural fertility continued to decline at a consistent pace, decreasing from 5.4 births per woman to 4.5 births per woman, while urban fertility decline slowed significantly, only falling 0.4 births per woman between the 1998-2000 and 2004-2006 time periods.[34]

According to UNICEF data, TFR in 2011 was 3.3. The TFR in rural areas (4.2 births) was considerably higher than the rate in urban areas (3.2 births). Thus, there has been some narrowing of the rural-urban differential in fertility. However, Pakistan has a long way to go to meet the Millennium Development Goals target of 2.1 births per woman. The differentials in TFR by regions are quite modest. The lowest TFR of 3.0 births per woman is estimated for ICT Islamabad while the highest is in Balochistan (4.2 births per woman). For both Punjab and Gilgit Baltistan, the estimated TFR is 3.8 births per woman. The TFR estimates for Sindh and KPK are also the same, which is almost the same as the TFR for Punjab and Giglit Baltistan.[35]

Contraceptive use rates had hardly risen in the period 1950-91 and a rise in the contraceptive prevalence rate from 5 percent in 1975 to 9 to 12 percent in 1991. It hardly supported any fertility control within marriage. However, the 1990's were a period of distinct departure from this trend with a sharp rise in contraceptive prevalence rates. As per, the Pakistan Fertility and Family Planning survey of 1996-97, contraceptive prevalence among currently married women rose from 12 to 24 percent. It is currently projected to be 30 percent (2011), rising at about 2 percent a year. Thus, while earlier any change in fertility was attributed to factors other than contraceptive use, it is now a major contributor to the lower levels of fertility seen in the 1990's. Overall, 35 percent of married women in Pakistan are currently using a contraceptive method which is a five percentage point increase from 2006-07. Currently, married women in urban areas are considerably more likely to use contraception (45 percent) than those in rural areas (31 percent). Contraceptive use among currently married women is highest in ICT Islamabad (59 percent), followed by the Punjab (41 percent), Gilgit Baltistan (34 percent), Sindh (30 percent), and Khyber Pakhtunkuwa (28 percent), and it is lowest in Balochistan (20 percent).[36]

Child Mortality in Pakistan

Information on infant and child mortality is useful in identifying segments of the population that are at high risk so that programmes can be designed to reduce it. Pakistan is undergoing its demographic transition as exhibited by the slowing down of its population growth rate due to declining mortality as far back as the 1950s followed by the decline in fertility in the early 1990s. The death rates declined sharply from about 27 per 1000 population in 1951 to about 11 per 1000 population then to 7.2 in 2005-06.

According to 2012-13 PDHS, the level of under-five mortality is 89 deaths per 1,000 live births during the five-year period before the survey. It implies that one in every 11 children born in Pakistan during the period died before reaching their fifth birthday. The infant mortality rate estimated in the survey is 74 deaths per 1,000 live births. Comparison of mortality rates recorded in 2012-13 PDHS with the 2006-07 PDHS shows a small change in mortality overtime, falling below the rate of decrease needed to achieve the MDG target of reducing the under-five mortality to 52 deaths per 1,000 live births and infant mortality to 40 deaths per 1,000 live births by 2015. The estimated infant mortality rate in the 2006-07 PDHS was 78 per 1,000 live births in contrast to 74 per 1,000 live births in the 2012-13 PDHS.[37] The lag between changes in mortality and fertility rates has delayed the process of demographic transition in Pakistan by nearly 2-3 decades compared with many other countries in the Asian region. In this situation, it is important to achieve a sustained decline in fertility to reach replacement level of 2.1 children as documented in Pakistan's population policy (2010-15) and this would ultimately reduce the dependency ratio considerably and create an opportunity to benefit from demographic dividend.

Prospects for the Future

Pakistan has clearly seen its peak in population growth rates and in fertility levels, but the path ahead seems unclear. Much of the population growth rate will be determined by the speed of the fertility decline and population momentum.[38] The following table shows projected population by different scenarios.

Table 6: Total Projected Population of Pakistan by Different Scenarios (Millions)

	United Nations World Population Prospects: The 2008 Revision	*Current rate*	*Planning Commission Pakistan (2005)*	*Planning Commission Pakistan (2010)*
2005-2010	175.2	166.1	160.9	168.2
2010-2015	195.1	185.5	175.0	182.6
2015-2020	215.9	206.0	189.1	200.9
2020-2025	236.3	226.8	202.2	218.9
2025-2030	256.0	246.7	214.3	234.9
2045-2050	327.7	314.0	254.0	–

Sources: Population Council 2009, "Pakistan's Demographic Transition in the Development Context", Planning Commission, Government of Pakistan. http://esa.un.org/unpp/index.asp?panel=1.

Role of Public Policy

Pakistan is one of the first few countries which made a pioneering effort in the field of family planning. This initiative was taken by an NGO named 'Family Planning Association of Pakistan in 1953.[39] The Government of Pakistan, in the 1st Five Year Plan, 1955-60, endorsed the need for family planning and allocated Rs.5 million for disbursement to voluntary organizations for contraceptive advice and services. Because of the limited reach of the NGOs to cover population on a large scale, family planning services were provided through the outlets of the health departments during the 2nd Five Year Plan (1960-65). In 1964, evaluation revealed that the services were not reaching the target population through the health outlets as these were overburdened with the existing health care needs of the people. Consequently, a full-fledged National Family Planning Programme was launched during the 3rd Five year Plan (1965-70) and the prominent features of the programme were: involvement of "DAIS" as motivators, providers of conventional contraceptives and referrals for clinical services (IUD). In the 4th Plan period (1970-78), dais were replaced by literate (Matriculate) teams of male and female motivators for each union council. In the 5th Year Plan(1978-83), the programme strategy was changed from the single purpose family planning approach to multisectoral and multi-dimensional approach that involved the relevant public sector organizations providing broad-based programme coverage.[40]

A major initiative taken during 6th plan period was the establishment of NGO Coordination Council, with representatives from NGOs of all the provinces. Population Welfare Programme received substantial political support during the 7th Plan period, (1988-93), when the status of the Population Welfare Division was raised to that of a Ministry and it received considerably enhanced allocation of funds. In the 8th Five Year Plan, 1993-98, a village-based family planning workers (VBFPW) cadre was created. The Ministry of Health in 1994 launched a national programme of primary health care and family planning administered by 40,000 Lady Health Workers. The number of workers increased to 96,000 by 2007 Population Council. The Lady Health Workers were found to be very effective in delivering family planning services in 2001. However, during the 9th Five Year Plan, 1998-2003, programme was developed on the positive elements of the strategies of the previous plans, ensuring continuity and consolidation of gains.[41]

Population Policy 2002

Being signatory to the Programme of Action of the International Conference on Population and Development (ICPD: 1994), Pakistan adopted the National Reproductive Health Service Package in 2001, thus promoting family planning within the broader framework of reproductive health. In accordance to this, the population policy 2002 made a shift in focus from merely reducing population growth rate through Family Planning to a greater emphasis on providing broad based reproductive health services. It envisaged achieving universal access for family planning and reproductive health services by 2010 and the replacement level fertility (2.1) by 2020.[42] Similarly, Population Perspective Plan (2002-12) targeted to achieve CPR at 57% by 2012. However, in the prevailing circumstances, with the existing CPR at 30% and TFR at 2.6 and with high unmet need contraceptives of 25%, it failed to achieve these targets. In fact, current trends in fertility if extrapolated, the replacement level appears hardly achievable by 2020 as envisioned in population policy 2002.[43]

Proposed Pakistan Population Policy 2010

The proposed Population Policy deals with family planning as a health initiative by making family planning services a vital component of the essential services package.[44] It has both short and long term objectives.

The short-term objectives of the Policy 2010 are to:

- make available family planning services to the remotest areas of the country by 2015;
- reduce the unmet need for family planning from the current 25 percent to 20 percent by 2015;

- reduce the TFR from the current 3.6 births to 3.2 births per woman by 2015;
- improve maternal health by encouraging pregnancy spacing of more than 36 months, reducing the incidence of first birth among those mothers aged below 18 and discouraging the trend of mothers giving birth after age 34 and above.

The long-term objectives are to:

- attain replacement level fertility by 2030;
- achieve universal access to family planning services by 2030;
- reduce the unmet need for family planning from the current 25 percent to 5 percent by 2030.

The Population Programmes has, for the last many years, focused on promoting small family norms through awareness and motivational campaigns. This strategy has to certain extent able to raise the level of awareness of population issue but it has not been able to bring about the desired change in attitude and behaviour. The service delivery of the Programme focused more on promoting sterilization and less on pregnancy spacing. The PDHS 2006-07 shows that a significant proportion of Pakistani women continue to conceive and give birth in serious health and life risk conditions, such as childbearing in teen ages; childbearing after age 34; short birth interval; and four or more births. The trend of contraceptive mix shows female sterilization and use of traditional methods as the major means of practice, but they have had a limited impact on the TFR.[45] Over the years, four important issues have emerged:

- Decline in the use of three major methods of contraception (oral pills, injectables and IUCDs);
- Persistent unmet need for contraception;
- Widening gap between current and ever use of contraception indicating dropouts;
- High incidence of abortion (including induced).

To tackle all these issues Government agencies could not make an efficient use of the vast physical infrastructure of nongovernmental organization (NGO), including national and provincial Rural Support Programmes (RSPs). "Personal contact is perhaps the most effective mechanism for conveying family planning information, but the media has also been a successful channel for reaching large numbers of people. Contact either with a programme worker or exposure to the family planning message through media have been found to be critical factors in increasing contraceptive use among a sample of Pakistani women who want no additional children".

BANGLADESH

Bangladesh is the third largest populous country in South Asia, after India and Pakistan.[46] The United Nations Population Fund (UNFPA) estimated Bangladesh population at 15.5 million in 2011. This estimate is quite contradictory to Bangladesh census announcement of March 2011 which state the population of Bangladesh at 142.319 million and is likely to grow up to 172 million by the year 2020 and stabilize at or below 210 million by the year 2060, even if replacement level fertility (i.e. NRR=1) is achieved by the year 2010. However, if it is delayed by another 10 years i.e. up to 2020, population will be stabilized 25 years later (i.e. 2085) at 250 million.[47] The population density has increased from 907.5 of 1991 to 1174.33 people per square kilometer in 2011.[48] The following table shows the urban and rural population levels in Bangladesh:

Table 7: Total Urban and Rural Population Levels and Trends in Bangladesh (1961-2011)

Year	*Total population (Million)*	*Growth Rate %*	*Urban Population (Million)*	*Rural Population (Million)*
1961	55.2	-	2.6	52.6
1971	76.4	2.5	6.0	70.4
1981	89.9	2.4	14.1	77.8
1991	111.45	2.17	22.45	89.0
2001	129.25	1.48	28.8	100.44
2011				

Source: BBS, Population Census, 1981, 1991 and 2001.

From the above table it is clear that the rural-to-urban migration has increased. About one-third of Bangladeshis live in urban areas.[49] At the current growth rate, it is projected that by 2040 the total population will increase to 230 million people where 52% will live in urban areas. This would place severe stress on the national resources and constrain the efforts to improve the living standards of the people. Population stabilization, therefore, becomes an urgent national priority. Realizing the importance of such a policy, government prepared a Population Policy Outline in 1976, in which high population growth rate was identified as the nation's "number one problem". Since then, the above policy emphasis has been reflected in all successive 5-year plans and programmes. Moreover, the success in reducing the population growth rate from 3 percent in mid 70s to 1.4 percent by the year 2000, the work on creating conducive environment and opportunities for improved quality of life for the masses still remains to be fully realized. Traditionally in the developing world, large families is like an insurance policy against illness and poverty in old age. Clearly, a shift has occurred in the attitude towards family planning, but it is not enough to head off the potentially catastrophic effects of a rapidly increasing population against a markedly slower food production rate.[50] Population growth continues to constrain efforts to uplift the standard of living of the people

Trends in Fertility

Fertility in Bangladesh has been declining since the 1970s. The TFR declined sharply from 6.3 in 1971-75 to 5.1 births per woman in 1987-1989. This was, followed by another sharp decline of 1.8 births per woman to reach 3.3 births per woman in 1995-97. The TFR declined further by one child per woman during the current decade to reach 2.3 births per woman. Moreover, one witness a steady encourage decline in each subsequent DHS (9 percent 1999-2000 to 2004; 10 percent between 2004 and 2007 and almost 15 percent between 2007 to 2011. Between 2007 and 2011 the decline in fertility was greater in urban areas (17 percent) compared to the rural areas (11 percent). As expected, the TFR for rural women is higher than that for urban women (2.5 compared with 2.0 births per woman). Four of the seven administrative divisions (including Rangpur) have reached replacement level fertility (2.2) or below. Bangladesh's current health sector program, the Health, Population and Nutrition Sector Development Program (HPNSDP) 2011-2016 aims to reduce fertility to 2 births per woman by 2016. Khulna (1.9 births per woman) has reached that level already and Rajshahi and Rangpur are very close (2.1 births per woman).

Estimates of fertility are of crucial importance for a country in order to have an idea about population growth rate. It is evident from the about facts that total fertility rate showing a decreasing pattern over the period from 1990-2011 which is obviously a good indicator for Bangladesh, the country which is suffering from huge population pressure.[51]

Family Planning

In 2011 overall, 61 percent of currently married women in Bangladesh are currently using a contraceptive method. The majority of women use a modern method (52 percent) and 9 percent use traditional methods. The pill is by far the most widely used method (27 percent), followed by injectables (11 percent), female sterilization (5 percent), and condoms (6 percent). About one percent of women mentioned the use of male sterilization, IUDs, and implants.

Longer term trend in use of various methods shows that between 1991 and 2011 use of female sterilization among currently married women declined from 9 to 5 percent. At the same time, two methods gained popularity; the pills are being used by 27 percent of women almost double from the level in 1991 (14 percent). Use of injectables has also increased from 3 percent in 1991 to 11 percent in 2011, almost a four times increase. Currently only 8 percent of married couples use a long-acting and permanent method (LAPM), namely sterilization, IUD and implants, accounting for 13 percent of all contraceptive use. Comparatively use of LAPM was much higher (12 percent) in 1991 and accounted for 30 percent of contraceptive use. Use of LAPM started to decline from the early 1990s, stabilized in 2007, and hints at a slight increase in 2011.

Under HPNSDP, Bangladesh aims to increase overall use of contraception to 72 percent by 2016. This means an increase in 11 percentage points in 5 years or an average of 2.2 percentage point increase per year for the next five years. It will pose a major challenge for the government to achieve the target.

Child Mortality

Child mortality rate in Bangladesh is decreasing over the year. But Bangladesh shows a tremendous success in this case as child mortality, whether infant or under-five, halved during the last two decades.[52] This is clear from the following table:

Table 8

	Year	*Infant mortality*	*Child mortality*
BDHS, 2011	2007-2011	43	11
BDHS, 2007	2002-2006	52	14
BDHS, 2004	1999-2003	65	24
BDHS, 1999-2000	1995-1999	66	30
BDHS, 1996-1997	1992-1996	82	37
BDHS, 1993-1994	1989-1993	87	50

Source: GOB, Bangladesh Demographic and Health Survey, 2011, 2011.

Childhood mortality rates obtained for the five years preceding DHS surveys conducted in Bangladesh since 1993-1994 confirm a declining trend in mortality. Between the 1989-1993 and 2007-2011 periods, infant mortality declined by half, from 87 deaths per 1,000 live births to 43 deaths per 1,000 live births. Even more impressive are the 71 percent decline in post neonatal mortality and the 60 percent decline in under-five mortality over the same period. The corresponding decline in neonatal mortality was 38 percent. Comparison of mortality rates over the last four years show that infant, child, and under-5 mortality declined by about 20 percent. As a consequence of this rapid rate of decline, Bangladesh is on track to achieve the MDG 4 target for under-5 mortality target of 48 per 1,000 live-births by the year 2015.[53]

Population Policy in Bangladesh

Population Policy in Bangladesh was first articulated after the war of independence, when the economic compulsion forced the government to check the growth of containing population growth. In fact the First Five Year Plan

(1973-78) declared that "no civilised measure would be too drastic to keep the population of Bangladesh on the smaller side of 15 crores for the sheer ecological viability of the nation."[54] Lowering the birth rate was seen as the goal of population policy and contraceptive service delivery through a national family planning programme was seen as the primary means of achieving that goal. The exclusive thrust of the programme was to increase the use of modern birth control methods by married women in their childbearing ages through a doorstep delivery service. There was also a motivational campaign to promote the two-child norm and legitimise the use of modern methods of contraception.[55]

When the Bangladesh population policy was first unveiled in 1973 demographers found the logic of the programme to be faulty and seriously questioned the likelihood of success in controlling population growth. [56] The very supply of service delivery and implementation of the programme depending on centralised bureaucracy and an army of workers was seen as a "Herculean" task. And the motivational efforts to generate demand were thought extremely unlikely to change fertility behaviour in a context where high fertility was the best response individual couples made in adjusting to their own environment.[57] In short, the basic premise for the extreme skepticism was that change in fertility behaviour was linked with the socio-economic conditions which generated the demand for large families. In other words, the belief that "Development was the best contraceptive". The response was astonishing as the fertility levels started to decline from 1975. Fertility preferences also indicated a trend towards smaller desired families. Today, the vast majority of currently married women want either to delay their births or limit childbearing completely. Unfortunately, however, there appears to be a plateauing of the fertility level and further increase in contraceptive prevalence has not been translated into expected reductions in the birth rate.

To understand the problem of rapid increase in the demand for birth control, demographers now present a different picture. The argument put forward was that the availability of family planning services in a fairly widespread manner from the mid 1970s, which led to the rapid uptake of modern birth control techniques and caused the subsequent fertility decline because of the existence of a large "latent demand" for birth control.[58]

In the mid-1970s the government instituted the deployment of full-time, local family welfare assistants, who served as community-based family planning motivators and distributors. During the same period, a social marketing program to promote the sale of birth control pills and condoms was initiated. The population program involves more than 200 nongovernmental organizations (NGOs).[59] Since 1980 the family planning program has emphasized the importance of integrating health and family planning services. The goal is to provide an essential integrated package of high quality, client centered reproductive and child health care, family planning, communicable disease control, and curative services at a one-stop service point. This only came after the ICPD in 1994 to better reflect the goals of ensuring health and expanding choice in family planning.

Since 1998 the health programme in Bangladesh has drawn on the Sector-Wide Approach (SWAp). The SWAp programme aims to provide a package of essential, quality health care services that respond to population needs, especially those of children, women, the elderly, and the poor. The first SWAp—the Health and Population Sector Program (HPSP) was formulated as part of the fifth Five-Year Plan (1998-2003). It was followed by the second SWAp, which began in 2003 and expired in June 2011.[60]

Major Objectives of Population Policy 2002

The national population policy aims at improving the overall standard of living of the people of Bangladesh through improved reproductive health status and reduction of population growth rate. Specific attention will be given to under-served areas and vulnerable population groups:[61]

- To attain Net Reproductive Rate (NRR) equal to one by the year 2010 in order to stabilize the population size by 2060. One of the means to achieve this objective is to provide people at all levels of the society quality reproductive health and family welfare services that are affordable and accessible to rural and urban poor;
- To address the causes of maternal mortality including unsafe abortion and reduce infant mortality rate by adequately providing quality antenatal delivery and post-natal services, emergency obstetrics care where necessary and safe delivery practices;
- To undertake, on an urgent basis, necessary steps to ensure that trained and skilled health and family welfare workers attend up to 50 per cent of birth by the year 2005, and up to 100 per cent by the year 2010.

Bangladesh demonstrated how effective family planning efforts can help slows population growth. After its split from Pakistan in 1971, Bangladesh adopted the same family planning programme as Pakistan, but population control has been a high priority for its government. The Ministry of Health and Family Planning was put in charge of the national family planning programme and adopted a multi sectoral approach that allocated responsibility to eight different ministries. NGOs played an important role in awareness-raising and marketing exercises by distributing condoms and oral birth control. Further, the program was heavily funded by international donors. Essentially, the government worked with NGOs and the private sector to consistently promote contraception. Bangladesh has managed to considerably reduce its fertility rate from 6.3 in 1975 to 2.3 in 2011.[62] The Bangladesh case study concludes that "door step delivery of family planning methods and the participation of poor rural women in income-generating projects have led to an increased level of contraceptive use as well as a decreased level of desire for additional children".[63]

Conclusion

Improvements in public health are the key to initiating the demographic transition and contribute to better quality of human capital in the future. Improved sanitation, immunization programs, and antibiotics lead to declines in mortality that lead in turn to declines in fertility. Furthermore, there are economic reasons to invest in health. Mounting research indicates that a healthy population can abet economic growth and reduce poverty. Governments must make the political and financial commitments which are needed to ensure voluntary family planning policies and programmes that are equally accessible for all people, including adolescents. Effective family planning can accelerate the demographic transition, potentially enhancing the economic benefits and lifting nations out of a cycle of poverty. What is more important is that the policies in education, the economy, and governance are crucial for attaining demographic dividend.

- **Education and Health:** Fertility decline will have immediate and direct impact on the school going population and will give an opportunity to invest more on their education and health contributing to better quality of human capital in the future. Transforming a youthful population into a productive work force requires investment in education at all levels.
- **Invest in Women and Girls:** Governments must make the political and financial commitments, in education, health, and labour, needed to promote gender equality and empower women and girls.
- **Economic Policy:** Governments should prioritize policies that create jobs and decent work opportunities for youth, particularly girls. Government policies that lead to stable macroeconomic conditions are associated with the growth of productive and rewarding jobs. Labour-market flexibility and openness to trade are also important, but the relevant policy reforms must be undertaken gradually and in a manner that protects those who loses out in such transitions.
- **Good governance:** Governments should prioritize reforms, tack necessary steps for strengthening the rule of law, improving the efficiency of government operations, reducing corruption and guaranteeing contract enforcement.

The effects of successful policies in all of these areas can be mutually reinforcing, helping to create a "virtuous cycle" of sustained growth. Policymakers have a time-limited opportunity to capitalize on reduced fertility and the maturing of young populations. Policymakers of these countries should therefore act soon to implement the policies required to accelerate the demographic transition and to realize its benefits.

REFERENCES

1. C. Haub and O.P. Sharma, "India's Population Reality: Reconciling Change and Tradition", *Population Bulletin*, 2006 Vol. 61:3-5.
2. Census of India, Govt. of India 2012: 1-5.
3. India to be most populous country by 2028: UN report(2013), *the Hindu*,15 June, http://www.thehindu.com/todays-paper/tp-national/india-to-be-most-populous-country-by-2028-un-report/article4816016.ece
4. O. Singh, and A.K. Singh, "Population Growth and Family Planning in India: An Analysis" in "Strategies in Development Planning", Edited by Singh, A. Kumar and Rai, V. Kumar and Mishra, Anand Prasad, Deep & Deep Publications, New Delhi, 2000, pp. 355-367.
5. GOI, "Family Welfare Statistics in India", The Ministry of Health and Family Welfare, New Delhi, 2011, p.15.
6. The cumulative value of the age specific fertility rates at the end of the childe bearing ages give a measure of fertility known as Total Fertility Rates.
7. Government of India, "Indian Economic Survey 2009-2010", Ministry of Finance, New Delhi, 2010, [Online: web] Accessed on 22 July 2010, URL: http://indiabudget.nic.in/es2009-10/echap-08.pdf.
8. Government of India, "Indian Economic Survey 2011-12", Ministry of Finance, New Delhi, 2012, [Online: web] Accessed 23 may 2012, URL: http://www.indiabudget.nic.in/survey.asp, pp.3-70.
9. Government of India, "Indian Economic Survey 2009-2010", Ministry of Finance, New Delhi, 2010, [Online: web] Accessed on 22 July 2010, URL: http://indiabudget.nic.in/es2009-10/echap-08.pdf.
10. Government of India, "Indian Economic Survey 2011-12", Ministry of Finance, New Delhi, 2012 [Online: web] Accessed 23 may 2012, URL: http://www.indiabudget.nic.in/survey.asp, pp.3-70.
11. Government of India, "Population Projections for India and States, 2001-2026", Office of the Registrar General and Census Commissioner, New Delhi, 2006, p.3.
12. UNFPA: State of World Population, "Choice, Not By Chance: Family Planning, Human Rights and Development", 2012 [Online: Web] Accessed 5 March 2013, URL: http: http://www.unfpa.org/public/home/publications/pid/12511, p.3.
13. L. Visaria, "Mortality Trends and the Health Transition" in Twenty-First Century India: Population, Economy, Human Development, and the Environment", Oxford University Press, New York, 2004, pp.32-56.
14. Ibid.
15. S. Sharma, "UNAIDS Count Not Correct, Says Government," *Hindustan Times*, New Delhi, 1 June 2006, p.7.
16. L. Visaria, "Mortality Trends and the Health Transition" in Twenty-First Century India: Population, Economy, Human Development, and the Environment", Oxford University Press, New York, 2004, p.36.
17. L.S. Ashford, "New Population Policies: Advancing Women's Health and Rights", *Population Bulletin*, 2001, 56:1.
18. Gulati, A., and Ganga Shreedhar "Agriculture, poverty and malnutrition: linkages and synergies" International Food Policy Research Institute, New Delhi, 2010.
19. O. Singh, and A.K. Singh, "Population Growth and Family Planning in India: An Analysis" in "Strategies in Development Planning", Edited by Singh, Alok Kumar and Rai, Vinay Kumar and Mishra, Anand Prasad, Deep & Deep Publications, New Delhi, 2000, pp. 355-367.
20. Z. Sathar, and B. Zaidi, "Fertility prospects in Pakistan", Population Council, Pakistan, United Nations, New York, 2011 [Online: web] Accessed 2 October 2012, URL: http://www.un.org/en/development/desa/population/publications/pdf/expert/2011-

7_Sathar&Zaidi_Expert-Paper_FINAL_ALL-Pages.pdf, p.10-14.

21. United Nation World Food Programme, "Pakistan: Operation, facts and figure", 2009, [Online: Web] Accessed 5 March 2013, URL: http: http://home.wfp.org/stellent/groups/public/documents/communications/wfp202887.pdf, p.12-123
22. Z. Sathar and B. Zaidi, "Fertility prospects in Pakistan", Population Council, Pakistan, United Nations, New York, 2011, [Online: web] Accessed 2 October 2012, URL: http://www.un.org/en/development/desa/population/publications/pdf/expert/2011-7_Sathar&Zaidi_Expert-Paper_FINAL_ALL-Pages.pdf, p.4.
23. Government of Pakistan, "Population Policy of Pakistan", 2003, [Online: web] Accessed 6 October 2008, URL: http://www.mopw.gov.pk/event3.html, pp.8-15.
24. Ibid, p.10.
25. Government of Pakistan, "Pakistan Economic Survey 2012-13", Islamabad, 2013 [Online: Web] Accessed 22 December 2013, URL: http://www.accountancy.com.pk/docs/economic-survey-pakistan-2012-13-02.pdf, p.45.
26. UNFPA: State of World Population, "Choice, Not By Chance: Family Planning, Human Rights and Development", 2012, [Online: Web] Accessed 5 March 2013, URL: http: http://www.unfpa.org/public/home/publications/pid/12511, p.3.
27. GOP, "Poverty Reduction Strategy Paper-II", 2008, [Online: web] Accessed 24 June 2009, URL: http://www.finance.gov.pk/admin/images/poverty/PRSP-II.pdf
28. Z. Sathar, and B. Zaidi, "Fertility prospects in Pakistan", Population Council, Pakistan, United Nations, New York, 2011, [Online: web] Accessed 2 October 2012, URL: http://www.un.org/en/development/desa/population/publications/pdf/expert/2011-7_Sathar&Zaidi_Expert-Paper_FINAL_ALL-Pages.pdf, p.17.
29. Ibid, 23.
30. G. Feeney, and I. Alam, "New Estimates and Projections of Population Growth in Pakistan", *Population and Development Review*, 2003, vol. 29, 3:486.
31. Z. Sathar, and B. Zaidi, "Fertility prospects in Pakistan", Population Council, Pakistan, United Nations, New York, 2011, [Online: web] Accessed 2 October 2012, URL: http://www.un.org/en/development/desa/population/publications/pdf/expert/2011-7_Sathar&Zaidi_Expert-Paper_FINAL_ALL-Pages.pdf, p.23.
32. R. Stephenson, and M. Hennink, "Barriers to Family Planning Service use Among The Urban Poor in Pakistan, Opportunities and Choices", working paper no. 2 February, 2004, p.11.
33. Z. Sathar, and B. Zaidi, "Fertility prospects in Pakistan", Population Council, Pakistan, United Nations, New York, 2011, [Online: web] Accessed 2 October 2012, URL: http://www.un.org/en/development/desa/population/publications/pdf/expert/2011-7_Sathar&Zaidi_Expert-Paper_FINAL_ALL-Pages.pdf, p.11.
34. Government of Pakistan, "Population Policy of Pakistan", 2003,[Online: web] Accessed 6 October 2008, URL: http://www.mopw.gov.pk/event3.html, p.13.
35. Government of Pakistan, NIPS Report, 2011. http://www.nips.org.pk/abstract_files/Priliminary%20Report%20Final.pdf
36. Ibid, p.51.
37. Ibid, p.53.
38. Population Council, "Pakistan's Demographic Transition in the Development Context", Planning Commission, Government of Pakistan, 2009, http://esa.un.org/unpp/index.asp?panel=1;
39. Government of Pakistan, "Economic Survey 2006-07", Ministry of Finance, 2007, [Online: web] Accessed 2 November 2008, URL: http://www.accountancy.com.pk/.../economic-survey-of-pakistan-2006-07.pdf
40. Government Of Pakistan, "Pakistan Economic Survey 2007-08", Islamabad, 2009, [Online: Web] Accessed 22 December 2009, URL: http://www.accountancy.com.pk/docs/economic-survey-pakistan-2007-08-02.pdf, p.16-56.

41. R. Stephenson, and M. Hennink, "Barriers to Family Planning Service use Among The Urban Poor in Pakistan, Opportunities and Choices", 2004, working paper no. 2 February, p.21
42. Government of Pakistan, "Economic Survey 2006-07", Ministry of Finance, 2007 [Online: web] Accessed 2 November 2008, URL: http://www.accountancy.com.pk/.../economic-survey-of-pakistan-2006-07.pdf
43. Government of Pakistan, Population council, 2010, p.41.
44. Ibid.
45. Ibid., p.29
46. N.K. Kulkarni, "Population Control and Urban Family Planning in Bangladesh", *Searchlight South Asia*, 2011, http://urbanpoverty.intellecap.com/?p=229
47. Government of Bangladesh, "Bangladesh Agriculture Report," 2010, Dhaka [Online: web] Accessed 2 April 2012,URL www.mof.gov.bd/en/budget/11.../Chapter-7%20_Eng-2012_.pdf, p.34-39.
48. World Bank, "World Development Report 20010/2011: Attacking Poverty", Oxford University Press, New York, 2011, p. 73.
49. N.K. Kulkarni, "Population Control and Urban Family Planning in Bangladesh", *Searchlight South Asia*, 2011, http://urbanpoverty.intellecap.com/?p=229
50. Ibid.
51. Government of Bangladesh, "Ensuring Food Security through increased Agricultural Production with efficient Water Resource Management", Ministry of Agriculture, Ministry of Food & Disaster Management, Ministry of Water Resources and Ministry of Fisheries and Livestock, Dhaka, 2010 [Online: web] Accessed 29 March 2012, URL: http// www.lcgbangladesh.org/BDF-2010/.../BDF2010_Session%20III.pdf
52. R. Faridi, and S.N. Wadood, "An Econometric Assessment of Household Food Security in Bangladesh", *The Bangladesh Development Studies*, Vol. XXXIII, September, 2010, No.3:121
53. Government of Bangladesh, "Ensuring Food Security through increased Agricultural Production with efficient Water Resource Management", Ministry of Agriculture, Ministry of Food & Disaster Management, Ministry of Water Resources and Ministry of Fisheries and Livestock, Dhaka, 2010 [Online: web] Accessed 29 March 2012, URL: http// www.lcgbangladesh.org/BDF-2010/.../BDF2010_Session%20III.pdf
54. Government of Bangladesh, Health and Population Sector Strategy1997: 7.
55. Ibid.
56. D. Ray, "Population Growth and Economic Development", Development Economics, Princeton University Press, Princeton, 2000, p.42.
57. I. Sirageldin, and M. Hossain and M. Cain, "Family Planning in Bangladesh: An Empirical Investigation", The Bangladesh Development Studies, Vol. 3, 1:1, 1975, p. 26.
58. M.M. Hossain, "Consumption in Rural Bangladesh: Households, Lifestyles, and Identities", Consumer Economics Unit, Department of Economics and Management,University of Helsinki,Finland, 2011, p.11.
59. Government of Bangladesh, "Bangladesh Agriculture Report 2010", Dhaka, 2011, [Online: web] Accessed 2 April 2012,URL www.mof.gov.bd/en/budget/11.../Chapter-7%20_Eng-2010_.pdf, p.37.
60. Ibid.
61. Government of Bangladesh, Bangladesh Population Policy 2013: 1.
62. N. Desai, "A Different Explosion in Pakistan", Searchlight South Asia, 2013, http:// urbanpoverty.intellecap.com/?p=714
63. J. Chowdhury, R. Amin, and A.U. Amhed, "Poor Women's Participation in Income Generating Projects and their Fertility Regulation in Rural Bangladesh: Evidence From a Recent Survey", *World Development*, April 1994, pp. 555-564.

21

Food Security and India's Security Challenges

Shivendra Shahi

While the "energy security" has been in vogue for many years, the term "food security" seems to acquire much importance in the last decade of the 20th century. Food security is an essential feature of a country's independence and sustenance. It was 38 years ago when world leaders accepted, for the first time at the 1974 World Food Conference in Rome, the common responsibility of the international community to abolish hunger and malnutrition within a decade.[1] At the World Food Summit (WFS) in Rome in 1996, heads of state representing 186 countries affirmed their "common and national commitment to achieve food security for all" and agreed to work toward the achievement of the intermediate goal of "reducing the number of undernourished people to half the present number no later than 2015". Recognizing the multifaceted nature of food insecurity, the WFS 1996 Plan of Action also contained a number of commitments, each in a broad action area relevant for reducing the number of undernourished people and eventually achieving food security for all.[2]

Today, the world faces contradiction because of the persistence of food insecurity and the degradation of natural resources. The contradiction is also seen that the major portion of the globe is that half of the world is preoccupied with dieting and the other half is struggling for survival since they do not have enough to eat. International meetings have from time to time came up with official documents that would adopt such methods that will provide food security, reduce poverty, and work for sustainable management of natural resources. Though international bodies have succeeded in achieving some of the goals, but still, there are hundreds of millions of people where poverty is a major cause of concern as millions of children die every year from malnutrition.

History of Food Security

There appears to be agreement that concerns on food security have progressed over the last 50 years or so from purely physical availability at the global level to the provisions of food to individuals and the role of poverty in ensuring year round access to food. The interaction between agriculture/food policies and socio-economic factors at the micro and macro-level is now considered crucial to ensuring food availability.

Swaminathan divides the post-war era into 4 phases (mainly from an Indian perspective).[3]

(a) 1940/60s—food security was only considered in physical availability terms.
(b) 1970s—economic access to food was considered equally important.
(c) 1980s—food security must be considered at the level of the individual and not merely of the household (since within a household women and girl children tend to be undernourished).
(d) 1990s—recognition that micronutrients in addition to environmental hygiene and safe drinking water are important.

He concluded that today food security should be seen from the viewpoints of physical, social, economic and environmental access.

Maxwell has distinguished 5 phases since 1974, these are:[4]

(a) 1974-1980: Global food security—The world food crisis was evident from famines in Africa, doubling of international grain prices and large grain imports by the Soviet Union. FAO set up a committee on World Food Security and a World Food Council was established to monitor world food availability.
(b) 1981-1985: Food entitlement and structural adjustment—questions of poverty and access featured since it was clear that production on its own did not assure consumption, and people needed access to food. This era coincided with structural adjustment activities where poverty reduction and basic needs were subordinate to debt management, macro-economic stability, etc.
(c) 1986-1990: The golden age—The 1984/5 African famine and the drawbacks of the social costs of structural adjustment changed the perceptions of food security which rose up in the international agenda.
(d) 1990-1996: Poverty, not food security—poverty reduction was brought back to the front of the development stage and displaced food security; many donors abandoned or downgraded food security. Famines were seen to be far more associated with war and with drought (eg. Southern Africa in 1992) which appeared to be managed reasonably efficiently. Thus, the problem was not seen as a food security issue per se but rather

one of managing food supplies in complex political emergencies characterized by social and policy breakdown.

(e) 1996: Where next?—Another rise in food prices and renewed concern about the ability of the world to feed itself. Will the agenda shift back to Malthusian concerns of the 1970s with a focus on food production, often in high potential areas or will the concern with consumption and access be sustained?

Food Security as a Concept

Food security as a concept originated only in the mid-1970s, in the discussions of international food problems at a time of global food crisis. The initial focus of attention was primarily on food supply problems of assuring the availability and to some degree the price stability of basic foodstuffs at the international and national level. That supply-side, international and institutional set of concerns reflected the changing organisation of the global food economy that had precipitated the crisis.

The concept of food security has undergone many changes during the last 60 years or so not only in regional but also in international discourse. The Universal Declaration of Human Rights of 1948 provides that "Everyone has the right to a standard of living adequate for the health and well being of himself and his family, including food". Food security is a flexible concept as reflected in the many attempts at definition in research and policy usage. Even a decade ago, there were about 200 definitions in published writings.[5] Whenever the concept is introduced in the title of a study or its objectives, it is necessary to look closely to establish the explicit or implied definition.

In the development of the concept of food security public policy there are wider and complex technical and policy issues which need serious concern. The most recent careful redefinition of food security is that negotiated in the process of international consultation leading to the World Food Summit (WFS) in November 1996. The contrasting definitions of food security adopted in 1974 and 1996, along with those in official FAO and World Bank documents of the mid-1980s are set out below with each substantive change in definition underlined. A comparison of these definitions highlights the considerable reconstruction of official thinking on food security that has occurred over 25 years. These statements also provide signposts to the policy analyses, which have re-shaped our understanding of food security as a problem of international and national responsibility.

Food security was defined in the 1974 World Food Summit as: "Availability at all times of adequate world food supplies of basic foodstuffs to sustain a steady expansion of food consumption and to offset fluctuations in production and prices".[6]

In 1983, FAO expanded its concept to include securing access by vulnerable people to available supplies, implying that attention should be balanced between the demand and supply side of the food security equation, "Ensuring that all people at all times have both physical and economic access to the basic food that they need".[7]

In 1986, influential World Bank report "Poverty and Hunger", focused on the dynamics of food insecurity. It introduced the widely accepted distinction between chronic food insecurity, associated with problems of continuing or structural poverty and low incomes, and transitory food insecurity, which involved periods of intensified pressure caused by natural disasters, economic collapse or conflict. This concept of food security is further elaborated in terms of, "access of all people at all times to enough food for an active, healthy life", from individual to the global level.[8] However, access now involved sufficient food with the focus on protein-energy malnutrition. Hence, the definition was broadened to incorporate food safety and also nutritional balance. It reflected concerns about food composition and minor nutrient requirements for an active and healthy life.

The 1990 Life Sciences Research Office (LSRO) Report on Nutritional Assessment defined terms associated with food access, including food security, food insecurity, and hunger. Food security implies the ability to secure adequate food. According to the LSRO report, it is "access by all people at all times to enough food for an active, healthy life".[9]

Food security includes at a minimum: (1) the ready availability of nutritionally adequate and safe foods, and (2) an assured ability to acquire acceptable foods in socially acceptable ways (e.g., without resorting to emergency food supplies, scavenging, stealing or other coping strategies), In contrast, food insecurity implies a limited ability to secure adequate food. Specifically, food insecurity is having "limited or uncertain availability of nutritionally adequate and safe foods or limited or uncertain ability to acquire acceptable foods in socially acceptable ways".[10]

A broader perspective was adopted in the UNDP 1994 *Human Development Report*, which promoted the construct of human security, including a number of component aspects, of which food security was only one.[11] The concept of human security is closely related to the human rights perspective to development that has, in turn, influenced discussions about food security.[12]

Ideally, estimates of under nutrition would be based on combined health and nutritional assessments, including anthropometry.[13] The assessment requires representative cross sectional sample population. Practically, such surveys are uncommon, especially in those countries where under nutrition is likely to be most pervasive.

Consequently, measurement is typically indirect and based on food balance sheet and national income distribution and consumer expenditure data. The line of reasoning linking hunger and under nutrition with inadequate food intake allows the measurement of food insecurity in terms of the availability and apparent consumption of staple foods or energy intake.[14]

This definition is again broadly equivalent to the earlier narrower definitions of chronic food insecurity.[15] The 1996 World Food Summit adopted a still more complex definition: "Food security, at the individual, household, national, regional and global levels is achieved, when all people, at all times, have physical and economic access to sufficient, safe and nutritious food to meet their dietary needs and food preferences for an active and healthy life".[16]

This term is again refined in The State of Food Insecurity 2001, "Food security is a situation that exists when all people, at all times, have physical, social and economic access to sufficient, safe and nutritious food that meets their dietary needs and food preferences for an active and healthy life".[17]

"This new emphasis on consumption, the demand side and the issues of access by vulnerable people to food, is most closely identified with the seminal study by Amartya Sen". Eschewing the use of the concept of food security, he focuses on the entitlements of individuals and households.[18]

The concept of providing people with food security extends from the individual and local community level to the global level. At the individual level, the concept of food security implies that under all circumstances each man, woman and child has access to sufficient, good quality food to meet the individual dietary requirements consistent with normal active life. At the national and regional levels, food security implies an assured availability of food through production, stock drawdown, trade or food aid to meet minimum requirements per capita, and also to meet any unexpected shortfall over a limited period. The achievement of food security requires the utilization of both renewable and non-renewable agricultural resources and carries the risk of environmental degradation if managed inappropriately.

From 1804, when the world passed the 1 billion mark, it took 123 years to reach 2 billion people in 1927, 33 years to attain 3 billion in 1960, 14 years to reach 4 billion in 1974, 13 years to attain 5 billion in 1987 and 12 years to reach 6 billion in 1999. It will take 14 years to reach 7 billion in 2013, 15 years to reach 8 billion in 2028, and, with the slowing down of population growth, it will take 22 years to reach 9 billion, in 2050.[19]

In summary, food security is influenced by various social, political, economic, and technical variables—purchasing power of consumers, dietary patterns, soil quality, climate factors, among others. Nevertheless, food security is almost always a matter of "access" instead of "availability" (in other words, food is often available—and the global agricultural system is capable of assuring this availability—but people cannot always get access for various reasons: economic, social or political).

World food situation underwent dramatic changes during three decades since mid-1960s, when widespread food shortages in Asia caused predictions of disastrous recurring famines. The Green Revolution, featuring the adoption of high-yielding cereal varieties and rapid increases in irrigated area and fertilizer use, dramatically improved productivity in Asia and other developing regions, easing the fear of endemic famine. The Green Revolution peaked in much of Asia in the 1970s and early 1980s. The Green Revolution was really a revolution for many developing countries where they experienced rising incomes and shifting consumption patterns, which led to striking increases in consumption of livestock products, particularly in Asia.

The demand for food growth caused by expanding populations and shifting consumption patterns will necessitate future food production increases. But, if it remains then the role of technology becomes important. Proper use of technology will yield improvements. Empirical evidence has also proved that negative effects on the environment from inappropriately applied technologies can translate into productivity losses and threaten human health. Growing urban and industrial demands on existing water supplies and the need for improved water quality further complicate the situation.

Cereals play dominant role in India, Pakistan and Bangladesh's food scenario because of their paramount importance in the sub-region's diet. IFPRI baseline projections indicate that wheat imports in South Asia will grow at 6.4 percent per year between 2000 and 2020. This increase is due to continued strong demand growth (in part because of high population growth in Pakistan) together with a slowdown in production, especially in Pakistan, where the bulk of wheat demand will come from. Rice will be almost in balance, in contrast to the large export in the base year. This will result due to reduced rates of production growth, particularly in Bangladesh and Pakistan.

The Impact of Food Insecurity

Hunger, poverty and disease are interlinked, with each contributing to the occurrence of the other two. Hunger reduces natural defences against most diseases, and is the main risk factor for illness worldwide. People living in poverty often cannot produce or buy enough food to eat and so are more susceptible to disease. Sick people are less able to work or produce food. The UN Standing Committee on Nutrition concluded that nutrition is an essential foundation for poverty alleviation, and also for meeting MDGs related to improved education, gender equality, child mortality, maternal health and disease.[20]

Hunger is a major constraint to a country's immediate and long term economic, social and political development. Food security is also seen as a prerequisite for economic development. Losses in labour productivity due to hunger can cause 6-10% reductions in per capita gross domestic product (GDP). Undernourishment pre birth and of young children is associated with poor cognitive development, resulting in lower productivity and lifetime earnings potential. The UN Children's Fund (UNICEF) estimate that one third of the world's people do not reach their physical and intellectual potential due to micronutrient deficiencies caused by food insecurity.[21]

Factors Influencing Food Insecurity

Food insecurity is determined by the immediate causes of hunger, underlying determinants of conditions in a community (affecting poverty, food production, and ability to respond to shocks), and the impact of shocks.

Low access to food: It is not necessary that the available food in the country will provide social and economic security. Low incomes, lack of roads and infrastructure, safe drinking water, primary health care and education all impact on people's food consumption. In some cereal-surplus countries, there are more underweight children than in food deficit ones. For example, India has sufficient food production, and yet very high numbers of underweight children, probably due to low incomes, imbalances in household food distribution and weak social networks.[22]

Degradation of natural resources and increasing water scarcity: Degradation of natural resources is rampant in many resource-poor areas of developing countries, particularly those areas with fragile soils, irregular rainfall, relatively high population density, and stagnant productivity in agriculture. While natural resource degradation often is a consequence of poverty, it also contributes to poverty. Water scarcity is emerging as a most limiting factor for food security in many regions.[23]

Increase in Population Growth: While poverty and natural disasters are the most common factors for food insecurity, rapid population growth overburdens already strained financial and natural resources. This, in turn, greatly impedes efforts to raise incomes and reduce food shortages, particularly in rural areas where food insecurity is mostly concentrated.[24] In many developing countries rapid population growth makes it difficult for agricultural production to keep pace with the rising demand for food. Most developing countries already are cultivating virtually all arable land and are bringing ever more marginal land under cultivation.[25]

Urbanization: Most of the population increases in coming years will occur in cities and towns of developing countries. By the year 2020, a majority of the developing world's population will live in urban areas. This will present new challenges to provide employment, education, health care, and food. While current actions must continue to focus on the rural areas where the majority of the poor and food insecure people reside, future policy actions must pay increasing attention to the growing poverty and food insecurity in urban areas.[26]

Health, water and sanitation: Poor sanitation, health facilities and water sources contribute significantly to malnutrition by increasing the burden of illness. More than 1 billion people globally lack access to safe drinking water, increasing their exposure to bacteria and parasites.[27]

Climate change and natural disasters: Natural disasters and climate variability are major sources of vulnerability for the food insecure. They particularly affect those in countries that largely depend on rain fed farming and those highly dependent on agriculture. Poor people are also less able to cope with the impacts of climate shocks and variability. These events can result in massive crop losses, loss of stored food, and damage to infrastructure and consequent increases in food prices.[28] Climate change is increasing the frequency and size of such events.

Conflict: Armed conflicts continue to cause severe human misery in a large number of developing countries. The impact could easily be seen on food security, nutrition, and natural resource management. While humanitarian assistance may be effective in providing food and shelter for millions of refugees, policy action is needed to deal with the underlying causes and the resulting impact on the people in war-torn and neighbouring areas.[29] Achieving sustainable food security for all is unlikely to be possible in the midst of conflict.

Many other issues also affect food security. Access and rights to land, education, gender and social exclusion all have big impacts. Poor governance and corruption can affect hunger levels by disempowering vulnerable groups (such as women and minority, ethnic groups), and seriously undermine any policies in place.

Food Insecurity

Food insecurity refers to a lack of access to enough food. There are two kinds of food insecurity: chronic and transitory. Transitory food insecurity is a temporary decline in a household's access to enough food. Chronic food insecurity is a continuously inadequate diet caused by the inability to acquire food. It affects households that persistently lack the ability either to buy enough food or to produce their own. Hence, poverty is considered the root cause of chronic food insecurity.

Famines are the worst form of transitory food insecurity. They can result from several causes: wars, floods, drought, crop failures, the loss of purchasing power by groups of households, and market failures including sometimes high food prices and grain hoarding. All of these types of disruptions to food supplies can 'trigger' subsistence crises by threatening a population's access to food.[30] They are the immediate causes of famine. But these precipitating 'triggers' lead to famine only where particular groups of people are already vulnerable to it. The most vulnerable include: small-scale subsistence farmers, landless agricultural workers, other workers who are affected by a drop in real income in famine regions, pastoralists, female-headed households, children, and the elderly. The international community has accepted these increasingly broad statements of common goals and implied responsibilities. But its practical response has been to focus on narrower, simpler objectives around which to organise international and national public action. The declared primary objective in international development policy discourse is increasingly the reduction and elimination of poverty. [31] The 1996 WFS exemplified this direction of policy by making the primary objective of international action on food security halving of the number of hungry or undernourished people by 2015.[32]

The concept of providing people with food security extends from the individual and local community level to the global level. At the individual level, the concept of food security implies that under all circumstances each man, woman and child has access to sufficient, good quality food to meet the individual dietary requirements consistent with normal active life. At the national and regional levels, food security implies an assured availability of food through production, stock drawdown, trade or food aid to meet minimum requirements per capita, and also to meet any unexpected shortfall over a limited period.[33] The achievement of food security requires the utilization of both renewable and non-renewable agricultural resources and carries the risk of environmental degradation if managed inappropriately.

Food Security Challenges for India

India is classified by the Food and Agricultural Organisation (FAO) of the United Nations, as a low income, food-deficit country. With 212 million undernourished people, India has the largest number of undernourished[34] people in the world and the highest levels of child malnutrition, higher than most countries in Sub-Saharan Africa.[35] India has committed itself to attain the Millennium Development Goals (MDGs) by the year 2015.[36]

A brief look at the statistical data reveals the dramatic situation of under nourishment and poverty in India. 20 percent of the Indian population is undernourished,[37] of which 57 million children are malnourished and make up one third of the world's 146 million undernourished children.[38]

Almost half (47 percent) of the malnourished children are under the age of five years.[39] One in three women is underweight and is, therefore, at the risk of delivering babies with low weight and inheriting her fate to her children.[40] Nearly a third of children are born underweight (30 percent), which indicates that their mothers themselves are underweight and undernourished. Malnutrition also increases during early childhood, particularly for girls, reflecting persistent gender discrimination against girl children. From an estimated population of 1027 million people in India, 28.6 percent lives below the poverty line, of which 23.6 percent in the urban areas and 30.2 percent in the rural areas. Poverty prevents persons from fully realising their potential and enjoying their rights

Recent years have seen reforms in Indian economy and as a result growth rates have been among the highest in the world. The flip side, however, is that one in every five Indians suffers from overt or covert hunger. "Hunger," as stated by Amartya Sen and Jean Dreze, is "intolerable in the modern world" in a way it could not have been in the past, because it is "so unnecessary and unwarranted." India is a poignant example of how food sufficiency at the aggregate level has not translated into food security at the household level.[41] India has emerged as the capital of hunger, illustrated by the fact that per capita consumption has dropped from 178 kg in 1991—the beginning of the period of economic reforms—to 155 kg in 2000-2003. Daily calorie consumption of the bottom 25 per cent of the population has decreased from 1683 k.cal in 1987-88 to 1624 k.cal in 2004-05, against a national norm of 2400 and 2011 k cal/day for rural and urban areas respectively.[42] Therefore, a response on the food security front is really a response to a national emergency.

Whether India will follow the Chinese model of controlling the population growth has to be seen in a proper perspective. India could lend over other countries by farming land overseas and transporting the food products to India. Here, what is important is that India has to think over in maintaining and improving it current food stocks.

India is in the midst of major economic reform. If it succeeds, incomes in India will rise much faster than they have in recent decades, with profound effects on food demand and food security. India is projected to have an average annual economic growth rate of 5.5 percent during 1993-2020. Daily per capita calorie availability is projected to increase from around 2,266 calories in 1990 to 2,780 calories in 2020.[43]

People in developing countries are affected by high food prices, which create a situation where "food is available, but significant segments of the population do not have access to it". The State of Food Insecurity in the World 2009, a report by FAO and the WFP, says that of the 1.02 billion hungry people in the world today, 642 million are in the Asia-Pacific region, 265 million in sub-Saharan Africa, 53 million in Latin America and the Caribbean, 42 million in the Middle East and North Africa, and 15 million in industrialised countries.[44]

It is a well known fact that African children are better fed than Indians. Even if we establish the well-being of the people to a certain level of "basic needs", then food supply for all has to be secured and provided to them.

Hence, food insecurity is a world phenomenon, the intensity of which may differ from nation to nation. It is a complex notion and there are various of factors that vary across the regions, countries and social groups. These factors can be grouped in five areas i.e. availability, accessibility, affordability, adequate storage facilities and nutritional value of the food. All these are necessary for the requirements of healthy person. In aggregate, over one-third of the population suffers from chronic hunger. It highlights the fact that food insecurity in India is not necessarily the function of under-production and bad weather.

As of late 2007, increased farming for use in bio-fuels, world oil prices at nearly $120 a barrel, global population growth, climate change, loss of agricultural land to residential and industrial development, and growing consumer demand in China, Pakistan and India have pushed up the price of grains. Food riots have recently taken place in many countries across the globe. For instance in India during the early 1980s, the country was almost self-sufficient in wheat and was a leading rice exporter. Over time, domestic demand for food increased steadily because of rapid population growth. The growth in food grain production fell behind demand because of the consistent decline in world prices of food grains and a shortfall of investment in agricultural infrastructure and technology to improve production. As a result, domestic demand for food grains exceeded the domestic supply, and annual imports rose in the late 1990s. Even with these imports, food security is a growing concern in India given inequitable access to food and the declining purchasing power of the poor. People have shifted from agricultural sector to other business because of low returns and high risk and uncertainty. Inflation has affected the common man and increasing food prices mean that half of the country's population is facing "food insecurity".

It became important for India to ensure access to natural resources and income to feed oneself with adequate nutritious food for the enjoyment of all other rights. At international level, India has ratified core international human rights instruments that have strong reference to the right to food.[45] Nonetheless, in 2008 the Committee on Economic Social and Cultural Rights expressed deep concern over the high levels of food insecurity in the country, as well as on the reports of corruption, inefficiency and discrimination in distribution[46] that impede the realisation of the right to adequate food.[47]

In 2000, India adopted the UN Millennium Declaration. It was a joint effort to reduce poverty and hunger by 50% before 2015. But still food insecurity, corruption, inefficiency and discrimination in distribution remain. The Constitution of India provides a strong framework for the protection and promotion of the right to food. Article 21 secures the protection of life and personal liberty, while Article 47 states that "the State shall regard the raising of the level of nutrition and the standard of living of its people and the improvement of public health as among its primary duties".

In India there are a number of food entitlement programmes such as the Integrated Child Development Scheme (ICDS) tenable by all children under six, pregnant and lactating mothers, and the Mid-Day Meal Scheme (MDMS) available to all primary and upper primary school children. Food subsidy schemes in the form of Public Distribution System guarantees 35 kilogrammes (kgs) per month of subsidised food grains, and the Annapurna Scheme provides for 10 kgs of free food grain for indigent senior citizens of 65 years or above who are not getting old age pension also exist. Inspite of these programmes, 21% of India's total population remains undernourished,[48] with women, girls and older persons being the most affected. Since 1997, the country has experienced an average annual GDP rate of 7%, yet India still has the world's highest number of malnourished.[49]

Despite a significant decline in malnourishment in the last few years, the levels of malnourishment are still very high. According to a recent study,[50] 42% of children under five are underweight and 59% are stunted. Commenting on the issues, the Prime Minister stated: "*...what concerns me and what must concern all enlightened citizens, is that 42% of our children are still underweight. This is an unacceptable high occurrence.*"

Legal Sanctity

Since 2001, over 40 Supreme Court interim orders have treated the right to food as justiciable.[51] In 2001, when the food stocks reached unprecedented levels in the country while hunger in drought affected areas was immense, People's Union for Civil Liberties (PUCL) filed a petition against the Government of India, the Food Corporation of India (FCI), and six state Governments in the context of inadequate food relief.[52] Consequently, the case was expanded to include issues of chronic hunger and undernutrition and all the states were added under the list of petitioners. In its response, the central government stated that it had nine nutrition-related schemes[53] to deal with the situation and the Court started to review the implementation of these schemes. The Supreme Court began issuing orders instructing the central and state governments to implement nutrition-related schemes in letter and spirit, effectively turning the benefits under these schemes into legal entitlements. Over the past decade, the focus of the case has shifted from one scheme to another.

Public Distribution System (PDS)

India's PDS is the world's largest food subsidy programme. It means to ensure availability of selected commodities at affordable subsidised prices. It operates under the joint responsibility of the central and state governments. The state's responsibilities include the distribution of food grains to consumers through 'Fair Price Shops' (FPSs), the identification of families below poverty line (BPL), the issuance of BPL cards, as well as the movement and the storage of food grains.

A 2010 Right to Information (RTI) application revealed serious inefficiencies in the government's monitoring of storage facilities and distribution. In an affidavit to the Supreme Court filed in September 2010, the Ministry of Consumer Affairs, Food and Public Distribution, admitted that more than 67,000 tonnes of grains were rotting in the godowns of the Food Corporation of India (FCI).[54]

While being a progressive scheme, the shift from universal applicability of the PDS to a targeted one since 1997—providing subsidised food only to Below Poverty Line (BPL) card holders—has led to the exclusion of genuinely poor households. In fact, in 2004-05, 50% of poor rural households did not have a BPL card, while 18% of households in the richest quintile had one.

Other problems of implementation include: losses during transportation, poor storage, rotting grains and illegal sale. The proposal to introduce a 'cash transfer' programme in place of the PDS cannot solve the problem of incorrect identification of the poor, and will not benefit the already targeted poor since they would be receiving a fixed sum when prices of essential items, including food, are rising. A plethora of impediments that render cash transfers not a sensible plan to achieve food security: the availability, efficiency and accessibility of banks or post office systems, especially for people living in remote areas of the country; the irregular payments and corruption; the high rates of illiteracy; the lack of decision-making power over the household income by women who are the main providers of food; as well as the adverse impact on agricultural production owing to the lack of demand for subsidised grains. A 2011 survey has shown that people rejected the introduction of cash transfers in states where the PDS is functional, whereas many respondents were more open to the idea in states with a dysfunctional PDS. *"Overall, more than two-thirds of the respondents expressed a clear preference for food over cash; less than one-fifth were in favour of cash over food"*.[55]

National Food Security Bill

The *National Food Security Bill, 2011* (NFSB) is a very important step towards the elimination of hunger and under-nutrition in India. Its positive features include the recognition of women as heads of the household for the distribution of BPL cards and the statutory recognition of *Mid-Day Meals* and *Integrated Child Development Schemes*. However, the Bill also has shortcomings, as it fails to universalise the PDS and rather opts for a targeted approach. In addition, the current overwhelming focus of the NFSB on the PDS is not adequate. In order to make the right to food a reality, access to productive resources like land, water and forests should also be addressed and incorporated in the ambit of the Bill. The NFSB should include provisions to implement the state's obligation to facilitate access to resources for people to feed themselves, along with the state obligation to provide food if people cannot access such resources. In order to ensure food security, the NFSB has to be in conformity with India's human rights obligations and in compliance with orders of the Supreme Court.

On 12 March, 2012, several eminent development economists wrote an open letter to Prime Minister Manmohan Singh welcoming the tabling of the *National Food Security Bill* but also pointing out to its serious shortcomings. The experts suggested a simpler and more effective framework for the PDS that would require only minor amendments to the Bill.[56]

Conclusion

Sustainable food security for India depends upon strong political will. This agricultural growth and improved livelihood in rural areas are earmarked by following factors:[57]

- Remunerative prices are important for agricultural produce and products.
- New methods have to be adopted by the government for national agricultural education and research and extension systems (both public and private) so that it could generate and disseminate productivity-enhancing technologies.
- Food security will also depend upon proper infrastructure in the form of good roads and transport systems, power supply and irrigation systems.
- Means and methods are necessary for proper agriculture service. Its must be delivered in an adequate manner, especially for modern farm inputs, agro-processing and credit.
- Moreover, the farmers may be provided with liberalised markets so that they can make access to domestic and international markets. Food security in India is related to the creation of effective public institution in order to provide key services where these cannot be served by the private sector.

Today, India food security problem is a big challenge for India. To meet the challenge of achieving food security for country it is necessary to make progress in agriculture output since it depends on both *availability* of food as well as its *access* and affordability. For India, the notion of food security should move beyond a relatively static focus on food availability. Higher agricultural growth, particularly emanating from the crop sector, will provide food security by increasing supply, stabilizing prices, and raising incomes of poor farm households. To benefit from the current global food crises, there is an urgent need for India to change its policy-orientation from the current practice. The emphasis should be more on price control and move towards yield enhancement, structural issues such as poor crop management skills of farmers, use of cheaper seeds, lack of agricultural infrastructure and higher post-harvest losses, limited research as well as the gap between available research and practical applications, and inadequate funding for research and development. In India, agriculture will still remain the highest priority for the government to reduce poverty and enhance methods for improving food security.

India should depend on cost-reducing technology through domestic reforms, promote agricultural diversification and put pressure on the developed countries to open up their markets for value added agricultural products. In order to formulate an appropriate agricultural strategy there are some vital issues of great concerns: (a) Proper utilization of the emerging opportunities from liberalised trade for the diversification of economic activities in rural areas; (b) improving the purchasing power of the poor; and (c) Proper utilization of the domestic food security keeping in view fluctuating in international agricultural prices which can become volatile than domestic prices.

The major problem to food security in India comes mainly from the slow growth of purchasing power of the people in the rain-fed eco-systems. Efforts must be made to help them by developing drought resistant seeds, cost-effective dry-land farming techniques. In addition, rain water harvesting techniques, moisture conservation, inter-cropping are imperative to stabilize and improve the production in the dry-land areas. It is also necessary to take stringent measures for cost-effective expansion of irrigation. Besides there, appropriate pricing of water, electricity and fertilizer and rationalization of minimum support prices would augment resources available for investment in irrigation, rural infrastructure and prevention of soil degradation.

REFERENCES

1. United Nations, "Report of the World Food Conference", Rome, 5-16 November 1974, New York, p.6.
2. "Global Hunger and Food Security after the World Food Summit", ODI Briefing Paper, February. Overseas Development Institute, London, 1997, p.9.
3. D.O. Hall, "Food Security: What have sciences to offer?", 1998 [Online: Web] Accessed 9 September 2008, URL: http://www.icsu.org/gestion/img/icsu_doc_download/221_dd_file_foof_security.pdf, p.4.
4. Ibid.
5. S. Maxwell and M. Smith, "Household Food Security; a Conceptual Review", in S. Maxwell & T.R. Frankenberger (eds.), Household Food Security: Concepts, Indicators, Measurements:

A Technical Review, New York and Rome: UNICEF and IFAD, 1992, p.13.
6. United Nations (1975), "Report of the World Food Conference", Rome, 5-16 November 1974, New York, p.6.
7. Food and Agriculture Organization, "World Food Security: a Reappraisal of the Concepts and Approaches", Director General's Report, 1983, Rome, p.6.
8. World Bank, "Poverty and Hunger: Issues and Options for Food Security in Developing Countries", Washington DC., 1986, p.15.
9. S.A. Anderson, The Life Sciences Research Office (LSRO) Report on Nutritional Assessment defined terms associated with food access, *Journal of Nutrition*, 1990, 102:1559-1660.
10. World Bank, "Poverty and Hunger: Issues and Options for Food Security in Developing Countries", Washington D.C., 1986, p.7.
11. The list of threats to human security is long, but most can be considered under seven main headings: economic security, food security, health security, environmental security, personal security, community security, and political security.' UNDP, 1994, [Online: web] Accessed on 18 February 2010, URL: http://www.undp.org/: pp. 24-25.
12. At the end of the wider investigation into the role of public action into combating hunger and deprivation, Dreze and Sen (1989) found no separate place for food security as an organizing framework for action. Instead they focused on a wider construct of social security which has many distinct components including, of course, health and nutrition. M. Hubbard, "Public Administration and Development", May, Vol. 12, Issue 2, 1992, pp. 123-222
13. Undernutrition is a less intimidating concept than protein-energy malnutrition (PEM), its technical synonym. PEM is manifested through wasting, low weight for height, as an acute condition and a stunting, low height for age, as a chronic condition.
14. Food and Agriculture Organization, "The state of food insecurity in the world 2001", Maren Lieberum, Florence Egal and Sofie van Waeyenberge [Online: web] Accessed on 6 March 2010, URL: http://:www.fao.org/DOCREP/003/Y1500E/Y1500E00.HTM
15. World Bank, "Poverty and Hunger: Issues and Options for Food Security in Developing Countries", Washington D.C., 1986, pp.19.
16. Rome Declaration on World Food Security and World Food Summit Plan of Action. World Food Summit, 13-17 November 1996, Rome, p.5.
17. Food and Agriculture Organization, "The State of Food Insecurity in the World", Rome, 2002, p. 6.
18. A. Sen, "Poverty and Famines", Clarendon Press, Oxford, 1981, p.21.
19. World Bank, "World Development Report 2000/2001: Attacking Poverty", Oxford University Press, New York, 2000.
20. "Food Security in Developing Countries", POST note, Dec., 2006, Number 274 [Online: web] Accessed on 15 November 2008, [Online: web] Accessed 15 November 2008, URL: http://www.parliament.uk/documents/upload/post pn274.p2.
21. Ibid.
22. UN Task Force on Hunger, "Halving hunger: it can be done", 2005 [Online: Web] Accessed 22 October 2008 URL: http://www.unmillenniumproject.org/documents/HTF-SumVers_FINAL.pdf
23. FAO, "The State of Food Insecurity in the World," 2004, Rome, p.7.
24. "How Population Growth Affects Hunger in the Developing World", August 1, 2005 [Online: web] Accessed 22 June 2009, URL: http://www.populationaction.org/Publications/Fact_Sheets/FS30/Summary.shtml
25. "Winning the Food Race" Population Reports, The Johns Hopkins School of Public Health, Vol. XXV, No. 4, December, 1997, Maryland, USA [Online: web] Accessed 22 June 2009, URL: http://www.infoforhealth.org/pr/m13edsum.shtml#top
26. By 2030 this number will swell to almost 5 billion, with urban growth concentrated in

Africa and Asia. "Urbanization: A Majority in Cities: Population & Development: UNFPA" (2008) [Online: web] Accessed 23 March 2009, URL: http://www.unfpa.org/pds/urbanization.htm

27. UN Millennium Project, "Investing in Development: A practical plan to achieve the MDGs", 2005 [Online: Web] Accessed 22 October 2008, URL: http:// www.unmillenniumproject.org
28. "Adapting to climate change In developing countries" (2006), PTSO note, October, No. 269 [Online: Web] Accessed 22 October 2008, URL: http://www.parliament.uk/documents/upload/postpn269.pdf, p.4.
29. "Reaching Sustainable Food Security for All by 2020: Getting the Priorities and Responsibilities Right", International Food Policy Research Institute, Washington, D.C., 2002.
30. M.B. Saad, "Food Security for the Food-Insecure: New Challenges and Renewed commitments" Centre for Development Studies, University College Dublin, Ireland, 1999 [Online: web] Accessed on 15 Dec 2010, URL: http://www.earthsummit2002.org/wcaucus/Caucus%20Position%20Papers/food%20security.pdf
31. Ibid.
32. C. Edward, "Food Security: Concepts And Measurement" Paper for FAO Expert Consultation on Trade and Food Security: Conceptualising the Linkages, Rome, 11-12 July 2002.
33. United Nations Economic and Social Commission for Asia and the Pacific (ESCAP) (2000), "State of the Environment in Asia and the Pacific 2000" [Online: web] Accessed on 15 Dec 2010, URL: http://www.unescap.org/esd/environment/soe/2000/documents/CH10.PDF
34. Food Agriculture Organization, "The State of Food Insecurity in the World," 2006 [Online: web] Accessed on 2 Dec 2011, URL: http://www.fao.org/docrep/009/a0750e/a0750e00.htm
35. United Nations Development Programme, "Human Development Report", 2005 [Online: web] Accessed on 9 July 2011, URL: http://hdr.undp.org/reports/global/2005/
36. The Millennium Development Goals are eight goals that United Nations member states have agreed to try to achieve by the year 2015. These goals range from halving extreme poverty to halting the spread of HIV/AIDS and providing universal primary education, all by the target date of 2015—form a blueprint agreed to by all the world's countries and all the world's leading development institutions.
37. Food and Agriculture Organization, "The State of Food Insecurity in the World", 2002, Rome.
38. United Nations Children's Fund (UNICEF), Progress for Children: A Report Card on Nutrition, May 2006, [Online: web] Accessed on 9 Dec 2011, URL: http://www.unicef.org/progressforchildren/2006n4/
39. Food and Agriculture Organization, "The State of Food Insecurity in the World", 2002, Rome.
40. Ibid.
41. Report of the Working Group on Social Protection Policy—National Social Assistance Programme And Associated Programme, Government of India Ministry of Rural Development Krishi Bhawan, New Delhi [Online: web] Accessed on 2 Dec 2011, URL: http://planningcommission.nic.in/aboutus/committee/wrkgrp11/wg11_sppnsapap.pdf
42. V. Shiva (2011), "India's Food Security Emergency" [Online: web] Accessed on 19 Dec. 2011, URL: http://www.aljazeera.com/indepth/opinion/2011/07/20117810358528978.html
43. "The World Food Situation—Recent Developments, Emerging Issues, and Long-Term Prospects", International Food Policy Research Institute (IFPRI), International Centers Week, 1997, October 27-31, Washington D.C.

44. Food and Agriculture Organization, "State of Food Insecurity in the World", 2009, [Online: web] Accessed on 6aug 2010, URL: http://www.ftp://ftp.fao.org/docrep/fao/012/i0876e/i0876e.pdf
45. International Convention on Economic, Social and Cultural Rights (ICESCR Art. 11), the Conventional on the Elimination of All Forms of Discrimination against Women (CEDAW, Art. 24&27), and the Convention on the Rights of the Child (CRC, Art. 12&14).
46. CESCR's definition of adequate food availability, apart from the possibilities for feeding oneself, also refers to the possibilities for "well functioning distribution (emphasis added), processing and market systems that can move food from the site of production to where it is needed in accordance with demand. General Comment 12 of the UN Committee on Economic Social and Cultural Rights, 1999, E/C.12/1999/5, para. 12, available at: http://daccessdds-ny.un.org/doc/UNDOC/GEN/G99/420/12/PDF/G9942012.pdf?Open Element
47. Concluding Observations of the UN Committee on Economic Social and Cultural Rights, 2008, E/C.12/IND/CO/5, para, 28, available at: http://daccess-dds-ny.un.org/doc/UNDOC/GEN/G08/436/08/PDF/G0843608.pdf?OpenElement
48. Food and Agriculture Organization of the United Nations, India, available at: http://www.fao.org/countries/55528/en/ind/
49. Percentage of children under age five years classified as malnourished according to three anthropometric indices of nutritional status: height-for-age, weight-for-height, and weight-for-age, according to state, India, 2005-06: (1) Height-for-age (stunting): 48%; (2) Weight-for-height (wasting): 19.8%; and (3) Weight-for-age (underweight): 42.5%—International Institute for Population Sciences and Macro International, National Family Health Survey 3 (NFHS-3), 2005-06: India, Mumbai, available at: http://www.nfhsindia.org/nfhs3.html
50. Naandi, The HUNGaMA Survey Report 2011, available at, www.hungamaforchange.org/FlierA4copy.pdf
51. People's Union for Civil Liberties v. Union of India, Supreme Court, Writ Petition (Civil) No.196 of 2001 (India); Also see: Planning Commission affidavit to the Supreme Court on 20.09.2011.
52. PUCL *vs* Union of India and Others, Writ Petition (Civil) 196 of 2001.
53. These were: Integrated Child Development Services, Mid-Day Meal Scheme, Public Distribution System, Annapoona, Antyodaya Anna Yojana, National Family Benefit Scheme, National Maternity Benefit Scheme and National Old Age Pensions Scheme. Sampoorna Grameen Rozgar Yojana (SGRY) was also in the initial list, but this programme was phased out after the NREGA came into force.
54. *Hindustan Times*, Rotting grain more than Government claimed, September 7, 2010, available at: http://www.hindustantimes.com/News-Feed/India/Rotting-grain-more-than-Govt-claimed/Article1-596981.aspx. Also see: *Hindustan Times*, Not a grain of truth, September 8, 2010, available at: http://www.hindustantimes.com/News-Feed/ColumnsSamarHalarnkar/Not-a-grain-of-truth/Article1-597806.aspx
55. R. Khera, Revival of the Public Distribution System: Evidence and Explanations, *Economic and Political Weekly*, Vol XLVI, Nos. 44 & 45, November 5, 2011.
56. *The Hindu*, A simple proposal on food security, March 12, 2012, available at: http://www.thehindu.com/opinion/oped/article2985212.ece
57. "Reaching Sustainable Food Security for All by 2020: Getting the Priorities and Responsibilities Right", International Food Policy Research Institute, Washington, D.C., 2002.

Index